Communication
in
Organizations

Communication in Organizations

Dalmar Fisher
Boston College

West Publishing Company

St. Paul • New York • Los Angeles • San Francisco

PHOTO CREDITS: *Chapter one* Rick Winsor, Magnum; *Chapter two* Bill Belisle; *Chapter three* Roger Malloch, Magnum; *Chapter four* U. S. Department of Labor; *Chapter five* Lawrence Fried, Magnum; *Chapter six* Abigail Heyman, Magnum; *Chapter seven* U. S. Department of Labor; *Chapter eight* Abigail Heyman, Magnum; *Chapter nine* Charles Harbutt, Magnum; *Chapter ten* Henri Cartier-Bresson, Magnum; *Chapter eleven* U. S. Department of Labor; *Chapter twelve* U. S. Department of Commerce; *Chapter thirteen* U. S. Department of Commerce; *Chapter fourteen* Constantine Manos, Magnum

copy editing: Lenore Franzen Johns
cover design: Peter Thiel
internal design, illustrations, and composition: Cobb/Dunlop Publisher Services, Inc.

Printed in the United States of America
96 95 94 93 92 91 90 89   8 7 6 5 4 3
Library of Congress Cataloging in Publication Data

Fisher, Dalmar.
   Communication in organizations.

   Includes index.
   1. Communication in organizations—United States.
2. Interpersonal communication. I. Title.
HM131.F52   302.2   80-21287
ISBN 0-8299-0374-7

To my parents

Contents

PART ONE
Observing and Understanding
Organizational Communication   1

Chapter 1
Perspectives for Understanding: An Overview   3

The Scope of Organizational Communication / Models
for Understanding Organizational Communication /
Communication Barriers / Perception and
Communication / Language / Nonverbal
Communication / Interpersonal Dynamics /
Communication in Groups / Communication in the
Total Organization / Counseling and Helping /
Influence / Organization Development and
Communication

Chapter 2
Diagnosing Communication Within Organizations:
A Models Approach   21

A Situation for Diagnosis / Communication as Action
—Linear Models / The One-way Model / The
Interaction Model / Communication as Relationship—
Organic Models / The Two-person Relationship Model /
The System Model

Chapter 3
Communication Barriers   39

Implicit Assumptions / Barriers Related to Status /
Barriers to Downward Communication / Barriers to
Upward Communication / Barriers to Lateral
Communication / Communication Load /
Communication Overload / Communication
Underload / Some General Characteristics of Barriers

Cases for Part One   59

The Sounds of Silence / Gordon Foundry Co. /
Rudolph Carter

PART TWO
Fundamentals of
Interpersonal Communication   **67**

Chapter 4
Perception and Communication   **69**

Some Fundamentals of Perception and Communication /
Perceptual Selectivity / Perception of Other People
and Self / Defending or Adapting the Conceptual
System

Chapter 5
Uses and Misuses of Language   **93**

General Semantics: Definition and Importance / The
Multiple Functions of Language / The Symbolic
Process: The Symbol is not the Thing Symbolized /
Abstracting / Extensional and Intensional Meaning /
Reports, Inferences, and Judgments / Contexts /
Language and Thought / The Misuses of Language /
Toward Improved Use of Language

Chapter 6
Nonverbal Communication   **117**

Dimensions and Functions of Nonverbal
Communication / Body Language / The Voice:
Paralanguage / Proxemics and Environment / Time /
Implications and Recommendations

Chapter 7
Understanding Interpersonal Dynamics   **141**

The Two-person Relationship / Dimensions of
Interpersonal Relationships / Transactional Analysis /
Maladaptive Relationships / Adapting and
Improving Relationships / Using Exposure and
Feedback / Metacommunication: Addressing the
Problem of Communication / Dealing Directly with
Disagreement / Exercising Choice

Cases for Part Two   **165**

The Road to Hell / Drydocked / Ben Reed / Bob
Knowlton

PART THREE
Communication
in Groups   189

Chapter 8
Group Character and Communication   191

What Is A Group? / Primary and Secondary Groups /
Formal and Informal Groups / Phases of Group
Development / Group Structure / Group
Cohesiveness / Group Norms / Interdependence of
the Dimensions of Group Character

Chapter 9
Group Decision Making and Leadership   215

The Reflective Thinking Model / Factors Affecting
Group Decision Quality / Group Size and Composition /
Interaction Process / Decision-making
Mechanisms / Brainstorming / NGT and Delphi
Techniques / Risk Taking / Leadership in Groups /
Trait and Style Approaches / Contingency and
Path-Goal Approaches / Leadership as Functions /
Group Effectiveness Criteria

Cases for Part Three   238

The United Assemblers / Falls Church Concrete
Company / A Group Meeting / Ned Wicker

PART FOUR
Communication in the
Total Organization   251

Chapter 10
Communicating Within Organization Structures   253

Organization Design Issues that Affect Communication /
Division of Labor / Unity of Command / Span of
Control / Line-Staff Relationships / Centralization
versus Decentralization / Communication Within
Basic Organization Designs / Forms of Specialization /
Matrix Designs / Organization, Environment, and
Communication / Communication and the Informal
Organization / Advantages and Disadvantages of
Informal Organization / The Grapevine

Chapter 11
Managing Conflict in Organizations   275

Sources and Effects of Conflict-Laden Communication /
Sources of Conflict / Effects of Conflict /
Approaches to Managing Conflict Communication / A
Cyclical Model of the Conflict Process / Reactions to
Intergroup Conflict / Operational Steps to Managing
Conflict Communication / Organization Design and
Conflict Management / Communication and Role
Conflict

Cases for Part Four   301

The Case of The Missing Time / The Aircraft Brake
Scandal / Don't Ask Dumb Questions

PART FIVE
Improving
Organizational
Communication   323

Chapter 12
Counseling and Helping   325

Counseling in Organizational Life / Listening With
Understanding / Listening Orientation / Reflection:
The Technique of Chent-centered Listening /
Counseling in the Broader Perspective of Helping /
The Task / Factors in the Individual / Nature and
Stage of the Relationship / Organizational and Social
Surroundings / A Mode of Directive Helping:
Confrontation / The Appraisal Interview: A
Counseling/Helping Application / Typical Problems
in Appraisal Counseling / Toward Improved Appraisal
Interviews

Chapter 13
Influence Through Communication   353

Reinforcement Theory / Characteristics of Reinforcers /
Schedules of Reinforcement / Inadvertent
Reinforcement / Punishment / Phases in The
Influence Process / Unfreezing / Changing /
Refreezing / Some Major Factors Affecting the
Influence Process / Source / Message / Receiver /
Group and Organizational Settings / Some Specific
Persuasive Tactics

Chapter 14
Organization Development and Communication   **379**

The Process of Organizational Change / Specific
Approaches to OD / Individuals / Dyads, Small
Groups, or Teams / Intergroup Relations / The Total
Organization / Communication Problems and
Strategies in OD / Causes of Resistance to OD /
Strategies for Decreasing Resistance / Communication
Approaches for the OD Practitioner

Cases for Part Five   **402**

Sea Pines / Judd Curtis / Alice

Subject Index   **411**
Name Index   **414**

Preface

An organization is a vast mass of communications. In meetings, phone calls, discussions, memos, interviews, and over coffee in the cafeteria, the message traffic is thick. In such an atmosphere, it is hardly open to debate that a person who is to be a really effective member of the organization needs to be a competent communicator.

Given the pervasiveness and importance of organizational communication, it is remarkable that so few people have had any part of their formal education or training devoted to the subject. Instead, most organization members learn about communication the hard way—by suffering a failure, by getting involved in a destructive conflict, by living through a painfully unpleasant work relationship with a boss or another important associate, or perhaps even by getting fired. This book is intended to make possible a softer landing. By considering the examples from organizational settings and conclusions from scholarly research presented here, the reader will have encountered many of the kinds of communication problems that occur in organizations without having to experience them and will also be aware of useful approaches to dealing with them.

This book, then, includes a mix of theory and practice. The major concepts relating to organizational communication are explained by tying them to concrete examples. All of the chapters in parts two through four contain sections detailing specific ways of making communication more effective. The cases at the end of each part provide opportunities for the student to develop skill in identifying communication problems and devising corrective action.

Basic to the design of the book is the writer's belief that communication in organizations cannot be thought of simply as communication but must be understood with the contexts in which it occurs. Part One provides an overview of the many factors that either are contained in or affect organizational communication. Part Two zooms in for a close look at the process of interpersonal communication, including the factors of perception, language, nonverbal communication, and the structure of relationships. Part Three steps back for a look at the most immediate context within which communication occurs, the small group. Part Four widens the view to include communication in its broader context—the total organization with its inherent tendency to evoke conflicts. Part Five suggests some ways toward improved communication in organizations by examining the counseling and helping process, the process of influence, and the nature of organizational change and development.

It is impossible to acknowledge all the people who have contributed to this book, but there are some who surely must be mentioned. The people at West Publishing Company provided great support. My colleagues in Human Resources Organizational Studies at Boston College—Jean Bartunek, Jim Bowditch, Judy Gordon, Ed Huse, Jack Lewis, and Jack Rosin—were also helpful and supportive throughout. Deans Jack Neuhauser, Bill Torbert and Justin Cronin provided resources for manuscript preparation and other support for this project. Mary Gallagher did a fine job of editing new case materials, and Ann Schneider and Dan Finn helped in obtaining photographs. Barbara Haroz prepared the index.

A number of reviewers made valuable suggestions. I would like to acknowledge and thank Elmore R. Alexander III (Memphis State University), Dennis Brown and Darlene Brown (El Paso Community College), James H. Conley (Eastern Michigan University), Virginia A. Eman (Bowling Green State University), Myron Glassman (Old Dominion University), Don Hellriegel (Texas A & M University), Frederick N. Jablin (The University of Wisconsin at Milwaukee), Paul Marchinsky (Iowa State University), Larry E. Penley (The University of Texas at San Antonio), Elliott A. Pood (The University of North Carolina at Greensboro), Aubrey C. Sanford (The University of Southern Mississippi), John W. Slocum (Southern Methodist University), and Gordon I. Zimmerman (The University of Nevada at Reno).

Special thanks are due to Anne Shenkman, who typed the entire manuscript. She was always alert to keep things "looking right," always patient, and always cheerful.

Finally, my love and thanks to Laura and Deirdre, and to two who made extra efforts to keep somewhat quiet so daddy could "study," Nano and Omi.

Part I

Observing and Understanding Organizational Communication

Chapter 1

Perspectives
for Understanding:
An Overview

The Scope of Organizational Communication
    Models for understanding organizational communication
    Communication barriers
    Perception and communication
    Language
    Nonverbal communication
    Interpersonal dynamics
    Communication in groups
    Communication in the total organization
    Counseling and helping
    Influence
    Organization development and communication

After studying this chapter,
the reader should be able to

Define and use the following terms and concepts

Multiple perspectives
Communication barriers
Model
Organizational context
Mutually reinforcing behavior
Perception
Language
Nonverbal communication

Interpersonal relationships
Informal communication links
Organization design
Organizational conflict
Leadership
Influence
Organization development
Organizational communication

Understand

Several perspectives from which communication can be viewed
Why multiple perspectives are useful in understanding organizational
    communication

Why an orientation toward explanation is useful
A basic model of two person communication in an organization

1

Communication between people in organizations is an important and fascinating process. Its importance is acknowledged by statements organization members make so frequently, such as "Our basic problem is communication," or "I just can't seem to communicate with him." Communication, whether it is effective or not, takes place constantly in any organization. A continuous process, somewhat like the circulatory system in the human body, communication is inseparable from and essential to everything that is going on.

One cannot comprehend an organization and events that happen in it unless the communication component is understood. While at work, most people spend fifty to eighty percent of their time communicating.[1] The communication process is basic to whether work gets done effectively or ineffectively. Working relationships between people form, develop, or fail within the context of a communication process. Consider the following example. What would you say communication has to do with this story and its outcome?*

In April 1979, Jim Jacobs was hired as a project leader in a new department by Microcomp, a rapidly growing company in the minicomputer industry. On his first assignment—an independent project lasting about five months—Jim did an outstanding job and was recognized by upper management as well as his peers.

During this time the department was changing significantly. New people were being hired every week. Separate project groups were established, and Jim was assigned to head a group of five people of various backgrounds and technical skills. More attention was placed on work schedules and standard operating procedures within the department.

With these changes came a change in Jim Jacobs's behavior. Though Jim was never one to be punctual in arriving to work, his lateness became

---

*The Jim Jacobs case was written by Mary Louise Gardella.

more frequent and noticeable. He spent hours socializing with peers in the staff lounge. He would ignore his group members' requests for additional assignments and, at the same time, refuse new projects. In addition, he complained about the inadequacies of the members of the project group, other project leaders, and the manager of the department. Jim Jacobs became socially separate from his peers and finally resigned in December.

Many people would say Jim Jacobs was simply a poor choice for the job of project leader. Others would say the problem was a lack of communication. But do we know for sure that he could not have succeeded? And wasn't there in fact *a lot* of communication? Jim's lateness, coffee breaks, and complaints said a lot to others, and the fact that those who used to respect him now rejected him clearly said something to Jim.

Isn't this story more difficult to explain than it first appears? It raises many questions: Why didn't Jim's boss act to correct the situation, and why didn't Jim go to his boss for help? Why did Jim think his boss and coworkers were inadequate? Were these perceptions inaccurate, and could they have been corrected? What did Jim's constant complaining mean to those who listened to it? Did others fully read the meaning of his lateness and the time he spent in the staff lounge? Could Jim's problems more usefully and more accurately have been seen as something other than just the wrong man in the wrong job? Was the department properly organized? Were project groups the best structure for the type of work being done? Was part of the problem within Jim's project group? Could his subordinates have worked harder to build a better working relationship with him? Could Jim have been helped? Could he have been influenced to change his approach? Could he have been less punitive and more persuasive in expressing his own complaints?

Two things should be clear from the Jim Jacobs example. First, a number of questions can be asked about a seemingly simple interpersonal problem. Second, these questions cover a rather wide scope. These two points reflect the two primary objectives of this book:

1. To arouse the reader's desire to inquire into and explain communication processes that occur in organizations.
2. To provide a wide enough scope of topics and perspectives related to organizational communication that the reader's inquiries will cover these processes adequately.

These two objectives are called primary because they can be expected to lead the way to other highly desirable goals. Obviously, just asking questions would be a totally academic and very impractical pursuit unless the questions were to lead to some useful answers. But most people are pretty good at answering questions. Students, especially, seem able to give a reasonably convincing answer to almost any question. Their teachers have been asking them questions for years, thus giving them a lot of practice. But it is much less common for a teacher to say, "Here is something [say a novel or a historical event]; ask a comprehensive set of useful questions about it." We tend not to be as skillful at question finding as we are at question answering. In the Jim Jacobs situation, our tendency is to see as simple a situation that probably has multiple, interwoven causes, and to jump to a conclusion that is possibly wrong and very likely incomplete. As our earlier discussion showed, many questions can, and should, be asked. In this book, the reader will be encouraged to find answers to communication issues, and many such answers will be provided, but it is hoped that the reader's inquiries will be enriched by a heightened tendency to raise questions.

The two objectives listed earlier place heavy emphasis on *explaining* communication. This does not mean that we should always be coldly rational and never express feelings or make value judgments about interpersonal events. We do not need to be like the psychiatrist whose neighbor says, "Hello" to him in the morning, whereupon the psychiatrist looks down at the sidewalk, frowns, and mutters to himself, "Hm, I wonder what he meant by that." This book does not argue that people should only explain communication and never *do* any communicating. It does, in fact, suggest many ways in which people in organizations can communicate more effectively. The emphasis on explanation simply means that people usually do a better job of communicating if they understand what is taking place.

THE SCOPE OF ORGANIZATIONAL COMMUNICATION

The psychiatrist just mentioned was engaged in inquiry, but the scope of that inquiry was very narrow. Questions about communication, even about a single, simple encounter, can cover a large number of areas, as shown by the example of Jim Jacobs. Exhibit 1-1 classifies the questions raised by the Jim Jacobs situation into a number of different topic areas. These topics areas cover most of the chapter titles in this book. It is recommended that the student, when working at understanding and explaining communication processes, try to ask questions in as many of these areas as possible. The usefulness of looking at things from multiple perspectives has been pointed out elsewhere by the author and his colleagues.[2] Consider a 33 1/3 r.p.m. phonograph disc. If you look at the record from one angle, it appears to be a circle. From another angle it appears to be a rather thin, straight line, while from still another angle it looks elliptical, somewhat like a football. You need to see it from all these angles to understand what it is really like. In order that the reader may have an overview of the major topic areas covered in this book, an introduction to each of them is given in the sections that follow.

EXHIBIT 1-1
QUESTIONS AND TOPIC AREAS RAISED BY
THE JIM JACOBS SITUATION

Questions	Topic Areas (Chapters)
Could Jim's problems have been seen differently?	Communication Models (2)
Why didn't Jim go to his boss for help?	Communication Barriers (3)
Were Jim's perceptions accurate?	Perception, communication, and the self (4)
What did Jim's complaints mean to others?	The uses and misuses of language (5)
How did others read Jim's lateness and coffee breaks?	Nonverbal communication (6)
Could other people have built better relationships with Jim?	Interpersonal dynamics (7)
Was part of the problem within Jim's project group?	Communication in groups (8, 9)
Was the department properly organized?	Communication and organization structure/conflict (10, 11)
Could Jim have been helped?	Giving and receiving help (12)
Could the situation and/or the outcomes have been changed?	Persuasion/organization development (13, 14)

Models for Understanding Organizational Communication

It is impossible to understand anything without having in mind some sort of model of the thing being investigated. A good mental model leads to a useful understanding of some phenomenon. The same is true of a traveler, who can be aided in reaching his or her destination by a good map. Since territories, such as countrysides and cities, tend to be complicated, the traveler is especially helped by a map that highlights the important things.[3] A simple mental model, like a good map, can usually be expressed in the form of a diagram, and this book will present several such diagrams —ones that have proved useful in improving our understanding of communication processes.

Often a very simple model can lead to penetrating questions about communication. The basic model of two-person communication shown in exhibit 1-2 provides an example. This diagram shows Person 1 and Person

EXHIBIT 1-2
A BASIC MODEL OF TWO-PERSON
COMMUNICATION IN AN ORGANIZATION

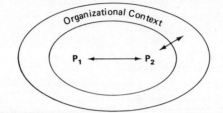

Source: Arthur N. Turner and George F. F. Lombard, *Interpersonal Behavior and Administration* (New York: The Free Press, 1969), p. 10. Adapted with permission of Macmillan Publishing Co., Inc. Copyright © 1969 Arthur N. Turner and George F. F. Lombard.

2 connected by a double-headed arrow and surrounded by an "organizational context." It is suggested that if this simple model were applied to an actual interpersonal event—say a misunderstanding between two managers—people in the organization could understand that event more fully and usefully. First, the model suggests that *both* 1 *and* 2 be included in the explanatory picture, thus counteracting any tendency to blame the misunderstanding on just one or the other. Second, the two-headed arrow connecting 1 and 2 suggests that their actions may be mutually reinforcing, that 1's behavior may be sustaining 2's, and vice versa. The two-headed arrow connecting the interpersonal relationship between 1 and 2 with its organizational context generates further questions. Is the disagreement between 1 and 2 partly a result of organizational factors, such as their jobs, departmental policies, or the ways in which decisions are being made? What about the human "climate" of the organization? Is it one of enthusiasm, team spirit, and mutual support, or perhaps the opposite? And is the nature of the organization being sustained partly by the way in which 1 and 2 are behaving toward each other? Are inappropriate policies made by top management both a cause and a result of the failure of 1 and 2 to deal constructively with their disagreement? People in organizations often see their communication problems as inevitable and yield to them with such remarks as, "If you're going to work in a place like this, what else can you expect?" A good model—even a simple one—conscientiously applied, can prevent such rapid and habitual jumping to conclusions that have nothing to recommend them other than an attitude of despair or overconfidence.

Communication Barriers

In most organizations, you will hear people complaining frequently about poor communication. Nothing is more commonplace in an office than to hear someone say something like, "Nobody told me what that new efficiency expert is working on. I hope he's not out to eliminate my job." Or,

"We were never told what our department is supposed to do on this project." Though such statements often do not represent a really useful diagnosis of the problem the speaker is experiencing, information in most organizations often does not get where it needs to go, or, if it does, it arrives in distorted form. If, as suggested above, communication events are explainable, then we should be able to identify the barriers that block or distort information. In fact, we can, and there are a great many of them.

The very nature of an organization makes communication problems unavoidable. Organizations exist to accomplish goals that cannot be achieved by one person alone. Large tasks are divided into smaller sub-tasks whose performance must be coordinated to achieve the overall goal. Since the division into subtasks means that people in organizations tend to become specialists, communication difficulties necessarily arise. Differ-ent specialists have differing concerns and may, in effect, "speak different languages," as any student who has a hard time tuning in on a philosophy professor after having just come out of a physics class knows. Where two or more specialists must coordinate their work closely, the language bar-rier can become especially difficult and significant.

Numerous other barriers can block or distort communication. Spatial distances and status differences between people, pressures for social con-formity, and personal defensiveness are just a few examples. Even this short list indicates that communication barriers can be found in individu-als, in their interpersonal relations, and in their social and organizational surroundings. In chapter 2 several kinds of barriers are discussed, as well as the important fact that barriers tend to occur not singly, but in inter-related clusters. Most communication problems are not understood well until several barriers have been identified.

Perception and Communication

A person's ability to perceive things is limited. No one is capable of sensing every word, shape, color, noise, or smell. There are just too many stimuli to attend to them all. Furthermore, individuals, being different, tend to see different things and to see the same thing in different ways. A good example comes from a study by DeWitt Dearborn and Herbert Simon.[4] Managers from various parts of a large organization were given a comprehensive set of facts about another company and then asked to state the most important problem it faced. The results showed that the problems the managers saw were a result of their personal concerns. Sales managers tended to say sales was the most important problem, for exam-ple, while production managers felt the need to clarify the organization was primary. An example provided by Floyd Mann's studies shows that supervisors and their subordinates have widely different views of the subordinates' freedom to discuss problems. For example, almost all fore-men and managers stated that they always or nearly always tell subordinates about changes affecting them or their work, but only about half of their subordinates agreed that this was true.[5]

Percepetual differences that result in conflict often begin when an individual's self-esteem is injured. In one typical case, a manager whose subordinates were performing project work for another manager became very upset, claiming that his people were underutilized and that the project was being managed too loosely. Later, it emerged that the real problem was that he felt hurt that the project manager hadn't recognized him and asked him to contribute his own ideas.[6] Chapter 4 will discuss more fully the ways in which people's perceptions, including their perceptions of themselves, are interdependent with their ways of communicating.

Language

A director of information services, explaining to a group of working supervisors from various departments why their organization had bought a new computer, said the following:

> The software enabled us to move our DOS/VS workload directly on. We attached full speed 3333 equivalent 7733 disc drives, thus providing higher speed secondary storage. The new equipment is configured with 256K bytes of core. We reduced running time without changing core allocations and expect to improve core availability by more effective I/0 blocking.[7]

While this is an extreme example, it is probably correct to say that no two people ever fully understand each other. To a greater or lesser degree, humans are engaged in a constant struggle to try to improve their effectiveness in using language. Those who make progress in this area tend to achieve more success in reaching task objectives. In a study of big city mayors, John Kotter and Paul Lawrence found that the more successful mayors were most often those who were most skillful in speaking the "languages" spoken in their cities. An aide described one successful mayor this way:

> When he is with the Irish, his ethnic background comes out and he looks like he grew up in Dublin. When he's at the university, he's a wise old man. Over at the Chamber, he is a shrewd capitalist. With the unions he is a cigar-chomping tough guy. He's not just "acting" either. He really knows how to talk the language of each of those groups.[8]

Chapter 5 gives special attention to two major topics related to language, the abstraction process and the multiple functions of language. We will see that while human language is weak and our skill in using it imperfect, we can make considerable improvement by first understanding some of the basics and then applying some simple techniques aimed at clearer thinking and communicating.

Nonverbal Communication

The student of organizations should assume that there is no such thing as "lack of communication." The phrase is too often used as a substitute for careful analysis leading to more useful understanding. Messages are constantly being sent or received even when no words are spoken. When the boss comes in and walks by Jones's desk without a word, after having said "Good morning" every day for the past six weeks, Jones is almost certain to receive a message, whether or not the boss had one in mind.

The importance of nonverbal communication is indicated in a study by Mehrabian and Ferris of types of communication that result in the changing of people's attitudes. They found that only seven percent of attitude change was accounted for by the verbal content of the message, while thirty-eight percent was accounted for by vocal characteristics (tone of voice, rate of speech, etc.), and fifty-five percent was accounted for by facial expression. Numerous other experimental studies have indicated that the face is more accurately judged than either tone of voice or speech. People tend to be more influenced by nonverbal cues (especially those they see) than by the words they hear.[9] This is not hard to understand when one considers that nonverbal aspects of communication can reveal such things as a person's mood, attitude toward other people, and degree of self-confidence.

The ways people use space and time often say more than the words they use in conversation. Edward Hall gives an interesting example in his book *The Silent Language.* Hall was asked to find out if nondiscriminatory labor practices could be adopted in the various departments of a city government. When he interviewed the department heads, they all said they would be willing to adopt nondiscriminatory practices. However, by observing how they used the nonverbal language of space and time, Hall concluded that only one department head was really willing to change. When he went to interview them, long waits were common, and interviews originally scheduled for an hour were cut to ten or fifteen minutes; some department heads forgot the appointments entirely. Hall was kept at an impersonal distance during the interviews, and only one department head came from behind the desk—this being the one who was really open to change.[10] Chapter 6 provides a number of aids for recognizing and understanding unsaid messages.

Interpersonal Dynamics

It is important to understand verbal and nonverbal messages, but it is probably even more important to understand the dynamics of interpersonal relationships. Communication problems and successes do not reside in individuals but in relationships *between* individuals. Probably the biggest block to understanding and improving communication lies in our stubborn tendency to believe that causality runs in just one direction. We tend to say, "If Joe would just pay attention to my point of view, things would improve." This statement contains the assumption that Joe is the single cause of the way things are. When we think this way, we are blind to any possibility that Joe's behavior may be partly in response to ours. Passively waiting for him to act may have convinced him that we didn't want him to pay attention to us.

Interpersonal relationships may be explained as exchanges of valued "commodities." Person 1 may give guidance and in turn receive esteem from Person 2. Relationships may also be seen usefully as transactions between certain kinds of internal states within the people involved, such as their motives, emotions, or degrees of self-awareness and openness. Chapter 7 provides some frameworks for understanding relationships that have proved to be useful for both explaining and improving interpersonal behavior.

Communication in Groups

Small groups have been said to be the most persistent and probably the oldest social form, fulfilling personal needs that no other form of organization can supply.[11] Small, face-to-face work groups occur throughout organizations in committee meeting rooms, in offices, and on the factory floor. In addition, such informal groups as car pools and lunch groups, formed spontaneously without official management sanction, contribute greatly to employee morale and often help accomplish tasks. For these reasons it is impossible to have a thorough understanding of organizational communication without understanding something about how small groups tick.

In some people's minds, groups are associated with ineffective task performance. One definition of a committee is that it is a group of the reluctant assigned by the imcompetent to do the unnecessary. It has also been suggested that a camel is a horse that was designed by a committee. The phenomenon of group-sanctioned output restriction among workers is also a familiar one.[12] On the other hand, John F. Kennedy and his advisors during the Cuban missile crisis[13] and the recent successful experience in Europe with autonomous work teams[14] indicate that groups can achieve both quality decisions and productivity. Therefore, it would be more useful to determine the difference between more and less effective groups.

Chapters 8 and 9 consider many of the aspects of communication in groups that make this difference. For example, attention is given to the patterns of communication, influence, and role-taking that occur in groups. These chapters also compare various group problem-solving procedures and their usefulness in particular kinds of situations. Differing styles of group leadership are examined, along with the conditions in which they tend to be effective. Overall, chapters 8 and 9 provide an array of important things to look for when observing or participating in group communication.

Communication in the Total Organization

The quality of communication that takes place in an organization is greatly affected by the overall design of that organization. There can be quite a difference, for example, between an organization that groups people according to their professional specialty, such as accounting, engineering, or sales, and one in which each unit is a self-contained team having the various specialists needed to produce a certain product or to serve clients in a given geographical area. In the first case, a person would be likely to spend more time talking with similarly oriented specialists. This organization could be expected to develop greater depth of expertise in the specialties because of the easy access of the specialists to one another for mutual sharing of knowledge. Coordination *between* different specialists —say a production supervisor and a sales engineer—could be much more difficult to attain in the first type of organization than in the second, however.

The communication gaps that exist in an organization because of its formal design are often bridged by spontaneous informal contacts. If the production supervisor and sales engineer have been friends since high school days, ample coordination may take place even though the company's official organization chart never provided for it.

Though many devices—formal and informal—may exist in an organization to help provide communication links, misunderstandings and interpersonal conflicts still inevitably occur. In fact, an organization that minimizes conflict is very likely complacent and not very effective. There is a difference, however, between productive conflict, where important issues are brought to light and dealt with, and the kind of conflict Sheldon Davis has referred to as "accumulated garbage," meaning disagreements that boil beneath the surface, sometimes for periods of years. These types of conflicts are often based on factors that are imagined rather than real and can draw large amounts of human effort away from productive work and into the task of maintaining the conflicts. As Davis puts it, "It takes effort to maintain a conflict; you have to work at it."[15]

Chapters 10 and 11 consider the relationships between organizational structure, communication, and task effectiveness. The roots of organizational conflict are examined along with the various ways that conflict can be handled.

Counseling and Helping

The final chapters address key areas in and by which organizational communication can be made more effective. The first of these, chapter 12, explores the counseling process—the means by which help is given and received. Counseling is obviously a vital process in the personal development as well as the working effectiveness of people in organizations, but the topic derives special importance from the fact that in actual practice, helping efforts are so often undertaken badly. A great many opportunities for useful exchanges of help pass by unrecognized. Potential receivers of help often disguise their requests, as was perhaps the case with Jim Jacobs's complaints about his boss and coworkers in the example at the beginning of this chapter. Would-be helpers, for their part, seem more often to fail than to succeed mainly because the helper fails to see adequately the receiver's point of view. The tendency to try to make judgments, evaluations, and decisions for other people is pervasive. In organizations, as elsewhere, a great deal of advice is given that is never taken. Chapter 12 develops a general model of the helping process, indicating that effective helping relationships vary depending on the nature of the surroundings, on the task, needs, abilities, and points of view of the helper and receiver, and on the kind of interpersonal relationship that exists between them.

Influence

It is impossible for an organization member to function effectively without exerting influence. The successful manager persuades his or her subordinates to achieve and maintain a high level of productivity. Subordinates get ahead by selling their bosses and others on new ideas. Problems are considered solved not just when a possible remedy becomes known, but when it is communicated persuasively. In addition, many communication events that are not explicit attempts to influence contain an element of persuasion. When people exchange information or advice, for example, they implicitly convince each other that the activity represents a worthwhile investment of time and effort and that what is being given by one person is being compensated in an adequate amount by the other.

Influence is not a one-way process. When people change their behavior in a direction someone else desires, they do so because they see the change as profitable to themselves.[16] In labor-management relations, for example, there have been cases where managements have conferred status on the union by giving them credit for certain improvements or providing them with valuable information, hoping thus to establish a bargaining climate of good faith.[17] Chapter 13 discusses influence within the framework of reinforcement theory. Reinforcement theory provides several insights into the kinds of two-way exchanges that are likely to result in a change in attitudes or behavior.

Chapter 13 also examines the complexity of the influence process, noting that there are multiple factors involved in persuasion. The credibility of the persuader is an important factor, as are the form and content of a persuasive message. The receiver's point of view and the group and organizational surroundings within which the influence attempt is being made are also significant.

The importance of organizational surroundings in the influence process is shown in an example given by George Strauss of a purchasing agent in a large scientific laboratory who was very skilled at reading the power realities of his organization. He had succeeded in extending his influence by always working through the laboratory manager when dealing with the heads of research departments. The lab managers were, as he put it, "a buffer between me and the department heads." However, he always dealt directly with the heads of other departments, such as equipment maintenance, since these department heads had a much lower status than the heads of the research departments, many of whom had Ph.D.'s. This agent knew when and how to use his organizational surroundings in order to exert influence. Strauss notes also that the purchasing agents who were most successful in extending their influence were those who rarely relied on their superiors to help them in interdepartmental disputes. The agents felt that such a reliance would weaken their relations both with the superior and with their fellow employees because it would indicate that they could not handle their own problems.[18] Clearly, the topic of influence is one which is subtle as well as complex. It is an area that cannot be overlooked in understanding organizational communication.

Organization Development and Communication

Organization development (OD) can be defined as a planned, organization-wide effort, managed from the top, to increase an organization's effectiveness and health through interventions that use behavioral science knowledge.[19] During the 1970s and early 1980s, OD has grown into a widely accepted field of professional practice encompassing such methods for organizational improvement as management by objectives, job enrichment, organization mirroring, confrontation meetings, and intergroup team building. The majority of OD methods use existing knowledge about organizational communication and have improved communication as part of their aim. Intergroup team building, for example, makes use of the fact that people in different organizational units often see one another in incomplete or distorted ways because their perceptions are colored by the nature of their jobs. This team building technique is usually used where two departments have had disruptive disagreements and difficulty in cooperating with each other. The two departments are brought together to express their perceptions after each department has first prepared a written statement of its view of the other department, as well as a statement of how it believes the other department will describe it. When successfully used, team building leads each group to see both itself and the other group more realistically and enables the two groups to find ways to achieve more effective on-the-job coordination.[20]

Organization development efforts are not always successful, and when they do fail, communication problems are often responsible. The author participated in an OD program in a big-city postal district in which all the middle managers and supervisors in the district were assigned to teams of six to ten members each. The teams met weekly to identify problems and prepare recommended solutions for submission to higher management. Although several weekly meetings were devoted to each recommendation and the recommendations were convincingly presented, the program was discontinued after an initial eight-week trial period. A major reason appeared to be that top management became overloaded with the large mass of information generated by the teams and were so slow in responding to the reports that the team members lost interest. Just as a doctor is aided when a patient is healthy enough to tell him where it hurts, OD efforts require a certain level of communication effectiveness in order to proceed.

In chapter 14 the communication implications of OD are considered in greater detail. Attention is given to the process of change in organizations, ways of reducing resistance to change, and the details of some specific OD techniques that have proved successful in practice.

Summary

The topic of this book can be defined thus: Organizational communication is the flow of messages within a network of interdependent relationships.[21] In order to be understood, however, the communication process needs to be examined from several perspectives. Most of this chapter has introduced a number of the perspectives that are covered more fully in the following chapters. These perspectives have practical application both in and out of an organizational setting; they can help show the differences between more and less effective communication; and those who understand these differences more fully are in a better position to communicate more effectively. Furthermore, these perspectives can help provide the reader with the excitement of seeing many new dimensions in events that comprise so much of everyday experience.

Questions for Review

1. In attempting to explain something, why is it useful to look for questions rather than answers first?
2. Why is it important to view the communication process from multiple perspectives?

3. What perspective does the psychiatrist lack when he mutters about his neighbor's "Good morning" greeting, "Hm, I wonder what he meant by that?"
4. How does the organization itself act as a barrier to communication?
5. Give an example showing how a person's self-perception can be an important factor in the quality of communication.
6. Why is it useful to assume that there is no such thing as "lack of communication?"
7. What does it mean to think in terms of interpersonal relationships, and why does this way of thinking represent an important perspective?
8. Give an example showing how organization design can affect communication.
9. How can an understanding of the influence process help a person improve organizational communication?
10. What is organization development, and what does it have to do with communication?

References and Notes

1. E. T. Klemmer and F. W. Snyder, "Measurement of Time Spent Communicating," *Journal of Communication* 22, no. 2 (1972): 142–58.
2. Edgar F. Huse, James L. Bowditch, and Dalmar Fisher, eds., *Readings on Behavior in Organizations* (Reading, Mass.: Addison-Wesley, 1975), p. 2.
3. S. I. Hayakawa, *Language in Thought and Action* (New York: Harcourt Brace Jovanovich, 1972), pp. 27–29; Fritz J. Roethlisberger, *Training for Human Relations* (Boston: Division of Research, Harvard Business School, 1954), pp. 24–27.
4. DeWitt C. Dearborn and Herbert A. Simon, "Selective Perceptions: A Note on the Departmental Identifications of Executives," *Sociometry* 21 (1958): 140–43.
5. From an unpublished study by Floyd C. Mann discussed in Rensis Likert, *New Patterns in Management* (New York: McGraw-Hill, 1961), p. 52.
6. Richard E. Walton, *Interpersonal Peacemaking* (Reading, Mass.: Addison-Wesley, 1969), pp. 20–23.
7. Adapted from Leslie H. Matthies, *The Management System* (New York, 1976), p. 10. Copyright © 1976 John Wiley & Sons. Reprinted by permission of John Wiley & Sons, Inc.
8. From John P. Kotter and Paul R. Lawrence, *Mayors in Action* (New York, 1974), p. 137. Copyright © 1974 John Wiley & Sons. Reprinted by permission of John Wiley & Sons, Inc.
9. Albert Mehrabian and Susan R. Ferris, "Inference of Attitudes from Nonverbal Communication in Two Channels," *Journal of Consulting Psychology* 31 (1967): 248–52. See also Belle N. DePaulo et. al., "Decoding Discrepant Nonverbal Cues," *Journal of Personality and Social Psychology* 36 (1978): 313–23; Paul Ekman and Harriet Oster, "Facial Expressions of Emotion," *Annual Review of Psychology* 30 (1979): 544.

10. Edward T. Hall, *The Silent Language* (Garden City, N.Y.: Doubleday, 1959), p. 15.
11. See George C. Homans, *The Human Group,* (New York: Harcourt, Brace and World, 1950), p. 454; Abraham Zaleznik and David Moment, *The Dynamics of Interpersonal Behavior* (New York: John Wiley & Sons, 1964), pp. 3–5.
12. See, for example, Donald Roy, "Quota Restriction and Goldbricking in a Machine Shop," *American Journal of Sociology* 57, no. 5 (1952): 430-37.
13. See Irving L. Janis, *Victims of Groupthink* (Boston: Houghton-Mifflin, 1972).
14. Edgar F. Huse and James L. Bowditch, *Behavior in Organizations* (Reading, Mass.: Addison-Wesley, 1977), pp. 372–77.
15. From comments made by Sheldon Davis, Vice President and Director of Industrial Relations for the Systems Group, TRW, Inc., in the film "Organizational Development," University of California Extension Media Center, Management Development Series, no. 9, (Berkeley, Calif.).
16. See, for example, George C. Homans, *Social Behavior: Its Elementary Forms* (New York: Harcourt, Brace and Jovanovich, 1974), pp. 119-24.
17. Richard E. Walton and John B. McKersie, *A Behavioral Theory of Labor Negotiations* (New York: McGraw-Hill, 1965), pp. 236–40.
18. George Strauss, "Tactics of Lateral Relationship: The Purchasing Agent," *Administrative Science Quarterly* 7, no. 2 (1962), 161–86.
19. Richard Beckhard, *Organization Development: Strategies and Models* (Reading, Mass.: Addison-Wesley, 1969), p. 9.
20. Ibid., pp. 33–35.
21. Gerald M. Goldhaber, *Organizational Communication* (Dubuque, Ia.: W. C. Brown, 1974), p. 11.

Chapter 2

Diagnosing Communication within Organizations: A Models Approach

A Situation for Diagnosis
Communication as Action—Linear Models
    The one-way model
    The interaction model
    The channel
    Encoding and decoding
    Noise
    Feedback
Communication as Relationship—Organic Models
    The two-person relationship model
    The system model

After studying this chapter, the reader should be able to

Define and use the following terms and concepts

Model	Indirect feedback
Linear models	Internal feedback
Organic models	External feedback
One-way model	Two-person relationship model
Interaction model	Self-view
Encoding	Organic interdependence
Decoding	System model
Channel	System environmental factors
Channel redundancy	Group controls
Sender noise	Group structure
Channel noise	Organizational factors
Receiver noise	Task characteristics
Feedback	Function
Direct feedback	

Understand

Four models for explaining communication (the one-way, interaction, two-person relationship, and system models)
How to diagnose a specific event using each model
The strengths of each model and what each omits
The difference between communication as action and as relationship
Aspects of effective diagnostic thinking
The errors that effective diagnosis helps minimize

2

A person attempting to service a TV set is helped by having a diagram of the circuits. In a similar fashion, someone trying to understand, and perhaps repair, a communication process can be aided by a model.

A model is a simplified way of thinking about something and can usually be expressed as a visual diagram. Models are a useful way of illustrating some of the components of communication as well as some of its processes. The fact that a model is a simplified representation is both an advantage and a disadvantage. It is an advantage because communication is a complicated process. The many perspectives or aspects of communication represented by the chapter titles of this book indicate its complexity. It would be impossible, and probably unnecessary, to attend to all of these aspects at the same time. A useful model is one that helps us focus on aspects that are critical in particular circumstances. The skilled observer of communication is a person who can select the particular model or models that provide the most applicable insights in specific situations. A disadvantage of models is that they tend to oversimplify. Like maps, they leave out things that may be important. The good driver is one who is aware of both the road and the map. Similarly, the skillful observer of communication keeps checking back and forth between the model and the actual communication events being observed. Students of communication sometimes confuse the model with the process it represents and end their investigation of the facts too soon. Models are helpful when used as aids to understanding events, not as distractions that cause us to lose touch with them.

Quite a number of models are presented throughout this book, not

Quite a number of models are presented throughout this book, not just in this chapter. For the most part, the models introduced in other chapters relate to specialized aspects of communication (e.g., language, communication in small groups, organizational conflict), while the models presented here are concerned with more general, pervasive features. All the models shown here and elsewhere in this book are intended to be used for one primary purpose: diagnosis. The models should be used in combination, for a single one cannot do the complete diagnostic job. Experienced observers of organizational communication have found that these models not only help them understand communication events and express their understanding, but, in some cases, encourage them to suggest or undertake action aimed at improvements.

A SITUATION FOR DIAGNOSIS

To demonstrate the process of diagnosis, a brief case example follows. The models introduced later in the chapter will be applied to this case.

Pam Gale was personnel manager for an unemployment office located in southwestern Wisconsin. Most of the Unemployment Commission's policies and procedures were established by the commission's head office in Madison and announced to the local offices through regional headquarters offices. The head office frequently consulted the regional managers about new procedures but seldom conferred with the local offices. Local personnel managers typically received current policies and procedures through the director of their local office.

Recently Pam had been bothered by one new procedure, which required that eighty percent of all new local office employees hired during any six-month period had to be minorities. She felt this would make it hard to hire qualified employees during the rest of the winter. There were four months to go, she thought, and the only people hired in the past two months were nonminorities. In effect, this meant no one could be hired except minorities for the next four months. This was typical, she thought, of the procedures one had to live with in this job.

One morning, as Pam was reading her mail, Chuck Carlada, the local office's client services director, walked into her office. "Pam, I've got a problem, and I need some help from you," Chuck began.

"What's up?" asked Pam. "I'll sure do what I can."

"It's about Bill Wilson," Chuck continued. "He's applying to be rehired after taking a try at the insurance business for a few months. He was one of our best client service coordinators, but your secretary tells me we can't reinstate him for four months because he's not a minority. What can we do about this? We certainly ought to reinstate Bill. We're way short of people, and he can do three times the work that an inexperienced person could do."

"Well," replied Pam, "the minority hiring procedure applies to newly hired employees, and that's what Bill would be. He was terminated, not put on leave. According to the procedure, there's no way we can hire him until four months from now."

Chuck looked incredulous. "I can't believe it! I really need someone to help cut the case backlog in my department, and you're saying we have to add to our workload, in effect, by bringing in new people to train. It just doesn't make sense. Sure, we could use Bill in four months, but he'll never wait that long for the job. He has other opportunities right now."

"Well, I know you've heard about the eighty percent minority hiring rule," said Pam. "It is dangerous to make exceptions to head office procedures, and we may not make the eighty percent even if we hire all minorities for the next four months. I agree that the procedure is a poor one, but if you want to change it, you'd better see the local office director, not me."

Chuck sighed. "Pam, I just need help in my department. They aren't going to fire you for being off a few percentage points in your affirmative action numbers."

"You know what happens when you start making exceptions to procedures," Pam replied. "If I let you hire Bill, I'll have all the other department heads in here saying, 'Hire this guy. He's not a minority, but you let Chuck hire Bill Wilson.' And what happens if we can't stay within affirmative action guidlines? We're an unemployment office. If we won't hire minorities, how can we expect other employers to hire all the minority clients we're trying to place? As I say, if you want to suggest a change, see the local office director."

Chuck was becoming exasperated. "Come on, Pam, this isn't the problem. I need someone, and here's a really competent person available. The people in my department are starting to lean on me about getting some help in to spread the case load. We have an especially bad backlog on our hands right now. You're not being very helpful."

"Well, you're the one who got yourself into this jam," argued Pam. "If you were bringing some lower-rated employees along by running a good training program for them, you wouldn't get caught short. You'd have a person all ready to step into a coordinator's job whenever you needed someone."

Chuck responded that he didn't see how this was relevant to his problem. "I need a coordinator right now, and you are refusing to help. This whole hiring issue is the most ridiculous thing I have ever experienced," he said as he stamped out of the office.

COMMUNICATION AS ACTION—LINEAR MODELS

Probably the simplest way to view the conversation between Pam and Chuck is to say that each of them was transmitting certain messages to the other. Each may be seen as a telegraph operator, sending a message to the other, getting a signal that the message has or has not been received, and then sometimes receiving a message in response from the other person. Looked at this way, communication is seen as action, with the action consisting of the beaming of messages on a line from a transmitting party to a receiving party. This linear-action picture of communication is the basis of two specific models which will now be discussed, the one-way model and the interaction model.

The One-Way Model

Probably the oldest model of communication is shown in exhibit 2–1. It is based on Aristotle's *Rhetoric,* the first formal treatise on communication. Aristotle observed mainly persuasive forms of communication: courtroom arguments, legislative assemblies, and public meetings where men and events were being praised. This may have led Aristotle to see communication as a one-way process flowing from a sender to a receiver. As Aristotle saw it, successful persuasion took place when a sender used the right techniques to present the right message to the right audience. He strongly emphasized the need for the sender to consider the characteristics of the audience, such as age and frame of mind. He noted, "the same thing does not appear the same to men when they are friendly and when they hate, nor when they are angry and when they are in a gentile mood."[1]

Though simple, the one-way model is a useful diagnostic tool. One of its major strengths is that it emphasizes the importance of the receiver. In the case of Pam and Chuck, for example, the way Chuck hears Pam's message is not caused purely by the content of her argument as to why Bill Wilson should not be hired but by the pressures Chuck was experiencing—namely, his worries about the heavy current workload and his subordinates' pleas for more help.

EXHIBIT 2–1
THE ONE-WAY MODEL

Sender	Message & delivery techniques →	Receiver

This model directs attention to another important area, the message and the way it is delivered. When using this model as an analytic tool, the diagnostician has to ask what all the parts of the message are, in what order they are being presented, and in what ways they are expressed. A complex, multipart message may not be received or accepted as fully as a simple one. The total message Pam sent Chuck contained a number of parts, including Pam's suggestion that if Chuck wanted to do something further about hiring Bill Wilson, he should go to see the local office director. Chuck gave no evidence that he even heard this suggestion, perhaps because it was just one part of a message containing so many other parts: her initial statement that she will "do what she can," her refusal to hire Bill, her support for the eighty percent rule (along with her statement that she feels the procedure is a poor one), her belief that other department heads would also want exceptions made, and so on. The suggestion about going to the local office director, even though made twice, was apparently lost in this shuffle of multiple message parts.

A minute's consideration of the one-way model should reveal that even though it is useful, it is vastly oversimplified. Probably the most obvious shortcoming of this model is that when communication is seen as a one-way action, feedback is ignored. Most messages that are sent receive some kind of response, especially in face-to-face conversation. Even on the telephone we make occasional grunts to indicate we are listening. Indeed, the fact that no response is given—that feedback is zero —can have a powerful influence on the subsequent messages the sender transmits. The one-way model also fails to give attention to any specifics of the sending and receiving processes. Messages vary in their quality, and they are sent in diverse ways. Sometimes a simple nod or wink conveys clear meaning, while a loud shout may be completely misunderstood. The next model provides for some of the one-way model's shortcomings.

The Interaction Model

The interaction model shown in exhibit 2–2 combines ideas from several prominent communication theorists.[2] The interaction model contains four concepts, which are additions to those contained in the one-way model: (1) the channel, (2) encoding and decoding, (3) noise, and (4) feedback.

EXHIBIT 2–2
THE INTERACTION MODEL

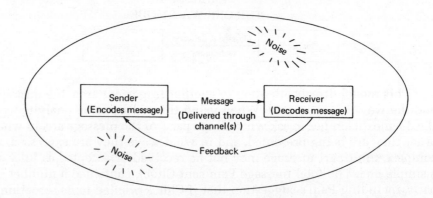

The Channel. Any medium by which messages can be conveyed is a communication channel. Spoken words, written prose, poetry, diagrams, nonverbal means, the telephone, and countless other channels exist. The choice of a channel can have an important bearing on the outcome of communication. Sometimes meanings can be conveyed more effectively in writing, as in the case of a complex financial analysis, while other messages are more appropriately delivered in a face-to-face conversation. If I have asked my boss to budget some money for a special project and he responds with a written memo saying, "Your request has been denied," I will probably gather a very different meaning than if he comes to my office and gives his response in person.

Marshall McLuhan gives many vivid examples of the effects of the channel. Some channels, he notes, have the effect of increasing the pace of activity.[3] People act faster on information that arrives by telegram than by letter. Another of McLuhan's examples concerns the effects of print media. He observes that "the uniformity and repeatability of print permeated the Rennaissance with the idea of time and space as continuous, measurable quantities."[4] He makes the point that the medium (or channel) itself tended to give people a sense of control over physical and political processes. McLuhan's well-known argument is that the medium *is* the message. While this seems overstated, it is important to realize that not only the message, but also the channel, can convey meaning.

A message may be sent and received over more than one channel. This *channel redundancy* can make a message more likely to be received and understood, as in the case of a televised sports event, where the video presentation is backed up by an audio description by the announcer. In the case of Pam and Chuck, Pam could not escape learning that Chuck was unhappy, since he expressed it in words and also by the pained expressions on his face.

The existence of multiple channels can sometimes lead to communication problems, as in cases where conflicting signals are sent over two different channels. For example, a persuasive speech can lose its effectiveness if the speaker's body language conveys nervousness. Furthermore, the capacity of a person to process information coming in over a large number of channels is limited. As mentioned previously in connection with multipart messages, people sometimes withdraw or tune out when an excessive amount of information comes at them.

Encoding and Decoding.   Encoding is the process by which the sender's ideas become converted into the symbols that comprise the message. Encoding really involves the sender making a prediction about the receiver. Some people claim that human behavior cannot be predicted; yet when we put an idea into words and say it to another person, we are typically making a prediction that they will understand us.

Since we cannot take our idea and put it directly into the head of the receiver, what we are doing is choosing to encode our idea into certain symbols, such as particular words and gestures, which we expect the receiver to decode into the same idea we have. When we view communication in this way, we can see that the accuracy of the predictions has a major effect on the quality of communication that takes place between people.

These predictions are often very accurate. Frequently one observes the effects of faulty encoding and decoding. Ed Huse, a colleague of the author, says he once left a stack of papers on his secretary's desk with a sheet on top saying "Xerox this." Later he found just one Xerox copy in his in-basket, a copy of the sheet that said "Xerox this." Occasionally, and to varying degrees, we all play the role of the young son in the following classic exchange:

Mom: Where are you going?
Son: Out.
Mom: What are you going to do?
Son: Nothing.

As these examples indicate, encoding and decoding problems cannot be fully separated from each other. Decoding refers to the process whereby the receiver interprets the symbols contained in the message. Recurrent states of mind, their surroundings, and other factors too numerous to mention could lead Mom in the above example to reach any number of conclusions. Information, in and of itself, has no meaning. It becomes meaningful only when people attribute meaning to it by interpreting it. Because of this, one might say that the important message is not the one the sender sends but the one the receiver receives. More generally, the encoder and decoder parts of the model are important because they lead us beyond the objective content of the message to ask what is on the inside of the sender and receiver and how their two points of view compare with each other.

Noise.   Noise may be defined as anything present in the perceived signal that was not part of the original intended message. Noise may originate with the sender. For example, the sender's mode of dress may distract from the message. Or noise may originate with the receiver. In the Pam and Chuck conversation, for example, Pam's preoccupation with the pressure of the minority hiring rule may have made it hard for her to hear Chuck's need for immediate help in handling his department's case load, a problem she might have addressed separately from the question of whether or not to hire someone new. Noise is always present in the channels. It can be audible noise, such as machinery starting up, phones ringing, or other people's conversations, or it can be the silent presence of something distracting, as when two people are talking while a third person is waiting for a chance to speak with one of them.

Feedback.   The biggest difference between the interaction model and the one-way model is that the interaction model includes the concept of feedback. Feedback suggests that communication includes a return channel by which the sender can obtain reactions from the receiver. Is the audience bored, upset, or pleased with my speech? Does the class understand the lecture, or are they confused? Does my client agree or disagree with the advice I am giving him? All of these questions indicate that the sender can open up a second line of communication and get some information back from the receiver.

Some senders make stronger attempts than others to obtain feedback. In the case of Pam and Chuck, Pam suggested twice that Chuck go see the local office director but did not try to get a response from Chuck. In this instance, our use of the feedback concept as a diagnostic tool helps us to see that Pam is really not as interested in seeing action taken to solve some of the problems she has "had to live with" as some of her other statements seem to indicate. Receivers, of course, also vary in the degree of effort they put into providing feedback to senders.

Various types of feedback can be distinguished. Feedback is sometimes *direct,* as in face-to-face exchanges of words and other expressions. *Indirect* feedback can occur, for example, when absenteeism or a decline in production indicates that managerial messages are not being favorably responded to. *External* feedback refers to responses from listeners. However, feedback may also be *internal* in the sense that when we are sending, we monitor the encoding and transmitting processes. We know when we have mispronounced a word and when our tone of voice has been harsh and argumentative if our internal feedback channels are open. If they are not, we may be surprised to find that the receiver is responding to us in ways we cannot explain. Internal feedback channels were not included in exhibit 2–2, but the reader may wish to draw them in.

Feedback is often spoken of as a good thing that no one can give or receive enough of. Nevertheless, there can be such a thing as too much feedback. For example, sometimes a sender needs to think about, encode, and transmit a message without being distracted by feedback before the transmission has been completed. Whether there is too much, too little, or the right amount in a specific case, the main point is that the feedback concept can be used as an aid to understanding what is happening when people are attempting to communicate. Instead of saying, "Aha, there's not enough feedback; *that's* the problem," and then sitting back satisfied, we need to use the feedback notion (as well as the other concepts contained in this model) as stimuli to further diagnostic questioning: Why isn't the receiver responding? What effects does the receiver's lack of response have on the sender? When the receiver does respond, what is the content of the response, and what is this doing to change or reinforce the behavior of the sender? Unless such questions are asked, communication can only be thought of as a one-way phenomenon rather than as an interaction between sender and receiver.[5]

COMMUNICATION AS RELATIONSHIP—ORGANIC MODELS

The interaction model accounts for quite a few of the most important aspects of communication. The concepts of *channel, encoding, decoding,* and *noise* allow us to begin to see how complex and how diverse the communication process can be. The interaction model adds substantially to the one-way model by including the concept of *feedback.* With this addition, we can begin to see communication not just as individual messages but as a series of messages, each of which evokes a response that, in turn, can affect subsequent messages. This model directs our attention to the two-way nature of communication, wherein the participants take turns being sender and receiver, each influencing the other in a series of multiple message-feedback interchanges.

Although the interaction model is a major improvement over the one-way model, it still falls short in two important respects. First, it suggests that communication proceeds sequentially, one step at a time—message, then feedback, then another message, then more feedback. Several commentators have noted that communication participants don't simply alternate this way. Instead, each is both sender and receiver simultaneously.[6] Even in a simple exchange of greetings between myself and another person, it is often impossible to specify the sequence. Did I say "Hello" in the manner I did because of the way the other person looked at me, or because it was what I thought he would expect? Did I say what I said because of how I felt in general that morning or because of what the other person said to me? Were my thoughts and feelings things that I brought to the situation, or were they evoked during the conversation? When we pursue questions like these, we find that the distinction becomes blurred as to who is sender and who is receiver; what is stimulus and what is response. We see that communication can usefully be viewed as an ongoing, mutual relationship in which aspects of the process are at the same time both causes and effects.

The second weakness of the interaction model is that it leaves out several important components of the communication process. The sender's and receiver's perceptions of each other and of themselves are not included, nor are context factors, such as the wider social and organizational settings in which the communication is taking place. The remaining two models to be discussed in this chapter, the two-person relationship model and the system model, help offset these deficiencies. The two-person relationship model gives special attention to the communication participants themselves, while the system model emphasizes factors that are in the environment surrounding the participants.

The Two-Person Relationship Model

The central focus of the two-person relationship model, shown in exhibit 2–3, is the two upper boxes connected by arrows going in both directions.

These arrows indicate that the communication process is a reciprocal one in which A's view of, and behavior toward, B is simultaneously affecting and being affected by B.

Straightforward as this may seem, it represents a way of thinking that runs strongly counter to our usual ways of understanding and explaining human behavior. Our dominant tendency is to reach conclusions like, "Joe has slowed down on the job because his boss never listens to the suggestions he makes." We grab onto the most convenient one-way cause and effect explanation: the boss's behavior causes Joe's. In doing this we blind ourselves to the fact that Joe doesn't look any more inspiring to his boss than the boss does to Joe; that Joe's lagging morale and output makes him seem to the boss like someone whose suggestions do not deserve much attention. Two mutually reinforcing entities—Joe and the boss—sustain the situation. In the case involving Pam and Chuck, we might tend to say that Chuck became angry and left because Pam would not try to help him solve his problem. However, the relationship model helps us see it is equally valid to say Chuck's anger and his reluctance to see the difficulty Pam was experiencing made it unlikely Pam would want to help him. It is especially important to have this sort of eye for the organic, interdependent nature of relationships if we want to bring about change and improvement in them. If Pam wanted to change things, she would do well to recognize that a simple change in her behavior (e.g., being more sympathetic) might not have much effect if no change occurs in Chuck's view of her. As long as he has her defined as the one who must take all the action and as being unreasonable for not doing so, the situation remains in a stalemate. If Pam and Chuck had thought in terms of the relationship model instead of one-way cause and effect, they might have more readily

EXHIBIT 2–3

THE TWO-PERSON RELATIONSHIP MODEL

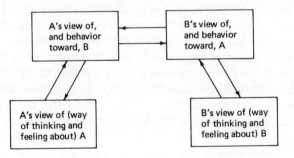

Source: Arthur N. Turner and George F. F. Lombard, *Interpersonal Behavior and Administration* (New York: The Free Press, 1969), p. 12. Adapted with permission of Macmillan Publishing Co., Inc. Copyright © 1969 by Arthur N. Turner and George F. F. Lombard.

seen the possibilities that existed for shared responsibility and collaborative action. Pam, for example, might have said to herself, "My insisting again and again to Chuck that we can't hire any nonminorities is reinforcing his impression I don't want to help him. Maybe I can change that impression by offering to go with him to see the local office director about the problem. At least it could improve the working relationship between me and Chuck."

The model suggests that we look not only at each person's explicit behavior but also at how each *perceives* the other. Explicitly, the following perceptions are focused upon the model:

A's perception of B and of B's behavior

B's perception of A and of A's behavior

Each person's self-perception

The third item in this list is addressed by the two lower boxes in the diagram. The model indicates that how A and B see and act toward each other is partly influenced by how each of them sees himself or herself. Pam, for example, seems to view herself as a manager who is very dependent on her superiors and the Unemployment Commission's procedures to determine her actions. She says she has had to live with such procedures as the one about minority hiring. Her view of herself as one who cannot take initiative leads her to see Chuck's request as a threat, since he wants her to take action. Her refusal helps her reaffirm her way of thinking and feeling about herself. The arrows pointing in both directions again suggest that we need to think in terms of two-way interdependence between factors. One's self-view is both a cause of, and at the same time is being caused by, the way one views the other person. How A behaves toward B is partly a result of A's self-view, but, at the same time, A's self-view is being reinforced or changed as a result of the kinds of behavior A is producing. The more Pam fails to act, the more she sees herself as a dependent person.

People tend to act in ways that confirm the view they have of themselves. If we had to be limited to one proposition from the behavioral sciences to explain human action, this one would be a good one to choose. The two-person relationship model, which directs us to sort out how people see their own and another's participation in their relationship, illustrates the strong influence self-view has on behavior. The importance of self-view, the perceptual point of view, and the concept of organic interdependence (or two-way causality) are the key ideas contained in this model.

The System Model

All communication takes place in some kind of environment. In the case of the Pam and Chuck conversation, certain features of the environment help explain why the relationship took the shape it did and help us to understand the total situation better. One example would be the organization's decision process, whereby policies and procedures are set without consultation with the local offices. It is easy to see how this could lead Pam to feel that procedures are things she just has to live with. Conversely, Pam's reluctance to make recommendations, or even to ask any questions of her superiors, helps reinforce this centralized decision process. Other important aspects of the environment would include Chuck's subordinates, the local office director, and the nature of the local community.

The three models already discussed in this chapter have stressed the importance of taking a close look at the communicators and their behavior. In the system model, shown in exhibit 2-4, it is as if the camera has zoomed out, revealing three major environmental factors in addition to the individuals and their communication behavior. These environmental factors are *group controls and structure, organizational factors,* and *task characteristics.*[7]

EXHIBIT 2–4
THE SYSTEM MODEL

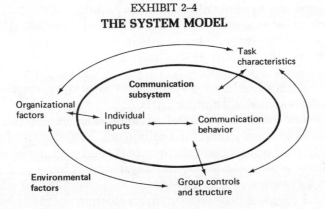

Group controls and structure are forces that exist in the group or groups to which the communicators belong. Group controls refer to the accepted standards or norms of how group members are expected to behave and the methods the group has for enforcing these standards. An example would be the complaints of Chuck's subordinates, who are saying that he should make their workload lighter by hiring more people. Group structure includes such aspects as the hierarchies of status and power that develop in human groups.

Organizational factors include the design of the organization, supervisory practices, information systems, policies, rules, procedures, and other aspects of the organization that are usually determined by management decisions. The nature of the work or problem about which communication is taking place is termed *task characteristics.* As already indicated, the two remaining parts of the model include the personalities, coding and decoding habits, and points of view of the communicating individuals (*individual inputs*) and their behavior in relationship to one another (*communication behavior*).

All parts of the model are connected to one another by double-headed arrows, indicating two-way interdependence, a feature that gives the model its designation as a *system* model. A system is a set of parts that depend on each other for the continuance of significant aspects of their present state of being.[8] Systems can be thought of as consisting of small subsystems, such as the communication subsystem shown in exhibit 2–4, contained within higher order systems (environmental factors). In the Pam and Chuck case, their conversation can be thought of as a communication subsystem, while their organization, the problems they are discussing, and the significant other people with whom each of them works are factors in the wider surrounding environment. The idea of a system existing in an environment is a notion that has been found useful repeatedly in sciences as different as physics and biology, and that has been called "a fundamental concept which is essential to scientific theory."[9] Systems and subsystems can be thought of as being in a state of mutual interdependency with their environments. Environments affect systems they surround and systems affect their environments.[10]

Implicit in the system model is the concept of *function,* which means that each part of the system plays a role in the maintenance or change of other parts and the system as a whole. The concept of function is an important one to keep in mind when applying the system model because it prevents us from looking at a system part separately, thus losing sight of its interdependence with other parts.

The system model has several advantages as an aid to analysis. It prompts us not to simply hunt for a villain or a hero in a complex human situation. By its emphasis on multiple parts and functional interdependency, it discourages us from judging a system part to be good or bad and encourages us to analyze and understand it thoroughly. In addition, the system model suggests that we see communication events as having multiple rather than single or simple explanations; that we see two-way interdependencies rather than one-way cause and effect relationships; and that we look for relationships between communication and the environment in which it occurs. If Pam Gale had thought in these terms, she might well have raised questions such as, Does higher management fail to consult with me partly because I always passively accept every directive they send me? In other words, she might have begun to see that her communication style was not just caused by her organizational environment but contributed to making that environment what it was.

The system concept is frequently misunderstood, partly because the word *system* itself is often used in ways other than the way the sciences define the term. The most common misconception is that the idea of system refers to something that is working smoothly and effectively like a well-tuned engine or a work group in which morale, efficiency, and productivity are all at high levels. The system model is not that limited. It can be used to understand healthy or unhealthy situations where communication is harmonious or conflict-laden, where system parts and environment factors are in states of mutual compatibility or mutual antagonism. The concept of system is one that has broad applicability and one that can lead to more than common insight into events.

Summary

This chapter began by noting that models can be helpful to the diagnostician. It is hoped that the remainder of the chapter has said something to the reader in an overall way about the importance of careful diagnosis above and beyond the specific models presented.

The models themselves, however, are ones of proven utility. The first one, the *one-way model,* stressed the importance of understanding the receiver's situation and the nature of the message being communicated. The *interaction model* was presented as a way of addressing certain factors in communication not included in the *one-way* model—namely the channel, the concept of encoding and decoding, noise, and feedback. Next, the *two-person relationship model* was described as giving special attention to the importance of people's perceptions of self and others and the usefulness of seeing communication as occurring within an organic process of interdependent parts. Finally, the *system model* reemphasized the notion of organic interdependency of factors, focused attention on key aspects of the environment in which communication takes place— namely, the social system, the organization, and the task—and implied strongly that a person successful at understanding communication events can avoid both single-cause thinking and the tendency to see things as good or bad. None of the four models is intended to be pictures of what communication ought to be like. They are offered as aids to understanding what kind of communication is taking place, why, and with what effects.

Questions for Review

1. A map is to a geographic area as a model is to what?
2. How is it that the models given in this chapter are useful even though each leaves out several important aspects of communication?
3. Give an example showing how a message can have different effects in different situations.
4. What are the major shortcomings of the one-way model?
5. Why is it often important in understanding communication to distinguish between the message and the channel?
6. Give examples of an encoding problem, a decoding problem, and three kinds of noise.
7. Can feedback sometimes consist of an absence of communication?
8. Give an example of how a person's self-view affected and was affected by communication with another person.

9. Give your appraisal of the following statement: "A system or subsystem is affected by its environment."
10. Refer to exhibit 2–4. What other important environmental factors could have been included in this diagram?
11. Define the term *function* as it is used in this chapter, and apply this concept to some aspect of the Pam and Chuck conversation described early in the chapter.
12. Explain how linear models differ from organic models.

References and Notes

1. Lane Cooper, ed., *The Rhetoric of Aristotle* (Englewood Cliffs, N.J.: Prentice-Hall, 1960), p. 91.
2. See David Berlo, *The Process of Communication* (New York: Holt, Reinhart and Winston, 1960), p. 72, for a description of his S-M-C-R (source, message, channel, receiver) model. For models introducing the encoding, decoding, and feedback concepts, see Wilbur Schram, "How Communication Works," in *The Process and Effects of Mass Communication,* eds. Wilbur Schram and Donald Roberts (Urbana, Ill.: University of Illinois Press, 1971), p. 24; Claude F. Shannon and Warren Weaver, *The Mathematical Theory of Communication* (Urbana, Ill.: University of Illinois Press, 1949), p. 9. The concepts of sender noise, channel noise, and receiver noise are taken from Jerry C. Wofford, Edwin A. Gerloff, and Robert C. Cummins, *Organizational Communication* (New York: McGraw-Hill, 1977), p. 45.
3. Marshall McLuhan, *Understanding Media* (New York: McGraw-Hill, 1964), chap. 1.
4. Ibid., chap. 18. For an empirical study showing channel effects, see Victor P. Wall and John A. Boyd, "Channel Variation and Attitude Change," *Journal of Communication* 21, no. 4 (1971): 363–67.
5. For a thorough discussion of the concept of feedback, see John Y. Kim, "Feedback in Social Sciences: Toward a Reconceptualization of Morphogenesis," in Brent D. Ruben and John Y. Kim, *General Systems Theory and Human Communication,* (Rochelle Park, N.J.: Hayden Book Co., 1975), pp. 207–21.
6. See, for example, George A. Kelly, "The Autobiography of a Theory," in *Clinical Psychology and Personality: The Selected Papers of George A. Kelly,* ed. Brendan Maher (New York: John Wiley & Sons, 1969), p. 47; Dean C. Barnlund, "A Transactional Model of Communication," in *Foundations of Communication Theory,* eds. Kenneth Sereno and C. David Mortensen (New York: Harper and Row, 1970); John Stewart, *Bridges Not Walls* (Reading, Mass.: Addison-Wesley, 1977), pp. 17–24; JoAnne F. Vandemark and Pamela C. Leth, *Interpersonal Communication* (Menlo Park, Calif.: Cummings Publishing Company, 1977), pp. 3–4; Donald K. Darnell, "Toward a Reconceptualization of Communication," *Journal of Communication* 21, no. 1 (1971): 5–16; Donald A. Clement and Kenneth D. Frandsen, "On Conceptional and Empirical Treatments of Feedback in Human Communication," *Communication Monographs* 43 (1976): 11–28.
7. The system model and the discussion of it given in this chapter draws upon ideas contained in Jay W. Lorsch and Alan Sheldon, "The Individual in the

Organization: A Systems View," in *Managing Group and Intergroup Relations* ed. Jay W. Lorsch and Paul R. Lawrence (Homewood, Ill.: Irwin-Dorsey, 1972), pp. 161–82.

8. John A. Seiler, *Systems Analysis in Organizational Behavior.* (Homewood, Ill.: Irwin Dorsey, 1967), p. 4.

9. Alfred North Whitehead, *Science and the Modern World* (New York: Mentor Books, New American Library of World Literature, 1948), p. 4.

10. George C. Homans, *The Human Group* (New York: Harcourt, Brace and World, 1950), pp. 90–92.

Chapter 3

Communication Barriers

Implicit Assumptions
Barriers Related to Status
    Barriers to downward communication
    One-way communication
    Differences in values and perceptions
    Mistrust
    The psychic conflicts of leadership
    Barriers to upward communication
    Attitudes of the subordinate
    Attitudes and actions of the superior
    Characteristics of the organization
    Barriers to lateral communication
    Increased specialization
    Lack of management recognition and reward
    Psychic suppression of differences and disagreements
Communication Load
    Communication overload
    Communication underload
Some General Characteristics of Barriers

After studying this chapter, the reader should be able to

Define and use the following terms and concepts

Microbarriers	Competition anxiety
Macrobarriers	The MUM effect
Implicit assumptions	Fayol's bridge
Downward communication	Communication overload
Upward communication	Communication underload
Lateral communication	Multiplicity of barriers
One-way communication	Interdependence of barriers
Status anxiety	Force field analysis

Understand

How to identify implicit assumptions
Several specific barriers to downward, upward, and lateral
    communication
What can be done to overcome specific barriers
Measures to correct communication overload and underload
The general characteristics of communication barriers
How to apply force field analysis

3

During Lyndon Johnson's presidency the words "credibility gap" were heard with growing frequency. This term referred to the public's increasing mistrust of statements coming from the White House, especially those relating to the war in Vietnam. It now appears that the Johnson administration's credibility problem with the public was related to incomplete information flow within the White House organization. For example, one story has it that Defense Secretary Robert McNamara's access to the president depended on his optimism. As McNamara became more pessimistic about the war, the president became less willing to see him alone.[1] Another anecdote suggests that Johnson neutralized disagreement on his staff by making fun of the critics. One day when McGeorge Bundy, an advocate of a more moderate approach to the war, arrived at a meeting, the president greeted him with, "Well, here comes Mr. Stop The Bombing."[2] It is said that the difficulty of disagreeing with the president's policies was such that the standing joke on the White House staff went as follows:

> "Of course I tell the president 'no'. Why I told him 'no' just the other day."
> "You did?"
> "Sure. He asked me if I had any objections to the way he was running things."[3]

Barriers to communication are obstacles that distort or block the flow of needed information. The Johnson anecdotes suggest at least three such barriers: (1) the reluctance of an individual to see other points of view; (2)

the hesitancy of lower-status members to communicate unpleasant information upward; and (3) the tendency for pressures from outside the organization (war, public protest, etc.) to make adequate internal communication difficult to achieve. Communication barriers tend to occur in bunches; one barrier evokes and sustains others and is in turn sustained by them.

Barriers do not shut communication off within an organization. That would be impossible, since people are always communicating. This is why solving organizational communication problems requires understanding the specific barriers that are present, not simply getting everybody, or certain people, communicating with each other. There is always communication but the difference for organizational effectiveness is communication *quality*—that is, the presence of the kind of communication necessary for effective performance, satisfaction, and development. The barriers that block or distort this portion of the total flow of communication in the particular situation need to be understood and acted upon.

There are so many possible barriers to communication that it is not useful to try to list them all. One author's search of 26 different writings in the management field yielded a list of 130 barriers.[4] An idea of their variety can be gained from the two lists that follow. The first can be termed *microbarriers,* since they refer to communication obstacles that can occur in small-scale, person-to-person communication.[5]

1. *Perceptual selectivity* - the fact that people can take in and understand only so much information at one time.
2. *Evaluating things and people as good or bad* - a tendency that can easily place the other person on the defensive.
3. *Implicit assumptions* - beliefs the communicator operates from without being fully aware of them and without having thought them through.
4. *Language differences* - the fact that the same words can mean different things to different people.
5. *Inadequate receiving* - the tendency to send so many messages that inadequate time and energy are devoted to listening to the other person.
6. *Excessive niceness* - reluctance to express negative thoughts or feelings for fear of damaging the relationship.
7. *Lack of feedback* - anything that keeps the sender from learning if the message has been received, acknowledged, and understood.

There are also obstacles which can be termed *macrobarriers,* since they concern the wider surroundings in which organizational communication takes place. Some examples are:

1. *Serial communication* involves the transmission of messages through one or more intermediate persons (up or down the organization's "chain of command," for example).

2. *Decision processes*, whereby persons affected by a decision, or capable of improving the decision, are not consulted.
3. *Geographic distance,* as between corporate headquarters and overseas divisions.
4. *Task specialization* of groups and individual organization members.
5. *Status, power, and authority differences* leading to mistrust between organization members and groups.
6. *Pressure,* such as that brought on by technological change, demands for increased productivity, and competition for rewards within the organization.

These lists could be extended indefinitely. The topic of communication barriers is somewhat the same as the topic of communication itself. Throughout this book numerous factors that can hinder effective communication are identified, ranging from defensive behavior by individuals to barriers resulting from inappropriate organization structures. To be adept at identifying barriers requires becoming skillful and knowledgeable in the full field of organizational communication. The more limited aim of this chapter is to examine a few important barriers not covered elsewhere in this book, and then to consider certain general characteristics of communication barriers that can help the reader to use the notion of barriers with maximum effectiveness as a diagnostic tool.

The sections that follow describe three kinds of barriers. The first is a microbarrier—the tendency of individuals to behave on the basis of implicit assumptions. The second is a macrobarrier—status-related difficulties that occur in downward, upward, and lateral communication in an organization. The third, also a macrobarrier, concerns the effects of the information load on organizational communication.

IMPLICIT ASSUMPTIONS

People often act on the basis of assumptions they are not aware they are making. This seems and is irrational, but it happens often. For example, a professor who lectures for the full hour, leaving no time for discussion, is operating under the assumption that the students have nothing worthwhile to contribute to the learning process. While this could be a consciously thought out and valid assumption, very often this is not the case, and, if asked about it, the professor would say, "Now that I think about it, I should have allowed discussion. Even if we hadn't covered as much material, the class might have learned more, and we'd have all enjoyed it better."

The distinguishing feature of implicit assumptions is that the individual has not "thought about it." Such assumptions may be defined as "a more or less unconscious taking for granted of certain basic but undefined conceptions of one's world."[6] These assumptions are not the same as beliefs, which are consciously held and recognized as having alternatives.

Implicit assumptions are the basis for automatic judgments and actions. They are not examined and revised because the individual is not aware of holding them.

Implicit assumptions tend to impede communication. Obviously, they foreclose discussion of areas where information exchange might be helpful. In addition, a person acting from an implicit assumption, not recognizing where he or she is coming from, often finds the responses of other people surprising and disturbing. They are responding to something the originator is expressing but isn't aware of. Unfortunately, such assumptions often yield results that tend to justify them. The professor in the above example, seeing glassy-eyed students slumped in their chairs, tends not even to consider whether such nonentities could enter into a worthwhile discussion.

Implicit assumptions are, of course, not directly observable. They are inferred from visible behavior. When a certain pattern of behavior recurs over and over in certain situations, and particularly when the behavior fails to solve problems, it is a clue that the observed behavior stems from rigid, unexamined, inarticulate assumptions. A few examples of implicit assumptions along with some typical behavior patterns that result from them are shown in exhibit 3-1. Implicit assumptions abound in most

EXHIBIT 3 - 1

**SOME IMPLICIT ASSUMPTIONS AND
RESULTING BEHAVIOR**

Assumptions	*Behavior*
I know all I need to know.	Lack of inquiry into the nature and causes of problems
My listeners understand what I have said	Not checking for reception and understanding
My listeners feel (or should feel) as I do	Not providing opportunities for others to express themselves
The environment is (or should be) unchanging	Treating problems as if, once solved, they will stay solved
The process of communication itself does not need to be examined	Failure to examine or study existing communication procedures

Adapted from Thomas R. Nilson, "Some Assumptions that Impede Communication," *General Semantics Bulletin,* 14 and 15 (1954): 41–44. Institute of General Semantics, Lakeville, Conn.

organizations. People who build skill in identifying implicit assumptions add a valuable tool for improving their own communication and for helping others to do the same.

BARRIERS RELATED TO STATUS

Certain communication barriers are associated with the direction in which messages are sent. *Downward* communication is the flow of information from superior to subordinate in the organizational hierarchy. *Upward* communication refers to messages sent from subordinate to superior. *Lateral* communication is the horizontal flow of messages among peers. Each is essential to effective organizational functioning. Downward communication commands and instructs; upward communication informs; lateral communication coordinates. But each has its special problems. Downward communications are often filtered by subordinates' mistrust of their bosses or by the fact that such messages may have been tailored more to motivate the subordinates than to provide them with full information. The quality of upward communication may suffer from subordinates' unwillingness to say anything other than what they feel the boss wants to hear. Lateral communication can become distorted by rivalry between persons of equal status and by conflict between groups in the organization whose specializations and goals differ. Some of the problems typical of each of the three directional forms of communication are examined in the following sections, beginning with downward communication.

Barriers to Downward Communication

Superior to subordinate, or downward, communication can be remarkably ineffective. One study showed that only twenty percent of downward-directed information ever reaches the bottom organization level. Another study found the figure to be a mere five percent.[7] Information losses tend to be substantial at each level from top to bottom (see exhibit 3-2). It is easy to see how messages can be unrecognizable by the time they reach lower-level employees. The seriousness of the problem is compounded by the fact that workers who are receiving information from above tend to want more, while higher-level personnel tend to overestimate the amount of information being received by people below them.[8] Lower-level people want more information; their superiors think it is getting through to them, but it is not. The frequent failure of downward communication has many causes, among them the following:[9]

One-way Communication. Downward communication is often a one-way message from superior to subordinates, providing no feedback. This problem is especially severe in the case of written and other kinds of mechanical communication methods (tapes, manuals, films, etc.). Face-to-

EXHIBIT 3 - 2
DILUTION OF INFORMATION IN DOWNWARD COMMUNICATION

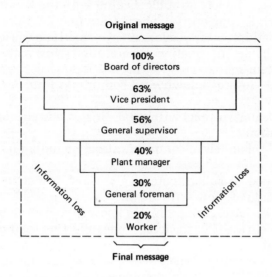

Figure derived from information found in Ralph G. Nichols, "Listening is Good Business," *Management of Personnel Quarterly* 1, no. 2 (1962): 2–9.

face communication allows for continuous correction until the message is understood.

Differences in Values and Perceptions. Superiors tend to be committed to the total organization; subordinates to their department or subgroup. Superiors' performance is usually seen in terms of long-term goals, subordinates' in terms of immediate outcomes. Superiors typically view their contribution in terms of achievements, while subordinates are more likely to see long hours and hard work as their contribution. Obviously these differences in viewpoint can cause parts of a downward-directed message to be filtered out and considered unimportant by subordinates.

Mistrust. Employees who mistrust a superior may misunderstand or block the relay of downward messages.[10] Reasons for mistrust include lack of frequent boss-subordinate contact, the fact that the superior is responsible for getting high productivity out of the subordinate, and the fact that the superior has control over the subordinate's rewards. Employees often feel their boss to be a more biased source of information than their own immediate co-workers or the organization's grapevine.

The Psychic Conflicts of Leadership. The pressures experienced by leaders often produce severe inner conflicts. Abraham Zaleznik has identified two such conflicts, *status anxiety* and *competition anxiety.* Status anxiety is experienced by the leader who is torn between the responsibilities of authority and the desire to be liked. Competition anxiety refers to the fears that arise in those who have trouble dealing with the inevitable fact that managerial work is competitive. These fears may be fears of success as well as fears of failure. Clearly, such inner turmoil can cause the manager to leave out or distort information in communicating with subordinates.

These problem sources suggest that the following steps can be taken by supervisors to improve downward communication.

1. Maintain adequate contact with subordinates, and encourage two-way communication.
2. Use multiple channels of communication, including face-to-face conversation.
3. Keep informed of subordinates' values and perceptions, and share personal points of view with them.
4. Build trust by letting subordinates know how decisions that are important to them are to be made, e.g., ones affecting their pay and career development.
5. Develop a keen sense of one's own reactions and a firm sense of personal identity.

Barriers to Upward Communication

Upward communication, when effective, provides feedback to management in response to downward directed messages, gives subordinates a channel for submitting their ideas, and enhances acceptance of decisions by allowing subordinates to participate in the decision process. It is not surprising that one study showed communication with superiors to be the type of communication organization members found to be the most important and the most satisfying.[11] Unfortunately, the same study showed it to be the type in which employees find it the most difficult to participate. The typical situation is that employees transmit upward messages they feel will improve their standing with their bosses and withhold information which they think might damage their image.[12] Evidence reflecting the inaccuracy and incompleteness of upward communication is contained in exhibit 3-3. Items 1 and 2 in the exhibit show that foremen and higher managers each see the quality of upward communication as being substantially more favorable than do their subordinates. Item 3 underscores the result: superiors think they understand subordinates' problems, but subordinates disagree. As was true in downward communication, numerous factors can lead to poor upward communication.[13]

Attitudes of the Subordinate. Being a subordinate, like being a leader, can bring out symptoms of underlying psychic conflict in some individuals. Not everyone copes well with the dilemma of whether to support and

EXHIBIT 3 - 3

DISAGREEMENTS BETWEEN SUPERIORS AND SUBORDINATES CONCERNING UPWARD COMMUNICATION

	Workers say about the foremen	Foremen say about themselves	Foremen say about higher managers	Higher managers say about themselves
1. Always or almost always gets subordinates' ideas	16%	73%	52%	70%
2. Is someone with whom subordinates can feel free to discuss important things about the job	51%	85%	67%	90%
3. Understands subordinates' problems well	34%	95%	51%	90%

Adapted from Rensis Likert, *New Patterns of Management* (New York: McGraw-Hill, 1961), pp. 47–53.

be guided by their superior or to challenge the boss for leadership. Maladaptive styles that border on extremes, such as rebellion or passive withdrawal, can badly mar communication. A strong desire by the subordinate to move up in the organization can act as an inhibitor to upward communication. Ambitious subordinates in some organizations feel that information is power and therefore should be held on to. They may be especially guarded with negative information such as failures, mistakes, or opposing viewpoints, not wishing to be seen as negative thinkers. Mistrust of the boss and a perception by the subordinate that the boss has a large amount of influence are further factors that can lead the subordinate to be less than candid in communicating upward. In addition, subordinates may see themselves, accurately or not, as less articulate and less persuasive than their superiors.

Attitudes and Actions of the Superior. It is easy for a superior to assume wrongly that he or she knows what subordinates think or feel. Superiors can find this assumption convenient for a number of reasons. Listening takes time, and many managers feel they are too busy to spend time attending to subordinates' ideas, reports, and complaints. Also, superiors, like anyone else, are more or less defensive about themselves and tend to resist information that indicates their performance has been less than perfect. Or, the superior, out of an exaggerated sense of duty, may feel it disloyal to listen to a subordinate's criticism of the organization. Such attitudes increase the likelihood that the superior will express impatience or annoyance when communicating with subordinates, avoid contact with them, or fail to act on matters they have brought to the superior's attention. The result is that subordinates lose confidence in the value of upward communication.

Characteristics of the Organization. Highly formalistic organization structures and procedures may block upward communication. In the Nixon White House, it is said, a cabinet official wishing to plead a program had to swim through a tight net to get to the president. Typically, the visitor would be ushered into the oval office by a top presidential aide who would explain that the visitor's proposal was complex and was being researched but was not yet ready for a decision. Thus intimidated, the visitor would often exchange brief greetings and then leave so as not to take any more of the president's time. A meeting that could have provided the president with a wide range of information would thus serve no value.[14]

Physical distance between superior and subordinates also restricts upward communication. This is true in large organizations where senior executives are located in a corporate or divisional headquarters building, remote from their subordinates. Even when the whole organization is within one building, managers' offices may be placed where they are not easily accessible.

Information-sharing norms in some organizations inhibit upward flows. One basis for such norms is the MUM effect, identified in research by Sidney Rosen and Abraham Tesser.[15] MUM, which stands for "minimize unpleasant messages," refers to the tendency of subordinates to try to create a favorable impression on their superiors by passing only plesant information upward through the organization.

A partial list of measures that can be taken to increase the quantity and quality of upward communication follows:

1. Subordinates can increase their willingness to build relationships (not simply to register complaints) with their superiors.
2. Superiors can develop skill in sensitive, objective listening in order to reduce subordinates' fear about communicating problems upward.
3. Superiors can work to increase the balance and coverage of upward communication by not allowing aggressive representatives from some departments to get all the attention, while others get none.
4. Superiors can increase their informal contacts with subordinates. Social events, ceremonial occasions, and occasional tours of the plant can be useful to this end.
5. Superiors can take action in response to upward messages. Subordi-

nates can increase their persistence in seeking responses from their superiors.

Barriers to Lateral Communication[16]

Lateral communication refers to exchanges between persons other than one's superiors or subordinates and is essential to the functioning of an organization. Back in 1916 management writer Henri Fayol recognized this form of communication and defined his "bridge" of organizational communication (see exhibit 3-4).[17] As the exhibit shows, lateral communication reduces the time and potential for distortion inherent in transmitting information through a long series of communication links. It enables coordination, information sharing, and problem solving between departments. It can serve as a substitute for upward and downward communication, allowing decisions to be made and conflicts to be handled without the intervention of superiors. Its value is attested by the fact that organization members—managers and nonmanagers alike—spend more of their time in lateral than in hierarchical communication. One study found that more effective supervisors spend a greater amount of time in contact with lateral groups, while poorer supervisors tend to devote more time and attention to their subordinates.[18]

EXHIBIT 3 - 4
**FAYOL'S BRIDGE OF LATERAL
COMMUNICATION**

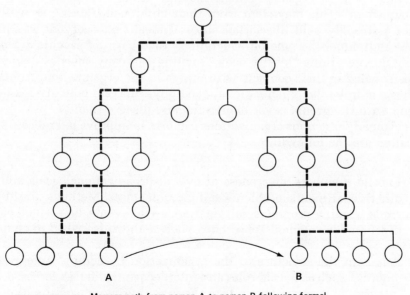

- - - - - - - Message path from person A to person B following formal organizational channels.

Message path from person A to person B following Fayol's bridge.

Though valuable, lateral interactions are not always trouble-free. People in different departments often have differing goals and viewpoints. Their disagreements range from minor misunderstandings to persistent and destructive conflicts. Within a department, people's willingness to share information with peers may be lessened by rivalry for recognition or promotion. Again, lateral communication problems in organizations have identifiable causes:

Increased Specialization. Produces a greater need for lateral communication because it increases the need for coordination. At the same time, specialization reduces the extent to which organization members share common interests. Increased specialization is a frequent problem for growing organizations, where lateral communication can proliferate in an uncontrolled fashion, clogging communication channels and reducing efficiency.[19]

Lack of Management Recognition and Reward. Numerous studies have shown that organizations encourage and reward vertical communication, while lateral communication typically does not lead to rewards.[20] Clearly, if lateral communication is not rewarded, its frequency and quality may well be below what is necessary for organizational effectiveness.

Psychic Suppression of Differences. Some people communicate less than candidly with their peers because they are afraid to express rivalry or disagreement. This may stem from their childhood training as well as from a strongly held libertarian cultural ideal that everyone is equal. Some individuals become bureaucratic as their form of psychic defense. They do everything "by the book," quoting company rules as a way of depersonalizing their contacts with others in the organization. Another defense is to be the organizational good guy—the one who always goes along with the group, never expressing any disagreement.

Among the actions organizations can take to improve lateral communication are the following:

1. Expand members' awareness of overall organizational goals and of other departments' problems and circumstances. Methods might include training programs, job rotation, social events, or various organization development approaches, such as those described in chapter 14.
2. Augment the structure of the organization by adding "integrative devices," such as liaison roles and interdepartmental task forces, or by integrating departments to take the main burden of coordination off of the specialists.[21]
3. Explicitly encourage and reward effective lateral communication.

4. Encourage the full expression, confrontation, and working through of disagreements.
5. Dispel the myth of equality by rewarding people differently depending on the excellence of their contribution.

COMMUNICATION LOAD[22]

The concept of load in communication is somewhat comparable to the power load on an electric circuit. If the circuit is underpowered, it will not fulfill its purpose. If the circuit is overloaded, it will blow a fuse. In communication, load has to do with the rate and complexity of the communication inputs an individual receives. Any student who has ever been assigned more reading than could be done in the time available has a good feel for load, as does the executive who cannot get the mail answered because of a steady stream of visitors and phone calls.

More specifically, load can be measured in terms of:

1. the number and difficulty of decisions or judgments to be made,
2. the time available,
3. the quality of information processing required, and
4. the predictability of the information inputs.[23]

Load increases as more decisions must be made in a given time period, as quality requirements and the effort given to processing increase, and/or as inputs become less predictable.

Many factors in the environment as well as in the individual determine load. Environmental factors include such things as the amount of coordination with others required by the individual's task, the extent to which work demands and performance standards are changing, and the individual's physical proximity to other people (since people located near one another tend to communicate). Individual factors include the person's capability and desire to communicate and process information, both in general and in the particular situation.

When appraising communication in an organization, it is important to consider not just the load on individuals, but on groups, departments, and the organization as a whole. In this connection one should be aware that higher-level systems are usually *less* efficient than the sum of their parts. An organization, for example, cannot process information as fast as the sum of its component groups.[24] Two reasons for this are the delay time involved in moving information around a larger system and the perceptual and language differences between different units. An awareness of this can aid organizational strategy. A certain commercial bank achieved a big increase in its volume of business loans by allowing individual loan officers to grant loans that formerly required a committee decision. This gave the bank a jump on its competitors, whose loan applicants had to wait longer for a larger system to make a decision.

Communication Overload

By now it should be clear that an excessive flow of information can itself be a barrier to communication. It is a common misconception that communication problems in organizations all result from blocked flows, and that the solution is to open up clogged communication channels. Often the problem is just the opposite; the amount and intensity of information flow is beyond the system's capacity to handle it. This is known as communication overload. As an example, the New York City superintendent of schools a few years ago ordered a moratorium on all written reports within the school system, noting that, "the number of unnecessary—and often unread—reports is beyond belief." It is not hard to see how an organization can drown in a sea of paper. Consider what happens when each official at the lowest level of a seven-level hierarchy generates one unit of information. Assuming the average superior has four subordinates, then 4,096 units of information are produced *at the bottom level alone.*[25]

Overload tends to perpetuate itself. The likelihood is that the overloaded individual will neglect to forward needed information to others, leading to errors and questions that further increase the communication load.[26] One of the functions of effective management and effective organization design is to avoid the overload barrier by restricting information flows. When this function is not being adequately performed, then the organization and individuals within it have an overload problem to cope with.

Individuals or groups experiencing overload can respond to the situation in a number of different ways. Some of the possible responses are more or less spontaneous, and may be termed "no-effort" strategies, some require the input of moderate resources or effort, while others are "major-effort" strategies.[27] No-effort strategies involve simply limiting the system's responses to those that can be made without additional effort. This can be done by allowing queues (waiting lines) to build up whenever messages exceed capacity, responding to only the highest priority messages, or by reducing the amount of response made to each message. Moderate-effort strategies include analyzing the responding system to find ways to improve its efficiency or adding personnel or other kinds of resources to increase response capacity. Major-effort strategies can involve measures such as large-scale computerized management information systems, the creation of special-purpose task forces, improving lateral communication (where the vertical channels are overloaded), or making major changes in the design of the organization.

Each of these strategies could be useful or maladaptive, depending on the particular circumstances. The no-effort strategies, for example, represent a breakdown in task performance if they involve a failure to respond to many important messages. On the other hand, they could mean improved performance, as in the case of the formerly harried executive who gets organized by learning to avoid responding to unimportant demands.

Obviously, response strategies involving major organizational changes depend on such considerations as financing, personnel, and environment, not just information processing. However, it is instructive to note the importance of information load as one of the key factors in such crucial organizational decisions.

Communication Underload

In organizations, communication underload is usually related to certain types of jobs, especially those that are repetitive, routine, dull, and boring. Once learned, such jobs require little information processing. Many factory jobs are of this type, as are the "paper pushing" jobs often found in offices.

The general coping response people often make to communication underload is that they manufacture message inputs to make up for the lack of inputs in their surroundings. Workers who find their jobs extremely boring typically turn their attention to things outside the job, such as friends, hobbies, problems at home, and worries. Since these things have nothing to do with their work, they have, in effect, compartmentalized their job-related thoughts into a relatively small portion of their total attention.[28] As this happens, the worker is less likely to correct the situation, say by complaining or suggesting improvements in the job. Underload thus becomes a communication barrier because it reduces the individual's openness to useful organizational communication.

Remedies for this situation can include redesigning the job to make it more challenging (see the topic of job enrichment in chapter 14). Personal counseling is another possible approach, aimed at increasing the worker's attention to opportunities for making suggestions or innovations or discussing possibilities for transfer to a more demanding job.

SOME GENERAL CHARACTERISTICS OF BARRIERS

The concept of barriers to high-quality communication is a useful diagnostic tool. Perhaps its major advantage is that a barrier, once identified, helps to suggest its own remedy. This has been shown in the preceding sections, where certain steps were aimed at reducing the barrier of implicit assumptions, barriers inherent in vertical and lateral communication, and those related to load. The relevance of these corrective actions could be seen once the barriers were identified and understood. In addition, there are three more characteristics of barriers that should be understood: (1) *multiplicity,* (2) *interdependency,* and (3) *restraining forces.*

The multiplicity of barriers means they tend to occur in clusters. When you find one, don't stop; look for others. The bored worker in the previous section suffers from communication underload, but the odds are good that other problems are also present. Internally, the worker could feel a strong resentment toward management and staff personnel. Also, this worker may be a member of an informal group whose members disapprove of anyone who helps management. These barriers might need to be dealt with before effective action could be taken on the communication underload problem.

The concept of interdependency suggests that barriers tend to sustain and reinforce each other.[29] For example, suppose the quality of communication between two managers is hampered because they mistrust each other and are geographically distant from each other. The geographic distance reduces the likelihood that the mistrust will be overcome, and, at the same time, the mistrust keeps them from bridging the distance to contact each other. Because of interdependency, we may act to remove one barrier, but the force of other sustaining barriers may counteract our effort. Interdependency suggests that multidimensional action, aimed at altering several barriers simultaneously, will often be more effective than trying to remove barriers one at a time.

Finally, it is helpful to understand the nature of barriers as restraining forces. This concept comes from the idea of a "force field" developed by Kurt Lewin.[30] Exhibit 3-5 diagrams a force field. The arrows represent forces being applied to the dashed line, which remains in place because of a balance of forces from each side. The length of each arrow represents its strength. If the sum of the strengths on either side were to change, the balance point would move until the sum of the forces again became equal. Thus, the balance point can be changed either by increasing the forces toward change or by reducing the restraining forces.

EXHIBIT 3 - 5
FORCE FIELD DIAGRAM

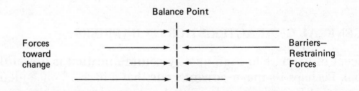

Force field analysis is applied to a specific communication problem in Exhibit 3-6, which shows the forces causing a certain individual to be rather reluctant to speak in a group. Notice that anyone wishing to increase this person's willingness to speak would have two approaches open, either to increase the "forces toward" or to decrease the "barriers against." Often, the wiser and more successful approach is to work to reduce the barriers rather than increase the forces toward. In the example, more pressure from the group toward speaking up might well induce more fear and resistance in the individual. Chris Argyris, a skilled facilitator of change, observes that most people are "culturally programmed" to resist change.[31] Therefore, a more effective approach is to reduce the strength of the resisting forces rather than to push harder in the directions that are already evoking resistance.

EXHIBIT 3 - 6
FORCE FIELD ANALYSIS OF AN INDIVIDUAL'S RELUCTANCE TO SPEAK IN A GROUP

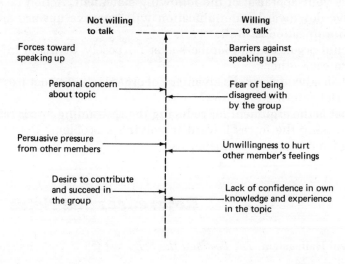

Summary

This chapter has provided an introduction to the kinds of barriers that limit the quantity or quality of communication in an organization. The discussion has included microbarriers, or those barriers that occur in direct, person-to-person communication, as well as the macrobarriers that relate to the wider organizational setting. Three kinds of barriers were examined in detail: implicit assumptions, barriers related to organizational status, and barriers related to load. Examples of some common implicit assumptions were given along with the behavior from which they can be inferred. Status-related barriers were those obstacles that tend to occur in downward, upward, and lateral communication in organizations. The concept of communication load was defined, and consideration was given to barriers arising from the conditions of both overload and underload. The chapter concluded with a statement of some further general characteristics of communication barriers—namely, multiplicity, interdependency, and the nature of barriers as restraining forces in a force field.

Questions for Review

1. Is it more convenient or more dangerous that a barrier tends to suggest its corresponding remedy? Explain.
2. Why are there more possible barriers to organizational communication than can conveniently be listed?
3. Why do people hold and act upon assumptions they aren't aware of? Why do these implicit assumptions impair communication?
4. Give your appraisal of the following statement: Action taken to improve downward communication will improve upward and lateral communication as well.
5. Should organization members ever purposely withhold information from each other?
6. Is it an advantage or disadvantage of organization structures that they restrict information flows?
7. What is the argument for reducing the restraining forces rather than increasing the forces toward in solving a problem? Does this argument hold in all circumstances?

References and Notes

1. David Halberstam, *The Best and the Brightest* (New York: Random House, 1972), p. 622.
2. Richard Tanner Johnson, *Managing the White House* (New York: Harper and Row, 1974), p. 192.
3. Lee C. White, "Symposium on the Office of the President: Formulation and Implementation of Domestic Policy", in *The White House Organization and Operations,* ed. Gordon Hoxie (New York: Center for the Study of the Presidency, 1971), p. 73.
4. Philip V. Lewis, *Organizational Communication* (Columbus, Ohio: Grid, 1975), p. 68.
5. The terms *macrobarrier* and *microbarrier* come from David S. Brown, "Barriers to Communication," *Management Review* 64, no. 12 (1976): 24–29, and 65, no. 1 (1976): 15–21.
6. Thomas R. Nilson, "Some Assumptions that Impede Communication," *General Semantics Bulletin* 14 and 15 (1954): 41–44. The ideas in the remainder of this section are adapted from this article.
7. Ralph G. Nichols, "Listening is Good Business," *Management of Personnel Quarterly* 1, no. 2 (1962): 2–9. Opinion Research Corporation, *Avoiding Failure in Management Communication,* Research Report of the Public Opinion Index for Industry (Princeton, N.J.: Opinion Research Corporation, 1963), p. 21.
8. S. Habbe, *Communicating with Employees,* Student Personnel Policy no. 129 (New York: National Industrial Conference Board, 1952); George Odiorne, "An Application of the Communication Audit," *Personnel Psychology* 7 (1954):

235–243; Rensis Likert, *New Patterns of Management* (New York: McGraw-Hill, 1961), pp. 47–53.

9. The ideas that follow draw upon Richard K. Allen, *Organizational Management Through Communication* (New York: Harper and Row, 1977), pp. 72–73; Samuel Deep, *Human Relations in Management* (Encino, Calif.: Glenco Publishing Co., 1978), p. 82; Gerald M. Goldhaber, *Organizational Communication* (Dubuque, Ia.: W. C. Brown, 1979), pp. 135–36; Abraham Zaleznik, "The Human Dilemmas of Leadership," *Harvard Business Review,* July-August 1963, pp. 49–55.

10. Glen D. Mellinger, "Interpersonal Trust as a Factor in Communication," *Journal of Abnormal and Social Psychology* 52 (1956): 304–09.

11. Norman H. Berkowitz and Warren Bennis, "Interaction Patterns in Formal Service-Oriented Organizations," *Administrative Science Quarterly* 6 (1962): 25–50.

12. See, for example, Sidney Rosen and Abraham Tesser, "On Reluctance to Communicate Undesirable Information: The Mum Effect," *Sociometry* 33 (1970): 253–63; Rosen and Tesser, "Fear of Negative Evaluation and the Reluctance to Transmit Bad News," *Journal of Communication* 22, no. 2 (1972): 124–41; John C. Athanassiades, "The Distortion of Upward Communication in Hierarchical Organizations," *Academy of Management Journal* 16 (1973): 207–26: Robert B. Johnson and Abraham Tesser, "The Effect of Prior Assistance/Non-Assistance and Norms Regarding Assistance on Transmission of Valenced Messages," *Communication Research* 3, no. 1 (1976): 37–52.

13. The ideas relating to upward communication are drawn from Athanassiades, "Distortion of Upward Communication," pp. 207–26; John E. Baird, Jr., *The Dynamics of Organizational Communication* (New York: Harper and Row, 1977), pp. 264–68; Richard C. Huseman and Elmore R. Alexander III, "Communication and the Managerial Function: A Contingency Approach," in Richard C. Huseman and Archie B. Carroll, *Readings in Organizational Behavior* (Boston: Allyn and Bacon, 1979), pp. 326–35; Earl Planty and William Machaver, "Upward Communications: A Project in Executive Development," *Personnel* 28 (1952): 304–18; William H. Read, "Upward Communication in Industrial Hierarchies," *Human Relations* 15 (1962): 3–15; Karlene H. Roberts and Charles A. O'Reilly III, "Failures in Upward Communication in Organizations: Three Possible Culprits," *Academy of Management Journal* 17 (1974): 205–15; Abraham Zaleznik, *Human Dilemmas of Leadership* (New York: Harper and Row, 1966), pp. 44–71.

14. Juan Cameron, "Richard Nixon's Very Personal White House," *Fortune,* July 1970, p. 104.

15. Rosen and Tesser, "Reluctance to Communicate," pp. 253–63.

16. The ideas about lateral communication are based mainly on Allen, *Organizational Management Through Communication,* pp. 77–79; Baird, *Dynamics of Organizational Communication,* pp. 270–73: Huseman and Alexander, "Communication and the Managerial Function," pp. 326–35; Ronald L. Smith, Gary M. Richetto, and Joseph P. Zima, "Organizational Behavior: An Approach to Human Communication," in Richard W. Budd and Brent C. Ruben, *Approaches to Human Communication* (Rochelle Park, N.J.: Hayden, 1972), pp. 269–89; Zaleznik, *Human Dilemmas of Leadership,* pp. 72–99.

17. Henri Fayol, *General and Industrial Administration* (New York: Pitman, 1949), p. 34.

18. O. Ponder, "Supervisory Practices of Effective and Ineffective Foremen" (Ph.D. diss., Columbia University, 1968).

19. Jerald Hage, Michael Aiken, and Cora Bagley Marett, "Organizational Structure and Communications," *American Sociological Review* 36 (1971): 860–71.

20. See, for example, Gerald Albaum, "Horizontal Information Flow: An Exploratory Study," *Academy of Management Journal* 7 (1964): 21–33; Joseph P. Schwitter, "Computer Work Group Problems," *Advanced Management Journal* 30, no. 4 (1965): 30–35; Eugene Walton, "Project 'Office Communications,' " *Administrative Management* 23, no. 8 (1962): 22–24.

21. Paul R. Lawrence and Jay W. Lorsch, *Organization and Environment* (Boston: Division of Research, Harvard Business School, 1967), pp. 54–83; Jay R. Galbraith, "Organization Design: An Information Processing View," *Interfaces* 4, no. 3 (1974), pp. 28–36.

22. This section draws on ideas contained in Allen, *Organizational Management Through Communication,* pp. 80–83; Richard V. Farace, Peter R. Monge, and Hamish M. Russell, *Communicating and Organizing* (Reading, Mass.: Addison-Wesley, 1977), pp. 97–125; Everett M. Rogers and Rekha Agarwala-Rogers, *Communication in Organizations* (New York: Free Press, 1976), pp. 90–94.

23. Farace, Monge, and Russell, *Communicating and Organizing,* p. 105.

24. Ibid., p. 113.

25. Anthony Downs, *Inside Bureaucracy* (Boston: Little, Brown, 1967), p. 117.

26. John T. Lanzetta and Thornton B. Roby, "Group Learning and Communication as a Function of Task and Structure 'Demands'," *Journal of Abnormal and Social Psychology* 55, (1957): 121–31; M. W. Shelley and J. C. Gilchrist, "Effects of Communication Requirements in Group Structures," *Journal of Social Psychology* 48 (1958): 37–44.

27. Farace, Monge, and Russell, *Communicating and Organizing,* pp. 117–24.

28. See, for example, Studs Terkel, *Working* (New York: Pantheon Books, 1974).

29. See, for example, Richard E. Walton, *Interpersonal Peacemaking: Confrontations and Third-Party Consultation* (Reading, Mass.: Addison-Wesley, 1969), p. 87.

30. Kurt Lewin, *Field Theory in Social Science* (New York: Harper and Row, 1951).

31. Chris Argyris, *Management and Organizational Development* (New York: McGraw-Hill, 1971), p. 185.

Cases

for Part One

The Sounds of Silence*

The mail was being distributed as Bill sat at his desk tackling a tough scheduling problem. "Thank you," he mumbled when an envelope dropped into the box marked "In." As he reached for it, his mind slipped back to the day he had opened his first company envelope. It was his senior year at Eastern Institute, and at the time he had been convinced that no one wanted an engineer fresh out of college with only a bachelor's degree. But from the letter it appeared that Phillips' Drilling Services had, and since it was his only offer, he grabbed it on the spot. There was only one catch—the job was located in Louisiana, and all his roots were in New England. "Well, the break has to be made someday," he said while packing the car for its southerly trek. And that's where it had all started.

Phillips' Drilling Services is a large firm concerned primarily with the evaluation of wells drilled for oil- and gas-producing regions of the United States. The company's offices are located in Baton Rouge, Louisiana, the capital city of that state. "Not a bad place to be," Bill decided, though he knew that his specific job as field engineer was low on the ladder of ranks. It would involve long, grueling hours of driving to and inspecting the wells, and evaluating and making recommendations about their condition. There would be long stretches without sleep or food. No warm cheery office to welcome him each morning—most of the time only the ringing of a telephone—for he would be on call for 24 hours a day, nine days straight. "Tough," he thought, "but I'm sure I can take it."

And he was right. He could take the new job, he could take the six weeks of classroom training, he could take the long hours. But there was one thing he didn't seem to accept as readily—orders from authority. "The supervisors here are jerks," he said to himself time and time again. But still he plugged on, and his persistence paid off. The job became more enjoyable, and the more interaction he had with his superiors, the more he realized that they were normal people, too.

That is, until Craig Michaels arrived on the scene. Craig, a newly appointed district manager, came from Alabama after Bill had been with Phillips' for about six months. He had worked his way up from junior field engineer after five years with the company, and this was his first managerial position.

Bill remembered the day he was introduced to Craig. "Even then I

---

*This case was written by Anne M. Schneider.

didn't like him," he recalled. "It was his attitude, I think. Kind of a cocky, 'I'm the boss' air, like he's better than the rest of us and he'll never let us forget it. And he isn't the most approachable guy even when you have a problem to discuss. Maybe that's because he doesn't like his job. I know he doesn't plan to stay in this place very long. You can tell by the way he only associates with higher-ups who can get him somewhere.

"And the way he walks all over people. I've never had any problem with him regarding my work, but when I think of the way he tore Tom apart in the memo regarding his performance, it just wasn't fair. First, because there was no warning, and second, the reprimand came in writing. At least he could have talked to him about it. I guess maybe he's better at speaking with his pen than face-to-face. Come to think of it, I never see him talking with any of the field engineers. I used to think it was just me, but now I know that's just a little paranoia on my part. As far as I can see, he plans to go to the top, and he isn't going to make any friends getting there.

"It really doesn't seem like anyone is friendly to him. I wonder if they all feel the way I do? I wouldn't be surprised. He must sense the feelings of dislike sometimes because just the other day he told me that if he ever gets fired, he's firing someone too. Boy, am I glad I've never had any trouble with my work performance or my supervisors. Otherwise I'd be nervous that it just might be me that he takes along."

This thought interrupted Bill's reverie and brought him back to reality. He was at his desk with the envelope, still unopened, in his hand. He slit the top and removed a sheet of white memo paper on which was printed:

TO: BP
FROM: CM
SUBJECT: Customer Problems
   Two times recently we have had extra problems with clients due to bad decisions on your part. This is not the first time I have been dissatisfied with your work, though I've kept these thoughts to myself until now. Bill, you seem to have trouble making decisions under pressure. I suggest you make an effort to take the time to think things through—then decide.
   This letter will go into a file separate from your personnel file. If within three months I perceive that your work has improved, then I will dispose of this memo immediately after that three-month period. If no improvement is perceived, your future with Phillips' may be open to question.

Bill sat staring at the memo for a long time, stunned by the contents. But the shock soon gave way to indignation and confusion. "How dare he accuse me of something without even telling me what I've done!" he said out loud.

Tom King, another field engineer, was passing by and saw the troubled look on Bill's face. "What's the matter, buddy?" he asked. "Michaels is finally getting on your case?" Bill looked up in surprise, "Yeah, how did you know?"

With a chuckle, Tom replied, "Well, I knew it would happen sometime. All the other field engineers have received at least one complaint from good old Michaels. We were all just waiting to see when you'd get one, too. For a while there I thought he really liked you better than the rest of us. I mean, he never corrected you in your work, and I know a couple of customers have gone to him with glowing praise of the job you've done for them. But I guess now he's changed his mind about you and decided that you're no better than the rest of us. Tough break, too, because he's not one to fool around with. His employees aren't his friends, you can see that.

"You know how when we are out on a job checking the well, we will clown around with the junior field engineers? You have to keep your sanity! Not Michaels! First of all, to see him at a well site would be a miracle in itself! He's not interested in seeing our performance on the job, he's just interested in the information he can get from others as he sits behind his desk. And second, about that clowning around, I don't think he knows the meaning of the word *enjoyment.* Oh well," he paused. "Listen man, the only thing I can tell you is to shape up. He means what he says, and I honestly believe he'd screw us to the wall if he had the chance." Tom shook his head as he walked away.

"Later," Bill mumbled, his mind already stewing over the memo. "I wonder what those 'two times' were? What did I do wrong? What do I do now? I can't let him do this to me! I'll show him!" Just then the phone rang and Bill was called out to a job that lasted three days. A month and a half passed and Bill didn't hear another word from Michaels on the subject. Bill saw him at least once a week, but they never exchanged words concerning the memo. It was as if it never existed. But the feeling of tension was there. They both knew that the other hadn't forgotten.

"I wonder when he'll say something?" Bill thought silently on his way home one afternoon. "Will he wait until three months are up and tell me I'm fired with no warning? Or, if I have improved in his eyes, how will he let me know?"

The answer to Bill's questions came the next morning. He received a call at home from Irene Goldman, Michaels's secretary, saying that Craig wanted to see him at one o'clock sharp that afternoon. "Here it comes," Bill thought, and took a quick glance at the help-wanted ads as he ate his breakfast.

It was 12:59 when Irene ushered Bill into Craig's office. "Come in, Bill," Craig said from behind the desk. "I've been meaning to talk to you for some time now. If you recall, almost two months ago I wrote a memo to you regarding your poor work performance. Well, I've been checking on you and up until today I hadn't perceived any significant improvement in your work quality. However, I received a letter yesterday from a customer regarding your performance on the job.

"Let me read a particular paragraph to you. It says, 'Bill responded above and beyond the call of duty. He was extremely friendly, helpful, and quick in evaluating where our troubles were. The recommendations he provided were logical, and within minutes our problem was solved. You should be proud to have such a dedicated and capable employee working for Phillips'.' "

Michaels looked up and smiled. "Bill, I had my doubts about you, but this letter proves that I was wrong. You've certainly shown us that you are just what our customer says—'a dedicated and capable employee.' Here is my copy of the memo I sent you. Do what you want with it, but as far as I'm concerned, it was never written. I hope we'll never have a problem like this again."

Without another word he went back to his work, and Bill, not knowing quite what to do, mumbled a word of thanks and quietly left the room.

Case Questions

1. What caused and sustained the communication problem between Bill and Craig Michaels? Were Michaels's outlook and behavior the only factors, or were other things involved?
2. What do you make of Michaels's statement that if he ever got fired, he'd fire someone, too?
3. What information was available to Bill that he either didn't pay attention to or didn't seek out? Would it have been worthwhile for him to try to gain a more complete picture of Michaels and his relationships with the other engineers?
4. Could Bill have taken any action at any time during the case to try and improve his relationship with Michaels? If so, what could he have said or done?

Gordon Foundry Co.*

Right after I graduated from the Provincial Technical Institute I accepted a position with the Gordon Foundry, a medium-sized firm located in a small town in one of the Eastern Provinces. It was a fine position for I was the assistant to Mr. Smith, who was general manager and president of the family-owned company. I was anxious to learn the foundry business and since I was living alone it was not long before I literally lived in the foundry. We had many technical problems, the work was intensely interesting, and my boss was a very fine man.

The foundry workers were a closely knit group and in the main they were older men. Several had spent a lifetime in the foundry. Many of them were related. They felt that they knew the foundry business from A to Z and they were inclined to "pooh-pooh" the value of a technical education. The president had mentioned to me when we discussed the

---

*Copyright 1956 by the University of Alberta. Reprinted by permission.

duties and responsibilities of the position that no graduate of a technical institute had ever been employed in the Gordon Foundry. He added, "You will find that the men stick pretty well together. Most of them have been working together for more than ten years which is rather unusual in a foundry, so it may take you some time to get accepted. But, on the whole, you will find them a fine group of men."

At first the men eyed me coldly as I went around and got acquainted. Also, I noticed that they would clam up as I approached. A bit later I became aware of cat-calls when I walked down the main aisle of the foundry. I chose to ignore these evidences of hostility because I considered them silly and childish. I believed that if I continued to ignore these antics the men would eventually stop, come to their senses and see the ridiculousness of their behavior.

One Saturday, about a month after I had started, I was down in the Enamel Shop. As I entered it I observed a worker who was busy cleaning the floor with a hose from which flowed water at pretty good pressure. It was customary to "hose-down" the Enamel Shop every so often. I was busy near one of the dipping tanks when, all of a sudden, I was nearly knocked down by the force of a stream of water. The worker had deliberately turned the hose on me. I knew that he had intended to hit me by the casual way in which he swung around as though he had never seen what he had done.

Case Questions

1. Students often say the problem in this case is that there is "a lack of communication." Do you agree or disagree?
2. Do you agree with the new engineer that the foundry workers' behavior was "silly and childish"? If so, can this behavior be explained?
3. What part, if any, did each of the following factors play in the situation that developed in this case: the way in which the new man's job was defined; his actual activities on the job; differences in age, status, and background; Mr. Smith's way of introducing the new engineer to the foundry.
4. Would it have been useful for Smith or the new engineer to act any differently than they did? If so, specifically how?

Rudolph Carter*

Rudolph Carter, a young electrical engineer, three years out of college, received an attractive job offer from the SEMA Co., a major sugar company in the tropics. At the time, Rudolph held a position of junior engineer with the local utility company in a small town. In the three years he had been with the company he had received one "very insignificant salary increase" based essentially on merit, and no promotions. Therefore, for the

---

*Used by permission of Leon C. Megginson, Research Professor of Management, University of South Alabama.

past year he had been actively looking around the surrounding industrial area for a more attractive job position with an increased salary.

The job offer from SEMA, therefore, came at a very opportune time and, although it represented a "very substantial increase in salary, good promotional promise, plus numerous fringe benefits" (company furnished home and utilities), it did have certain drawbacks. Rudolph was well aware of these as he had been born, reared, and educated through high school on a similar tropical sugar mill plantation where his father had been chief mill engineer until his death five years ago. Having reached manhood in this atmosphere, Rudolph knew well that one of the chief disadvantages was getting to know the local engineers, working with them, winning their acceptance, and coping with other human relations problems.

The position Rudolph had been offered by SEMA was that of assistant chief electrical engineer. He had further been assured that he would be groomed to take over the chief electrical engineer's job when the chief retired in three years and possibly prior to that time, since the chief engineer was in poor health and was considering retiring at an earlier date.

After considerable deliberation and weighing of pros and cons, Rudolph accepted the job and within two months reported for his first assignment.

His first few days on the job proved to be very difficult—not from a professional-technical standpoint, but because of the human relations problems. The chief engineer had suddenly been required to take some sick leave and had flown to the United States for medical treatment. He had left the electrical department in charge of his senior electrical engineer, Señor Jose Gonzales, a national who was a graduate of the technical college on the island. Gonzales was about 45 years old and had 16 years service with the department. The chief engineer had left full written instructions with Gonzales (with a copy for Rudolph) outlining Rudolph's job assignments and responsibilities. The instructions left little doubt that Rudolph was to assume full responsibility and authority for operating the electric plant.

The beginning of the crop-grinding season was two weeks away and Rudolph found himself in a crush of people rushing around trying to put all of the electric plant facilities in final operating condition. The plant force, all locals, numbered about 40, and while most of them could understand English, they could speak it only brokenly. This even applied to Gonzales, the senior electrical engineer.

It was at once apparent to Rudolph that Gonzales was indeed the key man of the entire operations, and that, in fact, he had been running the whole show for a good number of years. His word and directions were law as far as the workers were concerned and they all respected him very highly.

Rudolph quickly noted two things about Gonzales during his first day on the job. First, Gonzales was an extremely competent engineer, completely familiar with the plant operations, and although there was no formal organization procedure, he and his men performed all work very efficiently. Second, Gonzales was highly ambitious, with a strong desire and motivation to become the chief electrical engineer.

Gonzales very quickly and definitely let Rudolph know that his presence was resented; he offered no cooperation, advice, or help. There was only one factor which helped to establish a certain amount of rapport between the two men, and that was Rudolph's ability to speak Spanish. Without this accomplishment, his effectiveness would have been nil.

During Rudolph's second week on his job, and only three days prior to the grinding season, the plant manager requested a detailed report on start-up status of all plant electrical equipment. Being completely unfamiliar with such status reports, Rudolph requested a report from Gonzales, to which Gonzales immediately replied that everything was completely "O.K. and ready to go," and that he had never prepared such a detailed status and it wasn't necessary—the chief engineer always was content with just his word. In a search through the files, which were in a pitiful state, Rudolph was able to locate a status report for the year prior which had been submitted by the chief engineer. It was quite lengthy and in considerable detail, listing all electrical items, and showing everything in a "ready to go" condition. It had been directed to the plant manager with copies to no one.

Rudolph deliberated the problem at length, debating on whether merely to duplicate the prior status report, showing everything on a satisfactory basis and thus relying on Gonzales's verbal say-so, or whether to take the list to him and insist on witnessing the testing and operation of all components. Rudolph realized he was on fairly touchy grounds and that if he were to succeed at his job, one thing was fairly certain: he needed the confidence and cooperation of Gonzales. He surely did not want to antagonize him this early in the game, and yet he wanted to be positive that his first report to the plant manager would be correct and accurate.

He decided to talk to Gonzales, show him the list from the previous year, assure him that he, Rudolph, was willing to accept Gonzales's verbal say-so of equipment fitness, but to ask him to check the list for completeness, since during the past year there might have been some deletions or additions of equipment.

Gonzales was genuinely surprised at seeing the list, and immediately put himself on the defensive. However, after a few minutes of talking during which time Rudolph emphasized his willingness and confidence to accept Gonzales's assurance that all items were on the "ready-to-go" status and that all he was requesting was a recheck of equipment listing, Gonzales warmed considerably to the situation and cooperated graciously.

During the checking of the list, they did indeed find numerous items which had been physically deleted in the field and a few new installations. Gonzales even pointed out that at least one major piece of equipment had not checked out completely to his satisfaction and that he and his men were having some difficulty in hooking up test instrument equipment for checking it out further. When Rudolph suggested that they put their heads together and see if they could unravel the testing difficulties, Gonzales seemed somewhat relieved.

In reviewing the test hook-up, Rudolph quickly spotted the difficulty but instead of pointing it out directly, he was able to guide Gonzales's analysis to the point where Gonzales himself recognized it on his own, so to speak.

On the face of it, Gonzales's men were most impressed with the fact that their man, and not the new man, had located and corrected the difficulty. Inwardly, Rudolph could tell Gonzales fully realized that he had been very astutely steered toward recognizing the fault and had been allowed to "save face" with his men.

This, then, was the start of a very pleasant and cooperative relationship between Rudolph and Gonzales, with Gonzales recognizing and accepting slowly but surely Rudolph's position and authority over him.

Case Questions

1. What was Rudolph Carter's strategy for dealing with Gonzales? Why was it successful?
2. Did Carter skillfully diagnose the communication situation he was in, or did he simply use common sense?
3. What communication barriers did Carter manage to overcome?
4. Was Carter honest in his relationship with Gonzales? Did he manipulate or trick Gonzales in an improper way?

Part II

Fundamentals of Interpersonal Communication

Chapter 4

Perception and Communication

Some Fundamentals of Perception and Communication
Perceptual Selectivity
    Physiological aspects of perception
    Context
Perception of Other People and Self
    Forming impressions of others
    Self-concept
Defending or Adapting The Conceptual System
    Defense mechanisms
    Adapting

After studying this chapter, the reader should be able to

Define and use the following terms and concepts

Perceptual set	Halo effect
Perceptual selectivity	Balance theory
Access	Self-concept
Detection	Conceptual system
Interpretation	Competence value
Closure	Defensiveness
Context	Defense mechanisms
Consistency	Adaption
Stability	Supportive and defensive climates
Stereotyping	

Understand

The main determinants and effects of perceptual set
Why we do not directly experience our surroundings
How tendencies toward consistency and stability affect a person's viewpoint in a specific situation

The difference between defending and adapting the conceptual system
Six behavioral components of a "supportive climate"

4

Willard Mason, billing manager of Equity Insurance Company, had recently been having problems with some of the supervisors who reported to him. One morning Mason was particularly concerned about Sam Simpson, a widower in his late fifties who had been with the company for thirty years.

"Sam's an extreme example of the typical 'old line' supervisor," Mason complained to a fellow department manager. "He's just completely ineffective with people, constantly berating his subordinates for things like tardiness, talking on the job, and not cleaning up their desks. Also, he digs in and resists every procedure change I send him, especially if it has anything to do with the computer. Whenever the systems department sends us a new procedure, I take it to Alice Walsh, Sam's assistant."

Mason deplored the amount of time he had to spend on details that he felt Sam should be handling. He became particularly annoyed when worker complaints or special requests were brought to him either by Alice or by the workers themselves. As Mason put it, "I can see why Sam's people hesitate to go to him with these things, but it's getting so that I'm spending about twenty-five percent of my time handling matters that Sam should be handling."

From Sam Simpson's point of view, the situation looked somewhat different. "My problem is workers who just don't take pride in their work," he complained recently to a supervisor from another department. "Take Pat, for example. I constantly have to remind her she's behind schedule and correct errors she has made. The department head, Mr. Mason, doesn't back me up. He's always being lenient with the workers. I just can't see that approach. My section has the job of making billing adjustments, and they have to be done right. There's no room for opinions. How's a girl like Pat going to know how to handle cases she's never seen before if I don't tell her?"

"The workers don't come to me with their problems, they go to my assistant, Alice. I don't know who she thinks she is. I end up being just the taskmaster, assigning work, correcting mistakes, and finding out who's behind schedule. Naturally, they like Alice better, but what happened to the old days when a supervisor was *supposed* to be a taskmaster?"

The event that heightened Mason's worries about Sam had occurred the previous afternoon. About 2:30 P.M., Mason had phoned Sam to tell him that the payroll office had just announced the amounts of the year-end bonuses his workers would be receiving. Since Sam was away from his desk when Mason called, Alice answered and wrote down the amounts of each worker's bonus. She agreed when Mason suggested the workers should be informed of their bonuses before the end of working hours that afternoon. "We don't want our people to be the last ones to hear about their bonuses," she commented.

An hour later Mason's phone rang. It was Alice. "Mr. Mason, I'm afraid I've really done it," Alice began. "When it got to be three o'clock and Sam still hadn't returned, I figured I'd better go ahead and tell the people what their bonuses were. I'd just finished doing this when Sam came back. When I told him what I had done, he stood there for about twenty seconds just staring at me. Then he said, 'I guess I'm just not needed around here anymore,' and walked over, got his coat, and left the building."

Mason reassured Alice that she had done nothing wrong. "It's just another Sam incident," he said. "Don't worry about it, I'll handle it." Overnight, he had been wondering just exactly *how* he would handle it. His concern grew even stronger when he learned that Sam had not arrived at work yet this morning. By mid-morning the department was buzzing about the situation. Nobody could remember Sam ever having been late to work before.

SOME FUNDAMENTALS OF PERCEPTION AND COMMUNICATION

In this example it is clear that the things being communicated are affected by the fact that each person involved is perceiving the situation in a different way. Mason sees Sam as the problem ("It's just another Sam incident"). Sam, however, has his attention focused on his assistant, Alice, who he perceives to be taking over functions that rightfully should be his. These perceptions, in turn, are shaped by two important factors—the internal state of the individual and the external environment surrounding the individual.

The internal state depends heavily on previous learning and includes motives, attitudes, emotions, and concepts of self and surroundings. Sam, for example, having previously formed the attitude that Alice is taking over the supervisor's functions, perceives the current incident as an extension of that trend. The external environment includes things outside the individual, such as other people, objects, and events.

The particular internal state and external environment determine a unique *perceptual set*—the image we have of surroundings and self during a particular period of time. Because of these two determinants, our perceptual set can never be 100 percent accurate. We can only see what is present in our environment, and that often is not the whole story. Even things that are available in our environment become modified or go unnoticed because we are looking through glasses that are rose-colored, dark, or the wrong prescription. In effect, we never come into direct contact with our physical environment. Also, many events occur during short time periods, further limiting our perceptual accuracy. Exhibit 4–1 summarizes the factors that shape the perceptual set and the effects the perceptual set has on what we communicate, as well as how we see the results of our communication.[1] Implied within exhibit 4–1 are four major principles that will serve as the framework for this chapter.[2]

EXHIBIT 4–1
A MODEL OF PERCEPTION AND COMMUNICATION

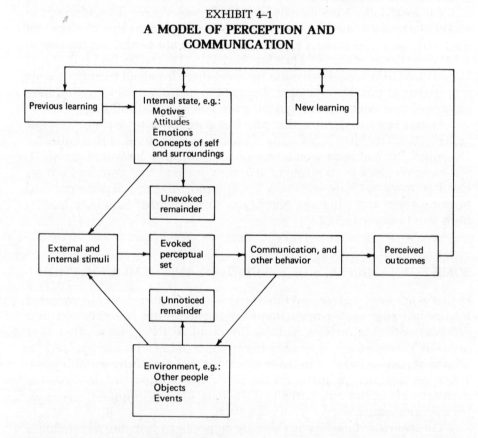

From Huse/Bowditch, *Behavior in Organizations,* © 1977, Addison-Wesley, Reading, Massachusetts. Fig. 4.1. As adapted from J. G. March and H. A. Simon, *Organizations,* New York: Wiley, 1958, p. 11.

1. *Human attention is highly selective.* As John Dewey has put it, "A stimulus becomes a stimulus by virtue of what the organism was already preoccupied with."[3] In the incident involving Sam and Alice,

Sam paid no attention at all to the question of urgency in getting the bonus information to the employees. He was totally preoccupied with his concern that Alice was taking over his supervisory role. The two "remainder" boxes in exhibit 4–1 represent the parts of the person's environment and internal state that do not become stimuli during a given time period. It is often the case, especially when the time period is short, that only a small part of a person's environment and internal state will become part of their perceptual set and thus have an influence on their behavior. In physical terms, for example, the human eye can handle about 5 million bits of information per second, but the brain can deal with only about 500 bits per second. Obviously, selection is inevitable.[4]

2. *The individual seeks consistency between self-concept, own behavior, and perceived information.* There is widespread agreement among psychologists as to the central role played by the self-image in a person's efforts to communicate. When Mr. Mason said to Alice, "It's just another Sam incident," his communication showed he was selectively perceiving Sam to be the sole source of the problem. This allowed him, at least for the moment, to retain a view of himself as a competent manager. He had nothing to do with the situation; it was all Sam's fault. It is not surprising that people try to behave in ways that are consistent with their self-images. It also seems to be true that people tend selectively to perceive things that are favorable to their predispositions. Research has shown that people are more likely to see and hear congenial communications than neutral or hostile ones.[5] Roger Brown has identified this as the principle of "cognitive consistency," referring to people's tendency to seek consistency between their own frame of reference and the information that is available to them.[6]

3. *An individual who cannot alter data often maintains cognitive consistency by distorting or avoiding it.* A person not only seeks consistency, as the preceding principle indicates, but frequently distorts reality to maintain a desired consistency. This is another way of saying that an individual's internal state has a major bearing on what is perceived and how it is perceived. The present principle, however, points out that the process of seeking consistency can produce harmful results for the individual who alters or screens out needed information. This process has been called *perceptual defense.* By perceiving inaccurately, the person doesn't have to make changes in his or her surroundings and self-image.[7] The employee who says "I wasn't promoted because my boss is unreasonable" may feel better in the short run but be less likely to do better the next time promotions are announced than the employee who is willing to say (less defensively) "Maybe I'd better find out what I can do to improve my job performance and my relationship with my boss."

4. *The perceiver's active participation tends to produce better retention*

of information and more useful changes in perceptions and internal states. This principle is the positive side of the coin whose negative side was shown in principle 3. It shows that defensiveness is not the only route to consistency. People may cope with their circumstances by actively giving and seeking information rather than by defending against it. According to this principle, the key to such adaptation is activity by the perceiver. When a person gives a speech, writes an essay, or in some way physically performs a task involving information, that information will be more fully retained and accepted than if the person is only involved as a passive listener.[8] And when people become actively involved with information, as in a discussion, attitude and behavior changes are much more likely.[9] Note that in exhibit 4–1, new learning follows action (communication and other behavior) by the perceiver. The implication is that perceptual accuracy can be increased through improved communication.

These four principles serve as the major topics for the remainder of this chapter. First, the selectivity of human perception is examined, with emphasis on the factors that determine what is perceived. Second, the consistency-seeking process is discussed, showing its effects on individuals' perceptions of other people and of self. Special attention is given to the importance of the self-concept in perception and communication. Finally, two modes of maintaining consistency, defending and adapting, are examined—a discussion showing how individuals can increase the validity of their own and other people's perceptions.

Perceptual Selectivity

Perception can be defined as a process of observing, selecting, and organizing stimuli and then making interpretations.[10] This definition highlights the important fact that it is the perceiver who forms the perception. We do not directly experience the things and people that exist in our surroundings. Instead, we receive a limited amount of data from them and then perform several operations on that data before forming an impression. Perception, therefore, refers to the way an object or situation appears to the perceiver, not to the object or situation itself.

For people engaged in communication, the fact that the perception is not the same as the thing perceived is an important distinction to keep in mind. The example at the beginning of this chapter illustrates what can happen when communicators do not try to anticipate how the other person will see things. If Mason and Alice had thought about how Sam would selectively perceive the way they were handling the information about employee bonuses, they might well have behaved differently, even if it meant waiting until the next day to get the information to the workers. One way we can increase our attention on perceptual selectivity is to understand its major causes—namely, the physiological nature of persons as perceivers and the context in which perception takes place.

Physiological Aspects of Perception.   Perception is an outcome of physiological processes and, as such, partakes of some of the strengths but also the limitations of human physiology. Three physiological aspects of special importance to perception are *access, detection,* and *interpretation.*[11]

Access refers to the fact that while we are all immersed in an ocean of stimuli—sights, odors, sounds, touches—not all of the stimuli in our environment are available to us. Physical location is one factor affecting access. When we watch a basketball game from a seat high in the second balcony, we form a different impression than when we are seated close to the baseline of the court under one of the baskets, where bodies can be heard colliding during rebounds. Also, we can only hear a certain range of sound waves, see a certain range of light waves, and feel a certain range of pressure. Furthermore, only so much information can be accepted by the sense organs in a given period of time, so a complex stimulus can easily overwhelm their capacity. Consider the experience of looking at a tree. How many of the individual leaves do you actually see? In organizations, a particular employee is perceived close up and in detail by coworkers and from a distance by others. These different perceptions may yield differing appraisals of the employee's helpfulness, trustworthiness, competence, etc.

Detection refers to our becoming aware, based on neural transmissions to the brain from the sense organs, that something has happened. These neural transmissions get evaluated in the context of whatever other neural activity is going on at the time. When we are very hungry, depressed, or excited, for example, we may tune some signals out and become sensitive to others. A student who has just had a test paper returned by the professor becomes tuned in to the grade on the paper and to comparative information that can be gained by peeking at other students' papers, to the exclusion of other information. Many professors hand back papers at the end of a class session, realizing that if they distribute them at the beginning of the hour, students' detection of the lecture is likely to be quite low.

Interpretation is the process by which we attach meaning to sensory information. Look at exhibit 4–2, and, before reading on, write down a title for this picture. Now consider the full range of possibilities: a vase, a candlestick, two faces, a drawing which may be seen as any of the foregoing, or an undifferentiated object. Now explain why you saw the drawing the way you did, and why you think others might be expected to see it in various other ways.

In your answers to the foregoing questions, you may have shown your awareness that factors such as the perceiver's frame of mind and past experience (e.g., "I've seen the vase-faces picture before") affect the interpretation made. Since individuals' predispositions vary, so do their inter-

EXHIBIT 4–2
AN EXAMPLE OF PERCEPTUAL INTERPRETATION

pretations. Notice also how one of the two images, the vase or the faces, fades from awareness when you focus on the other.

Interpretation is also affected by a pervasive human tendency known as *closure.* Closure is the tendency to form a complete mental image out of incomplete data. Consider exhibit 4–3. If you see figure A as a square rather than four separate lines, you are experiencing the closure tendency. In figure B, if you read the messages and saw the "meaning" words but missed the extra words, you can see the two-edged nature of the closure tendency. It is a human strength that we seek to arrange stimuli into meaningfully organized wholes. On the other hand, closure can lead people to reach conclusions based on insufficient information and contribute to missed communications. In general, interpretation adds another selectivity filter to the total process of perception.

EXHIBIT 4–3
EXAMPLES OF CLOSURE

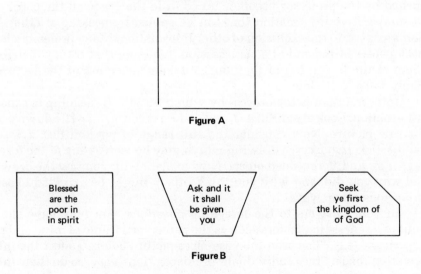

Figure A

Blessed
are the
poor in
in spirit

Ask and it
it shall
be given
you

Seek
ye first
the kingdom of
of God

Figure B

Context.   In addition to physiological constraints, perception is subject to another major cluster of determinants—namely, the setting or environment in which the perceiver is located. This context contains physical factors, such as lighting and distracting noise. It also includes social and emotional cues of various kinds. One study, for example, showed that managers often give higher evaluations to subordinates they see as sharing common values in such areas as work and religion.[12] It has also been found that a committee composed of socially congenial members who want to continue working in the same group will develop similar perceptions and will be more effective in reaching their goals than members who prefer not to work together.[13]

The time at which a message is transmitted can influence the way it is perceived. A staff member who has been accustomed to receiving a certain report at the end of each month may pay no attention to it if it is received on the 15th and put it aside for two weeks.

For people in organizations, a major context factor is the organizational position they occupy. As noted in chapter 1, people in different subunits of an organization (e.g., marketing, production, accounting) tend not to see things the same way, and superiors often see the same issues differently from their subordinates. Union-management controversies provide another example of how positions affect perceptions. The poor communication and lack of agreement typical of these situations stems in large part from the fact that neither side, because of their adversary roles, has full, direct access to the information and pressures that make up the environment of the other.[14]

Overall, context factors, when considered along with the physiological constraints, show that selectivity is a multistage process. First, we find ourselves in a particular context. Within that context we have selective access to certain stimuli, from which we selectively detect some and then interpret from those. The sheer complexity of this process makes it obvious that there is a high potential for error. The perceptual process tends to happen fast and spontaneously. People can improve the fidelity of their perceptions and communication by paying more explicit attention to the factors involved in selectivity and by being more open to the fact that they typically do not have the whole picture.

Perception of Other People and Self

The two-person relationship model presented in chapter 3 indicates there is a close interdependence between two kinds of perceptions, view of self and view of (as well as behavior toward) the other person. The importance of these factors is illustrated in the case of Sam Simpson and Willard Mason. Sam's self-esteem was slipping ("I guess I'm just not needed around here anymore"). This made it more likely he would see Mason and Alice as intentionally trying to shove him aside. Conversely, the more Sam perceived them in this way, the more his view of himself as slipping was reinforced. This was a destructive process, leading Sam to focus less and less on his strengths (e.g., his knowledge of how to make billing adjustments) and to reject the possibility that Mason and Alice may not really intend to crowd him out and might even be shocked (as Alice seems to be) to know the effects of their behavior on Sam. Because perceptions of other people and self are so prone to error and yet so central to communication, they are given special attention in the sections that follow.

Forming Impressions of Others. It has already been shown that perceptions are subject to distortion due to selectivity. This is especially true when the object of perception is another person. One reason is that people usually attempt to control the impression they make on a present observer. Erving Goffman has called this "the art of impression management."[15] Impression management is engaged in by the employee who sits upright and bright-eyed at his desk even though he is daydreaming, and who carries a stack of papers along so as to look busy on a trip to the water cooler. Another reason is that persons are particularly complex "objects." The perceiver simply cannot attend to all the information given, and hence has to "stereotype" the other person, paying attention only to those characteristics that enable the perceiver to decide which preestablished category to put the other person into.[16] People tend to form impressions of others on the basis of very slim information. Having seen a person, or even her picture for just a few moments, most of us would be willing to rate the person and say whether we would or wouldn't like to get to know her.[17]

The processes by which people perceive other people include two tendencies that help explain how impressions are formed from such limited information, *consistency* and *stability.* Consistency refers to our tendency to see others as unitary wholes rather than as a collection of disparate fragments stuck together. In doing this, we tend to organize our impression of a person around certain key traits. In a classic study, Solomon Asch presented one group of subjects with a list of traits: intelligent, skillful, industrious, warm, determined, practical, and cautious.[18] Another group was given the same list, except the word "cold" was substituted for "warm." This difference greatly affected the resulting impressions. When asked to describe the stimulus person further, subjects who had seen the "warm" list used such terms as generous, happy, good-natured, and reliable. The "cold" stimulus person was thought to be ungenerous, unhappy, humorless, and ruthless. This phenomenon is often referred to as the "halo effect"—the process of using one particularly favorable or unfavorable trait to color everything else the perceiver knows about the person. Asch argued that warm and cold were central traits that organized the observers' impressions into consistent form.

Evaluation plays a key part in the process by which consistency is attained. Once we see a person as favorable or unfavorable in one context, we often extend this impression of the individual to other situations and other seemingly unrelated characteristics. Research subsequent to the Asch studies has indicated that evaluation is often the most important underlying dimension around which we form coherent impressions of people.[19] A person usually is not seen as good and bad, intelligent and stupid, friendly and hostile. Even when there is contradictory information about someone, the person will likely be seen as consistent.

The consistency tendency helps explain many perceptual errors that occur in organizations. For example, research has shown that employment interviews are not a very reliable or valid means for selecting personnel. Too often, interviewers form an evaluation that is based on some of the applicant's attributes but overlooks other important ones.[20]

One representation of the tendency toward consistency is provided by Fritz Heider's P-O-X model shown in exhibit 4–4. This model concerns P's attitude toward another person, O, and toward X, an object or attitude they both perceive. Heider's theory, known as "balance theory," is that when P likes X and O, a balanced state exists if O also likes X. An important corollary is that if O approves of the things P values, P is more likely to accept and approve of O.[21] Heider's theory is a formal way of stating that people tend to agree with people whom they like and to like those with whom they agree. Later research has shown that an exchange of *reciprocal* approval between P and O can sometimes be of overriding importance. If O expresses approval toward P, P may like O despite their disagreement about X. Similarly, if P and O do not like each other, O's attitudes are not important to P.[22] Overall, balance theory and its refinements highlight the importance of evaluation in person perception and the extent to which we select and simplify our perceptions in order to achieve consistency.

EXHIBIT 4–4
HEIDER'S P-O-X MODEL

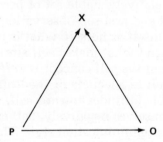

Stability is the tendency for our perceptions of other people to remain the same over time.[23] This often results from the fact that our information about others is limited. Data that would change our impressions may not get communicated. Social conventions, for example, make it more comfortable for people to say pleasant, rather than unpleasant, things to one another. As evidence of this, people in a group have more accurate knowledge of who likes them than who dislikes them, probably because indications of liking are expressed more readily than indications of disliking.[24] Problem relationships like those existing between Mason, Sam, and Alice often persist for long periods of time because of people's reluctance to discuss their negative evaluations of each other.

Stability can also be maintained by the phenomenon known as "self-fulfilling prophecy," a term which refers to the fact that perceptions may act to produce their own confirming evidence. Since Mason saw Sam as an ineffective "old-line" type, he worked more closely with Alice, which in turn made Sam look less and less proficient. A classic example of self-fulfilling prophecy is reported in a study showing that when teachers were told that certain randomly selected students would improve their IQ scores during the year, the IQ's of those students did, in fact, increase.[25]

Stability is not absolute. People's impressions of one another do sometimes change in response to new evidence or old evidence newly interpreted. However, stability is a strong and frequently observed tendency that, along with the tendency toward consistency, makes distorted perceptions of people an everyday occurrence.

Self-concept. Perceptions of self, like other perceptions, are indirect. This may at first seem contrary to our experience, since we tend to feel that we know ourselves thoroughly and have a direct apprehension of our natures. However, the versatile commentator on human affairs, S. I. Hayakawa, says that just as a map is not the territory it represents, the self-concept is not the self.[26] Psychologist Daryl Bem suggests much the same thing. He theorizes that people know themselves not by examining themselves inwardly but by inferring from their own external behavior. That is, people infer their own attitudes the same way they do other people's attitudes—by detecting external cues and making interpretations.[27]

Self-concept is the relatively stable set of perceptions an individual has formed from present and past self-observation. It is those things the person believes about himself or herself: what is unique about self, how self differs from others, and what makes self similar to others.[28]

A major component of the self-concept is *self-esteem:* the degree to which the person sees self as adequate or inadequate. People with high self-esteem have favorable attitudes toward self, while those with low self-esteem evaluate themselves negatively. Self-esteem is an important determinant of a person's communication style. The individual with low self-esteem is likely to be shy and anxious with others. High self-esteem would usually appear as social confidence and poise. People with low self-esteem frequently conform to the opinions of others even when they do not agree with those opinions, while people with higher self-esteem tend to have more confidence in their own judgments.[29]

The self-concept, including self-esteem, is the person's basic frame of reference. All perceptions acquire their meaning largely through their relationship to self. We are much more concerned about our own organization, our own job, and our own children than about others. Even when we do experience concern for matters relating to other people, it is typically because they are people with whom we identify. The self-concept, then, is a key factor in determining which incoming messages we will pay attention to as well as in selecting and shaping the messages we send.

The self-concept is formed through communication with others. We are influenced by the people who are significant to us. In an organization this may mean a superior who controls promotions and pay increases. We may become the kind of person the superior prefers, particularly if this produces rewards we want. On the other hand, our subordinates and peers have important rewards to offer, too, such as responsiveness to our leadership efforts and acceptance of us as friends and colleagues. Thus, we may adopt an identity as a result of deciding which category of other people we value the most. Or we may find we can somehow walk a middle ground and be the kind of person ("firm but fair," or "friendly so long as we don't take too much advantage of her,") that several or all of the people we feel are significant want us to be. Severe discomfort and lowered self-esteem can result when we are unsuccessful in such efforts or do not choose objectives wisely.

Of course, we need not be purely passive, having our self-concept shaped by other people's wishes. We can exert influence on those people who are significant to us. Overall, the formation of the self-concept is best viewed as a transactional process in which we test more or less thoroughly the limits of our social constraints and work out an identity consistent with people significant to us.[30] This transactional process is diagramed in exhibit 4–5.

EXHIBIT 4–5

**A TRANSACTIONAL MODEL OF THE
SELF-CONCEPT**

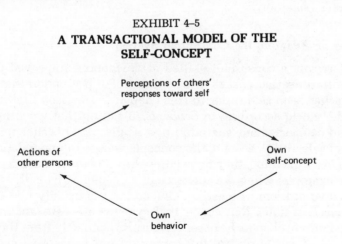

Adapted from John W. Kitch, "A Formalized Theory of the Self-Concept," *American Journal of Sociology* 68 (1963): 483, by permission of The University of Chicago Press. Copyright © 1963 by The University of Chicago.

Like perceptions of other people, self-concepts tend to have the characteristics of consistency and stability. An individual's self-concept is a system of values and views that has organization and integrity, with self-esteem as the central core around which the system maintains consistency. Behavior that seems inconsistent when viewed from outside may make perfect sense when understood in terms of the person's self-concept. Suppose a supervisor sternly criticizes and threatens a group of subordinates one minute and then becomes pleasant and submissive five minutes later while talking with the plant manager. From the supervisor's point of view, this behavior is completely consistent with a self-concept of having power and competence superior to that of the subordinates but less than that of the plant manager.

The self-concept has a high degree of stability. A rapidly changing self would not provide the solid frame of reference a person needs in order to cope with the ambiguities and variabilities of the world. Nor are self-concepts founded on a high sense of self-esteem the only ones resistent to change. Self-concepts in which the person appears very inadequate, dumb, or clumsy will often be defended to the end. It is widely recognized how hard it is to convince anyone having severe inferiority feelings of their true level of worth. They may be pleased with praise and encouragement but then continue to act in the same old way. College counselors are familiar with the phenomenon of such persons who, when told they received a high test score, respond, "There must be some mistake. That can't be me."

Once the self-concept has become established, it imposes a selective effect on perceptions. Experience gets interpreted with respect to that self. This selective effect can, in turn, contribute to making the self-concept still less likely to change. Its existence gives continuity to the person and the person's behavior.[31]

Defending or Adapting the Conceptual System

Roger Harrison, a consultant skilled at developing improved organizational communication, makes three points about perception that summarize what has been said so far in this chapter.[32] Harrison first notes that we see the world according to *concepts,* meaning that we simplify, abstract, and categorize our surroundings, as discussed earlier in terms of perceptual selectivity. Second, the concepts we use to understand a given situation are linked together by relationships, forming a *conceptual system.* For example, when we conceive of someone as friendly, we likely also conceive of them as trusting. One concept is usually tied to others. Third, Harrison notes that conceptual systems are *resistant to change.* This resistance to change, he observes, results primarily from the fact that our concept of self is central to so many of our conceptual systems. In Harrison's terms, our conceptual systems have *competence value* for us as individuals because they help us to be effective in our surroundings.

Harrison goes on to say that while our conceptual systems may have had competence value in the past, they are vulnerable to being disproved. Since our concepts represent the world as being more simple and stable than it really is, it is inevitable that there will be times when our expectancies get violated. This happened to Willard Mason and Alice Walsh when Sam walked off the job. Mason and Alice had both apparently conceptualized Sam as being indifferent to their excluding him from supervisory matters, since he had not vigorously objected when they had done so in the past. When their expectancies were violated, they faced a choice as to how to respond.

There are two general types of responses possible when expectancies have been violated, *defensiveness* or *adaptation.* Defensiveness refers to processes through which we may deny, falsify, or distort reality in order to maintain an existing conceptual system. Adaptation, on the other hand, involves examining the discrepant information, testing new ways of understanding it, our world, and ourself, and forming new and more adaptive conceptual systems. Both processes are described in more detail in the following sections.

Defense Mechanisms. When our expectancies are violated, our first spontaneous tendency is to respond defensively. This is a natural reaction because most of our existing conceptual systems have been formed and proven valid through repeated past experiences. We have reason to want to hold onto them. Thus, Mason's first response upon hearing Sam had left the office: "It's just another Sam incident." He spontaneously denies that the new occurrence tells him anything that would require a change in his view of Sam, the situation, or himself. This is typical of the way individuals defend against facts that might otherwise upset the conceptual systems that give stability and meaning to their experience.

Not all defending behavior is harmful.[33] It keeps us from being knocked into a state of confusion every time something occurs contrary to our expectations. It may enable us to hold onto a tentative view of a situation or issue long enough to test its validity. Also, it often protects our self-respect and relationships with others at times when we and they fail to measure up to our ideals. Defensiveness becomes a problem when it becomes habitual and prolonged, and when we persist in using words and other behavior that protect rather than test our viewpoints.

Because defensive behavior can become a habitual reaction to discrepant information, and because such behavior is maladaptive, it is useful to be able to identify one's own and others' defenses. Awareness of our own defenses can be especially important since our defensive behavior is often the stimulus that prompts defensiveness in the other person. A brief description of several frequently used defense mechanisms should aid in this identification process. Some of the most common defense mechanisms are *denial, avoidance, repression, projection,* and *rationalization.*[34]

Denial means refusing to admit that the threatening perception is relevant. This can take the form of denying its existence altogether ("This isn't so"), denying its relevance to self ("This has nothing to do with me"), or postponing the matter ("I needn't pay attention to this right now"). Since defense mechanisms often operate subconsciously, denial can take subtle forms, such as misunderstanding what another person has said or forgetting something. The behavior involved in denial may be more active, however. For example, a person may attempt to "snow under" a threatening perception by frantically working to enhance the self-concept. Thus, a man who has been criticized by his boss may drive home at breakneck speed, get in an argument with his wife, and in other ways seek superiority over whatever objects and people are most available at the time.

Avoidance involves finding ways of keeping out of the way of threatening perceptions. An example would be the person who does not talk in a committee meeting, thus avoiding the possibility of being disagreed with. Various styles of talking can also be associated with avoidance. A person may talk excessively, spinning a verbal cocoon to prevent incoming messages from getting through. People also hide from one another by "formula" communication—moralizing, sloganizing, and adhering to social conventions whereby safe topics are discussed instead of important ones. A frequent form of avoidance is indirection. Instead of speaking openly, people speak in double meanings. Humor often serves this end. A few witty remarks can make it impossible for anyone to explore personal differences seriously without being labeled as someone who can't take a joke.

Repression is a mechanism that protects the person from being aware of personal motives or emotions he or she thinks are undesirable. Feelings of hostility are often repressed. A manager or professional may repress anger toward a colleague because such relationships are believed to call for rationality rather than openness of expression. In the case of Sam, it seems likely that he has been repressing his true feelings about Mason's and Alice's encroachment on his supervisory role. Now his real feelings are coming out but in the form of an overreaction. Such explosions of long suppressed emotions can produce situations that are difficult or impossible to deal with constructively.

Projection may be seen as a variation on repression. Here, instead of burying unwanted feelings inside, the person projects them outside and attributes them to someone else. Thus, a person may believe "My boss is angry at me" rather than accept personal feelings of anger toward the boss. Once this belief is established, the internal feelings of anger can be justified as self-defense. Our judgments are strongly influenced by our own feelings. In one experiment, people were emotionally aroused and then asked to judge a set of facial expression pictures.[35] The judgments of the emotional states shown in the pictures were affected by the emotions of the judges. There is a tendency to project our own emotions onto others.

Rationalization is possibly the most frequently employed defense mechanism. We often hear people making up excuses or trying to explain away a frustrating situation. For example, a sales representative who loses an important customer may rationalize that this had nothing to do with his or her selling skill but resulted from not having been allowed a big enough expense budget for wining and dining the customer. Rationalization represents a process of selecting perceptions that are consistent with one's existing self-concept. People find "good" reasons for their behavior and its outcomes.

Adapting. Earlier, the principle was stated that the perceiver's active participation tends to produce better retention of information and more useful changes in behavior and internal state. This suggests that there is an alternative to defensiveness when people are presented with information that violates their expectancies. It consists of active involvement in a process of two-way communication aimed at understanding and resolving the discrepancy. This is the process of adapting. Its outcomes are, first, a correct assessment of the discrepant information as to its accuracy or inaccuracy. Then, if it is found to be accurate, the perceiver's conceptual systems are reorganized in order to accommodate it.

Adapting requires that people be willing to test their surroundings as well as make changes in existing conceptual systems. Willard Mason, for example, has initially made a defensive response to Sam's walking off the job. He sees Sam as the sole cause of the problem. To be adaptive rather than defensive, Mason would need to examine how Alice's behavior, that of the workers, and, most importantly, his own have contributed to the problem. He would have to be open to revising his concept that he has been fully effective in the way he has handled Sam in previous similar situations. To behave adaptively, Mason would have to talk with Sam and Alice with a willingness to listen as well as speak and be honest in viewing himself. Whether or not he will do these things depends on his willingness to tolerate some discomfort and the willingness of others around him to support his adaptive effort.

Roger Harrison notes that the urge to adapt is a human drive that competes with opposing motives toward such goals as comfort, stability, and a placid existence.[36] Since adapting requires examining and revising our assumptions about other people and groups, we may risk exposing ourselves to anxiety, producing personal feedback in which we find out that others do not see us the same way we see ourselves. To be willing to undertake adaptive effort, we need to be able to see that its rewards are worth the cost.

A person's willingness to take the risk of behaving adaptively is increased when he or she is surrounded by others who are supportive rather than threatening. People use their defenses the most when they are under threat or pressure. In such situations, they simply do not feel they can afford to give up conceptual systems that have served them in the past in favor of new, untested ways of looking at things. For this reason,

Harrison believes that people cannot really begin to engage in the kind of open communication required for adaptive learning without first building relationships of mutual support, respect, and trust. Such relationships then provide a climate in which people do not need to stay behind their defenses all the time.

Several characteristics of this kind of climate have been identified by Jack Gibb, following an eight-year study of small group discussions.[37] Gibb found that groups in which defensiveness was low were typified by behavior that contrasted sharply with that occurring in groups where defensiveness was aroused. The characteristics of supportive and defensive climates are summarized in exhibit 4–6. The supportive climate components may be summarized as follows:

1. *Description*—giving and asking for information. Presenting events, perceptions, or feelings in ways that do not imply that the receiver should change his or her behavior. Contrasts with *evaluation* (praising, blaming, passing judgment).
2. *Problem orientation*—mutual collaboration in defining problems and seeking solutions. Avoiding preconceived solutions. Contrasts with *control* (attempting to persuade others by imposing one's attitude on them).
3. *Spontaneity*—straightforward honesty, free of deception and hidden motives. Contrasts with *strategy* (the manipulation of others).
4. *Empathy*—identifying with other person's problems, feelings, and values. Respecting the other's worth. Contrasts with *neutrality* (expressing lack of concern for others; treating people as impersonal objects).
5. *Equality*—mutual trust and respect, participative decision-making, deemphasis of status, power, and positional differences. Contrasts with *superiority* (communicating a feeling of dominance and lack of willingness to enter into a shared problem-solving relationship).
6. *Provisionalism*—willingness to postpone taking sides on an issue, to experiment with one's own behavior, and to be open to information and help from others. Contrasts with *certainty* (being dogmatic, needing to be right, wanting to win an argument rather than solve the problem).

Gibb found that the more supportive the climate, the less people tended to read loaded meanings into the communication, and, thus, the more they were able to concentrate on the substantive meanings of messages. A major theme underlying Gibb's findings is the importance of openness—the willingness to be receptive to one's experience. A person who is open to experience copes with threat and change more skillfully. In a supportive climate people are more able to examine their own and each other's premises and discover what their real grounds for disagreement are, if, indeed, there are any. Where genuine differences do exist,

EXHIBIT 4-6
CATEGORIES OF BEHAVIOR
CHARACTERISTICS OF SUPPORTIVE AND
DEFENSIVE CLIMATES IN SMALL GROUPS

Supportive climates	Defensive climates
1. Description	1. Evaluation
2. Problem orientation	2. Control
3. Spontaneity	3. Strategy
4. Empathy	4. Neutrality
5. Equality	5. Superiority
6. Provisionalism	6. Certainty

Reprinted from Jack R. Gibb, "Defensive Communication," *Journal of Communication* 11:3 (1961): 143, by permission of the *International Communication Association.*

people who are open are more capable of dealing with them in a competent way.

Summary

At the start of this chapter, perception was depicted as the outcome of the individual's internal state and the environment in which the person is located. This basic conceptual framework showed that human perception is far from 100 percent accurate. Due to some environmental and internal factors, our perceptions are never in direct touch with objective reality.

Four principles served as the major topics in this chapter. The first three pointed to causes of perceptual inaccuracy: the fact that perception is selective; the fact that the self-concept plays a central role in the perceptual process; and the general tendency of people to distort or avoid incoming data to maintain cognitive consistency. Perceptual selectivity was explained by examining the physiological factors of access, detection, and interpretation, along with the factor of context. The self-concept was seen to be a special case of the way in which we perceive people in general. Our perceptions of others and of self were seen to be colored heavily by evaluation and limited in their accuracy by our needs to see people as having characteristics that are consistent with each other and stable over time.

The topics of perception of others, self-concept, and the tendency toward cognitive consistency were brought together into a transactional model of the self-concept. This model showed that as we interact with other people, an ongoing accommodation between how we see ourselves and them is achieved. Often this accommodation is a limited and limiting one in which we hold onto our self-concept by defending ourselves from any information that is inconsistent with it.

In the face of this seemingly discouraging state of affairs, a fourth principle proposed that it is possible for people to act in ways that will enable their perceptions to be more thorough and more accurate. This possibility was illuminated first by a discussion of the defense mechanisms that, unless they are kept in check, can prevent improved perception and communication. Adaptive behavior—the alternative to defensiveness—was then described along with the characteristics of a "supportive climate," the type of environment in which adaptive behavior is encouraged and sustained.

Questions for Review

1. Do you agree or disagree with the statement, "People behave in ways that make sense to them in terms of the way they perceive the world?" Why?
2. Why is the organization a context in which selective perception is likely to take place?
3. Explain the physiological aspects of perception by applying them to an example of selective perception you recently experienced.
4. Discuss the closure phenomenon in terms of the model of perception and communication in exhibit 4–1.
5. In the experiments conducted by Solomon Asch, why did the subjects form such widely differing impressions of persons described as "warm" versus "cold"?
6. Why does stereotyping occur?
7. Give an example of an incident that had an effect in forming your self-concept.
8. Identify the major parts of one of your own conceptual systems. Give an example of an instance in which you either defended or adapted this conceptual system.

References and Notes

1. The discussion of the determinants and outcomes of perceptual set is adapted from James G. March and Herbert A. Simon, *Organizations* (New York: John Wiley & Sons, 1958), pp. 9–11; William V. Haney, *Communication and Organizational Behavior,* (Homewood, Ill.: Irwin, 1979), pp. 56–63; Edgar F. Huse and James L. Bowditch, *Behavior in Organizations* (Reading, Mass.: Addison-Wesley, 1977), p. 118.
2. The four principles are adapted from Larry A. Samovar and Edward D. Rintye, "Interpersonal Communication: Some Working Principles," in *Small Group Communication: A Reader,* ed. Robert S. Cathcart and Larry A. Samovar (Dubuque, Ia.: Wm. C. Brown, 1970).

3. S. I. Hayakawa, *Symbol, Status, and Personality* (New York: Harcourt, Brace and World, 1950), p. 38.

4. Haney, *Communication and Organizational Behavior,* p. 57.

5. Bernard Berleson and Gary A. Steiner, *Human Behavior: An Inventory of Scientific Findings* (New York: Harcourt, Brace and World, 1964), pp. 529–30.

6. Roger Brown, *Social Psychology* (New York: Free Press, 1965), pp. 557–609.

7. Mason Haire and Willa F. Grunes, "Perceptual Defenses: Processes Protecting an Original Perception of Another Personality," *Human Relations* 3 (1958): 403–12.

8. Carolyn W. Sherif, Muzafer Sherif, and Roger E. Nebergall, *Attitude and Attitude Change: The Social Judgment-Involvement Approach* (Philadelphia: W. B. Saunders, 1965), p. 197.

9. Berleson and Steiner, *Human Behavior,* pp. 547–48.

10. Phillip V. Lewis, *Organizational Communication: The Essence of Effective Management* (Columbus, Ohio: Grid, 1975), p. 51.

11. The discussion of physiological aspects of perception draws upon Michael D. Scott and William G. Powers, *Interpersonal Communication* (Boston: Houghton Mifflin, 1978), pp. 115–18, 130–34; Kelly G. Shaver, *An Introduction to Attribution Processes* (Cambridge, Mass.: Winthrop, 1975), pp. 9–13; Harry C. Triandis, *Interpersonal Behavior* (Monterey, Calif.: Brooks/Cole, 1977), pp. 97–101.

12. John Senger, "Manager's Perception of Subordinates' Competence as a Function of Personal Value Orientations," *Academy of Management Journal* 14 (1971): 422–23.

13. Sheldon S. Zalkind and Timothy W. Costello, "Perception: Implications for Administration," *Administrative Science Quarterly* 7 (1962): 218–35.

14. Haney, *Communication and Organizational Behavior,* p. 59.

15. Erving Goffman, *The Presentation of Self in Everyday Life* (New York: Doubleday Anchor Books, 1959), pp. 208–37.

16. Shaver, *Introduction to Attribution Processes,* pp. 13–14.

17. Jonathan L. Freedman, J. Merrill Carlsmith, and David O. Sears, *Social Psychology* (Englewood Cliffs, N.J.: Prentice-Hall, 1974), p. 31.

18. Solomon Asch, "Forming Impressions of Personality," *Journal of Abnormal and Social Psychology* 41 (1946): 258–90. For a more recent experiment confirming several of Asch's findings, see Jesse Delia, "Change of Meaning Processes in Impression Formation," *Communication Monographs* 43 (1976): 142–57.

19. See, for example, Seymour Rosenberg and Karen Olshan, "Evaluative and Descriptive Aspects in Personality Perception," *Journal of Personality and Social Psychology* 16 (1970): 619–26.

20. See, for example, Marvin D. Dunnette and Walter C. Borman, "Personnel Selection and Classification Systems," *Annual Review of Psychology* 30 (1979): 477–525; T. D. Hollman, "Employment Interviewer's Errors in Processing Positive and Negative Information," *Journal of Applied Psychology* 48 (1964): 180–82; Michael D. Scott, James C. McCroskey, and Michael E. Sheehan, "Measuring Communication Apprehension," *Journal of Communication* 28, no.1 (1978): 104–11.

21. Fritz Heider, *The Psychology of Interpersonal Relations* (New York: John Wiley & Sons, 1958).

22. Stephen C. Jones, "Some Determinants of Interpersonal Evaluating Behavior," *Journal of Personality and Social Psychology* 3 (1966): 397–403; Kendall O.

Price, Ernest Harburg, and Theodore M. Newcomb, "Psychological Balance in Situations of Negative Interpersonal Attitudes," *Journal of Personality and Social Psychology* 3 (1966): 265–70.

23. The discussion of stability in person perception is adapted from Albert H. Hastorf, David J. Schneider and Judith Polefka, *Person Perception* (Reading, Mass.: Addison-Wesley, 1970), pp. 91–96.

24. Renato Tagiuri, Robert R. Blake, and Jerome S. Bruner, "Some Determinants of Positive and Negative Feelings in Others," *Journal of Abnormal and Social Psychology* 48 (1953): 585–92.

25. Robert Rosenthal and Lenore Jacobson, *Pygmalion in the Classroom* (New York: Holt, Rinehart and Winston, 1968).

26. S. I. Hayakawa, *Language in Thought and Action* (New York: Harcourt Brace Jovanovich, 1972), pp. 263–65.

27. Daryl J. Bem, "An Experimental Analysis of Self-Persuasion," *Journal of Experimental Psychology* 1 (1965): 199–218.

28. Arthur W. Combs and Donald Snygg, *Individual Behavior* (New York: Harper and Row, 1959), p. 127; Anthony G. Athos and John J. Gabarro, *Interpersonal Behavior* (Englewood Cliffs, N.J.: Prentice-Hall, 1978), p. 140.

29. Philip R. Constanzo, "Conformity Development as a Function of Self-Blame," *Journal of Personality and Social Psychology* 14 (1970): 366–74.

30. The foregoing discussion of self-concept and self-esteem is adapted primarily from William D. Brooks and Philip Emmert, *Interpersonal Communication* (Dubuque, Ia.: Wm. C. Brown, 1976), pp. 41–50; Combs and Snygg, *Individual Behavior*, pp. 145–57; Scott and Powers, *Interpersonal Communication*, pp. 88–90. Pro-action and the transactional approach to identity formation are discussed in Gordon W. Allport, *Personality and Social Encounter* (Boston: Beacon Press, 1960), chap. 3; Robert W. White, "Motivation Reconsidered: The Concept of Competence," *Psychological Review* 66 (1959): 297–334; David Moment and Dalmar Fisher, *Autonomy in Organizational Life* (Cambridge, Mass.: Schenkman, 1975).

31. The discussion of consistency and stability of the self-concept is adapted from Combs and Snygg, *Individual Behavior*, pp. 129–32; Prescott Lecky, *Self Consistency: A Theory of Personality* (New York: Island Press, 1945), chap. 4.

32. Roger Harrison, "Defenses and The Need to Know," *Human Relations Training News* 6, no. 4, Winter 1962–63, reprinted with adaptations in Paul R. Lawrence and John A. Seiler, *Organizational Behavior and Administration* (Homewood, Ill.: Irwin-Dorsey, 1965), pp. 266–72.

33. Ibid. See also Dean C. Barnlund, "Communication: The Context of Change," in *Perspectives on Communication,* ed. Carl E. Larson and Frank E.X. Dance (Shorewood, Wisc.: Helix Press, 1968), pp. 24–40.

34. The descriptions of defense mechanisms are adapted from Barnlund, "Communication," pp. 24–40; Combs and Snygg, *Individual Behavior*, pp. 272–84; Jerry C. Wofford, Edwin A. Gerloff, and Robert C. Cummins, *Organizational Communication* (New York: McGraw-Hill, 1977), pp. 122–23.

35. Allen Schiffenbauer, "Effect of Observer's Emotional State on Judgments of the Emotional State of Others," *Journal of Personality and Social Psychology* 30 (1974): 31–35.

36. Roger Harrison, "Defenses and Need to Know."

37. Jack R. Gibb, "Defensive Communication," *Journal of Communication* 11 (1961): 141–48.

Chapter 5

Uses and Misuses of Language

General Semantics: Definition and Importance
The Multiple Functions of Language
    Denotative and Connotative Functions
    The Expressive Function
    The Social Structuring Function
    The Directive Function
    The Ritual Function
The Symbolic Process: The Symbol Is Not the Thing Symbolized
    Abstracting
    Extensional and Intensional Meaning
    Reports, Inferences, and Judgments
    Contexts
Language and Thought
The Misuses of Language
Toward Improved Use of Language

After studying this chapter, the reader should be able to

Define and use the following terms and concepts

General semantics	Circumstantial context
Time-binding	Psychological context
Denotative function	Sapir-Whorf hypothesis
Connotative function	Codability
Semantic differential	The uncalculated risk
Expressive function	Bypassing
Social structuring function	Allness
Directive function	Indiscrimination
Ritual function	Polarization
Elementalism	Frozen evaluations
Extensional meaning	Intensional orientation
Intensional meaning	Blindering

Reports
Inferences
Judgments
Verbal context
Paralinguistic context

Undelayed reaction
Person-mindedness
Etc.
Indexing
Operational attitude

Understand

Why language-based malfunctions often occur in organizations
The multiple functions of language
Why words can never fully describe a person, event, or thing
The difference between reports, inferences, and judgments
How the Sapir-Whorf hypothesis applies to your own experience
At least five misuses of language

5

Language may well be the single most frequent source of error in human communication. Since meanings are learned through experience, and no two people have had the same set of experiences, no two people can have precisely the same meaning for the same word.[1] But we devote little attention to this problem. We take language for granted, assuming our words mean the same thing to our listeners as they do to us. Like fish, we swim through a sea of words, not recognizing the impact our verbal environment is having on our thinking and our efforts to act effectively. Here are some examples of the effects of language on communication, thought, and action.

> During World War II, the British Staff prepared a written plan they urgently wished to discuss, and informed their American counterparts that they wanted to "table it." To the Americans, however, "tabling" a plan meant putting it aside and delaying consideration of it until some indefinite future time. A long, tension-filled argument followed before the two parties finally realized they were agreed on the merits and both wanted the same thing.[2]

*   *   *

Harold Koontz, a highly respected management scholar, stresses the importance to any organization or program of clear, verifiable goal statements. Yet he notes that business goals are typically phrased in terms such as: "To make a satisfactory profit while producing a high quality product and being a responsible citizen in the community." Similarly a university may have the objective of "creating and disseminating knowledge." Projects and programs often have goals like "reducing credit losses to a minimum," or "improving the effectiveness of the sales department." Koontz notes that such statements, prevalent though they are, are all but meaningless. Their vagueness makes it impossible for anyone to know at a future point in time whether they have been achieved.[3]

* * *

A management consultant, J. Samuel Bois, reports how he improved the performance of industrial committees and task forces by having the members refer to themselves as "participants" rather than "members." The more they used the word "participant," the more active their involvement became. They in fact began to participate rather than being passive "members."[4]

The British-American example shows vividly that the same words can mean different things to different people. Koontz's commentary on goal statements indicates that words may seem to have meaning to people even when they do not refer to anything verifiable and factual. Finally, Bois's groups of "participants" show that language can affect behavior. It is ironic, therefore, that people's attempts to discuss and clarify the meanings of their words are often rebuffed by statements like, "Hey, let's not get hung up on semantics." As one teacher of communication, John C. Condon, has noted, calling something "a mere semantic problem" is itself a semantic problem. This chapter will show that language problems can be identified and dealt with for the improvement of communication effectiveness. It will be shown, as Condon puts it, that semantic problems "are not best regarded as trivial, irrelevant or *mere*."[5]

GENERAL SEMANTICS: DEFINITION AND IMPORTANCE

The term *semantics,* as it is currently used, refers to the study of words and their meanings. This chapter will broaden that focus to include the human behavior that results from the way in which language is used. In the 1930s, Alfred Korzybski, the Polish mathematician and engineer, applied the term *general semantics* to this broader area.[6] Korzybski viewed language as affecting all human behavior, including perceptions, assumptions, beliefs, and attitudes. General semantics, then, refers to the study of how language is used as well as the effects it has on thought and behavior.

One of Korzybski's basic principles is that a person is a "time-binder."

By this he meant that humans have the unique capacity to pass accumulated knowledge forward from one generation to the next, allowing each generation to build knowledge starting where the previous generation left off. The crucial factor in Korzybski's notion of time-binding is language. Language makes possible the accumulation, storage, and retrieval of knowledge. Obviously, the time-binding function of language is essential to progress in all areas of science and technology. Indeed, each of these fields, whether medicine, aeronautical engineering, or agronomy, could hardly operate without its own highly developed, and developing, special language.

For the nonscientist, language and other closely comparable kinds of symbols are equally associated with human progress. We live in a symbol-laden culture. Our alarm clock signifies that it is time to get up, making us independent of the sunrise and the rooster. The morning news on the radio, including its weather report and advertisements, conveys large amounts of information and meaning about things we cannot experience first hand. The traffic signs allow us to drive to work reasonably safely. Our wallets and purses are jammed with credit cards and licenses without which we might not even be able to prove who we are. The history of the development of human civilization is a history of the increasing pervasiveness of symbols.[7]

While symbol systems, including language, are instrumental in human progress, they are also closely associated with human difficulties. One major reason is that people often do not use the high symbolic capabilities they possess but instead behave as if they had no greater ability than an animal. As noted, humans can pass along accumulated past experience by means of symbols. The symbols "remind" us of the fuller content of the facts and knowledge they represent. In general, animals use signs rather than symbols. They respond in reflex fashion to a loud noise, a mating dance, or a danger signal given by another of their species. They cannot think about the many things the symbol may represent. As Wendell Johnson has put it, "To a mouse, cheese is cheese; that's why mousetraps work." People often make mouse-like reactions to certain words such as *Jew, feminist,* or *salesman.* Thinking immediately becomes restricted. This phenomenon helps explain why humans, along with their superb accomplishments, have shown themselves capable of cruelty and stupidity of many kinds and degrees.[8]

Another way language can result in difficulties is through the use of jargon. Terms such as *least squares, myocardial infarction,* and *reactive schitzophrenic* do not have clear meanings to most people who are not statisticians, physicians, or psychiatrists. As mentioned above, jargon has its positive value. It improves precision and saves time for those in the field who know its meaning. For others, however, it is confusing. Frequently, professionals are unaware of the technical nature of their vocabulary and do not realize it when they are baffling, intimidating, and antagonizing their nonspecialized listeners.

In organizations, language problems are frequent. Modern organizations are large, complex, and hierarchial, meaning they contain many groups of people who are separated from each other by physical location, specialty, and status. Language differences develop between these groups, further accentuating the differences. One study comparing two levels of management found that the words *sensitivity, solidarity, management,* and *strike* meant significantly different things to people in the two groups.[9] Studies also have shown that managers and their subordinates often differ in the meanings they attribute to varying aspects of the subordinate's job, and that these differences occur even if the manager has held the subordinate's job at an earlier time.[10] These studies show that even when people are located close together on the organization chart, the semantic gap between them can be large.

THE MULTIPLE FUNCTIONS OF LANGUAGE

Why is it that language can have the positive effect of furthering human development but can also have the negative effect of building barriers between people and between groups? As one answer to this question, we might say that since language is just an instrument, people can use it for whatever purposes they desire, whether constructive or destructive. This answer is not fully satisfactory, however. Semantic gaps often form and persist even when the people involved do not desire them. For example, most managers and their subordinates do not intend to use words that will be misunderstood by each other, but the studies just cited show that it happens nonetheless. A better answer is that language serves multiple functions, and that in using language, people sometimes understand and control these functions but sometimes do not.

Denotative and Connotative Functions

An important broad distinction can be made between two major functions of language, the *denotative function* and the *connotative function.* The denotative meaning of a word is that to which the word literally refers. Denotation is the explicit identifying of the thing referred to. The language of science is designed to be a denotative language. The attempt in science is to build a language in which the words have clear, constant, pointing meanings. In everyday, nonscientific language, on the other hand, words also have connotative meanings. These are the more general ideas, feelings, and action tendencies that speakers and listeners associate with a word.

Connotative meanings have been measured by means of a technique called the *semantic differential.*[11] Charles Osgood and his associates developed this technique by reasoning that when people are asked to define a word, they will usually try to give many other words they associate with it. Therefore, they present their subjects with words the meaning of which they wish to measure and accompany each of these words with a long list of paired adjectives denoting opposite ends of various dimensions, such as hard-soft, good-bad, and fair-unfair. The subjects were then asked to mark where on each of these dimensions the word being defined fell. Through the statistical technique known as factor analysis, the researchers found that three basic dimensions accounted for a large percentage of the variation in all definitions. These were evaluation (good-bad), potency (strong-weak), and activity (active-passive). According to later research, the evaluative component seemed to account for more of people's response to words than the other two components combined.[12]

These findings help explain why, in communication, a speaker may be intending to state a fact or denote an object, but the listener may be making a highly judgmental positive or negative response. Two nouns—"police officer" and "cop"—may have the same denotative meaning but differing connotations. Both refer to the same object, but the thoughts and feelings evoked by the two are different. Connotations are often manipulated to put a better-sounding label on something. A used car dealer may place the vehicles in an indoor showroom rather than a lot and refer to them as "preowned." A garbage collector may become known as a sanitary engineer. Of course, connotations are often more subtle, bringing about misunderstandings because the same word or phrase has not had the same associations for the listener as for the speaker.

Denotation and connotation are general functions. Language serves numerous more specific functions, each of which may be connotative, denotative, or both, depending on the particulars. Some of these specific functions are the *expressive* function, the *social structuring* function, the *directive* function, and the *ritual* function.

The Expressive Function

The expressive function refers to language as an expression of the condition or feelings of the speaker. There is usually something of the self contained in the statements people make, even those that seem to be statements about the outside world. If I enthusiastically say to a friend, "You're looking great!" I convey clear messages that I like the friend and that I am feeling well, too. S. I. Hayakawa observes that we often use language in the same way that animals snarl or purr. To call one's employer a "chisler" or a "gem" is to use a snarl-word or a purr-word.[13] The words say more about the speaker than about the employer. Typically, though, both speaker and hearer feel that something factual has been said about the employer. Communication can often be improved when we recognize that "language serves a man not only to express something but also to express himself."[14]

The Social Structuring Function

The social structuring function is best exemplified by small talk. When people discuss the weather or last night's ball game, they are building social cohesion in two ways. First, by the very act of talking with one another rather than remaining silent, people are establishing mutual acceptance. Second, people usually find many points of agreement in the topics of small talk. The more people agree that yes, it has been warmer than last winter, and yes, the race for governor does look closer than we thought it would be, and yes, the inflation rate is getting higher, the more mistrust diminishes and social solidarity is built. Thus, when the first few minutes of a committee meeting are spent in what seems like an irrelevant discussion of the morning's headlines, the time may not really have been wasted. A foundation for cooperation during the serious portion of the meeting may have been laid.

The form of language used can also function to confirm the relative standing of individuals in a group. One study of children showed that more popular group members used active language forms more than those members low in popularity. The more popular children used more directive forms of language and thereby gained and maintained influence.[15]

The Directive Function

The directive function represents one of the major uses of language. Whenever we say, "Come here!" or "Meet me in front of the library tomorrow," we are not describing an object or expressing feelings; we are trying to make something happen. Requests, commands, pleas, and orders are examples of language used directively. All directive statements contain a future-oriented element and, in addition, often contain the anticipation of a future reward. Thus, the basis for advertising is the promise that the listener will be better off after acquiring the product, voting for the candidate, etc. Another typical feature of directive language is its use of words loaded with strong emotional connotations and evaluations aimed at achieving a desired impact. For a fuller discussion of persuasive communication, see chapter 13.

The Ritual Function

The ritual function of language may be thought of as an especially powerful version of the directive function. In such rituals as marriage ceremonies, graduations, and inaugurations, the utterance of words transforms a person's position in society. In these rituals, as in the swearing in of a witness at a trial or the signing of a contract, the language carries the connotation that society is collectively imposing certain required behavior on those involved. Participation in other rituals may be more for expressive purposes, such as displaying the flag or cheering at a pep rally prior to a football game. Others, like convention banquets and company picnics, confirm the solidarity of the profession or organization. Ritual language can, of course, become antiquated and lose its power to persuade or satisfy if people find the words empty and not backed up by their experience.

Language, then, can serve multiple functions. Even a single word or phrase can have widely differing effects depending on its context and the way it is expressed. This would not be a problem if, as the late Fritz Roethlisberger suggested, people would label things as they said them; if, for example, they would say, "Now I am using language denotatively to point out to you that person standing over there." "Now I am expressing my feelings about that person." "Now I am urging you not to have anything to do with that person."[16] As speakers, we seldom do this. As listeners, we often ignore expressed meanings, assuming that the words we are hearing mean (denotatively) just what they say. Heightened sensitivity to the multiple functions of language can do much to improve communication effectiveness.

THE SYMBOLIC PROCESS: THE SYMBOL IS NOT THE THING SYMBOLIZED

Another reason people succeed as well as have difficulty in using language lies in the inherent nature of words as symbols. These symbols are not identical with the things they symbolize. The objects, events, and experiences we refer to with words are not as simple or unchanging as the words we use for them.

Over two thousand years ago, the Greek philosopher Heraclitus stated the point in a profound and simple way: one cannot step in the same river twice. Not only does the river flow and change, but the person who steps into it also changes from moment to moment. In more recent times, it has become a central notion of modern science that everything is in a state of process, flux, and change.[17] The preceding chapter on perception and communication noted that we cannot directly perceive this highly complicated, everchanging world-in-process. Likewise, our words can never fully and accurately represent a thing because things are complex and dynamic, while words are simple and static. This situation has been termed the *elemental* problem of language. Elementalism refers to the effect of using arbitrary, static words to represent processes. The concept of elementalism reminds us that language oversimplifies and divides the indivisible process of our experience.[18]

Because of the elementalism of language, we need to be on guard. For example, the innocuous little word *is,* which we use so frequently, produces many misevaluations. When we say, "George Jones is smart," we imply that we have examined George thoroughly and determined that this is the best way George can be described, and that he is always this way. We also imply that the smartness is in George rather than in our evaluation of him. We would communicate more clearly if we said, "I was impressed to hear that yesterday George found the error in the payroll program that the other programmers had been looking for all week." This statement points more accurately to a process and the speaker's role as observer, rather than reducing George to a rigid, elementalistic label.

Words are like maps. They are not the same thing as the territory they represent. This is why the *is* of identity in the statement "George Jones is smart" is misleading. It implies that the map-word *smart* is identical with George. To be useful, maps and words need to correspond fairly closely to the territory they represent. We reduce the risks of elementalism when we keep in mind that "the word is not the thing, the map is not the territory, the symbol is not the thing symbolized."[19]

Abstracting

Words vary in their level of abstraction. A word may indicate a very large class (dog), a more particular class (poodle), or a specific member of a class (Fifi). The process of abstracting is illustrated in exhibit 5-1, using George Jones the accountant as an example. The diagram shows that when we move up the abstraction ladder, we leave out more and more characteristics of George as we use more and more general categories to refer to

EXHIBIT 5-1

THE ABSTRACTION LADDER

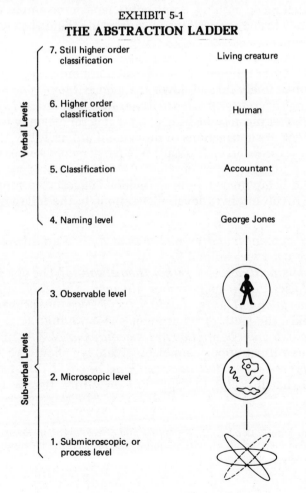

Verbal Levels

7. Still higher order classification — Living creature

6. Higher order classification — Human

5. Classification — Accountant

4. Naming level — George Jones

Sub-verbal Levels

3. Observable level

2. Microscopic level

1. Submicroscopic, or process level

him.[20] The name *George Jones* is the lowest *verbal* level, but even it is an abstraction, since it leaves out some attributes we can perceive (e.g., that George has lost weight since last month) and other microscopic and submicroscopic attributes.

Abstractions are useful even though they leave attributes out. The same group of objects may be classified (abstracted) in different ways for different purposes. Animals, for example, are classified one way by a meat cutter, a different way by a leather worker, another way by a furrier, and in a still different way by a zoologist. The test of a classification system is not whether it is true, but whether it is useful. None of the foregoing classifications is more true than the others, but each is useful. Even the very highest-level abstractions are useful. They aid us in understanding order and relationships. They include some of our most highly valued terms, such as love, life, beauty, reality, and justice.

But high-level abstractions are also involved in some of our worst language habits, including stereotypes, inflammatory rhetoric, and vague platitudes that mean nothing. Some politicians, for example, are noted for their tendency to dodge questions by answering them at a very high level of abstraction.

One rung on the abstraction ladder is not necessarily better than another. Clarity of thought and expression are enhanced when a person is able to move freely up and down the ladder. Moving down the ladder means giving concrete examples to illustrate a higher-level symbol. Moving up the ladder means attaching a more general meaning to a particular thing or event. Both directions of movement are useful. Malfunctions in thought and expression often result when a person becomes stuck on one rung, unable to move up or down.

To avoid being misled, John C. Condon suggests we submit terms or statements involving high-level abstractions to the following six tests:*

1. *Is the statement tentative rather than final?* Careful speakers recognize the need for caution.
2. *Is the statement probable rather than absolute?* The objective speaker seldom uses the terms *never* or *always.*
3. *Was the statement derived inductively?* Does the speaker know from experience the truth of what he or she is saying?
4. *Can the statement be applied to a specific example?* As in the previous test, when illustrations cannot be given, we should be suspicious.
5. *Does the statement tell us something new?* If the statement is so general that it seems to apply to everything, it may be telling us nothing.

---

*Adapted from John C. Condon, Jr., *Semantics and Communication, Second Edition* (New York: Macmillan, 1975) pp. 50–51, with permission of Macmillan Publishing Co., Inc. Copyright © 1975, John C. Condon, Jr.

6. *Does the term exist as a useful symbol, or is it regarded as a thing in itself?* Just because there are certain words does not necessarily mean there are things that correspond to them.

Extensional and Intensional Meaning

The main thrust of the preceding six tests is that useful abstractions are ones that can be checked against concrete, observable reality. The difficulty is that the abstractions (words) we use have personal meanings to each of us. Even a simple word like *chair* can evoke a picture of a simple wooden schoolroom chair for one person and an elegant, hand-carved museum piece for another.

In the terminology of semantics, the *extensional* meaning of a word is illustrated when the word *chair* is used to refer unambiguously to a particular chair—say the one in which you are now seated. The extensional meaning is that which can be verified by fact or observation. It is the physical thing the word stands for.

The *intensional* meaning of a word is the image that it evokes inside a person's head. Intensional meaning has to do with a person's reactions to words rather than the verifiable reality outside that person's mind.

It is easy to reach agreement and solve problems when extensional meanings are clearly understood. If someone says, "This room is too small for a rug that is fifteen feet long," the extensional meaning is clear and can be verified with a measuring tape. On the other hand, if we are talking with an office worker who complains, "My desk is too small," we need to listen more carefully. The worker may not be saying anything objectively verifiable about the desk but instead may be expressing feelings of alienation or lack of recognition in the organization.

Listening for another's meanings is difficult. It requires entering the other person's world, to a degree, and trying to understand what he or she is experiencing. In communicating, it is by far a safer rule to assume the other person's meanings are different from one's own than to automatically assume similarities.

Reports, Inferences, and Judgments

One way to stay alert to different meanings is to distinguish between three kinds of statements: (1) *reports,* (2) *inferences,* and (3) *judgments.* Reports are statements that point to the extensional level. They are statements that can be verified or disproved, such as, "Joe is a supervisor." Inferences are higher on the abstraction ladder. They are statements about the unknown made on the basis of what is known. "Joe looks angry" would be an inference. A judgment is an expression of the speaker's approval or disapproval of the thing referred to. For example, "Joe is a typical slavedriving boss."

There is nothing inherently wrong with inferences and judgments. If we never reached conclusions based on partial evidence and never expressed our likes and dislikes, it would probably be a sign of mental malfunction. Inferences and judgments are likely to bring trouble when we are not aware we are making them. When we make inferences and judgments with an attitude of finality, they often tend to stop further thought on the matter. The speaker who says, "Joe's a slavedriver," is committed to making every statement that follows consistent with that judgment. It is when inferences and judgments are treated as if they were reports that the danger of misevaluation increases.

Contexts

It is risky to classify a statement as being high or low on the abstraction ladder, or as being a report, inference, or judgment, unless people know the context in which it is made. Some words may indicate a wide diversity of meanings until the context provides clarification: *fast, thing, call, matter,* and *business,* to list just a few examples.

More than we realize, people use the context to make meaning out of statements they hear. A vivid illustration is provided by the British psychologist David Bruce.[21] Bruce recorded a set of commonplace sentences and played them in the presence of noise so intense that the voice was barely audible but not intelligible. The listeners were told they would hear sentences on some general topic, such as sports, and were asked to repeat what they heard. Then they were told a different topic and more sentences were played. This was done a number of times. On each trial the listeners repeated sentences appropriate to the topic they had been given in advance. At the end, when Bruce told them that they had heard the same sentences every time and that only the announced topic had changed, most were unable to believe it.

Statements exist simultaneously in a number of contexts. One is the *verbal context,* the other words and sentences that surround a particular statement. This is the context that public officials have in mind when they complain about being quoted "out of context." Then there is the *paralinguistic context* (discussed more fully in chapter 6) that makes "Lots of luck!" a cheerful, friendly wish when said in one tone of voice and a cynical expression meaning "I hope you fail!" when said in another. The *circumstantial context,* or the conditions in which the statement is made, can also be important. Early in a meeting, for example, a member who calls for fuller discussion of an issue may be seen as one who wants to see the group make the best possible decision, while the same request made late in the meeting may appear to be a tactic to delay the group's action on the issue. Finally, the *psychological context*—the listener's frame of mind while hearing the statement—can markedly affect the meaning that is derived. A manager with low self-confidence, for example, may take as a threat an announcement by senior executives that significantly higher standards of achievement are being set for the organization. Both senders and receivers of messages are prone to serious error if they ignore contexts.

LANGUAGE AND THOUGHT

To what extent does our language affect the way we think? Social scientists and philosophers have long been intrigued by this question. In 1929, linguist Edward Sapir argued that humans are "at the mercy" of their particular language. He reasoned that it is by the use of language that a person adjusts to reality and that what one considers to be the "real world" is built up, largely unconsciously, as a result of the language habits of one's group.[22] Later, anthropologist Benjamin Whorf continued this argument, saying that language is not simply a passive tool for reproducing ideas but is itself a molder of ideas, "the program and guide for the individual's mental activity, for his analysis of impressions. . . . We dissect nature along lines laid down by our native language."[23]

Numerous examples can be offered. For instance, Eskimos have several words for different kinds of snow, whereas people in the southern United States use just one. According to the Sapir-Whorf hypothesis, all snow is the same to the Southerner, while the Eskimo is able to differentiate many forms of snow. Similarly, Hopi Indian language has one word for everything that flies other than birds, whether it be an insect, an aviator, or an airplane. In German, there are two words for the pronoun *you*. The word *du* is used when addressing someone with whom you are very familiar, or who is of lower social status, while *Sie* is used when the relationship is more formal, or when addressing a superior. Since relationships can be damaged if these words are misused, Germans must constantly think in terms of these distinctions. If we were to switch to German suddenly, we might find our attention focused on aspects of interpersonal relationships we previously had not felt were important.

College freshmen and sophomores often complain that the many introductory courses they are required to take, whether in economics, biology, sociology, or history, consist largely of having to learn a huge mass of new words—namely, the terminology of each field. Most agree, at least grudgingly, that they need to have the terms in order to discuss the concepts of the particular field. But it may be necessary to have the terms in mind in order to be able to *perceive* instances of the concepts to which the terms refer.

In a study directly related to the language-cognition problem, investigators Roger Brown and Eric Lenneberg were interested in whether colors could be recognized more easily by persons who knew simple terms for them. First the "codability" of each of twenty-four colors for English-speaking persons was determined by showing patches of the colors to subjects and asking them to name them. Some patches were immediately given the same single word name by all the subjects. Other patches evoked a pause, followed by compound word names which varied from subject to subject. Four of the colors for which codability scores had been derived were then shown to a new group of subjects, who were asked to pick out the four colors from a large number of other colors. The results were that subjects were able to recognize highly codable colors (colors with short, well-known names) more easily than less codable colors. This study indicates that short simple words tend to be used more frequently, and that this in turn makes it more likely that judgments of similarity or difference corresponding to these words will be made.[24]

Not all theories of language agree with the Sapir-Whorf hypothesis. For example, the noted linguist Noam Chomsky argues that at an underlying level, all languages are comparable, since all share common principles of grammar and syntax.[25] Chomsky's followers assert that an individual who has learned not just words but the principles of his or her language is not bound to previously learned statements but is capable of generating new, unique utterances. Chomsky and his followers note that the English-speaking person *can* describe as many kinds of snow as the Eskimo, though not in as few words. Therefore, we should not assume that language always determines thought.

On balance, it should be noted that while the languages of different cultural groups, or even of production people and marketing people in an organization, may not differ in terms of what they are *able* to express, they do differ in what they habitually need to express and *do* express. Some things are more easily said in one language than in another. The new member of any society, whether a year-old infant or a new member of a profession, will learn a language that always uses the same simple terms for some things and uses long phrases, inconsistently applied, for others. It seems likely that to some degree this language will help shape the person's view of the world.[26]

For people concerned with effective communication, the relationship between language and thought takes on practical importance. We need to be concerned with the language systems of the persons with whom we are communicating. Is it hard for them to understand some thoughts? Do they lack certain words, which thereby makes it hard for them to grasp the concept we have in mind? Likewise, are they using expressions that are unfamiliar to us? Could this be why we do not see things the same as they do? If so, it may be useful to try to learn their language, at least in part. This can lead to clearer understanding and more successful problemsolving.

THE MISUSES OF LANGUAGE

It has been shown that the major characteristics of language are at the root of a large number of communication problems. Several specific misuses of language have been identified by William Haney.[27] Haney's list summarizes the most important language-based errors people tend to make in thinking and communicating. People who keep these items in mind will be aided in identifying and diagnosing language-related communication difficulties. The list can also help people "watch their language" so as to head off many communication problems before they occur. Haney's list, in slightly abridged and modified form, is as follows:

1. *The uncalculated risk.* The distinctions between reports, inferences, and judgments were discussed earlier. When we fail to calculate the risk involved in an inference and judgment, it is not so often a failure to perform a computation as it is a failure to realize an inference or judgment is being made. The three kinds of statements are often quite difficult to distinguish. To paraphrase an example given by Haney, the statement "Fisher wrote this chapter" is a report when made by the author, but, when made by the reader, it is an inference. Misunderstandings are less likely when people are aware of the inferences and judgments they are making.

2. *Bypassing.* When the same word means different things to different people, or when people have different terms for the same thing, there is a good chance they will "bypass," or talk past, each other. When bypassing occurs, the parties appear either to agree or disagree with each other, but the appearance is a deception. Bypassing results when people assume that meanings are in the words used rather than in the people who use them, are insensitive to contexts, and are reluctant to test their understanding of what another person has said by means of a query or paraphrase.

3. *Allness.* Allness is the attitude of someone who believes her statement on a certain subject is all there is to say or know about that subject. Statements like "What's the use in working hard around here; they'll just want more production" or "Today's workers have no pride in their work," spoken with an air of finality and absoluteness, are typical examples. Allness occurs when people are unaware they are abstracting—when the words they are using do not and cannot contain the full reality of the things referred to. Communication and problemsolving become difficult when individuals lock their minds in this way, becoming dogmatic, rigid, and probably closed to new ideas.

4. *Indiscrimination.* Statements like "Older workers are poor employment risks" or "All salesmen are big spenders" reflect indiscrimination—the process of assuming that all the people or objects we put into a particular category have identical characteristics. This phenomenon, often called stereotyping, reflects the fact that we are more prone to generalize than to differentiate. Special forms of indiscrimination include *polarization* and *frozen evaluations.* Polarization involves speaking in "either/or" terms about situations that really contain graded variations. The manager who feels "Each of my subordinates is either for me or against me" is polarizing, as are those who think

people are either motivated or lazy, sick or healthy, honest or dishonest. Polarization often leads to destructive conflict between persons who have opposite opinions and who refuse to recognize the middle ground. Frozen evaluations are failures to acknowledge that reality is a process, and that things change over time. For example, some employees assume their company will always take care of them. Many such workers, when laid off, return to work the next day refusing to believe they have been terminated.

5. *Intensional orientation.* As noted earlier, the map is not the territory. Nevertheless, people often respond to maps (symbols, concepts, theories, evaluations) as if they were responding to the territory (objects, events, people, relationships, etc.). It has happened on occasion that unknown political candidates have been elected because they had names connoting ethnic backgrounds that appealed to the voters. Haney describes a controversy in a college town involving intensional orientation.[28] Citizens and the press argued that since the college owned tax-exempt investment properties in the town, the amount of real estate thus removed from the tax rolls meant the citizens had to pay unreasonably high tax rates. The debate stayed at the level of concepts and feelings until finally it was revealed that the college's investment property actually amounted to only one half of one percent of the town's real estate. When confronted with the extensional reality, the disputants agreed that so small an amount was not worth worrying about. The conflict had persisted at the intensional level but was resolved as soon as someone pointed to the "territory." One common type of intensional orientation is referred to by Haney as *blindering.* Blinders are put on horses to narrow their vision. Similarly, people sometimes restrict their approach to a problem or situation by the way they think and talk about it. The word *atom* (derived from the Greek word for indivisible) may have long discouraged many capable scientists from thinking the atom could be split. Such timid phrases as "We've never done it that way before," or "That sounds impractical" are examples of blindering.

6. *Undelayed reaction.* People often respond without thinking. When this happens they are like Wendell Johnson's mouse, to whom cheese is cheese whether or not it is contained in a mousetrap. A young boy who hears his mother call "Johnny," to which he responds, "I didn't do it," is making a reflex-like response. So is the department manager who, seeing a member of the controller's staff approaching, immediately assumes there's going to be an argument about the budget. Some undelayed reactions are useful, such as slamming on the brakes when someone darts in front of the car, but communication problems occur when a word or situation is too quickly assumed to mean something it does not. The tendency to conclude quickly and uncritically that the boss is right because he or she is the boss or that a certain person with expert credentials is necessarily right are further examples of undelayed reactions.

TOWARD IMPROVED USE OF LANGUAGE

Semantic malfunctions can be fixed. S. I. Hayakawa has suggested we can, in effect, carry around a "tool kit" for this purpose.[29] Like the mechanic who has pliers and wrenches to use for prevention or repair purposes, we can have with us in our heads a set of mental tools, or rules, for keeping our use of language in good working order. The functions of these rules are to reduce the extent to which we take uncalculated risks, prevent bypassing, help us avoid the pitfalls of the allness fallacy and indiscrimination, keep us from getting caught in circles of intensional thinking, and prevent undelayed reactions. The rules listed below are not the complete solution to semantic problems, but, if kept in mind, they can at least get us started looking for better approaches when language-related difficulties arise. It should be noted that practice is necessary to develop one's ability to use the rules with speed and skill. Items 1 through 6 in the following list correspond respectively to the six language misuses listed in the previous section. They include the suggestions of several widely respected writers in the semantics field.[30]

1. *Be aware of information quality.* Confusion between reports, inferences, and judgments can be reduced by realizing that a report must be a statement of observation. This means that a report can be made only during or after observation, must not go beyond what the observer has observed, and can be made only by the observer. While reports, inferences, and judgments may sound alike, they are based on clearly different types of information. A checklist, adapted from one developed by Haney, can help in determining information quality:[31] (a) Did the speaker personally observe the thing being spoken about? (b) When statements of inference are made, are assessments of their probabilities included? (c) When inferences and judgments are made, are they labeled as such by the speaker? This checklist can help us be aware of the quality of information we are receiving from others and can also help us monitor and control the quality of our own informational output when we are speaking.

2. *Be person-minded.* Haney advises that we can reduce bypassing by becoming less word-minded and more person-minded, looking for the meanings of people's statements in the people rather than in the words they are using. According to Haney, the person-minded communicator frequently asks himself or herself questions like "What does this mean to the other person" or "What would I mean if I were in the other person's position?" Further steps in the direction of person-mindedness include asking questions when you are not sure you understand what has been said and testing your understanding by repeating, in your own words, what you have heard. Haney has noted that the latter device is "one of the oldest, simplest, most useful, and most neglected techniques in communication."[32]

3. *Use etc.* If we say or think *etc.* after a statement, we are kept aware

that, since words are abstractions, the statement has left characteristics out. We should mentally attach *etc.* to our own statements as well as to those made by others. We have not said it all, nor have we heard it all. The use of *etc.* should not be a ploy to make it appear we have more to say about a subject than we really do. Rather, it needs to be used with an attitude of humility and openness to self-examination.

A useful practice closely related to the etc. device is that of placing quotation marks around highly abstract terms as a reminder of their abstractness. The quotation marks alert both the sender and receiver that the word or statement is not precise and absolute but an approximation.

4. *Use indexing.* A library indexes its books, and an office indexes its files. The purpose of indexes is to keep items that are different in important ways separate from each other and identifiable. The habit of indexing the places, persons, things, and events we think and speak about is equally valuable. Worker$_1$ is different from worker$_2$, and worker$_2$ is different from worker$_3$. The small subscript, used as a mental device, helps combat the sort of indiscrimination that comes out in the form of statements like "The workers are lazy." It may be called a *which index* because it leads us to be more specific and ask *which* workers? It jogs us to remember important differences between the performance of different workers and their situations. Two other indexes are the *how much index* and the *when index.* The how much index enables hot$_{110 \text{ degrees}}$ to be distinguished from hot$_{80 \text{ degrees}}$, and a lot$_{5 \text{ pounds}}$ not to be mistaken for a lot$_{500 \text{ pounds}}$. The when index simply involves indexing things by their dates. It reminds us that things are not static but in a process of constant change. The United States$_{1980}$ is not the United States$_{1780}$. The boss, Ms. Smith$_{2 \text{ P.M.}}$ is not the same as Ms. Smith$_{9 \text{ A.M.}}$. When indexing becomes a mental habit, we are more likely to focus on facts rather than on abstract labels.

5. *Develop an operational attitude.* To operationalize is to move from the verbal to the nonverbal level—to perform the operation that will explain the abstract word or concept. An operational definition of the color red would be to say, "Go and look at the color of the topmost light on the traffic signal." Like indexing, the operational attitude keeps attention focused on the observable thing, person, or event rather than on an abstract symbol or map. Arguments about whether the Ajax Company is a good credit risk or whether George Johnson has executive potential are less likely to go on and on without resolution if an operational attitude is applied. The operational approach brings the disputants together in a search for relevant facts. By *operational* definition, a good credit risk means a prospective customer about whom we have obtained certain specific items of information and found that these facts measured up to established criteria. In the case of George Johnson, operationalism involves stating what we must do to identify the requirements of an executive job and to gather facts about Johnson

to see if he meets these requirements. The operational attitude makes it less likely that the decision will be swayed by someone's saying, "I've never seen as sharp a manager as Johnson," or "George is *really* terrific." It tends to lead to agreement through observation.

6. *Stop and think.* To counteract the destructive effects of undelayed reactions, a good habit to develop is that of waiting for a moment to size up the situation. "Don't just do something, stand there" is often a good rule to follow. The wait should not be passive, however. The purpose of the wait is to give yourself a chance to analyze what you have just heard before you commit yourself. Suppose someone has just made a remark about you or your group that sounds offensive. While the spontaneous tendency is to launch a counteroffensive, the better choice is delay. Consider the following: Was the remark really meant the way you heard it? What will be the results if you counterattack? Is it possible the remark was made as a joke? Why not give the other person a chance to clarify the matter? The idea is to gather facts, explore alternatives, index, and operationalize rather than to overreact.

Summary

This chapter began by noting that language, though usually taken for granted and used intuitively rather than carefully, can have profound repercussions. Language is an essential instrument for human progress. When not used carefully, however, language can be at the core of human problems, ranging from misunderstandings to wars. The multiple functions of language were examined, including the denotative-connotative distinction, as well as the expressive, social structuring, directive, and ritual functions. The diverse effects of language were seen to be partly a result of the differing uses to which language can be put.

An examination of the symbolic process showed further reasons why language can have both favorable and unfavorable effects. The elemental problem was discussed, as was the way in which we abstract, the distinction between extensional and intensional meaning, the difference between reports, inferences, and judgments, and the importance of contexts. The importance of language in human affairs was further emphasized in the discussion of language and thought. Here it was seen that the language a person knows can constrain in important ways the thoughts and perceptions that person is able to experience.

Six frequent and troublesome misuses of language were identified: the uncalculated risk, bypassing, allness, indiscrimination, intensional orientation, and undelayed reaction. Corresponding to each of these misuses, six steps toward improved use of language were described: be aware of information quality, be person-minded, use etc., use indexing, develop an operational attitude, and stop and think.

Questions for Review

1. Would you say the time-binding ability of humans helps explain human progress, human difficulties, or both?
2. Why is it important to listen for both connotative and denotative meanings? Give an example.
3. Explain the danger of misevaluation that is inherent in the word *is.*
4. What is the importance of understanding the difference between extensional and intensional meaning?
5. Why might it be useful for a manager who is making a hiring or promotion decision to keep in mind Heraclitus's saying, "One cannot step in the same river twice"?
6. Is one rung on the abstraction ladder better than another? Explain.
7. Recall the David Bruce "unintelligible sentences" experiments and the Brown and Lenneberg "codability" research. Based on these results, what advice about communication style would you give to a supervisor who works on a noisy factory floor?
8. Since it is true that humans are able to think and say things they have never thought or said before, does the Sapir-Whorf hypothesis really have any validity or importance? Discuss.
9. Explain the nature and usefulness of the following devices for reducing language-based communication malfunctions: etc., quotation marks, indexing.

References and Notes

1. Dan P. Millar and Frank E. Millar, *Messages and Myths* (New York: Alfred Publishing Co., 1976), pp. 38–39.
2. Winston Churchill, "The Second World War," *New York Times,* 28 February 1950, p. 31.
3. Harold Koontz, "Making MBO Effective," *California Management Review* 20, no. 1 (1977); 5–13.
4. J. Samuel Bois, "The Power of Words," *ETC.* 29, no. 3.
5. John C. Condon, Jr., *Semantics and Communication* (New York: Macmillan, 1975), p. 2.
6. Alfred Korzybski, *Science and Sanity,* 3rd ed. (Lakeville, Conn.: The International Non-Aristotelian Publishing Company, 1948), p. 8.
7. The discussion of the importance of symbols in cultural development is adapted from Condon, *Semantics and Communication,* pp. 5–6.
8. The discussion of signal reactions is adapted from Condon, *Semantics and Communication,* pp. 9–11.
9. Milton M. Schwartz, Harry F. Stark, and H. R. Schiffman, "Responses of Union and Management Leaders to Emotionally-Toned Industrial Relations Terms," *Personnel Psychology* 23 (1970); 361–67.
10. Norman R. F. Maier, L. Richard Hoffman, J. G. Hooven, and William H. Read, "Superior-Subordinate Communication: A Statistical Research Project," *AMA*

Research Report no. 52 (New York: American Management Association, 1961), pp. 9–30; Norman R. F. Maier, L. Richard Hoffman, and William H. Read, "Superior-Subordinate Communication: The Relative Effects of Managers Who Held Their Subordinates' Positions," *Personnel Psychology* 16 (1963); 1–11.

11. Charles E. Osgood, George J. Suci, and Percy H. Tannenbaum, *The Measurement of Meaning* (Urbana, Ill.: University of Illinois Press, 1957).

12. Donald K. Darnell, "Semantic Differentation," in *Methods of Research in Communication,* ed. Philip Emmert and William D. Brooks (Boston: Houghton-Mifflin, 1970), p. 183.

13. S. I. Hayakawa, *Language in Thought and Action* (New York: Harcourt Brace Jovanovich, 1978), pp. 38–40.

14. Statement by G. von der Gabelentz, quoted by C. K. Ogden and I. A. Richards in *The Meaning of Meaning* (London: Routledge and Kegan Paul, 1952), p. 152.

15. Fred Rosenthal, "Some Relationships Between Sociometric Position and Language Structure of Young Children," *Journal of Educational Psychology* 48 (1957); 483–97.

16. Fritz J. Roethlisberger, *Management and Morale* (Cambridge, Mass.: Harvard University Press, 1941), p. 91.

17. Wendell Johnson, *People in Quandries* (New York: Harper & Brothers, 1946), pp. 23–25.

18. Condon, *Semantics and Communication,* p. 38.

19. Hayakawa, *Language in Thought and Action,* p. 27. The *is* of identity and the map-territory analogy were introduced by Korzybski, *Science and Sanity,* p. 11.

20. The idea of the abstraction ladder was developed by Hayakawa in *Language in Thought and Action,* pp. 154–56, based on Korzybski's concept of "the structural differential" presented in *Science and Sanity,* pp. 386–411.

21. David Bruce, "Effects of Context upon the Intelligibility of Heard Speech," in *Information Theory,* ed. Colin Cherry (London: Butterworths, 1956), pp. 245–52.

22. Edward Sapir, "The Status of Linguistics as a Science," *Language* 5 (1929); 207–14.

23. Benjamin Lee Whorf, "Science and Linguistics," in *Language, Thought, and Reality,* ed. John B. Barroll (Cambridge, Mass.: MIT Press, 1956), pp. 212–13.

24. Roger W. Brown and Eric A. Lenneberg, "A Study in Language and Cognition," *Journal of Abnormal and Social Psychology* 49 (1954); 454–62. See also Brown's *Words and Things* (Glencoe, Ill.: The Free Press, 1958), pp. 235–36.

25. Noam Chomsky, *Aspects of the Theory of Syntax* (Cambridge, Mass.: MIT Press, 1965); idem, *Studies on Semantics in Generative Grammar* (The Hague: Mouton, 1972).

26. A balanced view between the extremes of the Sapir-Whorf hypothesis and Chomsky's argument has been offered by many commentators, including David Krech, Richard S. Crutchfield, and Edgerton L. Ballachey, *Individual in Society* (New York: McGraw-Hill, 1962), pp. 302–03; Dan I. Slobin, *Psycholinguistics* (Glenview, Ill.: Scott, Foresman, 1971), chap. 5; Condon, *Semantics and Communication,* pp. 29–33; William D. Brooks and Philip Emmert, *Interpersonal Communication* (Dubuque, Ia.: W. C. Brown, 1976), pp. 104–05.

27. William V. Haney, *Communication and Organizational Behavior* (Homewood, Ill.: Irwin, 1979), chap. 8–17.

28. Ibid., pp. 472–73.

29. Hayakawa, *Language in Thought and Action,* p. 280.

30. The six rules for improved use of language were derived by consulting Richard W. Budd, "General Semantics: An Approach to Human Communication," in Richard W. Budd and Brent D. Ruben, *Approaches to Human Communication* (Rochelle Park, N.J.: Spartan Books, 1972), pp. 97–119; Stuart Chase, *Power of Words* (New York: Harcourt, Brace, 1954); Condon, *Semantics and Communication,* pp. 50–51; Hayakawa, *Language in Thought and Action,* p. 280; Korzybski, *Science and Sanity,* pp. 386–411; Arnold E. Schneider, William C. Donaghy, and Pamela Jane Newman, *Organizational Communication* (New York: McGraw-Hill, 1975), p. 19.

31. Adapted from Haney, *Communication and Organizational Behavior,* pp. 259–63.

32. Haney, *Communication and Organizational Behavior* (Homewood, Ill.: Irwin, 1973), p. 271.

Chapter 6

Nonverbal Communication

Dimensions and Functions of Nonverbal Communication
Body Language
    Body Shape and Appearance
    Posture
    Gestures
    Touching
    The Face
    Eye Contact and Gaze
The Voice: Paralanguage
Proxemics and Environment
    Territory and Space
    Buildings, Rooms, and Seating Arrangements
    Artifacts and Objects
Time
Implications and Recommendations

After studying this chapter, the reader should be able to

Define and use the following terms and concepts:

Nonverbal communication
Sign language
Action language
Object language
Kinesic slips
Paralanguage
Proxemics
Body types
Display rules
Eye contact

Visual dominance behavior
Voice qualities
Vocal characteristics
Vocal qualifiers
Nonfluencies
Territoriality
Informal space
Intimate, personal, social, and public distances
Sociopetal and sociofugal settings

Understand

Examples of body language, paralanguage, proxemics, and time
How nonverbal cues can affect the impact of a verbal message
How working relationships can be affected by nonverbal factors
Why a single nonverbal cue cannot be interpreted in isolation
How managers and others can improve their nonverbal communication

---

6

One of the most important keys to understanding communication is to realize that much of it is never put into words. A nonverbal message can be transmitted by a nod of the head, a frown, an enthusiastic tone of voice, leaving one's office door open or closed, or arriving late for an appointment. Actions often speak louder than words, as the following examples show:

A student took a summer job in rural Missouri interviewing farmers about water supply availability. The first few days he went out on the job wearing a suit and tie. He got little cooperation from the farmers. He thought the way he was dressed might have something to do with it, so he began wearing jeans and a workshirt rather than the suit and tie. The farmers were much more cooperative.[1]

*   *   *

In the late 19th century a German horse named Hans became famous for knowing how to add. If asked to add 2 and 3, for example, he would paw the ground five times. Strangely, he could do this only in the presence of human beings. A simple explanation for his "talent" was later discovered: when he unknowingly reached the answer, he would see his audience relax, whereupon he stopped pawing.[2]

*   *   *

In *My Fair Lady,* Professor Higgins and Colonel Pickering coach the flower girl, Eliza Dolittle, to a point where she can pass as a dutchess.[3]

Higgins and Pickering, however, put little effort into teaching Eliza *what to say*. Most of their energy is devoted to training her in the sound and rhythm of aristocratic speech, how to dress properly, how to walk with elegance, and how to use "correct" gestures. The implication is that little had to be done to improve the substance of what she said.

* * *

A young lawyer was one of several who came into the firm at about the same time. One day he was told by the director to move to another office. The move was purely so he would be near another man with whom he was working on a long-range project. However, nobody believed that. As he put it, "We get practically no information on how we're doing in the firm." Thus the others at his level immediately began wondering what the move meant for them. Some considered looking for another job since the young man with the new office location obviously had the "inside track."[4]

Some scholars estimate that more than sixty-five percent of all social meaning in interpersonal communication is carried by nonverbal signals.[5] The face alone is said to be capable of producing 250,000 different expressions.[6] A study by Albert Mehrabian indicated that overall meaning is conveyed ninety-three percent by vocal, facial, and body cues and only seven percent by words. Various studies have shown that people are likely to be more strongly influenced by nonverbal cues than by the words being spoken.[7]

Nonverbal communication influences decisions, shapes careers, and in many other ways affects the quality of working life in an organization. A revealing pair of experiments showed, first, how the nonverbal behavior of white interviewers differed depending on whether they were interviewing black or white applicants. The interviewers sat farther away from the blacks and evidenced less "total immediacy," a measure consisting of scores for forward lean, eye contact, and shoulder orientation (directness). They also ended their interviews with blacks sooner and made more speech errors, such as stuttering and breaking off sentences. In the second experiment, white male subjects were interviewed by interviewers who were really confederates of the experimenters, trained to exhibit either immediate or nonimmediate behaviors. Interviewees who received nonimmediate behavior showed less composure and performed less adequately in the interview. These interviewees also rated their interviewers as less friendly and less effective.[8]

Every verbal communication is accompanied by a nonverbal context. Every spoken phrase is said in a certain time and place and is spoken at a certain rate, with particular inflections. Furthermore, most people actually speak words for only ten to eleven minutes a day. They spend hours every day in conversations, but the time actually spent uttering words is only ten or eleven minutes. Obviously, there is a great deal of time devoted to communicating nonverbally. We spend twelve or more years taking English courses, which give instruction in the use of words, but formal education pays little, if any, attention to nonverbal communication. We need to be more aware of the nonverbal messages that are shouting constantly, even at times when they consist of mere whispering or saying nothing at all.

DIMENSIONS AND FUNCTIONS OF NONVERBAL COMMUNICATION

The term *nonverbal* is commonly used to refer to all communication events that transcend spoken or written words.[9] Nonverbal communication may be classified in several ways. One of the simplest schemes, developed by Jurgen Ruesch and Weldon Kees, consists of three areas: (1) *sign language*—the use of gestures in place of words, numbers, and punctuation signs; (2) *action language*—all movements (such as walking) that convey meaning even though not used exclusively as signals; and (3) *object language*—material things (e.g., clothes, art objects, furniture, architecture) that express something about the one who displays them or about the situation.[10] Other schemes of categorization include:[11]

1. *Body motion or kinesic behavior*—gestures, facial expressions, eye behavior, touching, and any other movement of the limbs and body.
2. *Physical characteristics*—body shape, physique, posture, body or breath odors, height, weight, and hair and skin color.
3. *Paralanguage*—voice qualities, volume, speech rate, pitch, nonfluencies (saying "ah," "um," or "uh"), laughing, yawning, etc.
4. *Proxemics*—the ways people use and perceive space, including seating arrangements, conversational distance, and the "territorial" tendency of humans to stake out a personal space.
5. *Environment*—building and room design, furniture and other objects, interior decorating, cleanliness, lighting, and noise.
6. *Time*—being late or early, keeping others waiting, cultural differences in time perception, the relationship between time and status.

Nonverbal cues function or "work" in three principal ways: (1) they significantly influence the type of relationship that forms between persons; (2) they express emotions; and (3) they greatly affect the meanings that are conveyed verbally.[12] Relationships between people in organizations are continuously and strongly affected by nonverbal signals. The executive who sits behind a massive desk while talking with others is likely to establish more formal, less open relationships than the one who comes out from behind the desk and sits on the couch. A worker who is always hunched over a machine, almost never glancing in anyone else's direction, will probably not be fully trusted or accepted by other members of the work group.

Relationships are often shaped by nonverbal cues. From your own experience, how do you know that someone is a close personal friend of yours? Probably not because the person has said to you, "I am your close personal friend." More likely you know by the person's facial expressions, tone of voice, and the amount of time he or she spends with you.

Emotions are often expressed nonverbally as well. Sorrow, anger, enthusiasm, pain, or fear are hardly ever communicated by words alone. The nonverbal expressions are much more important. Words can best convey discrete bits of information, one bit at a time, but the body, because it can send out many signals simultaneously, does a better job of expressing complex attitudes and feelings and in generating interpersonal rapport.[13]

Nonverbal cues can operate in several ways to affect the impact of verbal messages. Five ways that verbal and nonverbal signals can be interrelated are mentioned in the following list.[14]

1. *Repeating,* as when verbal directions to some location are accompanied by pointing.
2. *Contradicting,* as in the case of the person who says, "What, me nervous?" while fidgeting and perspiring anxiously before giving a speech. This is a good example of how the nonverbal message can be more believable when verbal and nonverbal signals disagree.
3. *Substituting* for verbal messages, as when Dad comes home with a beaten expression that says, "I've had a horrible day at the office" without a word being spoken.
4. *Complementing* the verbal message by adding to it, e.g., when a worker blushes with embarrassment while discussing poor work performance with the supervisor.
5. *Accenting* a verbal message by, in effect, "underlining" it with a pound on the table, a grip on the shoulder, or a tone of voice indicating the importance the speaker attaches to the message.

It should be noted that nonverbal communication is closely related to verbal communication. The two should not be considered in isolation from one another. Neither is adequate by itself. When a tone of voice conveys an attitude, words say what the attitude is about. When information is expressed in words, accompanying muscle tensions show how the speaker feels about it. An experiment showing the cumulative effect of verbal and nonverbal cues had judges first listen to the voices of unknown persons, then see their gestures, then their facial expressions, and finally their interactional behavior. The observers' impressions of the strangers, recorded after each set of cues, shifted as each new class of cues became available.[15] This cumulative effect principle should be kept in mind throughout this chapter. Separate attention will be given to nonverbal cues eminating from the human body, the voice, physical environment, and time. In an ongoing communication event, all these aspects are present, however, each adding dimensions of meaning to the overall pattern. No single aspect or cue is meaningful except in the context of others.

Body Language

The body sends a continuous flow of cues. As Erving Goffman puts it, even if a person stops talking, ". . . he cannot stop communicating through body idiom; he must say either the right thing or the wrong thing. He cannot say nothing."[16] In *Roosevelt in Retrospect,* John Gunther provides an example when he describes Franklin D. Roosevelt in this way: "In twenty minutes Mr. Roosevelt's features had expressed amazement, curiosity, mock alarm, genuine interest, worry, rhetorical playing for suspense, sympathy, decision, playfulness, dignity and surpassing charm. Yet he *said* almost nothing."[17]

Presidents are not the only people who can communicate a lot while saying little. We all use "body English." We lean, we point, we look away. Our hands move to punctuate our sentences. We frown, smile, fold our arms, move toward, then move away. We express our liking of another person, for example, by looking at them attentively, asking questions, and leaning forward, while with someone we don't like we remain silent, look away, and lean back.[18] We tell something about our social or organizational status by walking tall or hunching down, relaxing or being tense, gazing steadily or blinking frequently.

An introduction to the communicative functions of the body may be gained by recognizing the importance of six aspects: body shape and appearance, posture, gestures, touching, the face, and eye contact and gaze.

Body Shape and Appearance.   The body conveys meaning even when it is not in motion. Most people have beliefs about the personalities and temperaments that go with certain body types. Three general body physiques have been identified: (1) *ectomorph* (thin, frail, and tall), (2) *endomorph* (fat, soft, round, and short), and (3) *mesomorph* (muscular, athletic).[19] In a 1961 study, subjects were shown pictures of the three body types. Ectomorphs were rated as tense, nervous, less masculine, stubborn, pessimistic, and quiet. Endomorphs were seen as old-fashioned, weak, talkative, warm, dependent on others, and trusting. Mesomorphs were said to be strong, masculine, adventurous, mature, and self-reliant.[20] Obviously, there are no necessary connections between physique and behavior, but people tend to expect them and base decisions on them whether they realize it or not. Research has shown that higher salaries tend to be paid to taller employees even when their qualifications are equivalent to those of shorter employees.[21] Tall men are likely to be perceived as more credible than shorter men.[22]

Skin color and gender also affect communication, however little they may be related to the verbal content of messages. In upper-class, predominantly white communities, for example, whites are perceived as more credible than blacks. Men also tend to be seen as more credible than women, even by women. Naturally, these results would vary in localities having different cultural norms, but they do show that physical attributes have a significant impact on one's attempts at communication.[23]

Dress is also a form of nonverbal communication. It would be impossible to list all the things that can be communicated by clothing; the list would vary greatly with time, place, and situation. Suffice it to say that skillful communicators attend to their apparel. Robert Guest documents how the "old beat-up jacket" worn by a new plant manager helped him to be quickly recognized by his subordinates as approachable and trustworthy.[24] When Nixon aide John Ehrlichman went on trial, he wore light blue suits and glasses with thin gold frames, much less foreboding than the dark pinstriped suits and dark-rimmed half-glasses to which he was accustomed. Some have speculated that this image change may have contributed to his receiving a relatively light sentence.[25] Whether it did or not, it is certainly true that such factors can influence communication quality.

Posture.   The way people carry themselves communicates messages. The workman who stands around with his weight back on his heels and his hands in his pockets probably will not be on the job long. The executive with his feet up on his desk likewise says something by his posture.

The kind of interpersonal relationship that exists between people is often indicated by their posture.[26] For example, when a group of people are turned inward toward each other in circular fashion, it is an indication they do not wish to include other people. Similarly, when two people are positioned face-to-face, a high rate of interchange in conversation between them is virtually required, while a side-by-side positioning indicates a less intense relationship that is more open to outsiders. Also, the extent to which people in conversation assume postures that are congruent carbon copies or mirror images of each other can be a tipoff as to their interest in and agreement with one another. Differences are often signaled by noncongruent postures.

Posture can be a means by which status differences between interacting parties are communicated. People tend to relax most with a person of lower status, a bit less equal, and least with someone whose status is higher than their own.[27] Erving Goffman observed at staff meetings in a hospital, for example, that doctors sat in relaxed, "undignified" postures, while lower-status people sat more rigid and straight in their chairs. Similarly, doctors had the right to saunter casually into the nurses' station and lounge on the counter while joking with the nurses. Others participated in these informal gatherings only after they had been initiated by doctors.[28]

Gestures.   The Italians are famous for enriching their speech with gestures, though all cultures do so to some degree.[29] Certain gestures differ greatly in meaning across cultures, however, and can convey unintended meanings. Americans, for instance, make a circle with the thumb and forefinger to signify "okay," but to a Brazilian this would be an obscene sign of contempt. Within the contemporary American scene, middle class WASPS do not gesture as broadly as Italian Americans or as frequently as Eastern European Jewish Americans. Furthermore, many WASP children are taught not to gesture because it is "impolite."[30]

Nonetheless, many gestures do have widely understood meanings. Footshaking and fingertapping usually signify nervousness, impatience, or boredom. A clenched fist typically indicates hostility or anger. Opening one's hands to another suggests openness, sincerity, and acceptance. Putting fingertips together to form a "steeple" can indicate confidence or superiority. Scratching, digging, or picking at one's own hands or body is usually taken to indicate nervousness, hostility, or conflict.

Head nodding is a gesture having special importance in keeping conversation going. It serves two functions, to reinforce the speaker and to control the flow of speech. Occasional nods signal the other person to keep talking, while rapid nodding conveys that the one nodding wishes to speak.[31]

Specialists in the study of body movements, such as Ray Birdwhistell and Albert Scheflen, emphasize strongly that no single gesture carries meaning in and of itself.[32] The gestures discussed above do not always mean the same thing. To understand a person's meaning we must pay attention to all the cues they are emitting and the context in which they are occurring, not just to a single gesture.

Touching. All people begin their lives as infants using touch to communicate. This is virtually the only method of communication a mother has to influence a child. Though American culture, unlike many others, disapproves of touching among adults in public, it is still a meaningful mode of communication.

Consider the handshake. A firm handshake conveys decisiveness, while a limp one usually evokes negative feelings in Americans, who interpret it as a lack of interest or vitality. A damp hand is considered a sign of anxiety. A prolonged handshake is usually unacceptable because it suggests too much intimacy.[33]

Higher-status people usually feel freer to touch lower-status people. Thus, touching is a clue to the extent to which people perceive hierarchical distance between one another, or the extent to which one person is, or is trying to be, dominant over another. Research has shown a person is more likely to touch when giving information, advice, or orders, when asking a favor, or when trying to persuade—all situations where at least a brief period of dominance is implied.[34] President Lyndon Johnson was a master of the persuasive touch. As one of his "targets" described it, "Lyndon got me by the lapels and put his face on top of mine and he talked, and talked and talked. I figured I was either getting drowned or joining."[35]

As with other forms of nonverbal communication, one should be aware of "kinesic slips" in this area. A manager attempting to reassure a subordinate about his or her chances for advancement may add a touch to strengthen the message, but if the touching is stiff and nervous, it may act to contradict the message instead.

The Face.   Because it is the most expressive part of the body, the face is probably the single most important source of nonverbal communication. The many muscles within the face make it capable of conveying several emotions simultaneously. Faces are sometimes hard to read, as in the case of the Mona Lisa, but our high fascination with the ambiguity of that particular face shows we are accustomed to getting clearer readings from facial expressions.

Research by Paul Ekman shows there is a set of facial expressions that can be interpreted with great accuracy by most people. Based on observation of specified areas of the face, he has developed a coding system for six emotions: happiness, sadness, surprise, anger, disgust, and fear. His results indicate that (1) happiness is conveyed by the lower face and eye area; (2) sadness is revealed most by the eyes; (3) the eye area and lower face communicate surprise; (4) the lower face, eyebrows, and forehead reveal anger; (5) the lower face is most revealing of disgust; and (6) fear is conveyed most by the eye area.[36]

Although the face can communicate a great deal, it also seems to be the type of nonverbal behavior that people are best able to control. People lie best with the face, and since the face is so dominant in communication, it is difficult for a casual observer to determine whether or not a communicator is sincere. One experiment has indicated that the "leakage" of feelings that a person does not intend to reveal can be picked up only by observers who concentrate on watching parts of the body other than the face.[37] From early childhood, we learn to make the right faces. We qualify our emotional expressions according to sets of "display rules" established by our culture (e.g., New Englanders are not supposed to smile much), situation (in this office you're expected to look happy), and self-concept (I'm a strong person who does not show fear).[38] Thus, while faces usually suggest clear meanings, they should be interpreted in context and with caution.

Eye Contact and Gaze.   Eye contact takes place when two people look at each other's eyes. It tends to occur when one person is seeking feedback about another's reactions, when people wish to signal that the communication channel is open, when people want to signal a desire for affiliation, involvement, or inclusion, or when one person wants to put the other under stress. Women generally engage in more eye contact than men. Eye contact diminishes when people have something to hide or are in competitive settings, where there is dislike, tension, or fear of deception, when the people are physically close to one another, during long utterances, or when a person does not wish to maintain social contact. People tend to establish eye contact more often and for longer periods of time the more they like each other. Of course, the long, icy stare can also convey antagonism.[39]

The gaze is a nonverbal cue that both signals and works to maintain status differences. Ralph Exline and his colleagues have identified a pattern they call visual dominance behavior, which they find to be characteristic of people in high power positions. Their studies show that people of high status look more at another person when they speak than when they listen. It is also typical of high-status people to look less than lower-status people at the other person.[40] Managers, supervisors, or staff experts in organizations might find it revealing to observe the amount of eye contact they receive from others as a measure of the extent to which they are seen as high-status individuals.

The Voice: Paralanguage

When President Dwight Eisenhower hoped to persuade Senator John Bricker to soften his proposed amendment to limit the president's treaty-making powers, he decided a good tactic would be to invite the senator over to the White House for a friendly chat. The move backfired, however. The warm and sympathetic tone of the conversation gave Bricker the impression Eisenhower was more willing to compromise than he really was, which led to an undermining of the president's position.[41] Paralanguage, or voice quality, like other forms of nonverbal behavior, often transmits more meaning than the words that are uttered. The importance of paralanguage is affirmed by such often-heard comments as, "I wasn't upset by what he said, but the way he said it," "Say it as if you mean it," or "You don't sound like a professor." Albert Mehrabian makes the point by explaining vocal information as "what is lost when speech is written down."[42]

Anthropologist George Trager coined the term *paralinguistics* to refer to something beyond or in addition to language itself. He divides the topic into four parts: *voice qualities, vocal characterizers, voice qualifiers,* and *vocal segregates.*[43] Voice qualities refer to such factors as pitch, range, resonance, rhythm, and rate of speaking. Vocal characterizers include laughing, crying, whispering, groaning, yawning, whining, coughing, and clearing the throat. Vocal qualifiers are momentary variations in volume (overloud or oversoft) or pitch (very high or very low), while vocal segregates are nonfluencies, such as "ah," "uh," and "um," silent pauses, and intruding sounds.

Any one of these ingredients can convey a lot.[44] A high-pitched voice can indicate excitement, while a low-pitched voice can show seriousness, sadness, or affection. Anger and emphasis are often signaled by loudness. Rate of speech can significantly affect meaning—rapid speech tending to indicate excitement and importance. Nonfluencies, such as "ah" and "er" are thought to mar a speaker's presentation, but there is also evidence indicating that too fluent speech may be perceived as "slick" and, therefore, untrustworthy.

Much research on paralanguage has focused on whether the voice can accurately convey the speaker's personal characteristics and feelings. Concerning personal characteristics, it has been found that age and sex can be identified rather accurately through voice quality. So can social class, as intimated by the Eliza Dolittle example at the beginning of this chapter. But people are generally less able to judge someone's occupation, body type, or personality traits by this means. Concerning feelings the research results are mixed, but there are clearly occasions when the voice conveys more accurate information about the speaker's emotions than do the words spoken. While verbal expression is often constrained by social or organizational norms, feelings can sometimes be expressed, perhaps unconsciously, by nonverbal means.[45]

Leadership and influence can be confirmed or disconfirmed by paralinguistic means. A bitter example was revealed in the Watergate tapes. During Richard Nixon's last year as president, his principal aides, John Ehrlichman and H. R. Haldeman, virtually extinguished his influence by vocally treating him as less than an equal. They did not call him "sir," interrupted him frequently, contradicted him, and often responded to him with monosyllabic answers or with long pauses. Influence in a group can usually be plotted with accuracy by ranking people according to the number of successful interruptions they achieve, minus the number of times they are interrupted. In general, people who talk more are seen as showing more leadership, as are those who manifest control over the speech or silence of others ("Speak only when I speak to you"). Laughter can also often be a clue to power relationships, because jokes tend more often than not to be told by higher-status people, with lower-status people being the ones to whom jokes are told. There is truth to the old admonition, "You'd better laugh at the boss's jokes."[46]

As with other categories of nonverbal behavior, paralinguistic cues need to be interpreted in context. Who is the speaker? What is the situation? How does the speaker see the situation? What are the norms of the speaker's culture? A key factor in improving a person's skill in this area is recognizing a change in a speaker's normal voice quality (increased rate, lower pitch, more nonfluencies, etc.). Assigning in-context meaning to differences in a speaker's voice quality can often significantly increase a person's understanding of the speaker's meaning.[47]

Proxemics and Environment

Up to this point, this chapter's discussion of nonverbal communication has been limited to the signals that come directly from persons themselves, first from their bodily appearance or movements, and then from their voices. The focus now turns to a third major category of unspoken messages, those transmitted through proxemics and environment. Proxemics is the study of how people use territory and space. This section also looks at the communicative functions of such environmental factors as building and room design, seating arrangement, and the presence of significant artifacts and objects.

Territory and Space. In any organization, one can observe that there are norms relating to the use of space.[48] There are places where a factory manager cannot go without creating the impression among the workers that they are being spied upon. Military officers keep away from enlisted men's quarters except during scheduled inspections. School and college administrators stay out of classrooms unless there is an emergency or the visit has been arranged in advance.

These phenomena are examples of *territoriality,* which may be defined as the tendency of organisms to lay claim to and defend space.[49] Like animals, people mark off boundaries that others recognize without having to be told. Have you ever gone looking for a place to study in a building filled with classrooms? If so, you undoubtedly passed by a room in which a single student was already studying and so you kept on looking for one where *you* could be the possessor of your own private space. As in basketball, where the home court advantage is well known, organization members also sense the benefit of being on one's own "turf." An experienced union negotiating team would never agree to hold major talks in the management's offices, and, since the management's team would feel the same way, the talks are usually held on a neutral site.

Territory can have very specific effects on a message. For example, if an employee approaches a manager in a neutral territory, such as the coffee lounge, to ask about a pay raise, the manager's response will probably be, "Come to my office and we can discuss it." At least part of the reason for the manager's preference is that he or she will feel more in command of the situation when on home territory.

Higher-status members of an organization typically have more control over space than do those of lower status. Thus one writer, Gerald Goldhaber, has stated the following three principles relating the concept of territory to organizational status:[50]

1. *Persons of higher status will have more and better territory.* You will notice around a university that four or more graduate students are given the same size office as two faculty members or one department chairman. In corporations, executive offices tend to be spacious, are located on the top floors of the building, and have carpets and fine quality furniture. The most senior offices will be at the corners, so they will have windows on two sides.

2. *The territory of higher-status people is better protected than that of lower-status people.* Consider how much more difficult it would be for you to arrange to visit the governor of your state than for the governor to arrange to visit you. Chief executives have been described as "controlling the area which is least accessible, sealed away from intruders by several doors and a handful of minions."[51] Even junior-level managers and many staff personnel are "protected" by having an office with a door and a secretary who answers their phone.

3. *The higher one's status, the easier it is to invade the territory of lower-status people.* A superior typically feels free to "walk right in

on" subordinates, while they in turn are more careful to ask permission or make an appointment before visiting the superior.

An awareness of the concept of territoriality can help an individual maintain the kinds of interpersonal relationships that are normally accepted in the organization. In general, good working relationships are sustained when people recognize and respect the territorial rights of other individuals and groups. At times, however, a desired change in normal communication patterns can usefully be signaled by not adhering to the usual territorial patterns. Thus, a superior who wants to have a free exchange of ideas with a subordinate may decide the best place to do so would be in a neutral territory, such as the cafeteria. Similarly, a department with grievances against higher management or another department may arrange to meet jointly and discuss the problems at an off-site location, perhaps during a weekend.

An important kind of space in interpersonal relations is that which anthropologist Edward Hall has termed *informal space.* This is the space that people place between each other when they interact. Hall defines four patternings of informal space among middle-class Americans; *intimate, personal, social,* and *public distances.*[52] Intimate distance, from direct contact to eighteen inches, is the space for lovers, parents, and small children, or close friends discussing a secret. When this distance occurs otherwise, such as on crowded elevators, defensive devices (e.g., looking at the floor) protect against it. Personal distance, from eighteen inches to four feet, is the range for most conversation, the distance depending on the relationship between the parties and their feelings toward each other. Social distance, from four to twelve feet, is the distance for most work-related interactions, with the closer distances used for informal conversations and by those who work closely together. The greater distances allow more formal business and social events to be conducted with maximum interchange but minimum emotional involvement. Finally, public distance is from twelve to twenty-five feet. It is typically used for one-way communication by a speaker to an audience.

There are significant differences in informal space between cultures. For example, one may distinguish high-contact (Arab, Latin American, and southern European) from noncontact (Asian, Indian-Pakistani, and northern European) cultures.[53] It is well to be aware of another person's concept of informal space. Several studies have shown that when their space is invaded, people feel uncomfortable, anxious, and sometimes even angry and aggressive.[54] Along with Hall's classifications, it is also useful to be aware of the distances that are considered appropriate for different purposes. Incongruence between distance and the type of message involved (e.g., giving a formal speech in a small, close group) can mar communication effectiveness.

Buildings, Rooms, and Seating Arrangements. Certain buildings and rooms seem to welcome people to come in and talk, while others seem to say, "Go away." As an example of the former, consider the Law School building at the University of New Mexico, a building purposely designed to promote social contact.

> As you enter the building, you come into the middle of a large circular foyer with a diameter of approximately 30 feet. The foyer is furnished with large, comfortable black leather chairs arranged in groups of three or four around coffee tables. The design calls for several circles within a circle. Faculty, students, and administrators all must pass through the foyer to get anywhere in the building. Thus, the design of the building greatly facilitates human interaction.[55]

Obviously, many tasks in an organization require human interaction (e.g., selling merchandise, checking information, trading ideas, meeting to identify issues or make decisions). Therefore, physical facilities that discourage needed personal contact can hurt the organization's performance. Fred Steele, a consultant on physical settings, quotes one manager's description of the route to his boss's office.

> I go from my office out past the receptionist and down the hall to the other end of the building. I take the elevator up to 12, get off and take another one to 21. I get off and walk to the other end of the building, turn and pass through three doors, and I'm at his office—about 100 feet straight above where I started![56]

Confirming the obvious, this manager commented dryly, "We don't see each other nearly as often as we should." Some managers, aware of the benefits of frequent contact, try to have their office located as close to their boss's as possible.

A large office may look coldly impersonal or warm and casual, depending on how its furniture is arranged. Banks often have multiple partitions separating customers from officers and employees and a "regimented arrangement of furniture (side-by-side seating alongside a wall or rows of desks for employees who face each other's backs.)"[57] One writer, Humphrey Osmond, has referred to the *sociopetal* and *sociofugal* aspect of settings. These terms refer, respectively, to the tendency of arrangements to bring people close together or to push them apart. The esthetic quality of an area also affects communication. One study showed that subjects in a "beautiful" room rated pictures of faces more favorably than did subjects who looked at the same pictures in an "ugly" room. Subjects in the ugly room described the faces as "fatigued, weary, displeased, and irritable," while those in the beautiful room were more likely to use terms such as "energetic, zestful, and content."[58] It is clear that both the physical arrangement and the overall appearance of a room are likely to affect the quality of communication that occurs in it.

Seating arrangements have important effects on the amounts and kinds of interaction that take place between people and on the emergence of leadership in groups. You may have noticed when students are seated row-by-row in a classroom that those in the forward rows and the center sections of each row tend to participate more. Though these center and front locations are usually the ones chosen by the most interested students, the phenomenon has also been observed in classes where seating is alphabetical.[59] Where group members are seated around a table, there is a tendency for people seated across from each other to converse with one another more frequently than those seated side by side, given a minimum of direction by a designated leader. When there is strong, directive leadership, the opposite occurs; more conversation is directed to neighbors than to those sitting opposite.[60]

Seating patterns also appear to be related to interaction quality. Research by Robert Sommer shows people prefer side-by-side seating for cooperative transactions and a face-to-face arrangment for competitive discussions. Another study shows that people expect friendliness between pairs of group members to be less the farther apart they are sitting. This tendency is mitigated by situations permitting easy eye contact (e.g., where the pair are seated at the head and foot of the table).[61]

The spatial position a person occupies in a group can have an important bearing on whether he or she emerges as a leader.[62] While those seated at the end positions typically tend to be seen as the leaders, an interesting additional insight comes from a study of five member groups, arranged with two on one side of the table and three on the other. More leaders by far emerged from the two-person side than from the three-person side. The reason appeared to be that since interaction and influence is more likely to occur across the table rather than around it, those on the two-person side could influence three people, whereas the three could influence only two.

It is clear that the designs of buildings, the appearance and arrangement of rooms, and the patterns of seating all have major effects on the communication environment. One final spatial-environmental factor will now be discussed, the influence of artifacts and objects.

Artifacts and Objects.   The presence of certain furnishings can play an important role in shaping interaction.[63] An office containing paintings, items of sculpture, family photos, or small momentos picked up by the occupant during travels can be useful as conversation pieces. On the other hand, one executive reportedly removed all art objects from the office after finding that visitors became so involved in discussing them that they never got down to business.

The objects in an office often convey clear signals about the occupant's status. One consultant says a wooden desk and area rugs are essential if power and authority are to be enhanced.[64] Writing in a way that is facetious yet revealing, *Boston Globe* columnist Susan Trausch lists the objects that can help one to "become powerful" in an organization.[65] First, a chair with arms is important. It allows you to "rest elbows on chair arms, clasp hands together, put chin on hands, and say, 'hmm.' " Next, a spare chair or couch is a must, since it suggests that you are important enough to have visitors. This is so necessary that if you have room for nothing else, a folding chair, folded, will do. A work table next to your desk is helpful. It connotes that you have so many important papers one desk will not hold them all. Some sort of shelving is helpful to give your space "intellectual depth," and, finally, a grandfather clock should be considered, since "people lower their voices around a grandfather clock." Trausch says that with the help of these objects, you will "go places." This claim is one that had better be interpreted with caution, however. If you are the junior cost clerk whose desk is located in the fifth row of the accounting department bullpen, bringing in a grandfather clock might start you moving in the wrong direction.

The objects around a person's desk or office can convey more than just status. The next time you visit other people's places, notice how much they declare about themselves. What things do they enjoy having around? What people are important to them? What books or magazines do they find important or enjoyable? Is everything neat and clean? Does this person prefer orderliness or informality? In the same fashion, try looking at your own spaces to find the messages others will read about you and your preferences.

Time

Time talks, as anthropologist Hall has noted in *The Silent Language*.[66] The time of day, for example, can speak clearly concerning the importance of a message. If you place a phone call at midnight, the receiver of the call will perceive it as much more important than if you had placed the same call at 3:00 in the afternoon. By the same token, a plant manager in the United States is undoubtedly aware that by calling the workers together to make an announcement during the middle of the morning or afternoon —times that take them away from their work—the significance of the message is enlarged. Indeed, when an important announcement is to be made, the first question managers are likely to ask is, "When should we let them know?"

Small increments of time can be highly meaningful. In a revealing study, subjects viewed a series of silent films in which two actors played the roles of executive and visitor, switching roles for different takes.[67] In each take, the visitor knocks on the door and then enters the executive's office. Subjects who observed the films were consistent in rating the relative status of the two men, with time as a major factor. The quicker the visitor entered the room, the more status he was perceived as having. On the other hand, the longer the executive took to answer, the higher status *he* was seen to have. This study is also related to the topic of territoriality, discussed previously. Subjects saw the visitor as having the least amount of status when he stepped just inside the door after entering, more status when he walked halfway up to the desk, and the most status when he walked directly up to the seated executive.

Cultures differ widely in the ways they conceive time. Promptness, for example, is highly valued by Americans, who become insulted much faster by being kept waiting for an appointment or a visitor's overdue arrival than do people from most other cultures. Hall notes that Americans typically apologize for even a five minute delay in keeping an engagement. He tells of an American ambassador in another country who misunderstood how time was thought of by the local diplomats. To them, an hour's tardiness was equivalent to our five minutes. They did not want to arrive exactly on time, since they felt that might connote a relinquishing of their freedom to act to the United States, so they arrived fifty minutes late. This was just right to their way of thinking, but the American ambassador was indignant. To him they were undependable—unable to keep an appointment and unwilling even to apologize.

Americans think of time as a road or ribbon to be divided up into discrete segments in which we do "one thing at a time." Hall describes a North American who arrived for an appointment with a Latin American businessman and was highly annoyed to find fifteen other callers there at the same time. The Latin concept is that a lot of things go on simultaneously. Business that might be finished in a quarter of an hour sometimes takes the whole day. Americans are unable to "shift the partitions" of scheduled time periods the way members of other cultures can. The amount of time scheduled for a certain purpose should be used in that way —no more, no less. This is quite unlike the Arab concept, which is that time is what occurs before or after an event. The Arab concept is that when an event starts, it proceeds until it is finished without regard to a preestablished schedule. The Greeks somewhat similarly believe that once meetings on an issue are begun, they should continue until all aspects are resolved. Once an American mission to Greece tried to limit the length of meetings by reaching an agreement on general principles and then leaving the details to subcommittees. The Greeks regarded this as a device designed to deceive them, and the result of the misunderstanding was a string of unproductive meetings in which each side deplored the other's behavior. From these examples it should be abundantly clear that special sensitivity to the time dimension is essential for those whose work involves communication across national boundaries.

Summary

This chapter began by stressing the importance of nonverbal cues through examples showing that in many instances, more meaning is communicated nonverbally than through words. The major dimensions and functions of nonverbal communication were defined, with the main body of the chapter consisting of an introduction to each of the principal nonverbal domains. Body language was discussed, with specific attention to body shape and appearance, posture, gestures, touching, the face, and eye contact and gaze. Paralanguage, or voice quality, was another area containing several subcategories of important cues, such as pitch, rate, and nonfluencies. The communication implications of space and environment were then considered, with attention given to the topics of territoriality, informal space, building and room design, seating arrangements, and artifacts and objects. The section on time showed how times of day, timing, and culture-based concepts of time play important parts in producing communication outcomes. Finally, a list of recommendations for using nonverbal forms of communication was given.

IMPLICATIONS AND RECOMMENDATIONS

At several points in this chapter, implications for managers and other organization members have been pointed out. For purposes of review and emphasis, three recommendations can usefully be stated.[68] They are the following:

1. *Become a better nonverbal observer.* Organizational communication is likely to improve if members increase their sensitivity to as many of the nonverbal areas as possible: from architecture to seating arrangements; from posture to tone of voice. Working relationships can be improved if it is recognized that nonverbal signals are helping to define these relationships. As more nonverbal signs are observed, people's predictions about one another are likely to get better. Their simplistic, black-and-white stereotypes can develop into more usefully complex inference systems. Better decisions can be made by those who have allowed themselves to be informed by all available channels. Attention to nonverbal cues can sometimes help a communicator from being deceived. Research has shown, for example, that when people are lying, they tend to reduce the extent to which they "talk with their hands."[69]

2. *Make improved use of nonverbal signs in sending messages.* Communicators can improve their effectiveness as senders by increasing their "band width"—that is, by using nonverbal as well as verbal channels. Managers who are trying to motivate subordinates should not settle for a narrow verbal band when they could give their messages more power and impact. A staff specialist trying to sell an idea needs to give it impact. Such aims can be greatly aided when the communicator knows about and uses the effects of such nonverbal dimensions as territory, clothing, posture, and voice quality. Messages sent within organizations often fail to achieve the results the sender desires because they are delivered in a tedious monotone or in a dull memo.

3. *Do not oversimplify nonverbal cues.* The importance of under-standing nonverbal signals in relation to their context has been mentioned more than once. The same cue does not always mean the same thing. A man may fold his arms across his chest to signal belligerence, but he may also do so because he's nervous or feels cold. The same signal can mean different things to different senders and to different receivers. The relationship between the communicators is important, as are the time, place, and other aspects of the situation. Whether one is preparing information for transmission or trying to read the meaning of someone else's message, it is important not to focus on single cues in isolation but rather to attend to the whole communication system.

Questions for Review

1. Do you believe that emotions can be conveyed better nonverbally than verbally? Discuss.
2. Think about the office of the most important person you ever visited. What conclusions can be reached about that person from the artifacts, use of space, and other nonverbal cues?
3. Think about a situation you have been involved in or have observed where different nonverbal cues contradicted each other. Was the contradiction resolved? Why or why not?
4. Describe the difference between sign language, action language, and object language.
5. Assume that as an employee you feel you are not given adequate recognition by your boss. How might you use your knowledge of nonverbal communication to improve this situation?
6. Suppose that you wish to develop a cooperative, trusting work relationship with an employee at the same level as you in another department. What nonverbal factors would be important ones to pay attention to in developing this relationship?
7. Flora Davis, a popular writer on nonverbal behavior, once wrote that "every little movement has a meaning all its own." Do you agree or disagree? Why?
8. What are some ways an organization member might use nonverbal means to increase his or her power and influence? What limits might there be to this undertaking?

References and Notes

1. William D. Brooks and Philip Emmert, *Interpersonal Communication* (Dubuque Ia.: Wm. C. Brown, 1976), p. 126.
2. O. Pfungst, *Clever Hans, the Horse of Mr. Von Osten* (New York: Holt, 1911).
3. Alan Jay Lerner and Frederick Loewe, *My Fair Lady.*

4. Fred I. Steele, *Physical Settings and Organization Development* (Reading, Mass.: Addison-Wesley, 1973), p. 53.
5. Randall Harrison, "Nonverbal Communication: Explorations into Time, Space, Action, and Object," in *Dimensions in Communication,* ed. Jim Campbell and Hal Hepler (Belmont, Calif.: Wadsworth, 1965), pp. 158–74.
6. Ray L. Birdwhistell, *Kinesics and Context* (Philadelphia: University of Pennsylvania Press, 1970), p. 8.
7. Albert Mehrabian and Morton Wiener, "Decoding of Inconsistent Communication," *Journal of Personality and Social Psychology* 6 (1967): 109–14. See also Bella N. DePaulo et al., "Decoding Discrepant Nonverbal Cues," *Journal of Personality and Social Psychology* 36 (1978): 313–23; Paul Ekman and Harriet Oster, "Facial Expressions of Emotion," *Annual Review of Psychology* 30 (1979): 527–54; David W. Johnson, Kenneth McCarty, and Thomas Allen, "Congruent and Contradictory Communications of Cooperativeness and Competitiveness in Negotiations," *Communication Research* 3, no. 3 (1976): 275–92.
8. Carl O. Word, Mark P. Zana, and Joel Cooper, "The Nonverbal Mediation of Self-Fulfilling Prophecies in Interracial Interaction," *Journal of Experimental Social Psychology* 10 (1974): 109–20.
9. Mark L. Knapp, *Nonverbal Communication in Human Interaction* (New York: Holt, Rinehart and Winston, 1972), p. 20.
10. Jurgen Ruesch and Weldon Kees, *Notes on the Visual Perception of Human Relations* (Los Angeles: University of California Press, 1956), p. 189.
11. Adapted from Starkey Duncan, "Nonverbal Communication," *Psychological Bulletin* 72 (1969): 65–68; Gerald M. Goldhaber, *Organizational Communication* (Dubuque, Ia.: Wm. C. Brown, 1979), pp. 152–87; Knapp, *Nonverbal Communication,* pp. 5–12. See also Randall P. Harrison and Mark L. Knapp, "Toward an Understanding of Nonverbal Communication Systems," *Journal of Communication* 22, no. 4 (1972): 339–52.
12. John Stewart and Gary D'Angelo, *Together: Communicating Interpersonally* (Reading, Mass.: Addison-Wesley, 1975), pp. 54–56.
13. Dean C. Barnlund, *Interpersonal Communication* (Boston: Houghton Mifflin, 1968), pp. 525–26.
14. Knapp, *Nonverbal Communication,* pp. 9–11; Paul Ekman, "Communication through Nonverbal Behavior," in *Affect, Cognition, and Personality,* ed. Silvan S. Tomkins and Carroll E. Izard (New York: Springer, 1965), pp. 390–442.
15. Ernst G. Beier and John Stumpf, "Cues Influencing Judgment of Personality Characteristics," *Journal of Consulting Psychology* 23 (1959): 219–25.
16. Erving Goffman, *Behavior in Public Places* (New York: Free Press, 1963), p. 35.
17. John Gunther, *Roosevelt in Retrospect* (New York: Harper, 1950), p. 22.
18. Albert Mehrabian, *Silent Messages* (Belmont, Calif.: Wadsworth, 1971), p. 2.
19. William H. Sheldon, *Atlas of Men: A Guide for Somatyping the Adult Male at All Ages* (New York: Harper & Row, 1954).
20. William D. Wells and Bertram Siegel, "Stereotyped Somatypes," *Psychological Reports* 8 (1961): 77–78.
21. S. D. Feldman, "The Presentation of Shortness in Everyday Life—Height and Heightism in American Society: Toward a Sociology of Stature," reported in Ellen Berscheid and Elaine Walster, "Physical Attractiveness," in *Advances in Experimental Social Psychology,* vol. 7, ed. Leonard Berkowitz (New York: Academic Press, 1974), pp. 178–79.

22. Charles D. Ward, "Own Height, Sex, and Liking in the Judgment of the Heights of Others," *Journal of Personality* 35 (1967): 381–401; Paul R. Wilson, "Perceptual Distortion of Height as a Function of Ascribed Academic Status," *Journal of Social Psychology* 74 (1968): 97–102.

23. Elliot Aronson and Burton W. Golden, "The Effects of Relevant and Irrelevant Aspects of Communicator Credibility on Opinion Change," *Journal of Personality* 30 (1962): 135–46; Franklin Haiman, "An Experimental Study of the Effects of Ethos in Public Speaking," (Ph.D. diss., Northwestern University, 1948); "The Case against Chauvinism: A 20-Year Bill of Particulars," staff report in *Human Behavior* 1, no. 3 (1972): 46–49.

24. Robert H. Guest, Paul Hersey, and Kenneth H. Blanchard, *Organizational Change through Effective Leadership* (Englewood Cliffs, N.J.: Prentice-Hall, 1977), p. 121.

25. Nancy M. Henley, *Body Politics* (Englewood Cliffs, N.J.: Prentice-Hall, 1977), pp. 87–88.

26. Albert E. Scheflen, "The Significance of Posture in Communication Systems," *Psychiatry* 27 (1964): 316–31; idem, *How Behavior Means* (Garden City, N.Y.: Anchor Press, 1974), pp. 53–65.

27. Albert Mehrabian, "Communication Without Words," *Psychology Today* 1 (1968): 53–55.

28. Erving Goffman, *Interaction Ritual* (Garden City, N.Y.: Doubleday, 1967), pp. 78–79.

29. Several of the examples in this section come from Anthony G. Athos and John J. Gabarro, *Interpersonal Behavior* (Englewood Cliffs, N.J.: Prentice-Hall, 1978), pp. 29–31; Marianne LaFrance and Clara Mayo, *Moving Bodies* (Monterey, Calif.: Brooks-Cole, 1978), pp. 48–49; Steward L. Tubbs and Sylvia Moss, *Human Communication* (New York: Random House, 1974), p. 154.

30. Albert E. Scheflen and Alice Scheflen, *Body Language and Social Order* (Englewood Cliffs, N.J.: Prentice-Hall, 1972), p. 88.

31. Michael Argyle, *The Psychology of Interpersonal Behavior* (Baltimore: Penguin Books, 1972), p. 42.

32. Birdwhistell, *Kinesics and Context,* p. 45; Scheflen, *How Behavior Means,* pp. 179–81.

33. Tubbs and Moss, *Human Communication,* p. 154; Mehrabian, *Silent Messages,* p. 7.

34. Henley, *Body Politics,* pp. 101–08.

35. Alfred Steinberg, *Sam Johnson's Boy* (New York: Macmillan, 1968), p. 13. Used by permission of the author.

36. Paul Ekman, Wallace W. Friesen, and Silvan S. Tomkins, "Facial Affect Scoring Technique: A First Validity Study," *Semiotica* 3 (1971): 37–58. See also Knapp, *Nonverbal Communication,* p. 127.

37. Paul Ekman and Wallace V. Friesen, "Nonverbal Leakage and Clues to Deception," *Psychiatry* 32 (1969): 88–106.

38. Paul Ekman, "Universals in Facial Expressions of Emotions," in *Nebraska Symposium on Motivation,* vol. 19, ed. James K. Cole (Lincoln, Neb.: University of Nebraska Press, 1972).

39. Goldhaber, *Organizational Communication,* p. 160–62; Michael Argyle and Janet Dean, "Eye Contact, Distance, and Affiliation," *Sociometry* 28 (1965): 289–304; Phoebe C. Ellsworth and Linda M. Ludwig, "Visual Behavior in Social Interaction," *Journal of Communication* 22, no. 4 (1972): 375–403.

40. Ralph V. Exline, "Visual Interaction: The Glances of Power and Preference," in *Nebraska Symposium on Motivation,* ed. Cole; Ralph V. Exline, Steve L. Ellyson, and Barbara Long, "Visual Behavior as an Aspect of Power Role Relationships," in *Nonverbal Communication of Aggression,* ed. Patricia Pliner, Lester Krames, and Thomas Alloway (New York: Plenum, 1975), pp. 21–52.

41. Richard Tanner Johnson, *Managing the White House* (New York: Harper and Row, 1974), pp. 103–04.

42. Mehrabian "Communication Without Words," pp. 53–55.

43. George L. Trager, "Paralanguage: A First Approximation," *Studies in Linguistics* 13 (1958): 1–12.

44. The examples in this paragraph are drawn from Brooks and Emmert, *Interpersonal Communication,* pp. 131–33.

45. The conclusions in this paragraph are drawn from research summarized in Knapp, *Nonverbal Communication,* pp. 151–64. See also Roland J. Hart and Bruce L. Brown, "Interpersonal Information Conveyed by the Content and Vocal Aspects of Speech," *Speech Monographs* 41 (1974): 371–80.

46. The ideas and examples in this paragraph are drawn from Henley, *Body Politics,* pp. 68–70; LaFrance and Mayo, *Moving Bodies,* p. 103.

47. Merwin A. Hayes, "Nonverbal Communication: Expression Without Words," in Richard C. Huseman, Cal M. Logue, and Dwight L. Freshley, *Readings in Interpersonal and Organizational Communication* (Boston: Holbrook Press, 1977), pp. 55–68. See also Owen Robbins, Shannon Devoe, and Morton Wiener, "Social Patterns of Turn-Taking: Nonverbal Regulators," *Journal of Communication* 28, no. 3 (1978): 38–46.

48. The examples in this paragraph are drawn from Robert Sommer, *Personal Space* (Englewood Cliffs, N.J.: Prentice-Hall, 1969), p. 19.

49. See Robert Ardrey, *The Territorial Imperative* (New York: Atheneum, 1966), p. 3; Edward T. Hall, *The Hidden Dimension* (Garden City, N.Y.: Doubleday, 1966), pp. 7–10; idem, *The Silent Language* (Greenwich, Conn.: Fawcett, 1959) p. 51.

50. Goldhaber, *Organizational Communication,* pp. 170–72.

51. Abne M. Eisenberg and Ralph R. Smith, Jr., *Nonverbal Communication* (New York: Bobbs-Merrill, 1971).

52. Hall, *The Hidden Dimension,* pp. 111–29.

53. O. Michael Watson, *Proxemic Behavior* (The Hague: Mouton, 1970); Robert Shuter, "A Field Study of Nonverbal Communication in Germany, Italy, and the United States," *Communication Monographs* 44 (1977): 298–305.

54. Paul M. Insel and Henry Clay Lindgren, *Too Close for Comfort* (Englewood Cliffs, N.J.: Prentice-Hall, 1978), pp. 21–26.

55. From: Goldhaber, Gerald M., *Organizational Communication, Second Edition,* 1979, Wm. C. Brown Company Publishers, Dubuque, IA.

56. Fred I. Steele, *Physical Settings and Organization Development,* © 1973, Addison-Wesley, Reading, Massachusetts, p. 65. Reprinted with permission.

57. Mehrabian, *Silent Messages,* p. 17.

58. A. H. Maslow and N. L. Mintz, "Effects of Esthetic Surroundings," *Journal of Psychology* 41 (1956): 247–54.

59. Sommer, *Personal Space,* pp. 111–19.

60. Gordon Hearn, "Leadership and the Spatial Factor in Small Groups," *Journal of Abnormal and Social Psychology* 54 (1957): 269–72.

61. See Marvin Shaw's review of research on seating arrangement and interaction quality in his *Group Dynamics* (New York: McGraw-Hill, 1971), pp. 130–35.

62. The findings relating to seating arrangements and leadership are drawn from Fred L. Strodtbeck and L. Harmon Hook, "The Social Dimensions of a Twelve-Man Jury Table," *Sociometry* 24 (1961): 397–415; Lloyd T. Howells and Selwyn W. Becker, "Seating Arrangement and Leadership Emergence," *Journal of Abnormal and Social Psychology* 64 (1962): 148–50.

63. The ideas in this section come from Michael B. McCaskey, "Place, Imagery, and Nonverbal Cues," in Athos and Gabarro, *Interpersonal Behavior,* pp. 63–73; Randall P. Harrison, *Beyond Words* (Englewood Cliffs, N.J.: Prentice-Hall, 1974), pp. 148–49.

64. John T. Molloy, *Dress for Success* (New York: Wyden, 1975), chap. 10.

65. Susan Trausch, "Things HBS Won't Tell You," *Boston Evening Globe,* 15 December 1975.

66. Hall, *The Silent Language,* p. 15. Several of the examples in this section are drawn from pp. 15–30 and 128–45.

67. Cited by Sommer, *Personal Space,* p. 19.

68. The three recommendations and the discussion that follows draw primarily on Harrison, "Nonverbal Communication," pp. 188–89; Stewart and D'Angelo, *Together: Communicating Interpersonally,* pp. 45–57.

69. Paul Ekman and Wallace V. Friesen, "Hand Movements," *Journal of Communication* 22 (1972): 353–74.

Chapter 7

Understanding Interpersonal Dynamics

Two-person Communication in a Superior-Subordinate Relationship
The Two-person Relationship
    Dimensions of Interpersonal Relationships
    Transactional Analysis
Maladaptive Relationships
Adapting and Improving Relationships
    Using Exposure and Feedback
    Metacommunication: Addressing the Process of Communication
    Dealing Directly with Disagreements
    Exercising Choice

After studying this chapter, the reader should be able to

Define and use the following terms and concepts

Content level	Game
Relationship level	Scripts
Interpersonal need compatibility	Disconfirmation
Interpersonal reflex model	Partial confirmation
Transactional analysis	Paradox
Parent ego state	Lockstep reciprocal
Adult ego state	Johari Window
Child ego state	Exposure
Complementary transaction	Feedback
Crossed transaction	Metacommunication
Ulterior transaction	Constructive fighting
Time structuring	

Understand

The difference between the content and the relationship levels
Three models for understanding interpersonal relationships

Examples of types of maladaptive relationships
How people can act to improve interpersonal relationships

7

What takes place when two people talk with one another? Thinking about the many factors involved, including differences in background, emotion, perception, and motivation, makes it seem amazing that anyone ever understands another person and gets understood. Communication between two people consists of a two-way flow of (a) whatever informational content is being discussed, (b) feelings about that information, (c) concepts and feelings about one's self and the other person, and (d) responses to the contexts in which the conversation is occurring. Very likely the reader can think of several other components that could be added to this list. Suffice it to say that interpersonal communication is complicated.

This list, as well as the models of the communication process presented earlier in this book, suggest that it is helpful for persons communicating to be as aware as possible of the complexity in which they are involved. If such awareness exists, they are able to make better choices about whether or not to continue behaving the way they are. Quite often people involved in communication do not have enough of this awareness. They miss important components of what is happening in the interaction and thus lose their ability to make effective behavioral choices. The following conversation between a young research scientist and his superior serves as an illustration. While reading this conversation, try looking for thoughts, feelings, and facts being communicated that one or both of the communicators do not seem clearly aware of.

Two-Person Communication in a Superior-Subordinate Relationship*

In this case, Dr. Dodds, a young researcher, talks with his superior, Dr. Blackman, the director of research, a man in his late forties with consider-

---

*Adapted and abridged from the full length version contained in Abraham Zaleznik and David Moment, *The Dynamics of Interpersonal Behavior,* pp. 257–260. Copyright © 1964, John Wiley & Sons, Inc., Publishers. Reprinted by permission of John Wiley & Sons, Inc.

able stature as a researcher and research administrator. Many ambitious and able young researchers wanted to work in Blackman's laboratory. Dr. Dodds was a promising young scientist who had recently been assigned to the laboratory as a staff scientist. Dodds, who had earlier requested the meeting with Dr. Blackman, entered Blackman's office and showed him a letter from Professor Wilkin of another research institution offering Dr. Dodds a position.

Dodds: What do you think of that?

Blackman: I knew it was coming. He asked me if it would be alright, and I told him to go ahead if he wanted to.

Dodds: I'm really quite happy here. I don't want you to get the idea that I am thinking of leaving. I thought I should go and visit—I think he expects it—but that doesn't mean I'm thinking of leaving here. Unless, of course, he offers me something extraordinary.

Blackman: It's up to you.

Dodds: What do you think?

Blackman: Well, what? About what? You've got to make up your mind. Sooner or later you are going to have to make up your own mind where you want to work.

Dodds: That depends on the offers, doesn't it?

Blackman: Not really. A good man always gets offers. Isn't there a factor of how stable you want to be?

Dodds: But I'm not shopping around. I already told you that. All I said was I think I should visit him, and to you that's shopping around! You really don't think I could find a better job than the one you have offered me here?

Blackman: I don't know. I'm not thinking about that.

Dodds: How would it look if I were to leave?

Blackman: To me, if you wanted to go, I'd say fine, if that's what you want. But frankly, I think there would be a few raised eyebrows if you were to leave now.

Dodds: Look, I came in here, and I want to be honest with you, but you go and make me feel all guilty. I didn't come in here to fight. I don't want to disturb you.

Blackman: I'm not disturbed. We can get another plasma physicist any day, just as good as you. They are standing in line to get in here.

Dodds: I can't understand you. You really think that no one will ever be able to make me an offer that will make me want to leave this place.

Blackman: All I'm saying is that it would look funny, so soon after you've come here.

Dodds: All I said was I would consider his offer if it was so good I couldn't afford to turn it down. Do you think I should turn it down even if it is a better job?

Blackman: All I'm saying is maybe it's too fast. If you leave this year, it would look like you had a lot of opportunism and self-interest. Like you were restless. It would not look good.

Dodds: I don't understand you. I came in here to be honest with you, and you make me feel guilty. All I wanted to do was to show you this letter and let you know what I was going to do. What should I have told you?

Blackman: That you had read the letter and felt that under the circumstances it was necessary for you to pay a visit to Wilkin, but that you were happy here and wanted to stay at least until you had established a record of performance.

Dodds: I can't get over it. You think there isn't a place in the world I'd rather be than here in this lab.

This conversation begins as a calm exchange of information but quickly escalates into anger and mutual resentment. This happens despite the avowed intent of both men to remain detached and rational. Though Dodds simply states his desire to visit the other lab and Blackman says "It's up to you," they become entangled in a bitter exchange that could seriously affect their future working relationship.

Each man shows he is unaware of certain important feelings being expressed by himself as well as by the other person. Dodds says he's quite happy and not thinking of leaving, but his other statements indicate differently. He denies having any feelings of dependency ("You really think that no one will ever be able to make me an offer that will make me want to leave this place") but repeatedly asks Blackman for advice. Blackman also shows lack of awareness. He says, "I am not disturbed," though his anger has already been evident when he answered Dodd's innocent question, "What do you think?" by sharply replying, "Well what? About what? You've got to make up your mind." Blackman's attention does not focus clearly on Dodds. When Dodds asks, "What should I have told you?" Blackman responds by saying what he wishes Dodds had said. Throughout the conversation, Blackman does not sense Dodd's between-the-lines expression of concern about lack of acceptance, status, and recognition in the lab and in his career. If he had, he might have wondered what problems Dodds was experiencing in his current work situation in the lab and turned the conversation in that direction. Instead, the growing resentment and the struggle by each man to control the other sapped energy that might otherwise have been used for mutual fact finding and problem solving. The content of their conversation was limited because of the process by which they went about talking with each other—a process that was characterized by lack of agreement as to the nature of their relationship.

This chapter examines the nature of interpersonal relationships. Frameworks are presented that can enable a person to do better than Blackman and Dodds did in recognizing what is happening in a two-person conversation. Longer-term interpersonal relationships are also discussed with emphasis on the kinds of malfunctions that can prevent working relationships from being productive and satisfying. Attention is then given to ways in which two-person relationships can be improved.

THE TWO-PERSON RELATIONSHIP

Why do people like Blackman and Dodds sometimes grate so hard against each other when all they intended was a calm exchange of information? Why do others handle similar information and even solve problems with much less strain? The first step toward an answer is to note that whenever two people communicate, the messages occur on two levels: content and relationship. For example, when Manager A says to Manager B, "Bring in the Ajax file," two messages are sent. The content message has to do with transporting the file; the relationship message is that Manager A has the right or obligation to tell Manager B what to do. Whenever people communicate, they signal a definition of the relationship. It is impossible for individuals to relate to one another only on a content basis.

Conflicts at the content level are relatively easy to resolve. Usually the parties can look the answer up in a book, tell each other what they actually saw and heard, or go and ask someone who has more information. On the relationship level, however, conflicts are much more difficult to resolve. This is partly due to the fact that the relationship is seldom explicitly discussed by the two parties. Manager A does not say, "I have the right to direct you to bring items to me." Instead, relational definitions are indicated by such cues as who speaks first, who speaks the most, tone of voice, and gestures.

Each party forms a view of the relationship as well as a view of how the other party is defining the relationship. In effect, each takes the role of the other and modifies his or her own behavioral intentions in light of how he or she expects the other to react. This also occurs in the content area, where each person has a view of how the other sees the issue the two are discussing.

The presence of these multilevel perspectives on content and relationship means there are many ways for conflict to arise. For example, two people may mutually agree and understand each other on the content level, but one of them may misperceive the other's definition of the relationship. Or, each may see accurately how the other defines the relationship, but the two definitions may disagree. (For example, both may wish to control the relationship.) Or, they may understand and agree with each other about the relationship but disagree or misunderstand concerning the content. These examples do not include all the possible conflict configurations, but they are enough to show that two-person interactions cannot be understood without considering relationship perspectives as well as content.[1]

Dimensions of Interpersonal Relationships

It is useful to know that interpersonal communication takes place on both a relationship and an issue level. But it is also important to know why people develop certain relationship perspectives. This section character- izes two closely related frameworks; the concept of *interpersonal need compatibility* and *the interpersonal reflex model.*

We all intuitively accept the everyday expression "Different strokes for different folks." Everyone has interpersonal needs. These needs differ from person to person and from time to time. Communication can be seen as people's attempts to satisfy their needs.

William C. Schutz suggests that there are three basic interpersonal needs that are the driving forces behind all interpersonal behavior.[2] These are the need for *inclusion, control,* and *affection.*

The need for inclusion refers to the need to associate with others, to be a member, to be accepted, and to accept others. Inclusion needs vary for different people. A person with a very low inclusion need (termed *undersocial* by Schutz) is the social isolate who maintains distance be- tween self and others. At the other extreme, the *oversocial* person puts so much effort into interacting with and angling for attention from others that other goals, such as work, are neglected. A third type, the *adaptable- social* type, is a person who can be either a high or low participator, depending on the situation.

The need for control represents the need to exercise power and au- thority. It also varies in different people. At the extremes, some people have a strong urge to dominate, while others avoid exerting influence and are happiest when others control them by making decisions for them. People in the middle range are able to function well both in situations where they are in control of others and in situations where others have control over them. They do not feel it necessary to constantly be asserting their influence, but they do not avoid taking leadership when it is appro- priate.

The affection need has to do with the need for close, personal, positive feelings between people. Like the other needs, it can vary between ex- tremes. There are those who suppress or deny their need for affection by being openly antagonistic or by being emotionally neutral, treating every- body the same. Others, afraid of not being liked, go all out to please everyone. In between are those who are able to be close to others but do not lose all sense of personal worth if someone does not like them.

In Schutz's scheme, each of the three needs—inclusion, control, and affection—has two aspects. One aspect is what the person *expresses* to- ward other people. The other aspect is what the person *wants* from other people. A summary of the expressed and wanted behaviors in the three need areas is given in exhibit 7–1. According to this model, a mutually satisfying relationship between two people would be a complementary one—that is, where each person wants the kinds of behavior the other is expressing. The conversation between Dr. Blackman and Dr. Dodds is an example of a relationship lacking in compatibility. Blackman is high in expressed control. He states a clear preference for how he wants Dodds to behave—to stay in the lab until he establishes "a record of performance." Dodds, however, is low on wanted control, desiring the freedom to look at the new job offer and choose for himself.

EXHIBIT 7–1

EXPRESSED AND WANTED ASPECTS OF
THREE INTERPERSONAL NEEDS

Expressed inclusion:	I join with others and ask others to join with me
Wanted inclusion:	I want others to ask me to join them
Expressed control:	I influence and decide for others
Wanted control:	I want others to influence and control me
Expressed affection:	I act toward others in a close and personal way
Wanted affection:	I want others to be close and personal toward me

The absence of interpersonal compatibility can substantially reduce productivity in an organized work setting. Research conducted by Schutz indicates that persons who are compatible tend to outperform significantly those who are incompatible on tasks requiring cooperation.[3] The implication of Schutz's framework is that people in organizations can better understand and manage their own and others' interpersonal communication if they understand the needs that motivate it. People can often disentangle themselves from misunderstandings and address issues more clearly and directly if they are aware of the needs behind their behavior.

Interpersonal behavior is not only driven from the inside by individuals' needs, as Schutz's framework suggests. People also evoke, or "pull" behavior out of each other.[4] Clinical psychologist Timothy Leary called this the "interpersonal reflex" and explained it by classifying interpersonal behavior around two axes, dominance-submission and hostility-affection. Many researchers have found these same two dimensions to be basic components of interpersonal behavior.[5] Exhibit 7–2 diagrams the two axes according to Leary's scheme.

EXHIBIT 7–2
THE INTERPERSONAL REFLEX MODEL

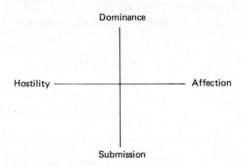

The dominance-submission axis is comparable to the control area in Schutz's framework, while the hostility-affection axis might be thought of as a combination of Schutz's inclusion and affection categories. According to Leary's scheme, interpersonal actions are located around these axes. The center point represents emotional neutrality: emotional intensity becomes greater as the distance from the center increases. Interpersonal acts may lie between the axes. For instance, a given behavioral act may be both dominating and affectionate (as in the case of "smotherly love").

Each interpersonal act is a "bid" for a complementary act. For example, controlling, bossing behavior by one person tends to evoke obedience from the other, while antagonistic, unfriendly actions provoke hostility. Along the vertical axis, an act of one kind tends to evoke an opposite act. Submissive behavior by one person is a bid for dominance by the other, and vice versa. Along the horizontal axis, acts of a given kind tend to evoke the same kind of act—affection encourages affection and hostility provokes hostility in return. Of course, one person's bids are not always fully reciprocated by another. A bid may be rejected in part or fully. The conversation between Dr. Blackman and Dr. Dodds can be seen as an instance of partial, but not complete, reciprocation. Each man does respond in kind to the other's increasing hostility, but since they differ in the way each defines the relationship, neither is willing to accept the other's efforts at influence and control. At the end of their talk, with each one telling the other, in effect, "You shouldn't be saying what you're saying," they are both competing for possession of a spot in the upper left quadrant of the two-dimensional diagram in Exhibit 7–2.

An important implication of the interpersonal reflex model is that behavior and its intentions often are not consciously thought out, nor deliberately executed, but happen reflexively, as the eye blinks in response to a dust particle. A person who is aware of the two-dimensional model can more readily recognize the nature of his or her behavior, observing how it affects and is affected by that of another person. This awareness can lead to more conscious choosing of a broader range of responses, enabling the parties to "move around" in interpersonal space rather than being boxed into, or struggling blindly to get into, a single small sector.

Transactional Analysis

One of the most insightful approaches to understanding interpersonal behavior is that of *transactional analysis* (TA), a somewhat imposing term for a rather simple set of concepts. Popularized by its originator, Eric Berne, in his best-selling books *Games People Play* and *What Do You Say After You Say Hello?*, and by Thomas Harris in *I'm O.K.—You're O.K.*, transactional analysis has received much attention in organizations as a possible way of improving communication through better understanding of the interpersonal processes.

In a sense, transactional analysis combines the approaches of the Schutz and Leary models by looking at both the internal states of individuals (ego states) and their outward behavior toward each other (transactions). TA also considers the ways people structure their time (time structuring) and the interpersonal roles people learn to play over and over again (scripts).

The Ego States. According to Berne, an ego state is "a consistent pattern of feeling and experience related to a consistent pattern of behavior."[6] An ego state cannot be directly observed but can be inferred from a person's behavior. Each individual's personality contains three ego states, the Parent, the Adult, and the Child. These ego states have no relationship to the age or family status of the individual. Instead, they are somewhat like internalized "tape recordings" people build up by observing and experiencing their own and others' behavior.

The Parent ego state is the set "recordings" one develops by observing and interacting with parents and other authority figures. The capital "P" indicates that the ego state is an internalized role, not an actual, biological parent. When in the Parent ego state, a person acts and speaks parentally —setting standards, making moral judgments, controlling, or being comforting and nurturing. As indicated in exhibit 7–3, these different modes within the Parent have open boundaries between them, represented by the dotted lines. For example, the standard-setting Parent may also be controlling.[7]

Cues that a person is "coming from" the *Parent* ego state are words and phrases such as "always," "never," "should," "shouldn't," "we've al-

EXHIBIT 7–3
THE EGO STATES

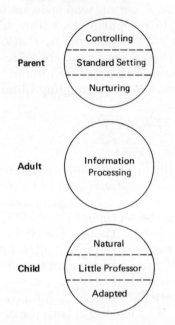

ways done it this way," "if I were you," "why don't you listen," "you are good," "bad," "all wet," "let me fix that for you," "let me help you," "don't worry." The Parent is often expressed in such postures and gestures as pointing an accusing finger, impatiently tapping a hand or foot, coming around to check up on whether someone is doing their job, or giving a pat on the back or a supportive touch. The Parent's tone of voice can be harsh, sneering, patronizing, sympathetic, or supportive. Facial expressions of the Parent include scowls, clenched teeth, tightly pressed lips, or smiles. In short, the Parent judges, criticizes, sets limits of what is good and bad, gives advice, guides and deciphers behavior, nurtures, and encourages and supports other people.

The *Adult* is the part of a person that seeks and gives factual information and uses logic to reach conclusions. The Adult ego state may be thought of as the minicomputer within each person. It is unemotional, calm, and inquiring, asking questions like "how," "what," "why," "when," and "where," and making statements such as "What can we learn from this situation," "What can we predict based on previous statistics," "That's opinion, not fact," or "Have you checked out other possible suppliers?" Nonverbally, the Adult indicates attention and interest, has a straight but not stiff posture with eyes straight and level, and wears a facial expression conveying attentiveness, alertness, thoughtfulness, and interest. The Adult's tone of voice is likely to be confident, clear, and calm without inflections indicating emotion or judgment.

The *Child* ego state is the repertoire of behavior, thoughts, and feelings that an individual learned as a child. This includes the impulsive, uninhibited release of emotions such as joy, excitement, anger, or rebellion (the Natural Child), compliance with the demands of authority figures (the Adapted Child), and intuitive, creative, or manipulative behavior (the Little Professor). Words and phrases that are typical of the Child include "won't," "don't want to," "don't blame me," "it's all your fault," "he's a jerk," "help me," "wow," "terrific," "oh, no, not again," "let's forget work and have some fun," "let's really show them," "you make me mad." Some nonverbal cues to the Child ego state are nail biting, moving uninhibitedly, slumping in dejection, whistling or singing, making obscene gestures, whining, laughing, teasing, talking loudly, pouting, flirting, and looking sad, excited, or rebellious.

Everyone has all three ego states. At any point in time, a person's behavior tends to be either Parent behavior, Adult behavior, or Child behavior. None of the three ego states is necessarily better or healthier than another; in fact, a person whose behavior is limited to only one ego state would probably be considered mentally ill. It is normal for people to shift quickly from one ego state to another.

Transactions. Any interaction between people may be looked at as a transaction between their ego states. Furthermore, all transactions can be classified as either (1) complementary, (2) crossed, or (3) ulterior.[8]

Complementary transactions are those in which, within each of the parties, the same ego state that is doing the sending is the one that is being addressed by the other person. Two examples are shown in exhibit 7–4. Notice that complementary transactions may involve the same ego state in both parties, or different ones. In either case, the ego state from which each person is speaking is being responded to by the other person. Also,

EXHIBIT 7–4

**EXAMPLES OF COMPLEMENTARY
TRANSACTIONS**

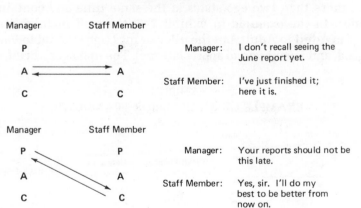

the ego state in the other person toward which each is beaming their messages is the ego state that is currently active. "Complementary" does not mean the parties are necessarily being agreeable or nice toward one another, but rather that the assumptions and perceptions each person has at the relationship level are getting confirmed and reinforced.

In *crossed transactions* this is not the case. A crossed transaction occurs when the messages do not have common origination and termination ego states for both parties. Thus, each person receives behavior from the other person that disconfirms their own position, their view of the other person, or both. Examples are given in exhibit 7–5. Because of their disconfirming nature, crossed transactions tend to be shorter lived than complementary transactions. When people become involved in crossed transactions, it is usually correct to predict that they will soon either break off communication and withdraw from each other or shift to a complementary transaction.

EXHIBIT 7–5

EXAMPLES OF CROSSED TRANSACTIONS

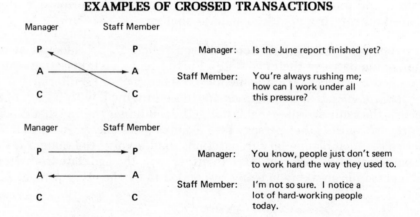

Manager | Staff Member

Manager: Is the June report finished yet?

Staff Member: You're always rushing me; how can I work under all this pressure?

Manager | Staff Member

Manager: You know, people just don't seem to work hard the way they used to.

Staff Member: I'm not so sure. I notice a lot of hard-working people today.

Ulterior transactions differ from the other two types in that they involve more than two ego states at the same time and contain hidden meanings. In the example in exhibit 7–6, the staff member's manifest message is Adult to Adult, but the ulterior message is Child to Parent (I've been good, and I want you to appreciate me). The manager's brief, disinter-

EXHIBIT 7–6

EXAMPLE OF AN ULTERIOR TRANSACTION

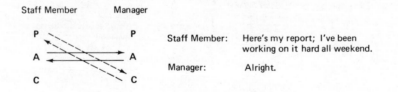

Staff Member | Manager

Staff Member: Here's my report; I've been working on it hard all weekend.

Manager: Alright.

ested response is likewise Adult to Adult on the surface, but in addition conveys an unspoken Parent to Child meaning (I do not put as much value on your weekend efforts as you feel I should). Ulterior transactions are the substance of "game" behavior. Games are one of the most intriguing and often destructive ways that people have of structuring their interpersonal time.

Time Structuring and Games. According to Eric Berne, there are six different ways people can allocate or "structure" their time: withdrawal, activities, rituals, pastimes, authenticity, and games.[9]

Withdrawal means avoiding other people either physically or perhaps psychologically, as by daydreaming. *Activities* center on things which realistically have to be done, such as work or caring for a family. *Rituals* are patterned, low-content transactions, such as, "How are you," "Fine, and yourself?" *Pastimes* are ways of occupying longer periods of time, as by gossiping. *Authenticity* means open, genuine sharing of thoughts and feelings with one another. Since authenticity usually involves taking risks, people tend to avoid it by engaging in withdrawal, activities, rituals, or pastimes, or by the more insidious and damaging method of playing games.

Games are defined as a recurring set of transactions that include: (1) a complementary transaction that seems to be socially acceptable; (2) an ulterior transaction that is the underlying message of the game; and (3) a predictable, negative payoff or putdown that ends the game and is its real purpose.[10] The game and its payoff keep the parties from being honest and authentic with one another, but usually one or both persons are not aware of this. Several specific games have been identified and named, and many of them are played in organizations. The rest of this section includes a few examples.

A game sometimes engaged in by bosses and their subordinates is called "Yes, But." The boss asks the subordinates for suggestions, and they offer some, but each is met by a "Yes, but" from the boss, who argues that the suggestion is unacceptable. On the surface, this appears to be Adult-Adult, but when the boss never accepts any of the suggestions and the subordinates have run out of ideas, the boss wins the game, having maintained power (as Parent) over the subordinates. In the game of "Kick Me," a person does something that seems satisfactory on the surface, but the ulterior message is, "Kick me, I've been naughty." The "Kick Me" game played by subordinates would reinforce a game of "Yes, But" played by their boss.

"See What You Made Me Do" is a game in which one person blames his or her error or problem on someone else. Dr. Dodds seemed to be playing this game when he complained that Dr. Blackman had "made him" feel guilty and angry. At the manifest level, Dodds was making a complaint, but at the ulterior level he was acknowledging that as he saw it, Blackman was in charge and should call the shots. Blackman, in turn, appeared to play a game called "I'm Only Trying to Help You." He appeared to offer suggestions, but he made them ambiguous and contradictory enough that they would frustrate Dodds rather than help him. But Blackman can claim he is just trying to help Dodds by giving him the facts he needs to know.

In theory, games can easily be stopped if either party refuses to "play." This is not always so simple, however, since the games people play are related to their fundamental ways of experiencing themselves and others. Berne and others refer to those basic underlying points of view as "scripts," because they serve as the basis for interpersonal roles that people play on a recurring basis.

Scripts. Scripts represent, in a sense, a programming of a person's behavior.[11] The script develops out of a person's previous experiences in interaction with other people. For example, childhood experiences may have exerted a strong influence in forming a script for an individual. A person who, as a child, was repeatedly told, "You'll never amount to anything" is likely to relate to people differently than one who is told, "You'll be a success." In general, scripts fall into four different categories, depending on the basic view the individual has toward self and toward others.

1. *I'm Not O.K., You're O.K.* In this class of scripts, the individual sees others as being well-adjusted and effected but sees himself or herself as inadequate. This person feels powerless compared to others and tends to withdraw or become dependent on others rather than compete.
2. *I'm Not O.K., You're Not O.K.* People with this perspective think badly of themselves as well as of other people. To them, nothing seems worthwhile, so they have given up. Communication is difficult for them, since they tend to put down both themselves and others. Attempts to support or help them are usually met with refusal, since the would-be helper is seen as "Not O.K."
3. *I'm O.K., You're Not O.K.* Here the person looks positively upon himself or herself but sees others negatively. This is a position of distrust and suspicion. This person frequently finds fault with others, putting people off in order to get elbow room to be more independent. Close relationships are sometimes formed, but the theme of the script then turns out to be, "Come close so I can let you have it."
4. *I'm O.K., You're O.K.* This is the perspective of a person who is potentially realistic and fully functioning and who avoids playing games and is able to solve problems constructively. This person feels positive about self, wants to progress and develop, and also feels confident about forming close relationships with other people.

The aim of transactional analysis is to provide frameworks that enable people, through improved understanding of their interpersonal behavior, to increase their likelihood of reaching the "I'm O.K., You're O.K." position. TA's concepts, together with the Schutz and Leary models, provide a versatile array of analytic tools toward this end. TA's ego states and Schutz's concept of interpersonal needs indicate the importance of knowing where individuals are "coming from." The interpersonal reflex model and TA's concept of the transaction provide ways of understanding the effects people have on each other when they interact. Finally, the notions of time structuring and scripts reveal the many modes of interpersonal behavior (other than authentic) that can exist.

It is impossible to say just how much time people spend playing games and otherwise avoiding being authentic, or what proportion of people are playing out scripts that include a "Not O.K." perspective. It is safe to say, however, that in relatively few relationships are the parties fully in the "I'm O.K., You're O.K." position. It is clear that interpersonal participants need to understand their relationships better.

MALADAPTIVE RELATIONSHIPS

In organizations, as elsewhere, there is a large potential for damage in human relationships. Virtually everyone's experience seems to abound with examples of "sick" associations between people. The author often gives students the assignment of writing case descriptions based on their own experience or observations, illustrating aspects of communication in organizations. The vast proportion of their cases—at least ninety percent —describe maladaptive relationships. Nearly everyone, it appears, has very recently experienced or is right now experiencing the pain of working for a boss they see as weak or unreasonable; the shock waves that go through an organization in which two senior executives are having a falling out with one another; or the helplessness of trying to work with someone from another department who "refuses to cooperate." Outside organizations the prevalence of divorce, alienation between parents and children, and the scarcity of close, long-lasting friendships confirms the fact that satisfying, effective relationships are not easy to build.

What causes maladaptive relationships? One explanation can be given in economic terms by saying that relationships malfunction when they do not provide a profitable exchange between the parties.[12] When one or both parties are not receiving what they feel they deserve based on their own inputs, they will be dissatisfied. Economic breakdown in relationships has been termed *disconfirmation.*[13] Disconfirming communication can take three forms: indifference, imperviousness, and disqualification. *Indifference,* the extreme form of disconfirmation, means treating another person as nonexistent. Even the ritual "Good morning" is not exchanged. *Imperviousness* is the failure of one person to become accurately aware of the other's perceptions or feelings, often shown by such statements as, "Forget it, you'll feel better tomorrow" or "I know you don't really mean that." *Disqualification* occurs when one person down-grades the other's concern by making an irrelevant or tangential response. An example would be a committee member who responds to the chairperson's call for suggestions on how to solve a problem by asking, "What time is lunch?" Instances of disconfirmation can often be explained in TA terms as crossed transactions or as a reluctance of the parties to reciprocate each other's "bids" in terms of the interpersonal reflex model. In Schutz's terms, disconfirmation is the failure of people to express behavior that fulfills each other's needs. Many disconfirming relationships once were confirming but have become disconfirming through changes over time in the interpersonal needs of the parties. The parties to disconfirming relationships are often kept together by their jobs or by habit and frequently do not believe there is anything they can do to improve the relationship.

In some maladaptive relationships the breakdown in the "economic exchange" is not as complete as it is in cases of disconfirmation. Some relationships, while not fully confirming, are partly confirming. To use the terms of the interpersonal reflex model, for example, suppose two work associates both behave in a friendly and dominant way toward each other. Each frequently volunteers advice to the other. It is never accepted, but both are always congenial with one another. In terms of the "reflex" concept, they are unresponsive to each other on the dominance-submission axis, but their mutual friendliness keeps them in the relationship. This type of relationship has been termed *symmetrical,* since each person matches the other's behavior. A problem with symmetrical relationships is their tendency to escalate. In cases like that of the two coworkers, there is an ever-present danger of competitiveness as each tries to outdo the other in helpfulness.[14]

Another form of partial confirmation occurs in relationships built upon paradoxes. A *paradox* occurs when people send messages that are self-contradictory.[15] A classic example of a paradox is a billboard saying

> IGNORE THIS SIGN

Interpersonal relationships sometimes form in which the messages sent are almost this hard to handle. For example, a person may attempt to control a relationship but at the same time send messages denying that he or she is in control. Consider the mother who responds when her daughter asks permission to go out with friends tonight by saying, "Oh, sure, go and have fun; don't mind lonely little me staying here by myself all evening." In the example at the beginning of this chapter, both Dr. Blackman and Dr. Dodds sent paradoxical messages. Blackman tells Dodds to make up his own mind about the job offer but then proceeds to tell him what the decision should be. Dodds wants advice but lashes out at Blackman when he gives it. Each puts the other in a "double bind" by making contradictory demands. In TA terms, paradoxes involve ulterior transactions that often develop into games. The person caught in them cannot act directly but must search for the ulterior meaning, vacillate, or freeze. Helpless confusion, frustration, or hostility are the likely by-products of such relationships.

Not all maladaptive relationships are ones in which the economic exchange is incomplete. Not infrequently, relationships that fully satisfy the participants' needs turn out to be traps. These relationships may be fully reciprocal in terms of the interpersonal reflex model and complementary in TA terms. But this very pattern of reciprocity may produce a "lockstep" effect that keeps the parties from growing.[16] Reciprocal, mutually satisfying relationships are an important source of stability in peoples' lives, yet, once established, they tend to become difficult to break out of, even when they are preventing development and change. Consider, for example, the relationships you have with the other members of one familiar organization, your family. Have some of these relationships remained the same even though you have grown older? When you visit your parents do you find yourself being drawn into some of the same old behavior? Well-developed interpersonal patterns can be hard to break.

One reason such relationships resist change is that they are based on what may be termed *unstated contracts.* Over time, the parties develop assumptions and expectations about how one another should behave that they are not fully aware of. The traditionally inferior role of women in organizations provides an example. The massive effort the various equal rights movements have had to devote to *telling* both women and men that the problem exists attests to the power of these unstated relational contracts. The danger of unstated contracts is that they may lock the parties into assuming that each should remain inadequate in some particular way. Each person avoids behavior he or she finds hard, and each finds that the behavior that comes easily for him or her is valued by the other person. Adherence to a contract of this sort can keep both parties from becoming richer, more effective people. A typical example was observed in a large urban hospital. The director of nursing habitually let the other administrators treat her as the "dumb blond," attractive but incompetent. This way, their discomfort at the idea that she might be both beautiful and competent was not aroused, nor was her own fear of being seen as an "aggressive bitch." She became aware of the problem and became determined to assert her considerable managerial skill in meetings with her peers. However, the others persisted in not taking her seriously. She ultimately left the hospital and took another job where she could have a fresh start.[17]

It is clear that maladaptive relationships can have seriously damaging effects on the productivity, satisfaction, and growth of people in organizations. When the relationship is either disconfirming or only partly confirming, productivity often suffers, since energy that the parties could otherwise be putting into task accomplishment needs to be devoted to coping with the damage caused by the relationship. Other relationships, though satisfying and productive, may trap the parties in an unchanging reciprocal pattern, thus inhibiting their development. Conversely, the developmental aspects of a relationship normally have to do with awareness, learning, problem solving, and choice. Though often difficult, it is possible for interpersonal partners to modify the nature of the relationship as their needs and the task situation change. The ability to adapt and improve relationships is a rare skill and one that is difficult to exercise. The effort is worthwhile, however, because the potential long-term payoff is high.

ADAPTING AND IMPROVING RELATIONSHIPS

Human relationships come in so many forms and degrees of complexity that it is impossible to give a simple step-by-step procedure for changing and improving them. Based on the notion that a sound diagnosis is the best basis from which to choose remedial action, most of this chapter has been devoted to introducing conceptual tools that can be used to understand important aspects of relationships, whatever their form. Consistent with this emphasis on diagnosis, there are four specific things that the parties can do to improve their interpersonal situation: (1) make effective use of exposure and feedback, (2) talk about the communication process, (3) deal directly with disagreements, and (4) encourage the exercise of choice.

Using Exposure and Feedback

Relationships tend to improve when the participants act to improve their knowledge of each other and of themselves. A well-known model called the Johari Window symbolizes this process (see exhibit 7–7). Named for its developers, Joseph Luft and Harry Ingham, the model symbolizes the fact that improving mutual awareness involves the behavior of both parties. Each interpersonal participant has a "window," but the size of each of the "panes" depends on the extent to which the individual enlarges his or her "arena," which represents the things known both to the individual and to the other person. The arena becomes enlarged through exposure and feedback. *Exposure* occurs when a person reveals things he or she knows to another person. Exposure is largely under the control of the individual and often serves as a means of building trust and legitimizing mutual exposures. *Feedback* takes place when one person actively solicits information he or she does not have but the other person does. Since the amount of feedback that actually takes place depends on the willingness of the other person to share, it is important that there be a climate of mutual exposure. Individuals who engage in exposure and soliciting feedback are taking the initiative to understand, develop, and strengthen the relationship. They reduce the likelihood that the relationship will freeze into a "lockstep" reciprocal or a destructive "game."[18]

EXHIBIT 7–7
THE JOHARI WINDOW

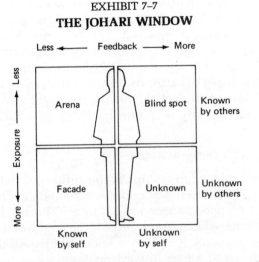

From Jay Hall, "Communication Revisited," © 1973 by the Regents of the University of California. Reprinted from *California Management Review,* volume XV, number 3, p. 58, only by permission of the Regents. Adapted from *Group Processes: An Introduction to Group Dynamics* by Joseph Luft by permission of Mayfield Publishing Company (formerly National Press Books). Copyright © 1963, 1970 Joseph Luft. See also, idem., *Of Human Interaction.*

Metacommunication: Addressing the Process of Communication

The parties to an interpersonal relationship often assume that their relationship itself—the process of communication between them—is not something that needs to be examined. This assumption is usually implicit; they aren't aware they are making it, but they behave as though they believe it by devoting all their time together discussing work, engaging in social banter, and otherwise addressing only "content," never "process."[19]

The health of a relationship is maintained and improved when the parties make it a point to appraise each other of their viewpoints concerning the relationship. This kind of discussion has been called metacommunication, or communication about communication, since it is an attempt by the parties to step out of their usual roles with respect to each other, take a transcendant point of view, and communicate about their relationship.[20]

Metacommunication is not always easy to do. Dodds, for example, made some attempts in his conversation with Blackman when he said, "You make me feel all guilty," and when he indicated he thought he had "disturbed" Blackman. In both cases, however, Dodds does not achieve enough detachment, and Blackman is not interested in discussing such matters. For process discussions to be useful, both parties must consider the effort to be worthwhile and recognize important and valid information about their relationship when they see or hear it. Efforts at metacommunicating lose their effectiveness when they are simply part of the "game" the participants habitually play. They need to be recognized as a different kind of message. It sometimes helps if the participants make it clear that they are calling a "time out" to talk explicitly about their communication patterns. Sometimes a third party "commentator" can also be of assistance. This is not to say that metacommunication has to take place in scheduled, structured discussions. In some instances it may be spontaneous and even nonverbal; in fact, this is probably the way it does occur most often in open, healthy relationships.

Dealing Directly with Disagreements

A frequent problem in relationships is the refusal of the parties to fight with each other. The norm in our culture, especially in "proper" business relationships, is to suppress anger and be "nice." This can lead to displaced aggression, as occurs when a manager who is angry at a superior, but is afraid to express it, takes it out on a subordinate. Alternatively, some people turn suppressed anger inward on themselves, despairing about their inadequacies and reducing their self-confidence. Suppressing disagreement makes sense to the individual on the basis that if the anger were expressed, it would damage the relationship.

Disagreements do not have to be destructive, however. Differences are a natural aspect of the human condition. When they are recognized as such and understood, they can serve to strengthen the relationship rather than divide it. Conflicts that are confronted and worked through by means of objective problem solving can serve to bring the parties closer together. This can occur when the parties bring to the confrontation a strong concern for the relationship, along with an equally strong concern for their personal goals.[21]

George Bach and Peter Wyden, in their book *The Intimate Enemy,* recommend ways that people may fight constructively—that is, in ways that improve the relationship.[22] Some of the important steps include having a clear, specific focus to the argument, maintaining active involvement in the argument by both parties, dealing with behaviors that the parties are capable of changing, and avoiding "hitting below the belt" (aggressing toward each other in ways that are unbearable). Bach and Wyden strongly recommend that each person in a fight reveal as much as possible of his or her relevant thoughts and feelings. This is referred to as "leveling." If important material is withheld, the parties do not know what is causing the conflict and may not discover how to develop a useful resolution. Bach and Wyden also suggest that disagreements be fought about one at a time and soon after they arise. They strongly advise against "gunnysacking"—keeping grievances covered up for long periods of time. When the sack of grievances gets so full that it finally bursts, the outpouring of anger is more than the parties can handle. Thus, Bach and Wyden conclude that the suppression of disagreement erodes the health of a relationship and constructive fighting improves it.

Exercising Choice

People in organizations have a wide latitude of freedom to choose their interpersonal style. Many are not aware of the breadth of freedom that is open to them. In a study of over 300 managers and professionals in three organizations, David Moment, Gerald Leader, and the author found many who talked and acted as though they were permanently rooted in a narrow, specialized mode of interpersonal behavior.[23] Their relationships with others were frozen into lockstep patterns. Some were reluctant to take initiative, feeling that it was higher management's job to make the decisions. Some remained consistently aloof and distant in dealing with other people; they explained that they had to be objective in their jobs and that it was dangerous to be too concerned with making and keeping human relationships. But in the same organizations there were others who were more versatile and who talked about how they chose and varied their behavior. These men and woman were typically seen as more effective by those with whom they worked. They were individuals who did not allow their action to be limited unnecessarily by ideological half-truths they held concerning their organization or their job. Instead, they took responsibility for their behavior.

Other researchers have also noted that interpersonal skill and organizational effectiveness tend to be accompanied by increased self-responsibility. Chris Argyris, for example, observes that people who have not adequately developed their interpersonal competence tend not to "look inward" to discover the extent to which they themselves might be causes of their own interpersonal problems. By contrast, when people are encouraged to increase their interpersonal competence, there is typically an increase in the extent to which they "own" their behavior.[24] In other words, relationships are likely to improve when the parties do not always say, "You (and others) make me act as I do," but begin to say, "I am behaving the way I am because I am choosing to do so."

Summary

It often happens that when two people communicate with each other, important aspects of what is going on escape their awareness. This chapter is based on the idea that communication and the health of a relationship can be improved if the parties understand the interpersonal process that is taking place. Specific frameworks for such understanding have been presented: Schutz's model of interpersonal need compatability, Leary's interpersonal reflex model, and Berne's transactional analysis scheme. These frameworks help identify important dimensions of interpersonal behavior and the "shapes" that two-person relationships can take. Major causes of unhealthy relationships were discussed, including total breakdown in the exchange process, partial breakdown, and the "lockstep" reciprocal relationship. Finally, some ways interpersonal participants can act to improve the health of their relationship were considered: the use of exposure and feedback, metacommunication, dealing directly with disagreements, and the exercise of choice.

Questions for Review

1. What pattern of interpersonal needs, both expressed and wanted, would you expect might be characteristic of two people who in their relationship with each other were able to fight constructively?
2. What aspects of interpersonal relationships are indicated in the interpersonal reflex model that are not specified in transactional analysis, and vice versa?
3. In what ways so far today have you expressed your Parent, Adult, and Child ego states?
4. When people structure their time, why do they tend to avoid authenticity? Explain in terms of interpersonal needs and the interpersonal reflex.
5. What is the relationship between "scripts" and "games?" Give an example.
6. Suppose you are the loser in a game of "Yes, But" played between you and your boss. You often have many new ideas you feel are good ones, but the boss always replies, "Yes, but." What could you do to try to stop this game and get your ideas attended to more satisfactorily?
7. Why are "lockstep" reciprocal relationships hard to change?
8. Think of a relationship in which you are or have been involved. In this relationship, what is the size of each of the "panes" in your Johari Window? Could the "arena" be/have been enlarged? How?
9. How is it possible to keep metacommunication from becoming just another game?

References and Notes

1. The comments on content and relationship perspectives and metaperspectives draws on ideas discussed by Paul Watzlawick, Janet Helmick Beavin, and Don D. Jackson, *Pragmatics of Human Communication* (New York: Norton, 1967), pp. 51–54; William W. Wilmot, *Dyadic Communication* (Reading, Mass.: Addison-Wesley, 1975), pp. 96–103.
2. William C. Schutz, *The Interpersonal Underworld* (Palo Alto, Calif.: Science and Behavior Books, 1966).
3. Ibid., pp. 128–35. See also pp. 57–80 for a description of *FIRO-B,* a pencil and paper test developed to measure the strength of expressed and wanted inclusion, control, and affection in an individual.
4. The ideas in this section draw upon Timothy Leary, *Interpersonal Diagnosis of Personality* (New York: Ronald Press, 1957), pp. 91–130; Zaleznik and Mo-

ment, *Dynamics of Interpersonal Behavior,* pp. 196–97; Robert C. Carson, *Interaction Concepts of Personality* (Chicago: Aldine, 1969), pp. 107–18; Stewart L. Tubbs, "Two-Person Game Behavior: Conformity-Inducing Messages and Interpersonal Trust," *Journal of Communication* 21, no. 4 (1971): 326–41.

5. See, for example, Robert F. Bales, *Interaction Process Analysis* (Reading, Mass.: Addison-Wesley, 1950); Edgar F. Borgetta, Leonard S. Cottrell, and John M. Mann, "The Spectrum of Individual Interaction Characteristics: An Interdimensional Analysis," *Psychological Reports* 4 (1958): 279–319; Earl S. Schaefer, "Converging Conceptual Models for Maternal Behavior and Child Behavior," in *Parental Attitudes and Child Behavior,* ed. John C. Glidewell (Springfield, Ill.: Charles C Thomas, 1961), pp. 124–46; Phillip E. Slater, "Parent Behavior and the Personality of the Child," *Journal of Genetic Psychology* 101 (1962): 53–68; Maurice Lorr and Douglas M. McNair, "An Interpersonal Behavior Circle," *Journal of Abnormal and Social Psychology* 67 (1963): 68–75; Roger Brown, *Social Psychology* (New York: Free Press, 1965), pp. 71–73.

6. Eric Berne, *Principles of Group Treatment* (New York: Oxford University Press, 1964), p. 364.

7. The descriptions of the three ego states draw primarily upon Muriel James and Dorothy Jongeward, *Born to Win* (Reading, Mass.: Addison-Wesley, 1971), chap. 2, 5, 6, 9.

8. Ibid., pp. 23–29.

9. Ibid., pp. 52–59.

10. Ibid., p. 30.

11. Ibid., pp. 33–34. The descriptions of the four categories of scripts also draw upon Thomas A. Harris, *I'm O.K.—You're O.K.* (New York: Harper and Row, 1969), pp. 43–53; Joseph A. DeVito, *The Interpersonal Communication Book* (New York: Harper and Row, 1976), pp. 108–10.

12. George C. Homans, *Social Behavior: Its Elementary Forms* (New York: Harcourt, Brace and World, 1961), pp. 51–82.

13. Evelyn Sieberg, "Confirming and Disconfirming Organizational Communication," in *Communication In Organizations,* ed. James L. Owen, Paul A. Page, and Gordon I. Zimmerman (St. Paul: West, 1976), pp. 129–49.

14. The ideas about partly confirming relationships, symmetrical relationships, and escalation are drawn from Carson, *Interaction Concepts of Personality,* pp. 147–48; Watzlawick, Beavin, and Jackson, *Pragmatics of Human Communication,* pp. 67–70, 107–08; Wilmot, *Dyadic Communication,* p. 108.

15. Wilmot, *Dyadic Communication,* pp. 130–35; Sara Kiesler, *Interpersonal Processes in Groups and Organizations* (Arlington Heights, Ill.: AHM Publishing Company, 1978), pp. 91–93.

16. The ideas in the remainder of this section relating to maladaptive reciprocal relationships draw upon Anthony G. Athos and John J. Gabarro, *Interpersonal Behavior* (Englewood Cliffs, N.J.: Prentice-Hall, 1978), pp. 277–79; Allan R. Cohen, Stephen L. Fink, Herman Gadon, and Robin D. Willits, *Effective Behavior in Organizations* (Homewood, Ill.: Irwin, 1976), pp. 184–87; Bobby R. Patton and Kim Giffin, *Interpersonal Communication* (New York: Harper and Row, 1974), p. 356.

17. Cohen et al., *Effective Behavior in Organizations,* p. 185.

18. The discussion of the Johari Window is adapted from Jay Hall, "Communication Revisited," *California Management Review* 15 (1973): 56–67. On the tendency for exposure by one person to encourage exposure by the other, see

W. Barrett Pearce and Stewart M. Sharp, "Self-Disclosing Communication," *Journal of Communication* 23 (1973): 409–25.

19. See Thomas R. Nilson, "Some Assumptions that Impede Communication," *General Semantics Bulletin,* 14 and 15 (1954): 41–44.

20. Watzlawick, Beavin, and Jackson, *Pragmatics of Human Communication,* pp. 40, 53–54, 179, 197.

21. Kenneth Thomas, "Conflict and Conflict Management," in *Handbook of Industrial and Organizational Psychology* ed. Marvin D. Dunnette (Chicago: Rand McNally, 1976), pp. 889–935.

22. George R. Bach and Peter Wyden, *The Intimate Enemy* (New York: Morrow, 1969).

23. David Moment and Dalmar Fisher, *Autonomy in Organizational Life* (Cambridge, Mass.: Schenkman, 1975), pp. 35, 38, 65–87, 98–105.

24. Chris Argyris, *Interpersonal Competence and Organizational Effectiveness* (Homewood, Ill.: Irwin-Dorsey, 1962), pp. 25–26, 154–156; idem, *Management and Organizational Development* (New York: McGraw-Hill, 1971), pp. 134–36.

Cases
for Part Two

The Road to Hell*

John Baker, Chief Engineer of the Caribbean Bauxite Company of Barracania in the West Indies, was making his final preparations to leave the island. His promotion to production manager of Keso Mining Corporation near Winnipeg—one of Continental Ore's fast-expanding Canadian enterprises—had been announced a month before and now everything had been tidied up except the last vital interview with his successor, the able young Barracanian, Matthew Rennalls. It was vital that this interview be a success and that Rennalls should leave his office uplifted and encouraged to face the challenge of his new job. A touch on the bell would have brought Rennalls walking into the room but Baker delayed the moment and gazed thoughtfully through the window considering just exactly what he was going to say and, more particularly, how he was going to say it.

John Baker, an English expatriate, was forty-five years old and had served his twenty-three years with Continental Ore in many different places: the Far East, several countries of Africa, Europe, and, for the last two years, the West Indies. He hadn't cared much for his previous assignment in Hamburg and was delighted when the West Indian appointment came through. Climate was not the only attraction. Baker had always preferred working overseas (in what were termed the developing countries) because he felt he had an "innate knack"—better than most other expatriates working for Continental Ore—of knowing just how to get on with regional staff. Twenty-four hours in Barracania, however, soon made him realise that he would need all of this "innate knack" if he was to deal effectively with the problems in this field that now awaited him.

At his first interview with Hutchins, the production manager, the whole problem of Rennalls and his future was discussed. There and then it was made quite clear to Baker that one of his most important tasks would be the "grooming" of Rennalls as his successor. Hutchins had

---

*This case was prepared by Gareth Evans for Shell-BP Petroleum Development Company of Nigeria, Limited as a basis for class discussion in an executive training program. Used with permission.

pointed out that, not only was Rennalls one of the brightest Barracanian prospects on the staff of Caribbean Bauxite—at London University he had taken first-class honours in the B.Sc. Engineering degree—but, being the son of the Minister of Finance and Economic Planning, he also had no small political pull.

The company had been particularly pleased when Rennalls decided to work for them rather than for the Government in which his father had such a prominent post. They ascribed his action to the effect of their vigorous and liberal regionalisation programme which, since the Second World War, had produced eighteen Barracanians at mid-management level and given Caribbean Bauxite a good lead in this respect over all other international concerns operating in Barracania. The success of this timely regionalisation policy has led to excellent relations with the Government —a relationship which had been given an added importance when Barracania, three years later, became independent an occasion which encouraged a critical and challenging attitude toward the role foreign interests would have to play in the new Barracania. Hutchins had therefore little difficulty in convincing Baker that the successful career development of Rennalls was of the first importance. Nigeria, Limited as a basis for class discussion in an executive training

The interview with Hutchins was now two years old and Baker, leaning back in his office chair, reviewed just how successful he had been in the "grooming" of Rennalls. What aspects of the latter's character had helped and what had hindered? What about his own personality? How had that helped or hindered? The first item to go on the credit side would, without question, be the ability of Rennalls to master the technical aspects of his job. From the start he had shown keenness and enthusiasm and had often impressed Baker with his ability in tackling new assignments and the constructive comments he invariably made in departmental discussions. He was popular with all ranks of Barracanian staff and had an ease of manner which stood him in good stead when dealing with his expatriate seniors. These were all assets, but what about the debit side?

First and foremost, there was his racial consciousness. His four years at London University had accentuated this feeling and made him sensitive to any sign of condescension on the part of expatriates. It may have been to give expression to this sentiment that, as soon as he returned home from London, he threw himself into politics on behalf of the United Action Party who were later to win the preindependence elections and provide the country with its first Prime Minister.

The ambitions of Rennalls—and he certainly was ambitious—did not however, lie in politics for, staunch nationalist as he was, he saw that he could serve himself and his country best—for was not bauxite responsible for nearly half the value of Barracania's export trade?—by putting his engineering talent to the best use possible. On this account, Hutchins found that he had an unexpectedly easy task in persuading Rennalls to give up his political work before entering the production department as an assistant engineer.

It was, Baker knew, Rennalls's well repressed sense of race conscious-ness which had prevented their relationship from being as close as it should have been. On the surface, nothing could have seemed more agree-able. Formality between the two men was at a minimum; Baker was delighted to find that his assistant shared his own peculiar "shaggy dog" sense of humor so that jokes were continually being exchanged; they entertained each other at their houses and often played tennis together—and yet the barrier remained invisible, indefinable, but ever present. The existence of this "screen" between them was a constant source of frustra-tion to Baker since it indicated a weakness which he was loath to accept. If successful with all other nationalities, why not with Rennalls?

But at least he had managed to "break through" to Rennalls more successfully than any other expatriate. In fact, it was the young Bar-racanian's attitude—sometimes overbearing, sometimes cynical—toward other company expatriates that had been one of the subjects Baker had raised last year when he discussed Rennalls's staff report with him. He knew too, that he would have to raise the same subject again in the forthcoming interview because Jackson, the senior draughtsman, had complained only yesterday about the rudeness of Rennalls. With this thought in mind, Baker leaned forward and spoke into the intercom. "Would you come in Matt, please? I'd like a word with you," and later, "Do sit down," proffering the box, "have a cigarette," He paused while he held out his lighter and then went on.

"As you know, Matt, I'll be off to Canada in a few days' time, and before I go, I thought it would be useful if we could have a final chat together. It is indeed with some deference that I suggest I can be of help. You will shortly be sitting in this chair doing the job I am now doing, but I, on the other hand, am ten years older, so perhaps you can accept the idea that I may be able to give you the benefit of my longer experience."

Baker saw Rennalls stiffen slightly in his chair as he made this point so added in explanation, "You and I have attended enough company courses to remember those repeated requests by the personnel manager to tell people how they are getting on as often as the convenient moment arises and not just the automatic 'once a year' when, by regulation, staff reports have to be discussed."

Rennalls nodded his agreement so Baker went on, "I shall always remember the last job performance discussion I had with my previous boss back in Germany. He used what he called the 'plus and minus' technique. His firm belief was that when a senior, by discussion, seeks to improve the work performance of his staff, his prime objective should be to make sure that the latter leaves the interview encouraged and inspired to improve. Any criticism must, therefore, be constructive and helpful. He said that one very good way to encourage a man—and I fully agree with him—is to tell him about his good points, the plus factors, as well as his weak ones, the minus factors. So I thought, Matt, it would be a good idea to run our discussion along these lines."

Rennalls offered no comment, so Baker continued. "Let me say, therefore, right away, that, as far as your own work performance is concerned, the pluses far outweigh the minuses. I have, for instance been most impressed with the way you have adapted your considerable theoretical knowledge to master the practical techniques of your job—that ingenious method you used to get air down to the fifth shaft level is a sufficient case in point. At departmental meetings I have invariably found your comments well taken and helpful. In fact, you will be interested to know that only last week I reported to Mr. Hutchins that, from the technical point of view, he could not wish for a more able man to succeed to the position of chief engineer."

"That's very good indeed of you, John," cut in Rennalls with a smile of thanks. "My only worry now is how to live up to such a high recommendation."

"Of that I am quite sure," returned Baker. "Especially if you can overcome the minus factor which I would like now to discuss with you. It is one which I have talked about before so I'll come straight to the point. I have noticed that you are more friendly and get on better with your fellow Barracanians than you do with Europeans. In point of fact, I had a complaint only yesterday from Mr. Jackson, who said you had been rude to him—and not for the first time either.

"There is, Matt, I am sure, no need for me to tell you how necessary it will be for you to get on well with expatriates because until the company has trained up sufficient men of your calibre, Europeans are bound to occupy senior positions here in Barracania. All this is vital to your future interests, so can I help you in any way?"

While Baker was speaking on this theme, Rennalls had sat tensed in his chair and it was some seconds before he replied. "It is quite extraordinary, isn't it, how one can convey an impression to others so at variance with what one intends? I can only assure you once again that my disputes with Jackson—and you may remember also Godson—have had nothing at all to do with the colour of their skins. I promise you that if a Barracanian had behaved in an equally peremptory manner I would have reacted in precisely the same way. And again, if I may say it within these four walls, I am sure I am not the only one who has found Jackson and Godson difficult. I could mention the names of several expatriates who have felt the same. However, I am really sorry to have created this impression of not being able to get on with Europeans—it is an entirely false one—and I quite realise that I must do all I can to correct it as quickly as possible. On your last point, regarding Europeans holding senior positions in the Company for some time to come, I quite accept the situation. I know that Caribbean Bauxite—as they have been doing for many years now—will promote Barracanians as soon as their experience warrants it. And, finally, I would like to assure you, John—and my father thinks the same too—that I am very happy in my work here and hope to stay with the company for many years to come."

Rennalls had spoken earnestly and, although not convinced by what he had heard, Baker did not think he could pursue the matter further except to say, "All right, Matt, my impression *may* be wrong, but I would like to remind you about the truth of that old saying, 'What is important is not what is true but what is believed.' Let it rest at that."

But suddenly Baker knew that he didn't want to "let it rest at that." He was disappointed once again at not being able to "break through" to Rennalls and having yet again to listen to his bland denial that there was any racial prejudice in his make-up. Baker, who had intended ending the interview at this point, decided to try another tack.

"To return for a moment to the plus and minus technique I was telling you about just now, there is another plus factor I forgot to mention. I would like to congratulate you not only on the calibre of your work but also on the ability you have shown in overcoming a challenge which I, as a European, have never had to meet.

"Continental Ore is, as you know, a typical commercial enterprise— admittedly a big one—which is a product of the economic and social environment of the United States and Western Europe. My ancestors have all been brought up in this environment for the past two or three hundred years and I have, therefore, been able to live in a world in which commerce (as we know it today) has been part and parcel of my being. It has not been something revolutionary and new which has suddenly entered my life. In your case," went on Baker, "the situation is different because you and your forebears have only had some fifty or sixty years' experience of this commercial environment. You have had to face the challenge of bridging the gap between fifty and two or three hundred years. Again, Matt, let me congratulate you—and people like you—once again on having so successfully overcome this particular hurdle. It is for this very reason that I think the outlook for Barracania—and particularly Caribbean Bauxite—is so bright."

Rennalls had listened intently and when Baker finished, replied, "Well, once again, John, I have to thank you for what you have said, and, for my part, I can only say that it is gratifying to know that my own personal effort has been so much appreciated. I hope that more people will soon come to think as you do."

There was a pause and, for a moment, Baker thought hopefully that he was about to achieve his long awaited "breakthrough," but Rennalls merely smiled back. The barrier remained unbreached. There remained some five minutes' cheerful conversation about the contrast between the Caribbean and Canadian climate and whether the West Indies had any hope of beating England in the Fifth Test before Baker drew the interview to a close. Although he was as far as ever from knowing the real Rennalls, he was nevertheless glad that the interview had run along in this friendly manner and, particularly, that it had ended on such a cheerful note.

This feeling, however, lasted only until the following morning. Baker had some farewells to make, so he arrived at the office considerably later than usual. He had no sooner sat down at his desk than his secretary walked into the room with a worried frown on her face. Her words came fast. "When I arrived this morning I found Mr. Rennalls already waiting at my door. He seemed very angry and told me in quite a peremptory manner that he had a vital letter to dictate which must be sent off without any delay. He was so worked up that he couldn't keep still and kept pacing about the room, which is most unlike him. He wouldn't even wait to read what he had dictated. Just signed the page where he thought the letter would end. It has been distributed and your copy is in your 'in tray.'"

Puzzled and feeling vaguely uneasy, Baker opened the "Confidential" envelope and read the following letter:

From: Assistant Engineer

To: The Chief Engineer, Caribbean Bauxite Limited

Subject: *ASSESSMENT OF INTERVIEW BETWEEN MESSRS. BAKER AND RENNALLS*

14th August, 198–

It has always been my practice to respect the advice given me by seniors, so after our interview, I decided to give careful thought once again to its main points and so make sure that I had understood all that had been said. As I promised you at the time, I had every intention of putting your advice to the best effect.

It was not, therefore, until I had sat down quietly in my home yesterday evening to consider the interview objectively that its main purport became clear. Only then did the full enormity of what you said dawn on me. The more I thought about it, the more convinced I was that I had hit upon the real truth—and the more furious I became. With a facility in the English language which I—a poor Barracanian—cannot hope to match, you had the audacity to insult me (and through me every Barracanian worth his salt) by claiming that our knowledge of modern living is only a paltry fifty years old whilst yours goes back two-hundred to three-hundred years. As if your materialistic commercial environment could possibly be compared with the spiritual values of our culture. I'll have you know that if much of what I saw in London is representative of your most boasted culture, I hope fervently that it will never come to Barracania. By what right do you have the effrontery to condescend to us? At heart, all you Europeans think us barbarians, or, as you say amongst yourselves, we are "just down from the trees."

Far into the night I discussed this matter with my father, and he is as disgusted as I. He agrees with me that any company whose senior staff think as you do is no place for any Barracanian proud of his culture and race. So much for all the company "clap-trap" and specious propaganda about regionalisation and Barracania for the Barracanians.

I feel ashamed and betrayed. Please accept this letter as my resignation which I wish to become effective immediately.

c.c. Production Manager
      Managing Director

Case Questions

1. What were Baker's intentions in the conversation with Rennalls? Were they or weren't they fulfilled, and why?
2. Was Baker alert to nonverbal signals? What did both Baker and Rennalls communicate to each other by nonverbal means?
3. How did Baker's view of himself interact with the impression he formed of Rennalls?
4. What kind of interpersonal relationship had existed between Baker and Rennalls prior to the conversation described in the case? Was the conversation consistent or inconsistent with that relationship?
5. What, if anything, could Baker or Rennalls have done before, during, or after the conversation to improve the situation?

Drydocked*

Jim Coyle had worked for twenty-five years as a boilermaker in the Naval Shipyard. When the yard closed ten years ago, he was retrained and was able to make a successful transition to another area of government service. Now, at the age of fifty-five, Jim is employed by the U.S. Navy as a contract negotiator. His chief duty in this capacity is the negotiation of prices for additional work arising after the awarding of a contract. Normally, the navy solicits competitive bids for the repair and overhaul of its vessels. After the close of bidding, a contract for a specified amount of work is awarded to the contractor whose bid is deemed to be the most advantageous to the government in terms of price and other factors.

The contract contains a detailed description of the work to be performed, specifies the time period for the job, and is valued at what is called a "firm-fixed" price. There would be very little need for negotiation if the actual work involved in the performance of a repair or overhaul job could be carried out exactly as originally specified. However, it is nearly impossible to write specifications that are complete and precise enough to remove the need of adding extra items of work, known as "growth work," as the job actually progresses. This is especially true in the case of an overhaul, which involves many varied and complex tasks. Jim's job is to negotiate with the contractor or his representative in order to arrive at an adjustment in contract price (and delivery date if necessary) for each additional work item the government has asked the contractor to perform.

---

*This case was written by Robert D. Rheaume.

Marty White had also been employed as a tradesman in the Naval Shipyard and at age thirty-five had become a supervisory machinist before the yard closed. Marty currently works within the same organizational unit as Jim. He is a ship's superintendent, and his job consists mainly of the on-site supervision of contracted repair jobs as they are being accomplished. He is also responsible for writing specifications to cover any extra items of work that are required once a repair job is in progress. Besides detailing the work to be accomplished, Marty also generates estimates of the cost for this work.

Mr. Al Crawford is the fifty-three-year-old general manager of Masterson Shipyard and Drydock, Inc. He is very much a self-made man, having achieved substantial success in business as a result of his widely recognized ability and forceful personality. For the better part of a year his firm has been engaged in the overhaul of the U.S.S. *Minot,* one of the navy's older active destroyers. The work had progressed fairly smoothly but had been accompanied by a considerable amount of growth work, not unusual for so old and problem-plagued a vessel. Most of the growth work items had been successfully incorporated into modifications of the original contract.

In September several troublesome items of additional work remained, which Jim Coyle found himself hard-pressed to negotiate. The difficulty arose due to the fact that the contractor's proposed price for the work was a great deal higher than the government estimate formulated by Marty White. Jim was getting pressure from his superior to resolve the conflict surrounding these items and to have them settled and incorporated into the contract as soon as possible. In an attempt to reconcile the widely divergent position of White and Crawford, Coyle had repeatedly been in contact with each of the men so that they might revise their figures into closer conformity. Thus far, his efforts to persuade each man into giving a little had been largely unsuccessful. Both White and Crawford remained quite intransigent, as the following phone conversation, held with Crawford in late August, indicates:

Jim: Hi, Al! How's the Navy's favorite contractor doing this morning?

Al: I'm fine, Jim, but how much is this phone call gonna cost me?

Jim: Don't be so suspicious, Al. I just thought we might be able to do some business.

Al: Sure, pal. What's on your mind?

Jim: Well, Al, I gotta tell you that your price on the new boiler item is not in our ballpark. Marty White claims that his estimate has been well thought out, and your figure doesn't come within a mile of his.

Al: Jim, you know as well as I do that that guy is living in a dream world. He doesn't have the slightest appreciation of my labor costs, and he thinks I can buy materials on sale at Sears!

Jim: Listen, Al, I hear what you're saying, but in this case Marty is being very persistent. After all, he isn't a newcomer to this business. He should have some idea of what he's talking about.

Al: Look, all I know is that every time that bum formulates an estimate, it seems like he's out to get me. As far as I know, I've never done anything to offend this guy, but he seems determined to give me a hard time.

Jim: Tell me about it! You don't know what a hard time is until you've heard my boss getting on my case about resolving these items. I know you well enough to know that there's some fat in the price you quoted us. How about making life easier for an old-timer and revising your proposal?

Al: Sorry, Jim, but I think my price is a fair one and I'm not prepared to budge until White shows some reason and good faith.

Another of Jim's conversations over the same matter, this time with Marty, went like this:

Jim: Marty, we've got a problem on that boiler item. Crawford says your estimate is unrealistic.

Marty: I ain't got no problem! My estimate is sound and reasonable, and that guy is out to rob us, as usual.

Jim: Well, how do you propose I reconcile his price of $50,000 and your estimate of $10,000?

Marty: Easy! Give him the ten grand and tell him he's lucky to get it!

Jim: Marty, you know I can't do that. I honestly don't think that he and I can come to any sort of agreement until you give a bit with your estimate.

Marty: It's your job to make the guy listen to reason. All I can do is give you a good, honest estimate.

Jim: I'm not asking you to do my job! I'm just suggesting that maybe you and he have a different concept of the scope of the job, and that once we understand each other better we'll have a basis for agreement.

Marty: I'll never understand the nerve that guy has to ask for the money he's asking. You can tell him I said Christmas is over, and now he has to work for his money.

Jim: You won't change your estimate then?

Marty: Not until I'm shown good cause to.

Jim: OK, I'll see what I can do to have Crawford justify or alter his price proposal.

Jim liked to think he was fairly objective with regard to the negotiation of these work items. He believed that Crawford set his prices high, but he also felt that the man could usually be persuaded into accepting a reasonable offer. He admired Al for his success, and he generally felt that he was no fool. Jim also had a fairly high regard for Marty White, but for very different reasons. He admired Marty's basic honesty and strength of conviction, but felt that he was a little too suspicious of contractors in general and that he could use a bit more tact and flexibility in his approach to them.

His separate dealings with each man having proved ineffective, Jim decided that his next move should be to meet with both Marty and Al, in the hopes that a face-to-face confrontation would enable the three men to resolve their differences. The men agreed to this suggestion, so a meeting was scheduled for the next morning at the contractor's plant.

Jim and Marty drove to the plant together, discussing the matter en route.

Marty: I tell you Jimbo, that SOB Crawford is a goddamn crook. He's trying to milk uncle [the government] for all he's worth on these items. He's got a hell of a nerve to ask for the kind of money he's looking for. I gave you my best estimate on these items and he's just way out of line.

Jim: Relax, Marty. I know how you feel, but I think we can work something out once we confront him with all your facts. Naturally, Crawford is out to get all he can, but my experience has been that the man can be reasoned with.

Marty: Well, maybe you know something I don't, but you can be damned sure he ain't gonna get rich off me. I know what my job is and I aim to do it!

Upon their arrival at the plant, the men were shown into Mr. Crawford's office.

Al: Come on in, boys! Have a seat. Can I get you some coffee?

Jim: Sure, Al. Make mine black.

Marty: No thanks.

Al: You know, boys, I'd like to get this business settled as much as you would. I've already committed my dough to doing this work, and I can't bill for a dime's worth of it till we agree on a price to put into the contract. All I'm looking for is a fair shake in terms of being paid for this work.

Marty: All I can say is that you got some kinda weird notion of what a fair shake amounts to.

Jim: Gentlemen! I'm sure we can talk this matter out and come to an agreement. Al, we realize that yours isn't a nonprofit organization. We only want to ensure that the final price is an equitable one for all concerned, and that we fulfill our obligations with respect to safeguarding the government's interest.

Al: Yeah, I know all that, Jim, so let's get down to business.

Al went on to describe the work involved in one particularly troublesome item. He talked about the difficulties encountered in performing the job, the many hours of labor that were required, and about expenses he had incurred with subcontractors. However, he didn't get very far in pleading his case before he was suddenly interrupted.

Marty: Wait a minute, Mr. Crawford! Are we talking about the same work item? All that stuff you're describing isn't in the spec I wrote. If you had followed the spec, you wouldn't be in this mess.

Al: Are you telling me how to do my job? You think this is the first ship I've worked on? Let me tell you something! If we followed your precious specifications like you want, this job would be so screwed up there'd be no unscrewing it!

Jim: Gentlemen, please!

Marty: Are you telling me I don't know how to write a spec?

Al: All I'm saying is that in the real world, jobs aren't as simple as they are on paper. You gotta understand what we went through to do this job.

Marty: When I was in the shipyard, a job like that would've been considered a piece of cake.

Jim: Hey, listen fellas! Maybe we're talking about apples and oranges. I mean, if we can come to an understanding of what the actual work amounted to and how it falls within the scope of the specification, then maybe the money angle will be easier to resolve.

Al: That's exactly what I've been trying to do, but this guy won't let me talk!

Marty: I can only listen to so much bull!

Al: Why you pompous little weasel! If brains were dynamite, you wouldn't have enough to blow your nose!

Marty: Jim, I don't have to sit here and take this abuse!

Al: That's right, you don't! So why don't both of you get the hell out of here right now! I'm a busy man. I gotta work for a living, and I ain't got time for any more of this foolishness.

A very unhappy Jim Coyle expressed the following thoughts after the abbreviated meeting: "Those two guys are like oil and water. They just don't mix. No one can get Crawford as mad as Marty can. White's so gosh darn stubborn and righteous: it's hard to negotiate when he's around. It's not that he doesn't have a leg to stand on. It's just that he's so darn undiplomatic in his approach. Besides, his estimates in general tend to be unreasonable. He always constructs his estimates as if the work were being done in the most efficient manner possible. It's almost like he thinks his job performance is measured by how low he can make his estimates. As long as he's doing the estimating on this job, I'll never get these items negotiated. That means we'll have to call in the auditors, and that we can expect to be dealing with claims from this contractor. It also means that the boss will be on my back even worse than before." Asked what he thought his role in the situation was, Jim replied, "To ensure that a price is negotiated that is fair to both parties, in as expeditious a manner as possible." When queried further as to the yardsticks used by his superiors to gauge his performance, Jim said, "Basically, the boss looks at the number of unnegotiated items I'm holding and my efficiency in resolving them."

Marty White had very different feelings to express after the meeting with Jim and Al. "I knew all along Crawford was a crook! He knows I'm right and he's wrong, but he'll never admit it. Coyle's no help either! You'd think he'd back me up more. After all, whose side is he on, anyway? He shouldn't have any doubts about my estimates. When's the last time he saw a ship, anyhow? He sits at that desk with his shirt and tie, and he has no idea what these work items are all about. He just wants me to make it as easy as possible for him to push his paper!" Asked how he would define his role in the situation, Marty replied, "My job is to make sure that the work is performed in accordance with the specifications, and that the government gets its money's worth. And I think I'm pretty good at what I do. You better believe that when I sign my name to an estimate, I make damn sure the contractor isn't given the opportunity to reap any bonanzas. When I stick my neck out, I make sure my backside is covered!" When asked if he felt that the huge discrepancy between his estimates and the contractor's proposals for certain items cast doubt on his ability to arrive at realistic estimates, Marty replied, "No, I don't! If he and I were always in close agreement on price, they'd think I wasn't doing my job!"

Al Crawford had very little to say after the meeting, save for a few terse comments. "I ain't runnin' no charity organization! Do they think I can work miracles with that old tub? They can pay me now or pay me later, but I'll get what's coming to me for the work I've done. Who the hell does that punk White think he is, anyhow? I don't like being treated like a crook when I'm only trying to make an honest buck. These bureaucrats have a hard time recognizing reality when it's staring them in the face. All they know is specifications, regulations, manuals, rules, and what the goddamn book says. It's a shame you have to deal with idiots when you work for the government!"

Case Questions

1. How do misuses of language help explain the communication problems that occur in this case?
2. What examples of selective and defensive perceptions (e.g., closure, halo effect, stereotyping, etc.) do you see in this case?
3. What seem to be the self-concepts and self-esteem levels of the three men? How do their self-concepts relate to the style of communication each employs?
4. Use Heider's balance theory and/or transactional analysis to explain why Jim Coyle was not successful in obtaining an agreement between Crawford and White.
5. What should Coyle have done differently, and, as of the end of the case, what should his next move be?

Ben Reed*

Shortly after Ben Reed, twenty-seven, graduated from the state university with a B.A. degree in psychology, he took a job as assistant office manager with the Acme Medical Association, a group health insurance organization. As assistant office manager, he was responsible for supervising approximately forty office employees who performed sorting, totaling, and recording operations concerning medical claims charged against Acme.

The office workers were situated at several rows of desks in a large open room. As assistant manager, Ben Reed had a desk in the same room but off to one side of the desks of the workers. His immediate supervisor, Charles Grayson, the office manager, had been with Acme for twenty years and had risen to his present position from a beginning job as a clerical assistant. During his career at Acme, he had watched the company grow and progress, and often referred to the increase in employees under his supervision with a great deal of pride.

According to Ben Reed, his work at Acme was not especially challenging. In describing his job he stated that his main duties were to check the time cards of the office workers each morning, to make sure that "everything was in order," and to answer questions concerning claims that might be brought to him. In addition, he did special statistical studies at the request of the controller's office or Grayson. These studies were infrequent, and during his first four months with Acme, Ben participated in only two such studies. He estimated that on the average he actually "worked" no more than one or two hours a day.

Partially because of some courses he had taken at the university, Ben Reed had some strong convictions concerning the supervision of the office employees. He was concerned about the situation at Acme for two reasons: the high turnover of office employees—which averaged about forty-eight

*Copyright, 1976 Professor Harry R. Knudson. Reprinted from *Organizational Behavior: A Management Approach,* Harry R. Knudson and C. Patrick Fleenor, Winthrop Publishers, Inc., Cambridge, Mass. 1978.

percent per year—and the apathy of many of the employees toward their work. He realized that he was new in the organization but nevertheless felt obligated to make some suggestions which he felt would improve the situation with regard to the office force. Grayson, his immediate superior, often did not agree with these suggestions.

For example, in order partially to utilize his unproductive time, Ben suggested that, as he had had several courses in physiology as a pre-med student before transferring to psychology, it might be helpful if he could spend an hour or two a week in instructing the office staff in some of the basic fundamentals of physiology. The nature of the work was such that knowledge of the various functions and systems of the various functions and systems of the body would, he felt, be helpful in speeding up the sorting and processing of claims that came in. Ben suggested to Grayson that he would be happy to conduct these informal classes as a part of his regular duties. Mr. Grayson, however, did not feel this was a good suggestion and did not permit Ben to go through with his idea.

Ben also had a disagreement with Grayson over the handling of the case of D. Martin. Martin, a clerk-typist, approached Ben one day while Grayson was out of the office to report feeling sick. Ben made the necessary arrangements for Martin to have the rest of the day off. When Grayson heard of this incident he was very upset. He told Ben that he did not have the authority to make these kinds of decisions and that he, Grayson, would make all such decisions in the future. Although Ben felt that, because of his position as assistant office manager, because Grayson was not in the office at the time the situation occurred, and because Martin was obviously sick, he had made a good decision, he let the matter drop.

On December 10, Robert Colvin, controller of Acme Medical Association, called Ben into his office to discuss plans for a new electronic data-processing installation that the company was considering putting in to speed up the processing of claims. He spent about two and one-half hours with Ben explaining the proposed system and concluded the interview by stating that he felt that as new people often had good ideas for improvement, he would welcome any thoughts that Ben might have.

Ben was enthusiastic about Colvin's approaching him, and spent several hours that night at home working out a plan that would permit the new process to be installed in his area with a minimum of difficulty. He submitted his ideas to Colvin the next morning.

Colvin was very impressed with Ben's ideas and immediately called a meeting of several of the officials of Acme, including Grayson, to review Ben's plan. This meeting was held during the early afternoon of December 11. About three o'clock that afternoon Grayson entered the area in which the workers' and Ben's desks were located, approached Ben's desk, and slammed down the folder containing Ben's plans, exclaiming, "What in the hell is this?" Before Ben could reply, Grayson commenced in a loud voice to lecture on the necessity of going through channels when submitting reports, ideas, and suggestions. His remarks attracted the attention of the office workers, most of whom stopped work to watch the disturbance. Ben Reed interrupted Grayson to suggest that they might continue their discussion in Grayson's office, which was glass-enclosed and out of ear-shot. Grayson snatched the folder from Ben's desk and stalked into his office. Ben followed.

The discussion in Grayson's office consisted mainly of a continuation of Grayson's diatribe. After Grayson had concluded, Ben stated that he had not been satisfied with his relationship with Acme and intended to sub-mit his resignation in the very near future. He then left Grayson's office.

The next day, December 12, Grayson asked Ben to step into his office for a few minutes. He apologized to Ben for his conduct of the previous day, remarking that he had had several things on his mind which had upset him and that he certainly had full confidence in Ben's abilities. Ben accepted his apology, remarking that he might have flown off the handle a little bit himself. The meeting ended on a cordial note.

On December 13, Ben Reed submitted his resignation and subse-quently left the Acme Company on December 24. At the time of his departure he did not have a new job.

Case Questions

1. Can Grayson's diatribe after the meeting in which Ben's plan was reviewed be explained? Where was Grayson coming from? How did he perceive Ben?
2. What specific actions by Ben during his time with Acme may have been significant in shaping Grayson's view of Ben, and in what ways?
3. Prior to the data processing project, could Ben have picked up any signals that his relationship with Grayson needed corrective attention?
4. Consider the Grayson-Reed relationship in terms of the transactional analysis model and the methods for adapting and improving relationships discussed in chapter 7. What could Ben or Grayson have done in an effort to improve their relationship?

Bob Knowlton*

Bob Knowlton was sitting alone in the conference room of the laboratory. The rest of the group had gone. One of the secretaries had stopped and talked for a while about her husband's coming induction into the Army, and had finally left. Bob, alone in the laboratory, slid a little further down in his chair, looking with satisfaction at the results of the first test run of the new photon unit.

He liked to stay after the others had gone. His appointment as project head was still new enough to give him a deep sense of pleasure. His eyes were on the graphs before him but in his mind he could hear Dr. Jerrold, the project head, saying again, "There's one thing about this place that you

---

*This case was written by Professor Alex Bavelas of the University of Victoria and is reprinted with his permission.

can bank on. The sky is the limit for a man who can produce!" Knowlton felt again the tingle of happiness and embarrassment. Well, dammit, he said to himself, he had produced. He wasn't kidding anybody. He had come to the Simmons Laboratories two years ago. During a routine testing of some rejected Clanson components he had stumbled on the idea of the photon correlator, and the rest just happened. Jerrold had been enthusiastic; a separate project had been set up for further research and development of the device, and he had gotten the job of running it. The whole sequence of events still seemed a little miraculous to Knowlton.

He shrugged out of the reverie and bent determinedly over the sheets when he heard someone come into the room behind him. He looked up expectantly; Jerrold often stayed late himself, and now and then dropped in for a chat. This always made the day's end especially pleasant for Bob. It wasn't Jerrold. The man who had come in was a stranger. He was tall, thin, and rather dark. He wore steel-rimmed glasses and had on a very wide leather belt with a large brass buckle. Lucy remarked later that it was the kind of belt the Pilgrims must have worn.

The stranger smiled and introduced himself. "I'm Simon Fester. Are you Bob Knowlton?" Bob said yes, and they shook hands. "Doctor Jerrold said I might find you in. We were talking about your work, and I'm very much interested in what you are doing." Bob waved to a chair.

Fester didn't seem to belong in any of the standard categories of visitors: customer, visiting fireman, stockholder. Bob pointed to the sheets on the table. "These are the preliminary results of a test we're running. We've got a new gadget by the tail and we're trying to understand it. It's not finished, but I can show you the section that we're testing."

He stood up, but Fester was deep in the graphs. After a moment, he looked up with an odd grin. "These look like plots of a Jennings surface. I've been playing around with some autocorrelation functions of surfaces —you know that stuff." Bob, who had no idea what he was referring to, grinned back and nodded, and immediately felt uncomfortable. "Let me show you the monster," he said, and led the way to the work room.

After Fester left, Knowlton slowly put the graphs away, feeling vaguely annoyed. Then, as if he had made a decision, he quickly locked up and took the long way out so that he would pass Jerrold's office. But the office was locked. Knowlton wondered whether Jerrold and Fester had left together.

The next morning, Knowlton dropped into Jerrold's office, mentioned that he had talked with Fester, and asked who he was.

"Sit down for a minute," Jerrold said. "I want to talk to you about him. What do you think of him?" Knowlton replied truthfully that he thought Fester was very bright and probably very competent. Jerrold looked pleased.

"We're taking him on," he said. "He's had a very good background in a number of laboratories, and he seems to have ideas about the problems we're tackling here." Knowlton nodded in agreement, instantly wishing that Fester would not be placed with him.

"I don't know yet where he will finally land," Jerrold continued, "but he seems interested in what you are doing. I thought he might spend a little time with you by way of getting started." Knowlton nodded thoughtfully. "If his interest in your work continues, you can add him to your group."

"Well, he seemed to have some good ideas even without knowing exactly what we are doing," Knowlton answered. "I hope he stays; we'd be glad to have him."

Knowlton walked back to the lab with mixed feelings. He told himself that Fester would be good for the group. He was no dunce, he'd produce. Knowlton thought again of Jerrold's promise when he had promoted him—"the man who produces gets ahead in this outfit." The words seemed to carry the overtones of a threat now.

That day Fester didn't appear until mid-afternoon. He explained that he had had a long lunch with Jerrold, discussing his place in the lab. "Yes," said Knowlton, "I talked with Jerry this morning about it, and we both thought you might work with us for awhile."

Fester smiled in the same knowing way that he had smiled when he mentioned the Jennings surfaces. "I'd like to," he said.

Knowlton introduced Fester to the other members of the lab. Fester and Link, the mathematician of the group, hit it off well together, and spent the rest of the afternoon discussing a method of analysis of patterns that Link had been worrying over for the last month.

It was 6:30 when Knowlton finally left the lab that night. He had waited almost eagerly for the end of the day to come—when they would all be gone and he could sit in the quiet rooms, relax, and think it over. "Think what over?" he asked himself. He didn't know. Shortly after 5:00 P.M. they had all gone except Fester, and what followed was almost a duel. Knowlton was annoyed that he was being cheated out of his quiet period, and finally resentfully determined that Fester should leave first.

Fester was sitting at the conference table reading, and Knowlton was sitting at his desk in the little glass-enclosed cubby that he used during the day when he needed to be undisturbed. Fester had gotten the last year's progress reports out and was studying them carefully. The time dragged. Knowlton doodled on a pad, the tension growing inside him. What the hell did Fester think he was going to find in the reports?

Knowlton finally gave up and they left the lab together. Fester took several of the reports with him to study in the evening. Knowlton asked him if he thought the reports gave a clear picture of the lab's activities.

"They're excellent," Fester answered with obvious sincerity. "They're not only good reports; what they report is damn good, too!" Knowlton was surprised at the relief he felt, and grew almost jovial as he said goodnight.

Driving home, Knowlton felt more optimistic about Fester's presence in the lab. He had never fully understood the analysis that Link was attempting. If there was anything wrong with Link's approach, Fester would probably spot it. "And if I'm any judge," he murmured, "he won't be especially diplomatic about it."

He described Fester to his wife, who was amused by the broad leather belt and the brass buckle.

"It's the kind of belt that Pilgrims must have worn," she laughed.

"I'm not worried about how he holds his pants up," he laughed with her. "I'm afraid that he's the kind that just has to make like a genius twice each day. And that can be pretty rough on the group."

Knowlton had been asleep for several hours when he was jerked awake by the telephone. He realized it had rung several times. He swung off the bed muttering about damn fools and telephones. It was Fester. Without any excuses, apparently oblivious of the time, he plunged into an excited recital of how Link's patterning problem could be solved.

Knowlton covered the mouthpiece to answer his wife's stage-whispered "Who is it?" "It's the genius," replied Knowlton.

Fester, completely ignoring the fact that it was 2:00 in the morning, proceeded in a very excited way to start in the middle of an explanation of a completely new approach to certain of the photon lab problems that he had stumbled on while analyzing past experiments. Knowlton managed to put some enthusiasm in his own voice and stood there, half-dazed and very uncomfortable, listening to Fester talk endlessly about what he had discovered. It was probably not only a new approach, but also an analysis which showed the inherent weakness of the previous experiment and how experimentation along that line would certainly have been inconclusive. The following day Knowlton spent the entire morning with Fester and Link, the mathematician, the customary morning meeting of Bob's group having been called off so that Fester's work of the previous night could be gone over intensively. Fester was very anxious that this be done and Knowlton was not too unhappy to call the meeting off for reasons of his own.

For the next several days Fester sat in the back office that had been turned over to him and did nothing but read the progress reports of the work that had been done in the last six months. Knowlton caught himself feeling apprehensive about the reaction that Fester might have to some of his work. He was a little surprised at his own feelings. He had always been proud—although he had put on a convincingly modest face—of the way in which new ground in the study of photon measuring devices had been broken in his group. Now he wasn't sure, and it seemed to him that Fester might easily show that the line of research they had been following was unsound or even unimaginative.

The next morning, as was the custom, the members of the lab, including the girls, sat around a conference table. Bob always prided himself on the fact that the work of the lab was guided and evaluated by the group as a whole, and he was fond of repeating that it was not a waste of time to include secretaries in such meetings. Often, what started out as a boring recital of fundamental assumptions, to a naive listener, uncovered new ways of regarding these assumptions that would not have occurred to the researcher who had long ago accepted them as a necessary basis for his work.

These group meetings also served Bob in another sense. He admitted to himself that he would have felt far less secure if he had had to direct the work out of his own mind, so to speak. With the groupmeeting as the principle of leadership, it was always possible to justify the exploration of blind alleys because of the general educative effect on the team. Fester was there; Lucy and Martha were there; Link was sitting next to Fester, their conversation concerning Link's mathematical study apparently continuing from yesterday. The other members, Bob Davenport, George Thurlow and Arthur Oliver, were waiting quietly.

Knowlton, for reasons that he didn't quite understand, proposed for discussion this morning a problem that all of them had spent a great deal of time on previously, with the conclusion that a solution was impossible, that there was no feasible way of treating it in an experimental fashion. When Knowlton proposed the problem, Davenport remarked that there was hardly any use of going over it again, that he was satisfied that there was no way of approaching the problem with the equipment and the physical capacities of the lab.

This statement had the effect of a shot of adrenalin on Fester. He said he would like to know what the problem was in detail and, walking to the blackboard, began setting down the "factors" as various members of the group began discussing the problem and simultaneously listing the reasons why it had been abandoned.

Very early in the description of the problem it was evident that Fester was going to disagree about the impossibility of attacking it. The group realized this and finally the descriptive materials and their recounting of the reasoning that had led to its abandonment dwindled away. Fester began his statement which, as it proceeded, might well have been prepared the previous night although Knowlton knew this was impossible. He couldn't help being impressed with the organized and logical way that Fester was presenting ideas that must have occurred to him only a few minutes before.

Fester had some things to say, however, which left Knowlton with a mixture of annoyance, irritation, and, at the same time, a rather smug feeling of superiority over Fester in at least one area. Fester was of the opinion that the way that the problem had been analyzed was really typical of group-thinking and, with an air of sophistication which made it difficult for a listener to dissent, he proceeded to comment on the American emphasis on team ideas, satirically describing the ways in which they led to a "high level of mediocrity."

During this time, Knowlton observed that Link stared studiously at the floor, and he was very conscious of George Thurlow's and Bob Davenport's glances towards him at several points of Fester's little speech. Inwardly, Knowlton couldn't help feeling that this was one point at least in which Fester was off on the wrong foot. The whole lab, following Jerry's lead, talked if not practiced the theory of small research teams as the basic organization for effective research. Fester insisted that the problem could be approached and that he would like to study it for a while himself.

Knowlton ended the morning session by remarking that the meetings would continue and that the very fact that a supposedly insoluble experimental problem was now going to get another chance was another indication of the value of such meetings. Fester immediately remarked that he was not at all averse to meetings for the purpose of informing the group of the progress of its members—that the point he wanted to make was that creative advances were seldom accomplished in such meetings, that they were made by the individual "living with" the problem closely and continuously, a sort of personal relationship to it.

Knowlton went on to say to Fester that he was very glad that Fester had raised these points and that he was sure the group would profit by re-examining the basis on which they had been operating. Knowlton agreed that individual effort was probably the basis for making the major advances, but that he considered the group meetings useful primarily because of the effect they had on keeping the group together and on helping the weaker members of the group keep up with the ones who were able to advance more easily and quickly in the analysis of problems.

It was clear as days went by and meetings continued that Fester came to enjoy them because of the pattern which the meetings assumed. It became typical for Fester to hold forth and it was unquestionably clear that he was more brilliant, better prepared on the various subjects which were germane to the problems being studied, and that he was more capable of going ahead than anyone there. Knowlton grew increasingly disturbed as he realized that his leadership of the group had been, in fact, taken over.

Whenever the subject of Fester was mentioned, in occasional meetings with Dr. Jerrold, Knowlton would comment only on the ability and obvious capacity for work that Fester had. Somehow he never felt that he could mention his own discomforts, not only because they revealed a weakness on his own part, but also because it was quite clear that Jerrold himself was considerably impressed with Fester's work and with the contacts he had with him outside the photon laboratory.

Knowlton now began to feel that perhaps the intellectual advantages that Fester had brought to the group did not quite compensate for what he felt were evidences of a breakdown in the cooperative spirit he had seen in the group before Fester's coming. More and more of the morning meetings were skipped. Fester's opinion concerning the abilities of others of the group, with the exception of Link, was obviously low. At times, during morning meetings or in smaller discussions, he had been on the point of rudeness, refusing to pursue an argument when he claimed it was based on the other person's ignorance of the facts involved. His impatience of others led him to also make similar remarks to Dr. Jerrold. Knowlton inferred this from a conversation with Jerrold in which Jerrold asked whether Davenport and Oliver were going to be continued on; and his failure to mention Link, the mathematician, led Knowlton to feel that this was the result of private conversations between Fester and Jerold.

It was not difficult for Knowlton to make a quite convincing case on whether the brilliance of Fester was sufficient recompense for the beginning of this breaking up of the group. He took the opportunity to speak privately with Davenport and with Oliver and it was quite clear that both of them were uncomfortable because of Fester. Knowlton didn't press the discussion beyond the point of hearing them in one way or another say that they did feel awkward and that it was sometimes difficult for them to understand the arguments he advanced, but often embarrassing to ask him to fill in the background on which his arguments were based. Knowlton did not interview Link in this manner.

About six months after Fester's coming into the photon lab, a meeting was scheduled in which the sponsors of the research were coming in to get some idea of the work and its progress. It was customary at these meetings for project heads to present the research being conducted in their groups. The members of each group were invited to other meetings which were held latter in the day and open to all, but the special meetings were usually made up only of project heads, the head of the laboratory, and the sponsors.

As the time for the special meeting approached, it seemed to Knowlton that he must avoid the presentation at all cost. His reasons for this were that he could not trust himself to present the ideas and work that Fester had advanced, because of his apprehension as to whether he could present them in sufficient detail and answer such questions about them as might be asked. On the other hand, he did not feel he could ignore these newer lines of work and present only the material that he had done or that had been started before Fester's arrival. He felt also that it would not be beyond Fester at all, in his blunt and and undiplomatic way—if he were present at the meeting, that is—to make comments on his [Knowlton's] presentation and reveal Knowlton's inadequacy. It also seemed quite clear that it would not be easy to keep Fester from attending the meeting, even though he was not on the administrative level of those invited.

Knowlton found an opportunity to speak to Jerrold and raised the question. He remarked to Jerrold that, with the meetings coming up and with the interest in the work and with the contributions that Fester had been making, he would probably like to come to these meetings, but there was a question of the feelings of the others in the group if Fester alone were invited. Jerrold passed this over very lightly by saying that he didn't think the group would fail to understand Fester's rather different position and that he thought that Fester by all means should be invited. Knowlton then immediately said he had thought so, too; that Fester should present the work because much of it was work he had done; and, as Knowlton put it, that this would be a nice way to recognize Fester's contributions and to reward him, as he was eager to be recognized as a productive member of the lab. Jerrold agreed, and so the matter was decided.

Fester's presentation was very successful and in some ways dominated the meeting. He attracted the interest and attention of many of those who had come, and a long discussion followed his presentation. Later in the evening—with the entire laboratory staff present—in the cocktail period before the dinner, a little circle of people formed about Fester. One of them was Jerrold himself, and a lively discussion took place concerning the application of Fester's theory. All of this disturbed Knowlton, and his reaction and behavior were characteristic. He joined the circle, praised Fester to Jerrold and to others, and remarked on the brilliance of the work.

Knowlton, without consulting anyone, began at this time to take some interest in the possibility of a job elsewhere. After a few weeks he found that a new laboratory of considerable size was being organized in a nearby city, and that the kind of training he had would enable him to get a project head job equivalent to the one he had at the lab, with slightly more money.

He immediately accepted it and notified Jerrold by a letter, which he mailed on a Friday night to Jerrold's home. The letter was quite brief, and Jerrold was stunned. The letter merely said that he had found a better position; that there were personal reasons why he didn't want to appear at the lab any more; that he would be glad to come back at a later time from where he would be, some forty miles away, to assist if there was any mixup at all in the past work; that he felt sure that Fester could, however, supply any leadership that was required for the group; and that his decision to leave so suddenly was based on some personal problems—he hinted at problems of health in his family, his mother and father. All of this was fictitious, of course. Jerrold took it at face value but still felt that this was very strange behavior and quite unaccountable, for he had always felt his relationship with Knowlton had been warm and that Knowlton was satisfied and, as a matter of fact, quite happy and productive.

Jerrold was considerably disturbed, because he had already decided to place Fester in charge of another project that was going to be set up very soon. He had been wondering how to explain this to Knowlton, in view of the obvious help Knowlton was getting from Fester and the high regard in which he held him. Jerrold had, as a matter of fact, considered the possibility that Knowlton could add to his staff another person with the kind of background and training that had been unique in Fester and had proved so valuable.

Jerrold did not make any attempt to meet Knowlton. In a way, he felt aggrieved about the whole thing. Fester, too, was surprised at the suddenness of Knowlton's departure and when Jerrold, in talking to him, asked him whether he had reasons to prefer to stay with the photon group instead of the project for the Air Force which was being organized, he chose the Air Force project and went on to that job the following week. The photon lab was hard hit. The leadership of the lab was given to Link with the understanding that this would be temporary until someone could come in to take over.

Case Questions

1. Could Knowlton's resignation have been prevented by improved communication? If so, what kind of communication, and between whom?
2. What does Jerrold's statement, "The sky's the limit for a man who can produce" mean to Knowlton? What was Knowlton's view of himself and how did it relate to his perceptions of Jerrold and Fester?
3. What was on Knowlton's mind that he didn't express to Jerrold or to Fester? *Could* he have said more? *How* could he have tried to resolve his concerns in a way that he himself would have seen as acceptable and comfortable?
4. If you had been in Jerrold's position, would you have anticipated the problem that developed?
5. Through what patterns of communication and interpersonal relationships can organizations successfully accommodate a person like Fester who is brilliant and productive but who tends to create a social disaster area around himself?

Part III

Communication in Groups

Chapter 8

Group Character and Communication

What Is A Group?
    Primary and Secondary Groups
    Formal and Informal Groups
Company 3: The Development of a Group
Phases of Group Development
Group Structure
    Communication Networks
    Patterns of Status and Power
    Subgrouping
    Patterns of Role Taking
Group Cohesiveness
Group Norms
Interdependence of the Dimensions of Group Character

After studying this chapter, the reader should be able to

Define and use the following terms and concepts

Primary groups	Status incongruence
Secondary or reference groups	Index of influence
Formal groups	Subgrouping
Phases of group development	Coalition formation
Group structure	Task roles
Communication networks	Group building and maintenance roles
Centralized and decentralized networks	Self-oriented roles
Status	Group cohesiveness
	Group norms

Understand

The differences between the major types of groups: primary, secondary, formal, informal

The value to a group member of knowing the typical phases of group development

How to observe various dimensions of group structure

Why cohesiveness and communication quality are not directly related

How to identify the norms of a group

How to describe interdependencies between elements of group character

---

8

It is not possible to understand human communication adequately without paying attention to the small group context in which so much of it occurs. This is especially true of organizational communication. Though many people think of workers as robotlike cogs on an assembly line, each doing individual work, most supervisors and managers know their subordinates as unified groups who share strong views about such things as working conditions, promotion procedures, and pay raises. Group formation that cannot take place on a noisy assembly line happens during breaks and lunch hours. Even executives and specialized staff experts, often seen by themselves and others as being "rugged individualists," actually spend little time working alone. They are members of a top management team, project groups, committees, and study groups, all of which strongly affect their activities and effectiveness in the organization.

Groups develop characteristics of their own that differ from the atributes of the individuals who make up the group. This is similar to the way in which a molecule of water differs from the hydrogen and oxygen atoms that come together to form it. In the molecule, forces emerge that hold the parts together to form a structure that has a certain character. In human groups, forces also emerge. These forces come about through communication, and communication is in turn affected by them. Unlike water molecules, however, human groups come in a great many shapes, sizes, and kinds. Every group, in fact, has its own character.

Since we all spend some time in groups, we are somewhat familiar with the things that make up group character. You may recall one group in which you exerted a lot of influence and another in which you were just one of the followers. You have probably been in some groups that had real "team spirit" and others where apathy was the dominant theme. Think of a specific group in which you are now or recently have been a member. Is there a central "in-group" and some "fringe" members? To which category do you belong? How is the group controlled? Are all members equal, or is there a "pecking order?" How does the group expect its members to behave, and what happens when someone acts differently? These are the kinds of questions that are addressed in this chapter. Concepts and examples are presented to help the reader develop skill in understanding group character, how communication develops and sustains it, and the effects of group character on communication.

WHAT IS A GROUP?

A group is usually defined by social scientists as two or more persons who interact with each other in such a manner that each influences the other. Since the focus in this book is organizational communication, this definition should be tightened a bit by adding that a group must have a certain amount of predictability, usually in the form of shared goals and norms. In addition, because our focus is on *interpersonal* communication, we can further define group as being a small number of people who are aware of one another and who see each other as being part of a group.[1] Thus, a whole organization or a total department or union would not be a group because they typically do not interact and are not all aware of each other. However, subunits of departments, work crews, teams, committees, task forces, cliques, the "lunch bunch," and various other formal or informal affiliations among organization members would fit the definition.

Although most groups consist of people in close physical proximity to one another, this is not necessary to the definition of a group. A team of police officers tracking a fugitive and maintaining radio contact between their respective cars and helicopters is a group even though the individuals may be miles apart from each other.

On the other hand, six people standing at a bus stop are not a group, even though they are physically close to each other. This could change abruptly if a serious traffic accident were to occur on the street in front of them and the six began interacting in pursuit of a common goal: rescuing the passengers. The six would then become a group.

Primary and Secondary Groups

Groups can be classified as either primary or secondary depending on their size, the amount of face-to-face contact involved and, above all, the type of influence the group exerts on its members.[2] Primary groups are usually small enough to permit frequent interaction. This term is reserved for groups in which members are on close, familiar terms with one another and where members are markedly influenced as a result of their participation. Primary groups usually refer to an individual's family and closest friends or to close associations among work colleagues. As indicated by the definition of a group given earlier, the focus in this chapter is on primary groups.

Secondary groups, by contrast, are more impersonal, typically larger-scale associations. Being in such groups is a means to something else, such as earning a living, rather than an end in itself. The term *reference group* is often used to indicate a secondary group. Most people belong to many secondary or reference groups. An accountant in a large company, for example, is probably a member of one or more professional associations, a university alumni body, and perhaps a political party. The accountant's company, residential community, and ethnic-religious group are further examples. Reference groups reflect and affect the beliefs, values, and feelings of their members even though they may not involve any face-to-face contact.

Formal and Informal Groups

Most employees are members of one or more groups defined by their place on the organization chart (e.g., the group of subordinates reporting to a given superior), their location in the work flow, and their appointment to various committees and task forces. These are called formal groups because they are explicitly planned as part of the design of the organization.

On the other hand, some groups emerge spontaneously, without deliberate design. These informal groups consist of people who join together because of common interests, friendship, or social needs. Although they do not appear on the organization chart, they do exist. Their members converse together and have their unwritten rules about who belongs, who doesn't, and what behavior is considered appropriate. Some informal groups are rather dormant, providing a set of potential communication links that become activated only on occasion. Others are much more active, perhaps even so intense that they could be classified as primary groups.

The concepts of primary and secondary groups and of formal and informal groups are useful because they help alert the observer to the group context in which much organizational communication occurs. Further, they help explain why the character of a given group is what it is and exerts the impact on communication that it does. The lack of success of a given formal group, say a committee formed to suggest ways of reducing a hospital's computer expenses, might be partly understood in this way. Suppose, for example, a split occurs within the group along reference group lines, with computer experts forming one informal group, medical professionals a second, and administrative managers a third. Each group has its own ideas as to how the computer should be used. Unless the members can find reasons for identifying more strongly with the formal group (the committee) and less strongly with their reference groups and informal groups, agreement on cost reduction methods may never be possible.

A similar pattern appears in the case of Company Three, the student task team described in the following pages. This group does manage to overcome its split into opposing factions and provides examples of many of the other dimensions of group character to be discussed in the remainder of the chapter.

Company Three: The Development of a Group

At Urban University, Professor John Steven's course, Introduction to Management, was required for management majors but was also open to any other students who wished to take it as an elective. During part of the course, the class was divided into several groups, each assigned to "manage" a computer-simulated company in a "business game." Each group was in competition with companies managed by the other groups.

After studying historic data about their computerized industry provided by Professor Stevens, the groups were expected to make several sets of decisions over a period of weeks. When each decision set was due, all groups had to pass in a form containing their decisions on various items, such as product prices, advertising expenditures, research spending, production quantities, and plant capacitiy additions. After the decisions were computer processed, Professor Stevens returned the results to the teams so they could see them and begin work on the next set of decisions. Several graded reports were submitted by each company during the game, and the students' grades in the course depended in part on their company's business success in the computerized industry.

Professor Stevens assigned five members to Company Three. Mike and Mary were management majors, Ellen and Ed were economics majors, while Larry was majoring in English. In its initial meetings, the group seemed comfortable and in agreement. It was decided that no formal structure would be set up within the group. As Larry put it, "We're all responsible; we don't need to have anyone bossing anyone." It was also decided that each member would study all aspects of the company rather than specialize in a certain area, such as marketing or production. "This way all of us will see how all the pieces of the business fit together," said Mike. "All of us will be able to contribute to each decision. Also, we won't have to meet as often this way. It's hard to get this whole group together since you and Ellen live off campus," he said, nodding toward Ed.

The day the first decision set was due, a brief disagreement arose when Ellen and Ed, who carpooled to school together, showed the group a rather extensive statistical analysis they had worked out. It indicated the company's market had only a moderate long run rate of growth. Based on their analysis, Ellen and Ed argued that the company should not overexpand and that all decisions should be made conservatively.

Mike disagreed. "I don't really understand all your charts and graphs," he said. "In marketing class we are learning that a company can create new demand for its products. The game is just beginning. Now is the time to take some risk and see if we can be a real leader in this industry."

Mary supported Mike, and Larry added, "Yeah, let's play to win. Maybe the computer will pay off just like a slot machine."

Ellen and Ed expressed reservations but soon agreed to go along with the others. As Ellen put it, "Since this is a management course, maybe we had better take the advice of the management majors." The first set of decisions worked out well, Company Three placing near the top of the industry.

The next few meetings took on a tone of routineness. Ellen and Ed continued working on their statistical charts but mentioned them only briefly in the meetings. When time came for company decisions to be made, Mike and Mary did almost all the talking. Ellen and Ed missed one meeting, deciding to spend the time studying for a quiz in an economics course both were taking.

At the next meeting they were greeted by Larry with a booming, "Well, the President's Council of Economic Advisors is back and ready to lead us into a recession." After brief discussion of the quiz Ellen and Ed had taken and the results of the company's recent decisions, which continued to be favorable, the group settled into its usual pattern of activity.

Tension rose abruptly in the group, however, the day its first graded report was handed back. The report had been prepared and written largely by Mike. It was graded C minus and included, among other comments, the following summary remarks by Professor Stevens:

> Company Three is a very lucky business enterprise. You are doing well, but you do not know *why* you are doing well. Your report shows you have not yet discovered in the game data the key factors that determine demand for your products and your cost of operation. Unless you stop flying by the seat of your pants, I am afraid you will soon crash.
>
> In addition, your report is very badly written. What is the English major in your group doing—making economic forecasts?

This event threw the group into turmoil and bitterness. Ed and Ellen expressed particularly strong feelings toward Mike and Mary. At one point, Ellen summed up her feelings as follows: "You two have been running this whole show and not paying any attention to Ed's suggestions or mine. I understand how you feel a need to manage things, but now that all of our grades are hurting, maybe you'd better start looking at some facts, not just your own opinions."

Mike replied that some of the professor's detailed comments on portions of the report showed that Ed's and Ellen's economic analyses had not been completely "factual" either.

After the argument continued in this vein for several minutes, Mary intervened. "Look, obviously this game has turned out to be more complex than we thought. We need to make better use of the mathematical approaches Ed and Ellen have been using. In fact, the professor's comments show that Ed and Ellen had better start pushing even more numbers than they have so far. We're going to have to become more specialized. We can't each handle all these numbers without being superficial. At the same time, we've got to have some leadership in this group. We've been friendly and happy-go-lucky long enough, and now we're starting to suffer for it."

The group then turned its attention to developing new ways of proceeding. After giving serious and detailed consideration to a number of suggestions from all the members, it was decided to assign a specialized job to each individual. Ellen, for example, would specialize in market forecasting, while Mike would concentrate on production and inventory planning. Since this arrangement would require much more contact between the members before decisions could be made, it was decided that the group would meet at 7:30 A.M. on every class day until further notice. Mary was elected president of the company. It was further agreed that Larry would write the next report, based on information submitted to him by the others. His draft report would then be reviewed and edited by everyone in a meeting of the entire group.

Success did not come instantly. Company performance did slip, much as Professor Stevens had warned, during the next two decision sets. Nevertheless, the group's next report received a grade of B and the comment "Much improved" from the professor.

By the time the game reached its final phases, Company Three's decision quality had taken a sharp upward turn. In the last two decision sets, in fact, the company outperformed all the other groups in the class and finished with an overall record well up in the top half. Whenever the group experienced further tendencies toward a split along lines of management majors versus economics majors, the process was nipped in the bud. This was often aided by a comment from Larry to the effect of "Oops, here comes another revolution again," which helped break the tension as well as focus the group on its internal problems at times when they needed attention.

PHASES OF GROUP DEVELOPMENT

One thing that shows clearly in the story of Company Three is that the group was not static; it developed and changed over time. Soon after its formation, for example, the group had a relatively confident, comfortable atmosphere. The members shared a view that all were equally responsible and, therefore, no bosses were needed. Later, when the group received the results of its first graded report, the climate became much more tense.

It is typical for groups to move through a series of developmental phases. Many groups, in fact, never reach a state where they are not developing. Since communication and performance are strongly influenced by the group's developmental phase, a group really cannot be adequately understood unless its state of development is taken into account.

Various theories have been proposed to the effect that all groups tend to pass through the same sequence of developmental phases.[3] Bruce Tuckman, after reviewing various studies of group development involving observations of groups engaged in problem solving, production, military action, and therapy, has concluded that there are four stages of group development that groups have in common. He calls these stages *forming, storming, norming,* and *performing.* In another excellent synthesis of the group development studies, Rodney Napier and Matti Gershenfeld identify four phases similar to Tuckman's plus a fifth phase, which can be called *reforming.* These phases have the following characteristics:[4]

1. *Forming* In this first stage, the group is concerned with testing the boundaries of appropriate behavior. The climate tends to be a hesitant one, with members watchful to discern what they have to do to be accepted in the group, and whether it is worth it. Members at this stage usually feel dependent on either the leader, other members, or preexisting standards. While it sometimes happens that an individual makes a vigorous early grab for control, this is rare. Most people experience this first stage as a time of inhibted testing to gain familiarity with each other and the task they are supposed to do.
2. *Storming* In this stage, conflict arises. Members begin to seek personal recognition and their own spheres of influence. They take personal stands, and issues become polarized. Conflict occurs around both interpersonal and task issues, with members resisting the group's influence as well as the requirements of the task. Underlying issues at this stage involve matters of status, prestige, and power. If the group can face these problems and work on them, there will likely be a confrontation and an effort to get people together and back to work.
3. *Norming* In this third stage, a countermovement develops to reduce the growing hostility, reopen communication, and reorganize the group into a more effective working body. The climate becomes one of compromise and harmony as shared attitudes and values develop along with clearer role expectations, a division of labor, and standard modes of behavior. Personal feelings are subordinated to the group interest. Thus, in this phase there is often a sizable discrepancy between people's overt behavior and their underlying feelings.
4. *Performing* During this stage, members get on with the task. Since the structural and interpersonal issues have been solved, at least for the time being, energy can be channeled into work. There is a greater freedom to communicate during this phase, and more informality than before. People tend to feel a sense of shared responsibility for group goals along with a sense of personal accountability for a particular function.

5. *Reforming* Even effective working groups are not continually harmonious and free from tensions. Crises can arise in the form of a critical deadline, the arrival of new participants, or a controversial new idea. At such times, it may be necessary for the group to recycle back through one or more of the earlier phases. Old feelings and behaviors may reappear at these times. This is not necessarily a sign of group weakness or immaturity. Rather, the degree of strength is revealed in how well the group can cope with these very natural problems.

Communication and group performance can be significantly increased when members, especially those in leadership roles, know about this developmental sequence. For example, if members are unwilling to face and fight through their differences in the storming stage, this will impede the group's movement toward greater effectiveness. Efforts to exert dominance and a degree of interpersonal hostility are normal and need to be addressed before the group can reach agreements in the norming stage and go on to the performing stage. A leader who expects top efficiency out of a group that has not yet fulfilled the preliminary phases is fighting the developmental process. Many groups become stuck at one of the early phases. Alienated factory work groups are one example, but it happens to staff committees and even top management teams as well. This is less likely to happen in groups whose members share an awareness of the steps involved in group development.

The group development process should be kept in mind as the reader turns to the discussion of the major elements of group character that follows. These elements—group structure, group cohesiveness, and group norms—all are variables that can take on a wide range of forms. They do not remain fixed but change as the group moves through the developmental phases. Thus, describing a group in terms of its structure, cohesiveness, and norms helps not only to understand communication in the group at a point in time but also to sense where the group is located developmentally.

Group Structure

Most groups find it useful to develop some specialization of functions and responsibilities and some predictability in their internal communication. As different people in a group take on different functions, inequalities develop among them along a variety of dimensions. As these differences occur, mutually sustaining relationships develop between the differentiated parts of the group. This pattern of relationships is referred to as group structure.[5]

The business game team, Company Three, initially decided everyone would have the same role. Nevertheless, structural differentiation soon emerged as the split developed between the economics and management majors in the group. These two subgroups communicated more with one another than with the rest of the group, approached work problems in different ways, and soon developed a distinct power differential as Mike and Mary began to take the lead regularly in making final decisions. These differences arose as members began working in the ways their previous backgrounds had prepared them. The economics majors took a quantitative, more conservative approach, while the management majors took a qualitative, more aggressive approach.

When such differences become established in a group, they tend to persist. People need to be able to count on some degree of stability in their social environment, and out of this need for predictability come strong pressures on group members to assume and maintain certain stable relationships with other members. It is this recurring, persisting nature of the differences between members that gives the group a recognizable structure.[6]

When we think of the structure of some object, we think of an easily observable relationship of parts. Structural characteristics of groups do not always jump out at us quite so noticeably. Different structural characteristics vary in terms of how readily observable they are. Some structural features may be quite explicit and others more subtle. In effect, we need to take several looks at a group in order to discern its various structural dimensions. In discussing more specifically the properties of group structure, four dimensions will be considered: communication networks, patterns of status and power, subgrouping, and patterns of role-taking.

Communication Networks.   Communication networks are recurring patterns of who talks to whom. Group networks indicate where there are channels open for the flow of messages. In their first studies of communication networks, Alex Bavelas and Harold Leavitt compared the patterns shown in exhibit 8-1 as to their speed and accuracy in solving problems and how they influenced the morale of their members.[7]

EXHIBIT 8-1
**COMMUNICATION NETWORKS STUDIED BY
BAVELAS AND LEAVITT**

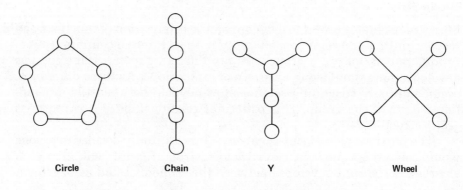

Circle   Chain   Y   Wheel

In Leavitt's experiment, vertical partitions were placed around the table to restrict communications to one of the desired patterns. Subjects had to communicate with each other by passing written notes. Each person was given a card containing five symbols out of a possible six. The group's task was to discover which symbol was held in common by all five members.

In general, the results showed the wheel network to be fastest and most accurate in solving the problem, while the circle was slowest, used more messages, and was least accurate. However, circle groups were more likely than the others to correct their errors. Moreover, overall group satisfaction was highest in the circle. In the chain, Y, and wheel networks, persons in central positions reported high satisfaction, while the satisfaction of other members decreased with their distance from the center of the network.

The networks studied by Bavelas and Leavitt are not the only possible structures. Obviously, in some groups each member communicates with all the others, or, there may be separate subgroups, connected to each other by one or more liaison persons. An important distinction between different kinds of networks is whether they are centralized or decentralized. The wheel and chain are examples of highly centralized networks because one individual is central to the communication flows. The circle or each-to-all patterns are decentralized networks because no one person is central to the flow of messages. Later research has confirmed the greater speed and accuracy of centralized networks for simple tasks, such as symbol matching. For more complex tasks, however, decentralized networks tend to be faster and more accurate.[8] This difference seems to apply especially to the early time phase during which the group is planning how it will do its task. A recent study by Alvin Snadowsky showed that centralized communication patterns were more efficient on all types of tasks during the actual doing of the task, but that decentralized networks developed better plans for performing complex tasks.[9] This makes sense because when individuals can communicate directly to each other, without having to go through a central person, they can express their ideas and opinions more freely, enabling the group to develop more creative and imaginative solutions.

The experimental studies of communication networks cannot always be directly applied to organizations.[10] Additional factors in the natural setting, such as noise, the location of needed information, and the members' skills and previous experience would, of course, affect productivity. Nevertheless, networks do occur frequently. Workers on an assembly line, for example, work in a centralized network, since the line arrangement allows only limited communication among individuals. A supervisor who wished to tap the workers' ideas for improving the efficiency of the line might meet with them in a setting where freer communication was possible. In the case of Company Three, the group's ability to shift its communication pattern when the need arose was a key ingredient in its performance improvement. During the blowup following the bad report grade, everyone spoke, giving a needed airing to pent up gripes and ideas. Then, to accomplish the more codified task of playing the game, a more centralized structure was set up, including the appointment of a company president. The difference between more and less centralized communication flows is important in actual work groups in organizations, not just student groups like Company Three. Such factors as seating arrangements, office locations, and the higher cost of long distance telephone calls, often produce networks that limit performance—a condition that can often be corrected if it is recognized.

Patterns of Status and Power. Though their members may believe strongly in equality, groups develop a power structure based on differences in the extent to which individuals are able to influence each other. Company Three was no exception. The group expressed equality as its ideology, but it was not long before Mary and Mike emerged as the key decision makers.

Influence is related to status. Status may be defined as a person's relative position in terms of the degree to which he or she possesses socially approved characteristics. Early in a group's life, status is usually related to each member's standing outside the group. In general, the higher a person ranks in such external factors as age, education (how much and where), work experience, ethnicity, sex, and region born in, the higher will be that person's status in the group. Of course, different groups rank status in different ways. Larry, the English major, was accorded low status in Company Three, but this might not have been true if the group's task had involved literary criticism instead of business decision making.

An exception to the rule relating to external status factors can occur in the case of an individual who is *status incongruent*—high on some factors but low on others. Such individuals, say assembly line workers, with advanced degrees, often become isolates in groups, rejected by other members because their behavior is unpredictable and therefore perceived as threatening.

In the long run, status is a result of the individual's degree of compliance with the standard of behavior that develop in the group. Those who conform most closely to the group's norms have the highest likelihood of emerging as leaders of the group. It is often the case, however, that early status rankings determined by external factors set a pattern that shapes the power structure of the group for the longer term.[11]

While it is difficult to measure pecisely the relative degrees of influence in a group, a rough idea may be derived by observing the ratio of each person's successful influence acts compared with total attempts. This ratio can be stated as follows:[12]

$$\text{Index of influence} = \frac{\text{Successful influence acts}}{\text{Total influence attempts}}$$

Influence acts can take forms ranging from autocratic direct orders to mere suggestions in which gestures, tone of voice, and facial expressions are meaningful. Hence, a clear power structure may exist in a group even though influence is exerted in a subtle, permissive way.

The distribution of relative amounts of influence in a group will reveal whether the group has a hierarchial power structure with one or a few members dominating, or if it is an egalitarian group—one in which power is shared on a widespread basis. Power distribution tends to have major effects on communication within a group. In hierarchial structures, for example, the dominant flow of communication tends to be from low-status members to high-status members, and this communication tends to be less aggressively toned than in groups where status differences are less pronounced.[13] There is also a tendency for high-status persons to be reluctant to communicate negative attitudes, criticisms, or confusions about their own roles to low-status persons.[14] While these particular relationships, though frequent ones, may not occur in every group, the main point is that the pattern of influence is an important dimension of group structure having significant bearing on communication. Group members who are alert to status and influence patterns can help the group improve its effectiveness. A committee chairman, for example, may notice that he has become so dominant in his influence that other members are reluctant to disagree or make suggestions of their own. To increase member contributions, he could decide to make fewer influence attempts and find ways of encouraging and rewarding influence attempts by others.

Subgrouping. In any group the possibility exists that some members will form subgroups. In fact, it is only in rare cases that cliques do not form within a group.

Theodore Caplow has developed a very explicit theory of subgroup formation. According to Caplow, group members are motivated to form coalitions in order to maximize their control over others in the group. Control is determined by the power resources of the group members. Using the triad, or three-person group, as a basis, Caplow identified several basic types of power distribution a triad might have and predicted the most likely coalitions for each distribution.[15]

The predictions are shown in exhibit 8-2. In Type 1, for example, where three individuals have equal power (A=B=C), the reasoning is that each member will want to join a coalition in order to control the excluded member. Since the members' power quantities are equal, they will have no preferences for coalition partners, so any coalition will be equally likely. In Type 2, where $A > B$, $B = C$, and $A < (B + C)$, Caplow predicts a BC coalition. Although A would want a coalition with either B or C, since A would then control both the coalition partner and the excluded member, B and C will not want this, since it will put them under A's control.

While Caplow's theory helps alert the observer to the importance of

EXHIBIT 8-2
CAPLOW'S PREDICTIONS OF COALITION FORMATION RESULTING FROM POWER DISTRIBUTION

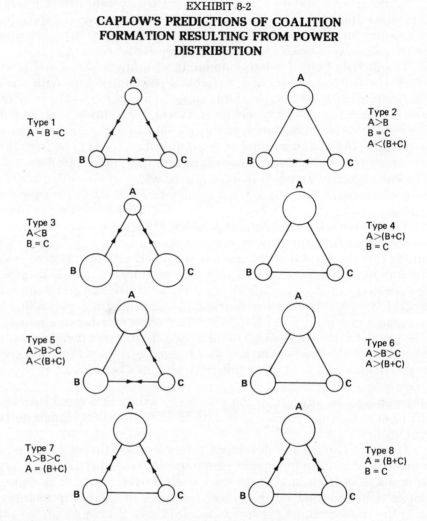

Type 1
A = B = C

Type 2
A>B
B = C
A<(B+C)

Type 3
A<B
B = C

Type 4
A>(B+C)
B = C

Type 5
A>B>C
A<(B+C)

Type 6
A>B>C
A>(B+C)

Type 7
A>B>C
A = (B+C)

Type 8
A = (B+C)
B = C

From Theodore Caplow, "Further Development of a Theory of Coalitions in the Triad," *American Journal of Sociology*, volume 64, p. 488, by permission of The University of Chicago Press. Copyright © 1959 by The University of Chicago.

power factors in the shaping of subgroups, it does not give attention to other factors of equal importance. In a given situation, similar attitudes, friendship, constraints imposed by physical location, the flow of work, or formally assigned associations might govern the formation of subgroups, as might any combination of the factors that have been mentioned. In Company Three, for example, the economics majors formed one subgroup while the management majors formed another. Power motives may well have played a part, but so did their similar academic backgrounds, their attitudes toward the strategy of the game, and the fact that Ed and Ellen commuted to school together.

The way to identify subgroups is to observe patterns of participation. Where subgroup members go for coffee together, or otherwise separate themselves physically from the total group, identification is not difficult. Observation can be more demanding in a discussion or problem-solving group, where directions of interaction from member to member must be noted as well as patterns of support and rejection of ideas. Subgroupings can often be observed at decision points by noting who repeatedly agrees with whom.[16]

The effects of subgroups on communication and group functioning may be either favorable or unfavorable. If subgroups are formed around differing but complementary task capabilities, they may enhance the performance of the group. Even if they are based primarily on social considerations, they may promote communication among members and facilitate task accomplishment. Of course, subgroups can have less desirable effects, serving as hindrances to communication or fostering nonproductive conflict. Whether the effects are positive or negative, subgrouping is a key aspect of group structure and the character of a group.

Patterns of Role Taking. The fourth and final dimension of group structure to be discussed here is patterns of role raking. Role taking refers to the behavioral acts of individuals in a group. A behavioral act can be said to be part of a role when it relates to some problem facing the group in accomplishing its task or maintaining its social stability. Over time, the role taking of members in a group usually develops some stability. When individuals have received the group's approval for certain acts in the past, such as coming up with new ideas or telling jokes to ease the tension, they tend to repeat them. This allocation of functions among members become the role-taking pattern of the group.

A useful set of categories for identifying roles of group members was developed by Kenneth Benne and Paul Sheats.[17] Benne and Sheats defined three main kinds of roles: (1) task roles, (2) group building and maintenance roles, and (3) individual roles.

Task roles relate to accomplishing group goals. These roles include being the seeker or giver of information, the initiator, the seeker or giver of opinions, the orienter, the evaluator, the elaborator, the energizer, the assistant to procedure, and the recorder.

Group building and maintenance roles relate to problems of group integration and solidarity. They include the encourager, the harmonizer, the compromiser, the gate-keeper (or expediter), the standard setter, the group observer/commentator, and the follower.

Individual or self-oriented roles relate to actions aimed to satisfying personal needs. They include the aggressor, the blocker, the recognition-seeker, the self-confesser, the dominator, the help seeker, and the special interest pleader.

It is not likely that a group member will constantly play just one of these roles. Over time, however, members tend to play certain roles more often than others, giving the group a discernable "profile" consisting of certain of the above roles, each played with a given frequency by a given number of members.

Role-taking profiles can affect group outcomes. One study, for example, indicated that groups that tended to be most productive and highest in member satisfaction were ones where ideas, guidance, and congeniality were contributed separately by different members. Where two or more of these functions were performed by the same member, the groups tended to attain lower performance, satisfaction, or both.[18] Thus, the committee chairman mentioned earlier who found himself dominating the group might usefully change his approach by divesting himself of the idea-contributing role and limiting himself to guidance—orienting the group and coordinating the members' suggestions.

Like subgrouping, role patterns can be beneficial or harmful to a group, depending on the roles performed, the circumstances facing the group, and the needs of the members. One role-taking pattern can splinter and immobilize a group, while another can provide a useful set of specialized functions along with the integrative effort needed to coordinate them.

Group Cohesiveness

While the dimensions of structure help identify the shape of a group—what kinds of "functioning parts" it has and how they are positioned in relation to one another—cohesiveness has to do with how tightly or loosely they are held together. As the term *cohesiveness* suggests, members of highly cohesive groups are more likely to stick together, cooperate, and participate in common effort.

Cohesiveness is defined as the extent to which members find the group attractive. It is a result of all the factors acting on the members to remain in the group. These factors include aspects of the group itself, such as its people and its activities. Also included are ways in which the group may help members satisfy needs outside the group, such as status and security.[19]

In general, cohesiveness and communication are positively correlated. Members talk more in highly cohesive groups.[20] The fact that a group is cohesive does not necessarily mean conversation will be warm and pleasant, however. In one study, in fact, it was found that more cohesive groups engaged in more objective problem solving, less friendly behavior, and more aggressive activity.[21]

One interesting study of the relationship between groups cohesiveness and communication was conducted by Kurt Back.[22] Back found that communication quality differed depending on what the factors producing cohesiveness were. When cohesiveness was based on members' personal attraction to one another, their conversations tended to be long and pleasant. When cohesiveness was based on attraction to the task, members wanted to complete the task quickly and efficiently and discussed only matters related to achieving their purposes. When cohesiveness was based on the prestige obtainable from membership, the members spoke cautiously, concentrated on their own activities, and were careful not to risk their status. Finally, in groups where cohesiveness was at a minimum, members acted largely independently, paying little attention to each other.

Cohesiveness can have a significant bearing on a group's results. It was clear in the case of Company Three that cohesiveness was relatively low during one phase of the group's development, evidenced by Ed's and Ellen's lack of attendance and the fact that only Mike and Mary participated in making the key decisions. During this period, the group's results in the game were below par, as was their report-writing quality. Numerous studies have shown that in highly cohesive groups, members are likely to take on more responsibilities, persist longer in working on difficult tasks, attend meetings more regularly, and remain members for a longer time.[23]

Cohesiveness does not directly affect a group's productivity, however. More accurately, it heightens members' susceptibility to influence. Therefore, cohesiveness can be a key factor in sustaining whatever level of productivity the group comes to value—whether high, low, or average.[24] In highly cohesive groups members typically conform more uniformly to group standards. Group norms are more strongly enforceable where individuals place high value on their membership in the group. Conversely, low cohesiveness enhances members' susceptibility to outside influence.[25]

Group Norms

The norms that exist in a group are another essential ingredient of the group's character. Like the structural dimensions and cohesiveness, group norms are closely related to communication processes in the group.

A norm can be defined as an idea in the minds of the members of a group concerning what kind of behavior is appropriate or inappropriate.[26] The nature of group norms can be shown best by stating some norms actually observed in a well-known study of a work group. The following examples were noted by researchers in the Bank Wiring Room at the Hawthorne plant of the Western Electric Company:[27]

1. You should not turn out too much work. If you do, you are a rate buster.
2. You should not turn out too little work. If you do, you are a chisler.
3. You should not tell a supervisor anything that will act to the detriment of an associate. If you do, you are a squealer.

4. You should not attempt to maintain social distance or act officious. If you are an inspector, for example, you should not act like one.

Through observation, the researchers could see these standards of behavior operating in the group. The workers themselves would not have stated them in such elegant form; in fact, it is often true that group norms are unspoken. Therefore, the surest way to identify a norm is by seeing its violator punished. When a group member is ignored, frowned upon, or openly criticized after behaving in a certain way, the norm involved can be seen by inference.

When people conform to group norms, it is due to a combination of personal and external factors. Conflict arises inside an individual who observes that his or her behavior or viewpoint differs from others in the group. From outside the individual come forces exerted by members who sense that a given type of behavior is important to the group in accomplishing its task, maintaining itself as a group, and establishing certain opinions as being valid. Basically, then, when people comply with norms, it is a social phenomenon. Men wear neckties on certain occasions not because they find it physically comfortable or convenient but because they know others expect it.

Strong forces toward conformity can be generated through the communication that occurs in a group, even to the point that members may renounce their sensory perceptions. A striking demonstration is found in Muzafer Sherif's classic research on the autokinetic effect—the tendency of a person to see a pinpoint of light in a darkened room as actually moving back and forth when, in fact, it is stationary.[28] The stimulus is very ambiguous and each person tends to estimate a different amount of movement. After testing subjects several times individually, Sherif then tested groups composed of people who had developed stable but widely differing individual perceptions to see if a group norm would emerge. Though the group members' estimates were at odds to begin with, the estimates within each group soon began to converge on a single distance. The experiment dramatically showed how marked is the tendency toward common judgments when people interact in a group, even when uniformity is not a conscious concern. In a final phase of the experiment, Sherif retested the subjects individually and found that they retained the newly acquired estimates they had arrived at in the group.

Once formed, norms influence the kinds and amounts of communication that occur. This influence is particularly strong at times when one or more members of a group fail to comply with the norms. An interesting study by Stanley Schachter showed how deviation from group norms affects the pattern of messages sent within a discussion group.[29]

In Schachter's experiment, confederates fulfilled three experimental conditions: (1) the *deviate,* who expressed views at the opposite extreme from the norm of the group, (2) the *mode,* who agreed with the group's position, and (3) the *slider,* who first took an opposing position but later came around to the group's stand. Other subjects were simply asked to participate in a discussion of a case problem involving a juvenile delinquent and had no reason to believe the confederates were playing planned roles. At the outset, messages were directed mainly toward the deviate and slider. The number of messages to the slider decreased, however, as the slider approached the position that was the group's norm. Messages to the deviate (who persisted in an opposing stance) increased up to a point and then decreased abruptly. The overall pattern was one of increasing efforts to get deviates to conform to the group's norms, followed by complete acceptance if they do conform and rejection and isolation if they maintained their deviant position.

The effects of norms on the activities and outcomes of a group depend upon their content. Some groups develop norms of active, open communication, others of guardedness. In some groups high task productivity is the standard, while other groups enforce the opposite. Social pressure in groups is sometimes thought to be a force that produces a uniform sameness of thought and behavior among members. This can happen, but it is not always the case. Some groups have norms of diversity rather than sameness. The earlier discussion of role-taking patterns, for example, indicated that groups may expect unique rather than uniform performances of their members. Similarly, in chapter 9 it is shown that effective decision-making groups often are ones that are able to draw out the diverse abilities of their members to contribute. It has been demonstrated experimentally that social pressure can influence people to follow their inner sense of how to behave rather than the dictates of an outside persuader or authority.[30] The wide variation in the possible content of group norms makes it essential that the norms be identified if the character of a given group is to be understood.

INTERDEPENDENCE OF THE DIMENSIONS OF GROUP CHARACTER

The several dimensions of group character provide a fairly thorough checklist for describing a group. Typically, group members could be more specific and thorough in understanding their group, and could in many cases improve performance and satisfaction, if they made use of this checklist. In Company Three, for example, prior to the time the professor made his written comments on the group's first report, there were a number of things the members did not seem to recognize that were true of the group. The norms seemed to be ones of equality and routineness. It was an unwritten rule that disagreements should not be fully confronted. Members did not recognize they were in the "storming" phase and that more heated discussion of internal issues and personal feelings would help move the group's development forward. The effects of the subgrouping along reference group lines (management majors and economics majors) was not openly recognized, nor were its effects on cohesiveness. It was only when some of the group's character traits began to be recognized that the group developed greater strength and improved its performance. After the warning comments were received from the professor, the group in effect sat down and went through many of the checklist items in an explicit and vigorous way.

It is useful, however, to think of the dimensions of group character as being more than just a checklist. The dimensions are interdependent with one another. One characteristic of a group tends to reinforce others and be reinforced by them. Thus, in Company Three the norm of not confronting group problems limited the group's ability to develop greater cohesiveness and was itself sustained by low cohesiveness in that members did not care enough about the group to want to assess its problems. Similarly, the power structure in the group, whereby the management major controlled decision making, reinforced the nonconfrontation norm by providing an "automatic" way of resolving issues. At the same time, the nonconfrontation norm sustained the power structure since it prevented any concerns the members may have felt about the group's way of doing business from being addressed. Similar reciprocal connections can be seen between all of this group's character traits.

Deeper insight into the nature of a group comes when the reinforcing connections between its characteristics are seen. This level of insight is of particular importance for those members who wish to bring about change in a group. They will then see that successful change requires changing not just a single attribute of the group but the whole pattern. As was true of the improvement brought about in Company Three, change requires new action along all the dimensions of group character and the establishment of a new pattern of interdependencies between them.

Summary

The thrust of this chapter has been to identify several key dimensions of group character. To begin with, four types of groups were discussed: primary groups, secondary or reference groups, formal groups, and informal groups. All four of these categories are useful in characterizing most groups. A primary group is affected by the particular reference groups its members consider important. Informal groups often exist inside formal groups and sometimes form across the boundaries between formal groups.

Phases of group development were discussed next. Forming, storming, norming, performing, and reforming were seen as a normal sequence of "character changes" through which healthy groups are continually moving. Less healthy groups may be frozen at a given phase, unable to move to the next. The phase definitions contribute to understanding the character of a given group by revealing which phase it is in and also by indicating what issues need to surface and be addressed in the group in order for it to move into the next phase.

The concept of group structure was introduced as a persistent pattern or differences within a group. This concept was made more specific by discussions of four kinds of group structure: communication networks, patterns of status and power, subgrouping, and patterns of role taking. In each case, these structural forms are produced by communication within the group, and, once established, they exert a strong influence on the kinds and amounts of communication that occur and on the group's task effectiveness. Though persistent, the dimensions of a group's structure often go unnoticed by those who are preoccupied by technical or personal matters. Charting the communication network or estimating the indexes of influence for the members of a group can make these important aspects of group character more explicit and real.

Two further elements of group character were considered. Cohesiveness, the extent to which members find the group attractive, was found to be a group character trait closely related to several aspects of communication, including openness, aggressiveness, persuasion, and problem solving. Finally, group norms—the standards of behavior considered appropriate within a group—were seen to be strong forces affecting communication and performance.

Questions for Review

1. Think of a group in which you are currently a member. What stage of development has this group reached? What evidence shows this? If the group has passed through earlier stages, describe what they were like.
2. How can members' knowledge of group development phases improve communication quality and group effectiveness?
3. Why do different communication networks tend to result in different levels of morale and success in problem solving?
4. What is the "index of influence," and how is it related to group structure?
5. Refer to Caplow's predictions of coalition formation resulting from power distribution, and give an example from your own knowledge or experience that confirms one of the predictions.
6. Think of a group with which you are familiar. What roles are taken within this group? How has this pattern of role taking affected the group's operation?
7. How is group cohesiveness related to communication? Are cohesive groups likely to be highly productive?
8. How is communication likely to be affected by the degree to which members comply or fail to comply with the group's norms?

References and Notes

1. See Marvin E. Shaw, *Group Dynamics: The Psychology of Small Group Behavior,* (New York: McGraw-Hill, 1971), p. 10; Dalmas A. Taylor and Bruce Kleinhaus, "Group Development and Structure" in Bernard Seidenberg and Alvin M. Snadowsky, *Social Psychology* (New York: Free Press, 1976), p. 377; Edgar H. Schein, *Organizational Psychology* (Englewood Cliffs, N.J.: Prentice-Hall, 1970), p. 81.

2. Charles H. Cooley, *Social Organization* (Glencoe, Ill.: Free Press, 1956), pp. 23–31.

3. See, for example, W. R. Bion, *Experiences in Groups* (London: Tavistock Publications, 1959), chap. 3–5; Herbert A. Thelen, *Dynamics of Groups at Work* (Chicago: University of Chicago Press, 1954), pp. 129–67; Warren G. Bennis and Herbert A. Shepard, "A Theory of Group Development," *Human elations* 9 (1956): 415–38: Robert F. Bales and Fred L. Strodtbeck, "Phases in Group Problem Solving," *Journal of Abnormal and Social Psychology* 46 (1951); 485–87; William C. Schutz, *The Interpersonal Underworld* (Palo Alto, Calif.: Science and Behavior Books, 1966), pp. 168–74.

4. The descriptions of the five phases of group development are based on Bruce W. Tuckman, "Developmental Sequences in Small Groups," *Psychological Bulletin* 63 (1965): 384–99; Rodney W. Napier and Matti K. Gershenfeld, *Groups: Theory and Experience* (Boston: Houghton-Mifflin, 1973), pp. 247–55.

5. Shaw, *Group Dynamics,* p. 234.

6. Darwin Cartwright and Alvin Zander, *Group Dynamics: Research and Theory* (New York: Harper and Row, 1960), p. 644.

7. Alex Bavelas, "Communication Patterns in Task-Oriented Groups," *Journal of Acoustical Society of America* 22 (1950): 725–30; Harold J. Leavitt, "Some Effects of Certain Communication Patterns on Group Performance," *Journal of Abnormal and Social Psychology* 46 (1951): 38–50.

8. Shaw, *Group Dynamics,* pp. 142–45.

9. Alvin M. Snadowsky, "Communication Network Research: An Examination of Controversies," *Human Relations* 25 (1972): 283–306.

10. For a summary of the criticisms of network studies, see Richard F. Farce, Peter R. Monge, and Hamish M. Russell, *Communicating and Organizing* (Reading, Mass.: Addison-Wesley, 1977), pp. 161–62. For a study in which networks helped explain group performance in an organization, see Peter Meers, "Structuring Communication in a Working Group," *Journal of Communication* 24, no. 1 (1974): 71–79.

11. A close relationship between external status factors and the long-run internal pattern of status and influence in a group is shown in Abraham Zaleznik, C. Roland Christensen, and Fritz J. Roethlisberger, *The Motivation, Productivity, and Satisfaction of Workers* (Boston: Division of Research, Harvard Business School, 1958), pp. 198–217.

12. Abraham Zaleznik and David Moment, *The Dynamics of Interpersonal Behavior* (New York: John Wiley & Sons, 1964), p. 70.

13. John W. Thibaut, "An Experimental Study of the Cohesiveness of Underprivileged Groups," *Human Relations* 3 (1950): 251–78. See also Kurt W. Back et. al., "The Methodology of Studying Rumor Transmission," *Human Relations* 3 (1950): 307–12.

14. Harold H. Kelley, "Communication in Experimentally Created Hierarchies," *Human Relations* 4 (1951): 39–56.
15. Theodore Caplow, "A Theory of Coalitions in the Triad," *American Sociological Review* 21 (1956): 489–93.
16. The ways of observing subgroups discussed here are those suggested by Zaleznik and Moment, *Dynamics of Interpersonal Behavior,* pp. 77–79.
17. Kenneth D. Benne and Paul Sheats, "Functional Roles of Group Members," *Journal of Social Issues* 4 (1948): 42–47.
18. David Moment, "Role Patterns, Performance, and Satisfaction in Student Project Groups" (Unpublished paper, Harvard Business School, 1964).
19. Cartwright and Zander, *Group Dynamics,* pp. 74–75.
20. A. J. Lott and B. E. Lott, "Group Cohesiveness, Communication Level, and Conformity," *Journal of Abnormal and Social Psychology* 62 (1961): 408–12.
21. John R. P. French, "The Disruption and Cohesion of Groups," *Journal of Abnormal and Social Psychology* 36 (1941): 361–77.
22. Kurt W. Back, "Influence through Social Communication," *Journal of Abnormal and Social Psychology* 46 (1951): 9–23.
23. Cartwright and Zander, *Group Dynamics,* p. 89.
24. Stanley Schachter et. al., "An Experimental Study of Cohesiveness and Productivity," *Human Relations* 4 (1951): 229–38; Stanley E. Seashore, *Group Cohesiveness in The Industrial Work Group* (Ann Arbor, Mich.: Institute for Social Research, 1954). See also John A. Cartright, "A Laboratory Investigation of Groupthink," *Communication Monographs* 45 (1978): 229–46.
25. Sidney Verba, *Small Groups and Political Behavior* (Princeton, N.J.: Princeton University Press, 1961).
26. George C. Homans, *The Human Group* (New York: Harcourt, Brace & World, 1950), p. 123.
27. Fritz J. Roethlisberger and Wilham J. Dickson, *Management and The Worker* (Cambridge, Mass.: Harvard University Press, 1943), p. 522.
28. Muzafer Sherif, *The Psychology of Social Norms* (New York: Harper and Row, 1936).
29. Stanley Schachter, "Deviation, Rejection, and Communication," *Journal of Abnormal and Social Psychology* 46 (1951): 190–207.
30. Stanley Milgram, "Liberating Effects of Group Pressure," *Journal of Personality and Social Psychology* 1 (1965): 127–34.

Chapter 9

Group Decision Making
and Leadership

The New Product Meeting
The Reflective Thinking Model
Factors Affecting Decision Quality
    Group Size and Composition
    Interaction Process
    Decision-making Mechanisms
    Brainstorming
    NGT and Delphi Techniques
    Risk Taking
Leadership in Groups
    Trait and Style Approaches
    Contingency and Path-Goal Approaches
    Leadership as Functions
Group Effectiveness Criteria

After studying this chapter,
the reader should be able to

Define and use the following terms and concepts

Reflective thinking model

Membership heterogeneity

Membership compatibility

Interaction process analysis

Interaction process balance

Group decision making
  mechanisms

NGT and Delphi techniques

Risky shift

Trait theories of leadership

Authoritarian and democratic
  leadership styles

Contingency theory of leadership

Path-Goal theories of leadership

Leadership as functions

Understand

How to spot strengths and weaknesses in a group's decision making operations

How to apply the reflective thinking model to a recent decision of your
   own
What factors other than information and logic affect group decisions
Alternative decision methods and their advantages/disadvantages
How interaction process "balance" is related to group decision quality
Various leadership theories and their relative merits

9

People who do managerial, professional, and staff work in organizations
typically spend a major portion of their time attending meetings. An
average of about ten hours a week was reported by executives surveyed
in one study and college faculty members in another.[1] Formal committees
make decisions on matters ranging from next year's budget to the handling of the United Fund campaign. Informal meetings add to the total.
A research manager calls the department together to decide which members will work on a certain new project. A group from an advertising
agency visits a client's office to propose details for a new ad campaign.

Ironically, despite the extensive use made of decision-making groups,
most people tend to take a dim view of them. Typical comments include,
"These meetings are a waste of time. I never have a chance to get my work
done," "What's the use. Whenever this committee recommends anything
it gets disapproved by the higher-ups," or "I've made a New Year's resolution not to go to any more meetings." Managers generally feel that committees take up too much time, engage in buck-passing, compromise
excessively, and accomplish too little.[2]

On the other hand, there is a convincing body of research that tells
us that groups are capable of very high levels of performance. With proper
training and the effective use of communication skills, groups often accomplish greater achievements corporately than any of their individual
members are able to do on their own.[3]

In one such study, managers who were trained in group methods
were compared to those who were untrained in their performance in the
Lost on the Moon Exercise.[4] This exercise asks people to imagine they are
lost on the moon and to make a priority order ranking of which items from
a fifteen-item list they would take with them as they set out to try to

rendezvous with the mother ship. After each person made a rank order list, the subjects were assigned to four- to six-person discussion groups and asked to reach a group consensus on a single ranked list. The individual and group lists were then compared with a master list of answers that are correct according to experts at NASA.

For seventy-five percent of the trained groups, the scores were better than the top individual score in the group. Even twenty-five percent of the untrained groups did better collectively than their best individual. The researchers concluded that there is nothing inherent in group processes that makes decision-making groups necessarily inept. To the contrary, groups can produce high-quality decisions if their members make them function effectively.

This chapter focuses on those aspects of decision-making groups that have a bearing on whether they function more effectively or less effectively. As a point of departure, the reader is invited to eavesdrop on a short meeting involving middle-level managers in a major food products company. This is not offered as an example of effective group decision making, but simply as a meeting that is very typical of the many conducted daily in organizations.

The New Product Meeting*

A product manager (PM) in a large food products company had been assigned responsibility for a new brand of cereal the firm was planning to introduce. At one point, with test marketing of the new brand scheduled to begin in a few weeks, the PM arranged a meeting with representatives of the company's manufacturing and accounting departments to bring them up to date, as well as to discuss certain problems that concerned him. The PM was charged with overall coordination of all activities relating to the new cereal, although he himself was a member of the marketing department, with no direct authority over the people from manufacturing and accounting.

After he walked into the conference room, the PM tossed an artist's mock-up of the package onto the table. As the package was passed around, the PM talked about its specifications, giving precise facts and figures and telling how they had been determined. He went on to present plans for direct mail sample promotion, shelf location, and several other matters, and the people from manufacturing and accounting nodded in agreement.

Things went less smoothly, however, when the PM asked the manufacturing people about quality control. A lengthy discussion followed in which, with minor variations, the parties repeated the following statements several times over:

---

*David Moment and Dalmar Fisher, *Autonomy in Organizational Life,* p. 69. Copyright © 1975, Schenkman Publishing Company, Inc., Cambridge, Massachusetts 02138.

PM: Exactly what are you going to do to insure this product's taste? I've been asked about this. My superiors expect me to know.

Mfg.: But we *know* how to do quality control. What's the matter, don't you trust us? We will use the same statistical techniques on this product that we do on other products having similar ingredients.

PM: I understand that this is your responsibility, but it's our concern as well. It's a bigger problem on this product. Would it be too much to ask you to send us a note saying that the quality will be what it is supposed to be?

Mfg.: You're going to have to accept that we do the job and have faith that we're going to do the same thing we do on the other products.

Finally, the PM reluctantly replied, "OK, OK, so I trust you," and changed the subject by asking, "OK, what about costs?" Another lengthy discussion resulted when the PM discovered that the cost estimates for the product were now considerably higher than those the accountants had made a few months earlier. At one point, the PM expressed his distress:

PM: Can't we stay with the old numbers? Look, I'm confronted with a situation where a pricing decision has already been made. Now, if people see a lower projected profit, I'll lose all I've fought for. I'll get drilled.

Acctg.: If you stay with the old numbers, you'll defeat our whole structure. As you see, right *here,* on our standard forms, are the costs. We can't go all the way back to the beginning on costs. You can see from these sheets how much is involved in putting these figures together.

The issue was not resolved and the meeting ended.

Clearly this was not a highly productive meeting. The two big goals the PM had hoped to reach were not attained. He received no "specific" assurances about quality control procedures, nor was it made clear whether this could or should be done. The pricing issue also remained to be resolved. This could easily qualify as one of those many meetings from which the participants walk away muttering, "Ugh! Meetings sure are a waste of time." Can the causes of low productivity in this meeting be understood? How can such meetings be improved?

THE REFLECTIVE THINKING MODEL

The most durable and widely accepted prescription for improving decision-making effectiveness is the reflective thinking model developed by John Dewey in the early 1920s.[5] Though Dewey intended the model to apply to the mental processes of an individual, it has been widely applied to groups. Dewey's model contains the following six steps:

1. *A difficulty is felt and expressed.* The important requirement in this first step is that the group as a whole agrees that there is a problem. If only one or two members sense a problem, or if uneasiness is vaguely felt but not discussed, problem solving may not move beyond this point. Obvious problems, such as, "We're out of money," move easily through this phase. Greater sensitivity is required for problems that are easier to ignore, like an individual who is reluctant to speak up in the group or a member who feels the group is ineffective when everyone else thinks it is doing well.

2. *The problem is located and defined.* The more specifically the problem can be defined and its scope delimited, the more likely that decision quality will be high. Care must be taken not to mistake a symptom for the problem. Falling sales may be due to a poorly designed product and not to inadequate sales efforts. Causes also need to be kept separate from the problem. If the ball team is losing, *that* is the problem. Prematurely concluding that the manager is the problem can lead to only one possible solution and may keep other more important causes from being seen.

3. *The nature of the problem is analyzed.* In this stage, the factors producing and sustaining the problem are identified. When the causes and interrelationships between causes are seen, the group will begin to see where the leverage points for solution may be and to sense how much effect it can realistically expect to have on them. Groups often omit this phase and instead recommend solutions they do not have the power to implement. Careful work at this phase sometimes leads to directing the problem to another group that has better potential for solving it or redefining the problem in more manageable terms.

4. *Generating alternatives.* Once a problem is understood, there is a tendency to jump quickly to a logical solution, screening out other possible alternatives. This tendency of groups and individuals to seek quick and obvious solutions is a primary reason why the decision-making process so often breaks down. Depending on the circumstances, this phase may consist of the group carefully building the details of a solution to fit clear predetermined criteria, or it may involve a freewheeling creative effort aimed at generating as many solutions as possible (see the section on brainstorming later in this chapter). In either case, it is important that members explore openly during this phase, avoiding advocacy positions until all possibilities have been put out onto the table.

5. *Selecting a solution.* In this stage proposed solutions are analyzed according to criteria the group has developed during its earlier discussions. Each potential solution is carefully weighed in terms of its limitations as well as its strengths. They key in this phase is to iden-

tify as thoroughly as possible all the important consequences of each choice. Many groups, anxious to move on, fail to explore unanticipated consequences, focusing only on the benefits to be gained.

6. *Implementation.* Anyone who has spent even a small amount of time on committees has probably had the experience of seeing the group develop a useful solution and then watch helplessly as this good idea, so carefully designed and agreed upon, is never implemented. This is sometimes because of failure to involve at an earlier stage those who have the power to kill the idea or those who will be affected by the decision. Equally important is the failure to build in accountability so that certain individuals feel responsible for putting the action into effect and answerable to the rest of the group. Implementation should include a mechanism for evaluating the success of the solution and the means for making adjustments when results are analyzed, thus keeping the whole process flexible and open to new approaches when needed.

The reflective thinking model is useful for pointing out many important strengths and weaknesses in a decision-making group. For example, comparison of the new product group meeting with the model reveals weakness in the initial stage. The group did not agree, as a group, that there were problems. The manufacturing managers felt quality control had been adequately provided for, and the accountants said the same about cost estimates. On the quality control issue, the PM thoroughly departed from the model, giving in to the manufacturing managers without any analysis or exploration of alternatives. On the cost issue, the problem was argued on the basis of expediency, with no examination of facts bearing on the new product's costs, and no solution was selected.

Though the reflective thinking model is a helpful diagnostic tool, it cannot be directly applied as a technique. Studies have shown that, used as a method, reflective thinking produces decisions that are no better, and sometimes worse, than those produced by other methods.[6] This can be understood if one realizes there are important factors the model fails to consider.

Most significantly, the model assumes people can be totally rational and gives no attention to socioemotional dimensions of group behavior and their interdependence with task dimensions. Since every group is uniquely different in its task and human composition, a single prescription cannot be applied indiscriminately from group to group. Accordingly, the next section of this chapter examines a number of factors involved in group decision quality that go beyond the pure logic of the reflective thinking model.

FACTORS AFFECTING GROUP DECISION QUALITY

Norman Maier has summarized the potential assets and liabilities of groups compared with individuals in decision making.[7] Among the assets he mentions the greater sum total of knowledge and larger number of approaches to a problem available in a group and the likelihood that group members, having themselves participated in making the decision, will understand it thoroughly and support it strongly.

Factors that can act as liabilities include social pressure (making for conformity and silencing disagreement), the tendency for the first strongly argued solution to be adopted, and the fact that when conflict develops in a group, winning the argument often becomes more important to members than finding the best solution. In addition, it is not uncommon for one member to dominate the decision process, rendering the group no more capable than one individual.

Finally, Maier lists certain factors that can become either assets or liabilities depending on how they are handled by the discussion leader. One of these factors is the propensity for disagreements and conflicting interests in groups. Another is the issue of which persons change their mind in the group. If persons with good solutions change, the decision may hurt more than if those who had less valid solutions do.

Obviously, a group will be more likely to be effective if it can maximize the assets and eliminate or minimize the liabilities. The subsections that follow examine several of the variables that are most important in determining whether or not, in a given group, the assets will outweigh the liabilities.

Group Size and Composition

The size of the group can be an important determinant of decision quality.[8] Some writers have argued for small size, saying that the optimum is just five or six members. Studies have shown that, in general, this size is preferred by experienced executives, yields greater satisfaction on the part of group members themselves, and leads to more effective operation than larger groups. As group size increases beyond this point, communication becomes more difficult. There tends to be less participation, and people feel less involved and less potent. In some large groups, this leads to polite superficiality, while in others members seek recognition by joining subgroups supporting certain issues. Issues may then become overvalued and polarized, relationships more complex than in a smaller group, and member needs more difficult for the group to satisfy.

On the other hand, there are advantages in larger groups. Adding more people adds to the available resources of the group, increasing the likelihood that problems requiring a wide range of knowledge can be solved. A larger group is also a larger sample of the total population (e.g., department, organization, or community) from which it is drawn. Thus, its members would be more likely to give a valid representation of that larger population and to make decisions acceptable to it. Overall, the relationship between group size and decision quality is a complicated one, depending on the total mix of factors present in a particular situation.[9]

In addition to raw size, the kind of membership composition a group contains is quite important. Two aspects of composition that are related to decision-making effectiveness are heterogeneity and compatibility.

Numerous studies have shown productivity to be higher in heterogeneous groups than in homogeneous groups. In one of the best known cases, Richard Hoffman and Norman Maier experimented with four-person problem-solving groups.[10] The group members had been given a standard personality test. Homogeneous groups were formed with members who had high positive profile correlations on their personality tests. Heterogeneous groups were made up of persons who had negative or zero correlations between their profiles. Heterogeneous groups produced more high-quality solutions and contained more members who reported that they had influenced their group's decision. The researchers suggest the heterogeneous groups performed better because their members brought more perspectives to bear on the problem.

Compatibility refers to the extent to which the needs or behavior patters of various group members mesh well with one another. William Schutz, for example, whose FIRO scheme was discussed in chapter 7, postulated that a group would function more effectively when the kinds of interpersonal behaviors *wanted* by certain members were *expressed* by others. For instance, a group having certain members with strong urges to exert control would be compatible if there were others in the group who wanted to be controlled. Schutz's studies showed compatible groups to be more productive in a wide variety of tasks, including decision making.[11]

Another study, conducted by Marvin Shaw, produced somewhat similar outcomes with the added result that the correlation between compatibility and productivity was highest in groups whose leaders were compatible both with their followers and with the communication structure in which they were placed (e.g., where highly controlling individuals had submissive followers and also were in the central position in structures, such as the wheel network discussed in chapter 8.)[12] Shaw's study, showing that member characteristics need to be considered along with communication structure and roles, serves as a useful reminder that group characteristics need to be considered in interaction with one another, not in isolation.

Interaction Process

The kinds of communication occuring in a group can be classified in numerous ways. The best known of all is Robert Bales's Interaction Process Analysis (IPA) scheme, illustrated in exhibit 9–1. Using IPA, an observer of a group can classify any communicative act into one of the twelve categories. Only manifest, observable behavior is classified. No attempt is made to guess the speaker's underlying feelings. Exhibit 9–1 fits the twelve categories into four major headings: questions, answers, and positive and negative social-emotional reactions.

EXHIBIT 9–1
BALES'S CATEGORIES OF BEHAVIOR IN GROUPS: INTERACTION PROCESS ANALYSIS

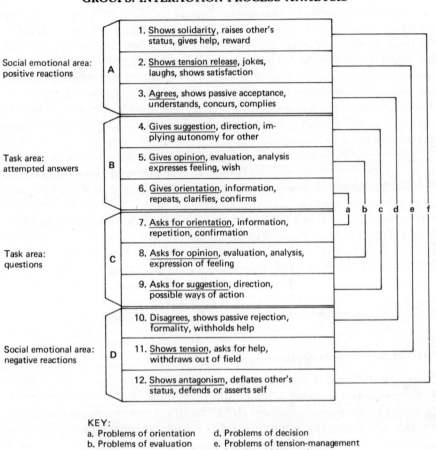

KEY:
a. Problems of orientation
b. Problems of evaluation
c. Problems of control
d. Problems of decision
e. Problems of tension-management
f. Problems of integration

Reprinted from *Interaction Process Analysis* by Robert F. Bales by permission of The University of Chicago Press. Copyright © 1950 by The University of Chicago.

Bales's research has shown that, on the average, fifty percent of all statements made in meetings are answers, while the other fifty percent consist of questions and reactions.[13] He suggests that something close to this fifty-fifty balance may be needed for successful problem solving. Answers—suggestions, opinions, information—are obviously needed to reach a decision, but if enough time is not allowed for questions and reactions, members may build up tensions that may reduce the level of effort they put into reaching the decision or implementing it once it has been made.

More generally, any of the twelve categories may be overelaborated or underrepresented in a given meeting, giving the group a behavioral profile that is out of balance. In the new product meeting, for example, there were virtually no positive social-emotional reactions. Even the PM's agreement on the matter of quality control was uttered grudgingly ("OK, OK, so I trust you."). This indicated a level of tension in the meeting, which made it unlikely that issues would be discussed fully. In most meetings, according to Bales, there are about twice as many positive reactions as there are negative.[14] Another imbalance may be related to the meeting's defensive tone: the large number of opinions and the meager factual content of the responses given to the PM's questions about quality and cost. On the quality issue, the manufacturing managers simply said, "Trust us." On costs, the accountants said their standard forms and sheets had been used but did not specify why the cost figures on those sheets should be taken to be valid.

The appropriate balance for a particular group depends on its circumstances. One important circumstance is the stage of development the group is in. Research using Bales's scheme has shown that exchanges of information are normal in the early life of a group, followed by a period during which conflicting opinions and feelings arise and need to be resolved. Then control-oriented interactions begin to predominate as members begin to suggest directions and come into line behind a group decision.[15] These phases are closely parallel to Tuckman's forming, storming, and norming stages discussed in chapter 8. As indicated there, performance quality often suffers when a group does not allow itself to pass through the normal sequence of developmental phases.

Decision-making Mechanisms

The way a decision is made by a group can strongly influence the quality of the decision, the speed with which it is made, and the willingness of the group's members to support it. Of the many mechanisms groups use to reach decisions, the following are the basic alternatives:[16]

1. *Decision by a single individual.* A decision may be completely determined by one individual within the group who may be a formal leader, an emergent informal leader, an expert, or an advisor. This method is appropriate when there is only one person in the group with the competence to contribute to the decision or, in an emergency, when there is no time for discussion. It is less desirable, however, in cases where the single decision maker goes unquestioned due to organizational power, personal charisma, or any factors that make other members unwilling to contribute according to their capabilities.
2. *Decision by a minority.* Often two or three people make the decisions for a group in which they are a small minority. They may carry along other members who believe the minority actually represents a majority since other members have remained silent. In one experiment, minorities of only about ten percent tended to believe that more than half the group agreed with them.[17] Obviously, this method may not

produce high-quality decisions unless the minority are the only ones in the group competent to contribute. It can also lead to a lack of support for the decision by those who did not participate.

3. *Decision by majority.* As a result of democratic ideology, a majority vote is probably the most popular group decision mechanism. Where discussion has involved broad participation and thorough examination of issues and facts, the results may be favorable. A danger is that after the vote, the losers may become embittered and the winners convinced that they are always right about everything.

4. *Decision by consensus.* Consensus means full participation by all group members until all members have become committed to a decision. It does not mean all agree with the decision, but that all accept it and will carry out their part.[18] Consensus can be obtained only when members freely express their opinions and keep working together to reach a decision that meets the approval of the group as a whole. Conflict-reducing techniques, such as voting and compromising, are avoided in order that the decision may be based on facts and full discussion. The consensus method tneds to bring the full resources of every member into play. Members are required to state their reasoning, not just to express agreement or disagreement.

As has already been indicated, the appropriateness of a given decision-making mechanism depends on the situation. The nature of the task is obviously an important situational factor. An early experiment reported by Robert Thorndike produced an intriguing result when it was found that groups were better than individual decision makers in *solving* a crossword puzzle, but that individuals did better than groups in *constructing* a crossword puzzle.[19] Solving a puzzle requires production of alternative responses that can be immediately tested for fit, with incorrect ones discarded and correct ones accumulated toward a complete solution. In constructing a puzzle, on the other hand, clear-cut, simple criteria of success are not available, and responses cannot simply accumulate. Instead, the task requires that more things be kept simultaneously in mind and worked into an integrated whole. In the construction task, the best product a group could produce was that of its best individual member.

A commentary by Terence Mitchell suggests that a group faced with an uncertain, unpredictable changing situation should employ the consensus method, while routine, predictable problems should be solved by individual specialists and by independent efforts with the group leader performing a coordinating role. Mitchell recommends voting methods when necessary to insure fairness in situations where conflicting organizational interests or responsibilities are involved.[20]

While there has not been much research on the effectiveness of alternative decision-making mechanisms, it is clear that group leaders and members should not just choose their method on grounds of ideology or habit. However much we may believe in majority rule, it is often a clear route to low-quality decisions. In many circumstances a sound decision cannot be made unless it is made by those who have the required technical competence. Likewise, while the consensus technique has gained favor in recent years, it should not be used uncritically. Although the task might be one seemingly well-suited to this method, it is unlikely to work effectively in a group whose members do not trust each other.[21] Ultimately, the choice must rest on managerial judgment aided by an awareness of the key factors involved in group performance.

Brainstorming

A specialized technique for facilitating the idea-generating portion of the decision process was first described by Alexander Osborn, an advertising executive.[22] Brainstorming, true to its origin, usually suggests a picture of a group of advertising specialists meeting to think up names or slogans for a new product. According to Osborn, a group can produce a maximum number of ideas by adhering to three rules: (1) ideas are expressed freely without regard to quality; (2) criticism of the ideas produced is not allowed until all ideas have been expressed; (3) elaborations and combinations of previously expressed ideas are encouraged. The suggestions are recorded by a secretary or tape recorder while the group members simply generate them as rapidly as possible. The theory is that creativity will build as one idea triggers another.

It has been shown experimentally that brainstorming does increase the production of new ideas.[23] However, in nine out of twelve studies comparing brainstorming groups with individuals working independently under brainstorming instructions, the individuals produced more ideas.[24] The reasons for this may be that individuals in a group are distracted by having to spend so much time listening to others' ideas and that some groups may develop "one track thinking."[25]

It appears that one reason for the lower productivity of groups compared with individuals in brainstorming researches has been the imposition of a time limit. Groups that are allowed to produce for longer work periods typically produce more ideas under brainstorming instructions than individuals. Most group continue to produce indefinitely, while individuals tend to taper off.[26]

Brainstorming might well be worth a try for a decision-making group despite its possible efficiency limitations. The experience tends to increase original thought on the part of low participators and those who usually do not express new ideas. It also teaches the need to listen to and tolerate the ideas of others. Thus, it is a technique that can help develop a group's capacity for effective communication.

NGT and Delphi Techniques

Two other well-known techniques are available for use by groups when creative, independent, equally treated ideas or judgments are needed.[27]

The nominal group technique (NGT) is designed for group meetings and involves a four-step procedure. Members silently and independently write their ideas about a problem. Each individual then reads one idea to the group, and the ideas are listed on a flip chart. After all the individual lists are exhausted, the ideas are discussed for clarification and evaluation. The meeting concludes with a silent secret vote on the ideas presented. NGT is aimed at reducing the adverse effects on decision quality of such factors as group pressures toward conformity and the tendency to reach decisions before all important aspects of the problem have been considered.

One writer, Richard Huseman, suggests that NGT may be used productively *prior to* a regular open meeting of a group because the technique is most useful for identifying problems and setting an agenda for group discussion. Huseman proposes that NGT is ideal for generating problem dimensions and alternative solutions, while the interacting group is most useful for synthesizing information, making evaluations, reaching a group consensus, and discussing the implementation of a final decision.[28]

The delphi technique is similar to NGT, but the group members are not physically present. Instead, a questionnaire is designed to collect opinions and ideas about a problem. The questionnaire is sent to a group of persons who may or may not be anonymous to one another. Responses are tabulated, summarized, and returned to the respondents. Delphi and NGT are quite similar, but Delphi might be preferred when it is difficult to assemble the group members or when the problem is so sensitive that anonymity is desired.

The NGT or delphi technique might well have proved useful to the product manager in the case about the new product meeting. The central underlying issue of interdepartmental differences in goals might have surfaced more clearly through use of one of these methods. The specifics of manufacturing's quality control procedures and the thinking behind accounting's numbers on the sheets might have had a better chance to develop, as would a set of alternative solutions to both the quality and cost problems.

Risk Taking

The notion that groups may be more willing than individuals to take risks has been a matter of some controversy. Some have argued that groups, especially management groups, foster a gray flanneled conservatism in their decision making. Nevertheless, laboratory studies conducted during the 1960s showed quite the opposite effect: decisions made by discussion groups tended to be riskier than individual decisions.[29] This phenomenon became known as the "risky shift." It was explained that the risk takers in a group tend to be the most persuasive speakers, and that individuals feel less need to be cautious in a group because the decision is the group's responsibility, not their own.

Later studies have shown that groups do not always produce a shift toward more risky decisions.[30] Instead, they tend to reinforce the prevailing attitudes within the group. If individual attitudes are initially on the conservative side of a neutral point, discussion usually moves the group toward more pronounced conservatism. On the other hand, if the dominant attitude at the outset is in favor of risk taking, discussion tends to produce a risky shift.

Caution should be exercised in interpreting laboratory research conducted mainly with college students as subjects, especially where the subject is risk. Student groups, temporarily together, are very different from groups of executives, medical doctors, or legislators who expect to work together in the future and have established status relationships and reference groups that influence their deliberation.[31]

LEADERSHIP IN GROUPS

Virtually everyone agrees that the content and quality of a group's work is dependent in large measure on the kind of leadership exerted in the group. We commonly feel that a certain city council, presidential committee, or student governing board is doing a good job because it has strong leadership, or a poor one because it doesn't. An annual example of this mode of thinking is the vote of the sportswriters that typically names as Manager of the Year the manager of the pennant-winning ball team. In a similar vein, we might feel that in the example of the new product meeting, the meeting went well during its early stages due to the PM's strong leadership (for example, his convincing use of precise facts, figures, and plans) and became less effective when his leadership faltered during the discussions of quality control and costs.

This line of thinking contains two assumptions. One is that leadership is vested in a person—usually a single person—within the group. The second is that certain styles of behavior constitute good leadership. Each of these assumptions has some validity and has prompted a large amount of research on the personal traits of leaders and on leadership style. Both assumptions also have important limitations, however.

Trait and Style Approaches

The trait approach aims at isolating the characteristics that distinguish successful leaders. One major study, for example, surveyed managers in ninety different companies and revealed several characteristics that were related both to organizational level and to performance effectiveness ratings made by superiors. Those traits included supervisory ability, initiative, achievement motivation, self-actualizing motivation, self-assurance, and decisiveness.[32] Thus far, however, researchers have not succeeded in identifying individual traits that relate strongly and consistently to success in a variety of organizations or situations. The trait approach also ignores the influence of the wants and needs of a particular group of followers. Finally, the trait studies do not consider whether one type of task may require a different kind of leadership than another.

The style approach focuses on how the leader behaves in carrying out the activities of being a leader. Unlike the trait approach, which attempts to understand leadership on the basis of what the leader *is,* the style approach tries to understand leadership on the basis of what the leader *does.*

Two styles, authoritarian and democratic, have been compared in numerous studies. As exhibit 9-2 indicates, the authoritarian leader exercises a high degree of power over the group and makes decisions unilaterally, while the democratic leader delegates power to group members, allowing them latitude in making their own decisions.

EXHIBIT 9–2
**THE CONTINUUM OF LEADERSHIP BEHAVIOR:
AUTHORITARIAN AND DEMOCRATIC STYLES
COMPARED**

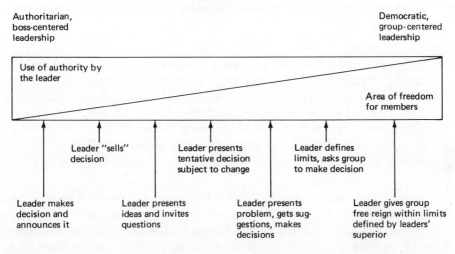

Reprinted by permission of the Harvard Business Review. Exhibit 1 from "How to Choose a Leadership Pattern" by Robert Tannenbaum and Warren H. Schmidt (May-June 1973). Copyright © 1973 by the President and Fellows of Harvard College. All rights reserved.

The results of research on leadership style have been inconclusive. Neither productivity nor group member satisfaction has been consistently associated with either authoritarian or democratic style by the leader.[33] As with the studies based on the trait approach, the style researches have revealed that there is not a single style that is best in all situations, with all kinds of group members, for every type of task, or in every organization. Therefore, the trait and style approaches to understanding leadership have given way to two more recent approaches, contingency theory and path-goal theory. Both are aimed at identifying circumstances in which different leadership styles are most effective.

Contingency and Path-Goal Approaches

Contingency theory derives its name from the concept that the success of a given leadership style is contingent upon the nature of the circumstances in which it is used. To date, the best known contingency model is one produced by Fred Fiedler based on data collected from a wide variety of groups, including military tactical problem-solving teams and executive boards of small businesses.[34] Objective measures of group effectiveness were available for all groups studied: training exercise scores for the military groups and company profitability compared to competing firms for the business groups. Fiedler found that directive, controlling leaders tended to be more effective in situations that were either highly favorable or highly unfavorable. Leaders who were less controlling and more group-centered were typically more effective in situations that were of a mixed nature—partly favorable and partly unfavorable.

In Fiedler's studies, the favorableness of the situation was defined by three factors:

1. *Task structure*—the more clearly defined and routine the task (a highly "structured" task), the more favorable the situation.
2. *The quality of leader-member relations*—the more the members like and trust the leader, the move favorable the situation.
3. *The leader's position power*—the more the leader has the power to hire, fire, promote, demote, reward, or punish, the more favorable the situation.

Exhibit 9-3 summarizes Fiedler's findings. As depicted in this exhibit, Fiedler's results indicate that where the circumstances are either very favorable or very unfavorable to the leader—that is, where leader-member relations, task structure, and leader position power are either very high or very low—a more controlling leadership style tends to be more successful. On the other hand, in the midrange, where the circumstances are more mixed, a more considerate, less controlling style seems appropriate. Fiedler explains that in very favorable circumstances the group is ready to be told what to do and welcomes the leader's direction, and that in extremely unfavorable circumstances the group will fall apart without the leader's active intervention. In mixed circumstances, however, the leader must provide a less threatening, less directive atmosphere if members are to feel free to make inputs and contribute to discussions.[35]

Fiedler's model makes a certain amount of intuitive sense, although the thoery does not prove true for every leader in every case. A leader's circumstances are not fully described by just three facts. Also, there are other important aspects of a leader's behavior in addition to degree of

EXHIBIT 9–3
GROUP EFFECTIVENESS AND LEADERSHIP STYLE, BASED ON FIEDLER'S RESEARCH

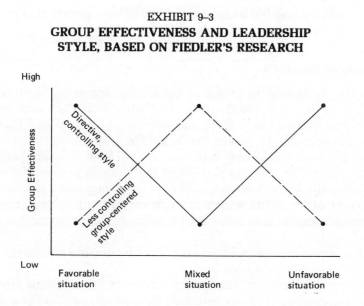

directiveness. Nevertheless, the contingency approach makes a major advance over other attempts to understand effective leadership without reference to the surroundings in which it is occuring.

Path-goal theory, proposed by Robert House, Charles Greene, and others, also takes a contingency approach.[36] House's notion is that successful leaders increase their followers' rewards for work goal attainment and make the path to such rewards easier to travel by clarifying it, reducing obstacles, and increasing opportunities for personal satisfaction along the way. Greene adds that the rewards offered must be of the kinds and amounts valued by the followers and must be linked to the followers' individual performances. House and Greene thus contribute an important "contingency,"—namely, that the success of a given leadership style depends in part upon the followers. To be effective, either a directive or a less controlling leadership style has to be seen by group members as an aid to their getting what they want.

In the case of the new product meeting, contingency theory and path-goal theory both help show why the PM did not attain his objectives. In path-goal terms, the manufacturing and accounting managers valued the clear, routine procedures to which they were accustomed. The PM therefore met resistance from theothers when he asked their help in developing new approaches. He did not show them how the new approaches he desired would be valuable to them. In terms of the Fiedler model, the PM was in unfavorable circumstances. He was not trusted by those present (as the manufacturing representatives state explicitly); he had no formal power over the group members, all of whom come from departments other than his own; and he was unsure how the tasks (quality control and pricing) should be accomplished. Fiedler would observe that in such circumstances, the PM should not have depended so heavily on inputs from the group but instead should have been prepared to get tough. Adaptability is a valuable characteristic in a leader.[37]

Leadership as Functions

One feature is shared in common by all the foregoing approaches to leadership, trait, style, contingency, and path-goal. Each assumes that leadership is centered in a particular person who occupies a leadership position in the group. However, this is not the way leadership takes place in actual practice. Leadership functions are performed in all groups, but by no means are they always performed by the same person. Viewed this way, leadership can be seen as a quality of the group or, as one writer has put it, "a set of functions which must be carried out by the group."[38]

Research on the role behavior of individuals in groups has shown that leadership is not always vested in a single person. More often than not, in fact, one member emerges as the task leader and a different person becomes the social-emotional leader.[39]

This specialization of leadership functions, observed in laboratory studies, was confirmed in a penetrating field study conducted by Richard Hodgson, Daniel Levinson, and Abraham Zaleznik.[40] The researchers observed first hand and at length the work activities of the three top administrators of a prestigious mental hospital—the superintendent, who spent a large share of his time on external contacts aimed at fund raising, the clinical director, and the research director. These three executives' behavior revealed a "division of labor" not just in terms of job specializations but also in terms of their performances as leaders. The superintendent was aggressive and demanding, insisting that things happen fast and that all personnel meet the highest standards of performance. The other two executives employed more permissive styles. They served as buffers between other staff members and the superintendent, helping their subordinates to recover and maintain their social and emotional stability in the face of the superintendent's aggressive style. Thus, the hospital had a "system" of leadership wherein the superintendent's style triggered the performances of the other two executives and was also sustained by them.

The functions approach may also be applied to the case of the new product meeting. Using this perspective reveals that the meeting was led not just by the PM but also by the manufacturing and accounting managers present who blocked his efforts. They determined the outcome of the meeting by arguing against his aggressive efforts to deviate from their departments' standard procedures. The accountants may have been more effective. By directing the PM's attention to the cost sheets, they blocked any decision from being made unless or until the PM could marshal a factual response to their argument. It may be less clear whether the manufacturing managers' eliciting of blind trust from the PM bodes as well for the success of the new product, but it is clear that from the function point of view it was leadership.

There is not yet an authoritative list of the various kinds of behavior that may serve leadership functions in a group. One useful list resulting from a synthesis of previous efforts is the following: initiating, socializing, protecting the group from outside threat, agenda setting, structuring the group's work, resolving conflict, managing information with the group, influencing participation within the group, rewarding and punishing, and productively working on the task.[41] As this list indicates, the functions approach widens our attention beyond persons to processes. The issue becomes not just "Who is the leader?" but "What leadership functions are being performed in this group?"

GROUP EFFECTIVENESS CRITERIA

Having considered in this chapter and chapter 8 several factors affecting the performance of small groups, it is appropriate to summarize some of the principal aims and characteristics of effective group communication. Accordingly, listed below are seven criteria for an effective task group. The list is not intended to be complete. It does, however, embody many of the points about group effectiveness previously stressed and also encompasses the principal items included on similar lists made by several respected authors.[42]

1. *Active verbal participation.* Communication is open and full. Divergent ideas are given a hearing. Disagreements are not suppressed or smoothed over until examined. Members do not withhold relevant information.
2. *Goal clarity.* Members understand and accept goals. Generalized objectives become increasingly specific and are reformulated when no longer relevant.
3. *Optimum use of available resources.* All members function in some way. Clear role differentiation allows the various leadership and membership functions to come into play when needed. Leadership is not exercised by just one person but moves around the group.
4. *Supportive relationships* are established. Members have a commitment to the group and to each other and have confidence and trust in each other.
5. *Reality orientation.* The group can assimilate, respond to, and learn from new information. Simplistic explanations and pat solutions are avoided. The group deals with the present real situation as it is, not in terms of stereotypes or clichés.
6. *Consciousness of own operations.* The group has self-knowledge; it knows why it does what it does. Members and leaders recognize and are patient with the group's developmental needs (e.g., group slowness during the "forming" phase). The group has the ability and willingness to criticize itself. Members do not look at the group through rose-colored glasses.

7. *Flexibility.* The group is able to adapt its structure, norms, and decision mechanism to meet changing circumstances.

Summary

This chapter began by noting that groups have a potential for high levels of decision-making competence, but that this potential is not always realized. John Dewey's reflective thinking model was presented as a useful tool for comparing a group with its potential with respect to how well it uses information and logic to reach decisions. Then a number of other factors relating to group decision quality were considered. These included group size and composition, interaction process (including Bales's concept of balance), alternative decision-making mechanisms and the circumstances in which they are useful, and the risk-taking tendencies of groups. Finally, the topic of leadership was addressed with major emphasis on two points: (1) that the success or failure of a particular leadership style cannot be explained without an understanding of the circumstances in which it is used; and (2) that leadership can usefully be thought of as a set of functions, not all of which are necessarily performed by a single individual within a group.

Questions for Review

1. Think of a group decision (e.g., among roommates, coworkers, classmates, family) in which you have been involved. What decision-making mechanisms were used? How did the performance of this group compare with the seven criteria listed at the end of this chapter?
2. Why do you suppose John Dewey's reflective thinking model has proved more useful as a tool for diagnosing a group's strengths and weaknesses than as an operational method for group decision making?
3. "The highest quality group decisions are those made by the consensus method." Do you agree or disagree with this statement? Why?
4. What are the assets and liabilities of a group as a decision-making entity? What factors might act as either assets or liabilities, depending on the circumstances?
5. Think of a small group with which you are familiar. Describe the approximate frequency of different types of behavior in this group using Bales's Interaction Process Analysis categories. What does the group's IPA "profile" help explain in terms of group effectiveness and member satisfaction?
6. Discuss the "risky shift" phenomenon. Why does it occur and why does it sometimes *not* occur?

7. Think of a leader you have observed (e.g., a supervisor or teacher). What leadership style did this person employ? To what degree was this individual an effective leader, and why?

References and Notes

1. M. Kreisberg, "Executives Evaluate Administrative Conferences," *Advanced Management* 15 (1950): 15–17; Gerald M. Goldhaber, *Organizational Communication* (Dubuque, Ia.: W. C. Brown, 1974), p. 214.
2. J. Allen Ofner, "Are Committees Worthwhile?" *Commerce Magazine* 56, no. 2 (March 1959): 64–65; Goldhaber, *Organizational Communication,* p. 214.
3. Barry E. Collins and Harold Guetzkow, *A Social Psychology of Group Processes for Decision Making* (New York: John Wiley & Sons, 1964), pp. 45–47; Dale G. Leathers, "Quality of Group Communication as a Determinant of Group Product," *Speech Monographs* 39 (1972): 166–73.
4. Jay Hall, "Decisions, Decisions, Decisions," *Psychology Today* 5, no. 6 (November 1971): 86–88.
5. John Dewey, *How We Think* (New York: D. C. Heath, 1910).
6. Ovid L. Bayless, "An Alternate Pattern for Problem-Solving Discussion," *Journal of Communication* 17 (1967): 188–97; Carl E. Larson, "Forms of Analysis and Small Group Problem-Solving," *Speech Monographs* 36 (1969): 452-55; Sandra W. Pyke and Cathie A. Neely, "Evaluation of a Group Training Program," *Journal of Communication* 20 (1970): 291–304.
7. Norman R. F. Maier, "Assets and Liabilities in Group Problem Solving," *Psychological Review* 74 (1967): 239–49.
8. Rollie Tillman, Jr., "Committees on Trial," *Harvard Business Review* 38 (1960): 7–12, 162–72; Philip E. Slater, "Contrasting Correlates of Group Size," *Sociometry* 21 (1958): 129–39; A. Paul Hare, "A Study of Interaction and Consensus in Different Sized Groups," *American Sociological Review* 17 (1952): 261–67.
9. For a thorough discussion of the group size issue, see E. J. Thomas and C. F. Fink, "Effects of Group Size," *Psychological Bulletin* 60 (1963): 371–84. For an interesting example of decision making in a very large group (10,000 members), see Amatei; Etzioni, Kenneth Laudon, and Susan Lipson, "Participatory Technology: The MINERVA Communication Tree," *Journal of Communication* 25, no. 2 (1975): 64–74.
10. L. Richard Hoffman and Norman R. F. Maier, "Quality and Acceptance of Problem Solutions by Members of Homogeneous and Heterogeneous Groups," *Journal of Abnormal and Social Psychology* 62 (1961): 401–07.
11. William C. Schutz, *The Interpersonal Underworld* (Palo Alto, Calif.: Science and Behavior Books, 1966), pp. 133–36.
12. Marvin E. Shaw, "Some Effects of Individually Prominent Behavior upon Group Effectiveness and Member Satisfaction," *Journal of Abnormal and Social Psychology* 59 (1959): 382–86.
13. Robert F. Bales, "In Conference," *Harvard Business Review* 32 (1954): 44–50. For more detail, see Robert F. Bales, "The Equilibrium Problem in Small Groups," in *Small Groups,* ed. A. Paul Hare, Edgar F. Bargatta, and Robert F. Bales (New York: Alfred A. Knopf, 1955), pp. 424–56.

14. Ibid.
15. Robert F. Bales and Fred L. Strodtbeck, "Phases in Group Problem Solving," *Journal of Abnormal and Social Psychology* 46 (1951): 485–95.
16. The list of four decision-making mechanisms that follows is adapted from Bernard M. Bass, *Organizational Psychology* (Allyn and Bacon, 1965) pp. 213–21.
17. Phil Stone and Joe Kamiya, "Judgements of Consensus During Group Discussion," *Journal of Abnormal and Social Psychology* 55 (1957): pp. 171–75.
18. The concept of consensus as commitment is drawn from Abraham Zaleznik and David Moment, *The Dynamics of Interpersonal Behavior* (New York: John Wiley & Sons, 1964), p. 142.
19. Robert L. Thorndike, "On What Type of Task Will a Group Do Well?" *Journal of Abnormal and Social Psychology* 33 (1938): 409–13.
20. Terence R. Mitchell, *People in Organizations* (New York: McGraw-Hill, 1978), p. 274.
21. See Dale E. Zand, "Trust and Managerial Problem Solving," *Administrative Science Quarterly* 17 (1972): 229–39.
22. Alexander F. Osborn, *Applied Imagination* (New York: Scribner, 1957). See also Arthur M. Coon, "Brainstorming: A Creative Problem-Solving Technique," *Journal of Communication* 7 (1957): 111–18.
23. See, for example, A. Meadow, S. J. Parnes, and H. Reese, "Influence of Brainstorming Instructions and Problem Sequence on a Creative Problem Solving Test," *Journal of Applied Psychology* 43 (1959): 413–16.
24. Helmut Lamm and Gisela Trommsdorf, "Group Versus Individual Performance on Tasks Requiring Ideational Proficiency (Brainstorming): A Review," *European Journal of Social Psychology* 3 (1973): 361–88
25. Donald W. Taylor, Paul C. Berry, and Clifford H. Block, "Does Group Participation When Using Brainstorming Facilitate or Inhibit Creative Thinking?" *Administrative Science Quarterly* 3 (1958): 23–47.
26. Marvin E. Shaw, *Group Dynamics* (New York: McGraw-Hill, 1971), pp. 72–73.
27. For a detailed description of NGT and delphi, see Andre L. Delbecq, Andrew H. Van deVen, and David H. Gustafson, *Group Techniques for Program Planning* (Glenview, Ill.: Scott, Foresman, 1975).
28. Richard C. Huseman, "The Role of the Nominal Group in Small Group Communication," in Richard C. Huseman, Cal M. Logue, and Dwight L. Freshley, *Readings in Interpersonal and Organizational Communication*, 3rd ed. (Boston: Holbrook Press, 1977), pp. 493–502.
29. Donald G. Marquis, "Individual Responsibility and Group Decisions Involving Risk," *Industrial Management Review* 3 (1962): 8–23; Daryl J. Bem, Michael A. Wallach, and Nathan Kogan, "Group Decision Making under Risk of Aversive Consequences," *Journal of Personality and Social Psychology* 1 (1965): 453–60; Michael A. Wallach, Nathan Kogan, and Daryl J. Bem, "Diffusion of Responsibility and Level of Risk Taking in Groups," *Journal of Abnormal and Social Psychology* 68 (1964): 263–74.
30. Ebbe B. Ebbesen and Richard J. Bowers, "Proportion of Risky to Conservative Arguments in a Group Discussion and Choice Shift," *Journal of Personality and Social Psychology* 29 (1974): 316–27; Earl A. Cecil, Larry L. Cummings, and Jerome M. Chertkoff, "Group Composition and Choice Shift: Implications for Administration," *Academy of Management Journal* 16 (1973): 412–22; Amiram Vinokur and Eugene Burnstein, "Effects of Partially Shared Persuasive Arguments on Group Induced Shifts," *Journal of Personality and Social Psychology* 29 (1974): 305–15.

31. Ross A. Webber, *Management* (Homewood, Ill.: Richard D. Irwin, 1975), p. 531.

32. Edwin E. Ghisell, *Explorations in Managerial Talent* (Pacific Palisades, Calif.: Goodyear, 1971).

33. Many comprehensive summaries have been made of the researches on leadership style. See, for example, Gary Dessler, *Organization and Management* (Englewood Cliffs, N.J.: Prentice-Hall, 1976), 158–69; James L. Gibson, John M. Ivancevich, and James H. Donnelly, Jr., *Organizations* (Dallas: Business Publications Incorporated, 1979), pp. 191–201.

34. Fred E. Fiedler, *A Theory of Leadership Effectiveness* (New York: McGraw-Hill, 1967).

35. Ibid., p. 147.

36. Robert J. House, "A Path Goal Theory of Leader Effectiveness," *Administrative Science Quarterly* 16 (1971): 321–38; Charles N. Greene, "The Satisfaction-Performance Controversy," *Business Horizons* 15, no. 5 (1972): 31–41. See also John E. Stinson and Thomas W. Johnson, "The Path-Goal Theory of Leadership: A Partial Test and Suggested Refinement," *Academy of Management Journal* 18 (1975): 242–52; H. Kirk Downey, John E. Sheridan, and John W. Slocum, "Analysis of Relationships Among Leader Behavior, Subordinate Job Performance, and Satisfaction: A Path-Goal Approach," *Academy of Management Journal* 18 (1975): 253–62.

37. See Julia T. Wood, "Leading in Purposive Discussions: A Study of Adaptive Behavior," *Communication Monographs* 44 (1977): 152–65.

38. Cecil A. Gibb, "Leadership," in *Handbook of Social Psychology,* vol. 2 ed. Gardner Lindzey and Elliot Aronson (Cambridge, Mass.: Addison-Wesley, 1954), p. 884.

39. See, for example, Philip E. Slater, "Role Differentiation in Small Groups," in *Small Groups,* ed. Hare, Bargatta, and Bales, pp. 498–515; Robert F. Bales, "Task Roles and Social Roles in Problem-Solving Groups," in *Readings in Social Psychology,* ed. Eleanor E. Maccoby, Theodore M. Newcomb, and Eugene L. Hartley (New York: Holt, Rinehart and Winston, 1958), pp. 437–47.

40. Richard C. Hodgson, Daniel J. Levinson, and Abraham Zeleznik, *The Executive Role Constellation* (Boston: Division of Research, Harvard Business school, 1965).

41. This list is a paraphrase, with modifications, of one developed by Michael Burgoon, Judee K. Heston, and James McCroskey, *Small Group Communication: A Functional Approach* (New York: Holt, Rinehart and Winston, 1974), pp. 147–48.

42. Douglas R. Bunker and Gene W. Dalton, "The Comparative Effectiveness of Groups and Individuals in Solving Problems," in *Managing Group and Intergroup Relations,* ed. Jay W. Loroch and Paul R. Lawrence (Homewood, Ill.: Irwin-Dorsey, 1972), p. 208; B. Aubrey Fisher, *Small Group Decision Making* (New York: McGraw-Hill, 1974), pp. 182–93; Rensis Likert, *New Patterns in Management* (New York: McGraw-Hill, 1961), pp. 162–77, Rodney W. Napier and Matti K. Gershenfeld, *Groups: Theory and Experience* (Boston: Houghton Mifflin, 1973), pp. 217–18; Edgar H. Schein, *Process Consultation* (Reading, Mass.: Addison-Wesley, 1969), pp. 61–63; Clovis R. Shepherd, *Small Groups* (San Francisco: Chandler, 1964), pp. 122–25. John W. Lewis III also contributed to the development of this list.

A Group Meeting*

Setting: 12:30 A.M. in a small short order restaurant. The crew has just finished cleanup for the night and are sitting together having snacks before going home.

Characters: Ted—manager/cashier
                      Frank—short order cook
                      Millie—senior waitress
                      Alice—junior waitress
                      Bobby—dish washer

Millie: I'm bushed. Does anyone know why the rush hit us so late tonight?

Bobby: Yes, there was a dance at the high school. I saw a lot of the kids coming in who were there.

Ted: Is that why you spent so much time out front tonight, Bobby?

Bobby: I did get a bit behind, I guess, and I'm sorry we ran out of cups for a few minutes.
(Pause)

Frank: I had more double-deckers tonight than I've had in the last month. Were you girls pushing them or something?

Ted: Yes they were, because I asked them to . . . why?

Frank: They're a lot of fuss and slow me down. At one point I got ten orders behind. I suppose they do make us more profit.

Alice: Not if it costs us customers. I had two tables walk out because their order took so long.

Millie: That wasn't because the grill was slow. You were hanging over the table of that "friend" of yours half the night.

Alice: That's not true. I bet when Ted looks over the checks, he'll see I handled more orders than you did tonight.

Ted: Now girls, let's not get into that one this evening. Actually, Millie, Alice is coming along fine these days.

Millie: She should be. You've assigned her the best section this week.

Ted: Didn't we all agree a couple of weeks ago that the two of you would rotate out front?

---

*This case was written by John W. Lewis III.

Millie: I guess so. That was because I kept getting one creep in the last booth, but he doesn't come in anymore.

Ted: Hey, I noticed the handle is loose on the meat cooler. Does anybody ...

Bobby I banged into it with a case of ketchup before we opened tonight. I'll bring some tools and fix it tomorrow.

Ted: That's OK. I have the refrigeration man coming tomorrow, and he can take a look at it. Be more careful, though, when you're moving stuff in, Bob.

Frank: Bobby does have a problem there, Ted. It's narrow in that space, and when I did that job, I had trouble moving stock in.

Ted: When we remodel in a couple of months, the cooler will be moved, which should solve the problem.

Millie: That won't solve *all* of our problems with Bobby. I hate to say it, but we've never had a dishwasher that turned out so many dirty cups and dishes.

Bobby: Get off it, Millie. You've been on my back since the first day I started. If you'd scrape them better to begin with, I could wash them better.

Frank: I think you could solve part of the problem by using a little more detergent, and rinsing them a bit longer. I agree, though, that it goes better if they come to you scraped properly.

Alice: I think we all must be tired. We don't usually talk like this to one another.

Ted: I have some news that will warm things up, I think. We are having a good year and I have decided to give you each a ten percent raise beginning Monday.

Frank: Weeeeeo! Right on, Ted. You gals can take all the double-decker orders you want, I'll put them out faster than you can catch them.

Ted: Well, this is one of the best crews I've had, and you've all earned it.... I don't know about anybody else, but I'm getting tired. Does anybody need a ride home?

Case Questions

1. What would you say is the character of this group? Is it a healthy group?
2. Try classifying each of the statements made during the conversation using Bales's Interaction Process Analysis categories from chapter 9. How many statements fell into each category? In IPA terms, what was the tone of the meeting?
3. What problems, specific and general, does this group have that need further attention and follow-up?
4. What is your assessment of Ted's leadership style during this meeting? If you had been in his position, what, if anything, would you have done differently?

Ned Wicker*

Ned Wicker is the manager of the Systems Proposal Department in the Graubart Electronics Company. The department was organized a year earlier to improve efforts by the company to gain new electronics systems business. Its functions were:

1. To carefully review and evaluate all incoming bid specifications for new electronic systems required by aerospace and other users of such equipment.
2. Then decide which of these (if any) would be potentially profitable, and within both the technical and fabrication capabilities of Graubart Electronics, and finally
3. Prepare the necessary business proposals to win contracts from potential customers.[1]

A graduate electronic engineer, Ned had been a senior proposal analyst with another company when he was hired by the president of Graubart to set up the new department. The new job coincided with his completion of an MBA degree and it was his first managerial position. He personally recruited and hired a diversified group of seven highly qualified engineers as systems proposal analysts, most of whom had prior experience with customer requirements in the industry. The president of Graubart Electronics, Ned's boss, was enthusiastic about the new group, especially Ned's aggressive approach in getting things organized and underway.

Since the work of generating and submitting technical proposals for potential customers can be both costly and time consuming, Wicker felt the key to his department's success would be the careful preliminary screening and selection of bid possibilities on which proposals were to be prepared by the group. It was largely for this reason that he built such an elite group of professionals to work with him, and he developed a procedure for full participation by the entire group in the RFP (request for proposal) selection process.[2]

The procedure called for all RFPs to be distributed and given a preliminary evaluation by individual analysts, who then made informal written "bid/no bid" recommendations to Wicker on Friday each week. On Mondays, a full morning review meeting involving the entire group

---

*Huse/Bowditch, *Behavior in Organizations,* © 1978, Addison-Wesley Publishing Company, Inc., pages 44 and 45 adaptation of "Participative Decision Making." Reprinted with permission.

[1]In high technology industries such as electronic systems, skillful bidding is critical. If a company bids too high, it rarely gets the business, or if it bids too low ("buying" the contract) it may get bled by the job. Also, the kinds of work a company bids on and gets determines the shape of the company's future.

[2]When an organization has a need for a device, system, or service from outside, it makes this need known to potential suppliers along with specifications through the means of a "request for proposal," which is an invitation to bid for the contract work.

was to be held, at which time each analyst would present in detail those proposals he had reviewed the preceding week and lead the group in discussing them. After RFPs had been reviewed in this way, final selections for making proposals were to be reached by group censusus.

The RFP review and selection procedure seemed to work effectively for the first three or four months, and three proposals submitted by the department resulted in major new contracts for the company. Discussions in the Monday morning review meetings about various RFPs were lively and involved the whole group. Frequently the sessions ran over into the early afternoon. The variety of individual backgrounds, consciously selected by Ned, provided the group with a broad technical perspecive for approaching its task. On only two occasions, based on information he had bained from top management staff meetings, Ned found it necessary to overrule the group's decisions. This was not done high-handedly, however, and he was able to lead members to see the wisdom in his final decision.

At the Monday meeting following the announcement of the second contract won by the group, the president paid a surprise visit just before lunch with a bottle of champagne for Ned and the group to show his appreciation of their efforts to date.

While Ned was very pleased with the quality of decisions made by the group during the first several weeks, two things began to bother him. Although the number of proposals being reviewed remained about the same, each successive week the Monday morning meetings seemed to last longer and would soon consume the entire day, a luxury he felt the department couldn't afford. He also had a nagging feeling that, as the manager, he needed to be better prepared to discuss the merits of the RFPs in order to assist the group in reaching the soundest decisions.

Since he received the written recommendations on Fridays, he decided to familiarize himself with them over the weekend and to arrive at his own tentative conclusions and priorities for making bid/no bid decisions of each RFP. His purpose was to have answers ready which might speed up group discussion on Mondays, but to do so in a way which did not directly influence members of the group as to his tentative conclusions.

Except for the fact he had less time for golf and weekend household chores, this additional effort on Ned's part appeared to bear results. And although the group's batting average with successful proposals declined in the second quarter, he felt better prepared on Monday morning, and the meetings began to shorten with discussions more to the point. This had the dual advantage of enabling the group to handle a larger number of proposals in the meetings and also freed up valuable time for the analysts to do the on-going work of the department.

A disquieting thing began to develop, however. Gradually, discussions in the group became more formal and at times, recently, became a dialogue between Ned and to analyst who had done the preliminary evaluation. The final blow came this morning, when the meeting lasted merely forty-five minutes, with Ned doing most of the talking. Since he considered this review meeting to be the heart of the RFP selection process, Ned became alarmed. While he still had complete confidence in the men and women he had selected, he felt more and more that in the review meetings they were holding back their ideas and technical judgment, both of which he knew were crucial to arriving at the soundest bid/no bid decisions.

As he mulled over the situation on his way to lunch, one of the analysts in the group who had received the second highest performance rating stopped Ned to say he was leaving to take a position elsewhere.

Case Questions

1. Why isn't Wicker getting the full participation he desires in the Monday morning meetings?
2. How does Wicker's leadership style fit the requirements of the situation he is in?
3. What decision-making mechanisms have been used by the proposal analysis group, and with what degrees of success?
4. What can Wicker do to improve the performance and morale of his group?

The United Assemblers*

John Ferguson, supervisor of the Mechanical Assembly Department of Supra Tech Corporation, found his department's rapid expansion was causing management problems. He thought over the events of the past year, his first with the company. What stood out the most was the amazing growth. In one year direct labor employees in the department had increased from fifteen to twenty-one, up forty percent. Along with the burgeoning ranks, for better or worse, had come more structure and a barrage of paperwork.

"It's the paperwork that's killing me," mused Ferguson. "At least I'll get relief now that the boss has allowed me another group leader." He remembered how difficult it has been to convince his boss, Tom Hanley, that the reason for his being two weeks behind schedule was due to lack of indirect labor support. Hanley had balked at the explanation. Only by repeatedly assuring him of a rapid return to the schedule had Ferguson been able to prevail in the discussion. Now, two weeks later, he felt compelled to find another group leader and get back on schedule.

He looked at Frankie Wong, who was busy at the drill press. Wong, an industrious twenty-four-year-old of Chinese heritage, had been hired eight months before and assigned to the four-man Heavy Assembly group. The work was rugged and very different than that of the Light

---

*This case was written by Charles Swanberg.

Assembly area, where instruments were made using simple hand tools. The heavy assemblers had always considered themselves a breed apart. After all, they were the "heavies" who performed "a man's job," as they were fond of pointing out. They were aloof, independent, and very proud. Though very capable workers, their output was only fair, a fact that perplexed Ferguson. The "heavies" had always stuck together and demanded loyalty. Unlike Frankie, the other "heavies" each had several years experience at the same job, and each had long before abandoned any notion of advancement. They made sure that the job got done, but within this framework, they set their own standards, which often meant extended break periods and periods of unproductive "shooting the breeze." Kevin, who set most of the standards, was fond of pointing out that if they worked hard consistently, the boss would expect that from them all the time.

Joe, Kevin, and Romero hadn't approved of Frankie's hard work and eagerness to please the boss, nor did they appreciate the fact that he conversed frequently with the light assemblers. Ferguson remembered that it had taken Frankie several weeks to be accepted by the heavy assemblers. The breakthrough had come when Frankie, a former art student, produced an excellent color sketch of the group. Entitled the *United Assemblers,* it depicted the four men dispatching the toughest jobs with ease, like so many comic book heroes foiling their foes.

Ferguson turned his thoughts to Karen Withers, his group leader of Light Assembly. He called her in. As she would be directly responsible for training the new group leader, he felt it imperative that she have an input into the decision-making process.

They quickly agreed that Frank Wong was the best choice, based on his organizational skills and motivation. Karen expressed reservations about his leadership ability, but Ferguson assured her that Frankie would "rise to the occasion."

After lunch break, Frankie Wong was called into the supervisor's office.

"Frankie," began Ferguson, "due to our fast growth, it looks as though we will need another group leader in the near future. You've done excellent work and seem eager to learn and progress. Would you be interested in training for the job?"

Caught off guard and somewhat puzzled, Frankie responded, "Sure, boss, whatever you say. Sounds like a good opportunity for me. What will I be doing?"

"Well, you'll work closely with Karen. She'll train you. If you do a good job you'll become group leader in a month or so." "Will I still be assembling during the training period?" "Part-time, yes. Don't worry, Frankie, I won't let you get away from assembly that easily!"

As Frankie left the office and resumed his work on the drill press he felt uneasy. He was confused by the boss's proposal. Whay had he been chosen? Frankie thought about his friends the heavy assemblers and what they might think. After all, they had been good to him, at least since he had been accepted by them. "It's going to be different now," thought Frankie. Counteracting his uneasiness was excitement and pride—pride that the boss had picked him over the others. This thought buoyed his spirits almost enough to erase the lingering doubts.

The next morning Frankie spent with Karen, learning a variety of new functions. He enjoyed it thoroughly and found the time flying— already it was coffee break. Kevin, the senior heavy assembler, approached him and began to question him.

"Why are you working with Karen? Only light assemblers answer to her."

Frankie explained lamely that the boss had asked him to assist Karen because of a paperwork build up. He assured Kevin that he would still be assembling with the group part-time.

"That's good, said Kevin. We were afraid you were becoming Karen's errand boy, and we'd hate to see that happen to one of the heavies!"

"Yeah," added Romero, the heavy assembler from Puerto Rico. "We thought you had sold out to become one of those lighweight stooges who sit at the bench all day!"

Frankie said nothing, finished his coffee, and reported back to Karen for more training. Later, while passing through the Heavy Assembly area, he was shocked to find his face obliterated from the *United Assemblers* portrait. Though shaken, he did his best to ignore it.

For John Ferguson the end of the day couldn't have come sooner. A two-hour weekly production meeting hadn't gone well. The latest production status showed his department slipping yet further behind. Not only that, but several flawed mechanical assemblies had reached the test floors, causing complaints from test managers. The only good news that he had been able to report to his boss was that the group leader search had finally been ended, thereby paving the way for rapid improvement.

On her way home, Karen stopped in to report the day's progress with Frankie Wong. She attested to his eagerness to learn the new skills and remarked on his apparent ability to manage the detailed paperwork of a group leader. John felt pleased that they had made a good choice and went home feeling relieved.

The next morning Ferguson was engrossed in an engineering change order when Frankie appeared at the door.

"Do you have a minute, boss?"

"Sure, Frankie. What can I do for you?"

"Well, I've thought over the group leader thing and decided I don't want it after all."

"Frankie, I don't understand. You said it was a good opportunity, and Karen said you liked learning the new skills."

"I just don't think it's for me. I'm sorry to disappoint you, boss."

No amount of convincing worked. Talk of career, progress, more earning power would not change Frankie's mind. He returned to the Heavy Assembly area and resumed his old duties.

For three days John Ferguson sought to discover why Frankie had changed his mind. At the end of the week the following conversation took place between John Ferguson and Frankie Wong.:

"Frankie, that decision you made earlier this week—was it yours or someone else's?"

"I didn't think it was the right job for me."

"Karen says the other heavy assemblers gave you a hard time. I thought that perhaps they had influenced your decision."

"Well, they're my friends and they mean a lot to me."

"Yes, Frankie, but it seems to me that a friend might respect your wish to advance. I think you've given this opportunity little chance. Do you want to think more about your decision?"

"Yes, boss, if you want I'll continue to work with Karen."

"No, Frankie, return to assembly. Until you decide where your loyalty lies, I cannot consider you for group leader."

A week later, Wong informed his supervisor that he was transferring to the Maintenance Department where he hoped to learn carpentry and advance his career. Ferguson urged him not to do it, on the grounds that the Maintenance Department was a dead end. His efforts were to no avail.

Ferguson fumed. How would he explain this to his boss at the next production meeting? And what about those rapid improvements he had promised?

Case Questions

1. What is the nature of the heavy assembly group? What specific components comprise its group character? Do these components reinforce each other? Is the group strong or weak? Healthy or not so healthy?
2. What could John Ferguson have done to avoid losing Frankie Wong from the department?
3. If you were in Ferguson's position, what would you do about the heavy assembly group? Let them remain as they are? Break up the group? Keep them together but try to influence them to change their attitudes? Why?

Falls Church Concrete Company*

Andy Johnson had just been promoted to senior driver for Falls Church Concrete Company. Andy had been with the firm for fifteen years, and when Jack Hobart retired as number one man, he seemed the likely replacement. Andy was pleased with his new appointment, for it not only meant driving a new truck but receiving a substantial increase in pay as well.

However, Andy was soon to find out that these new benefits also demanded new and greater responsibilities. Shortly after the first week, Andy's problems began.

---

*This case was written by Peter L. Knott.

Walt Richards, vice-president of Falls Church Concrete, had set up an appointment on Monday with Andy to discuss his new role and subsequent responsibilities. Andy already had a pretty good idea of what was expected, for he had kept a close watch on Jack since the announcement of his retirement. Andy knew that he would have to act as intermediary between the drivers and the dispatcher. In general, Andy would be the spokesman for driver interests. Also, he was to discuss daily job schedules with Nick Verenis, the dispatcher. (See the partial organization chart at the end of this case.) The coordination of job schedules and driver starting times was essential, and Andy was to make sure that enough drivers worked each day to handle the schedule, yet not too many drivers so as to be unprofitable. In other words, heavy schedules would require all six drivers, while light ones meant that some drivers were not needed.

Since schedules were based on seniority, those drivers who had been with the firm the longest would be called in first, and so on, until no more drivers were needed for the day.

At their appointment, Andy found Walt Richards to be quite concerned with coordinating these schedules. This did not surprise him, however, as Falls Church could only be profitable with effective use of each man on the clock. Still, Andy was a bit nervous.

Walt: You're in charge, Andy. You've had a week to get acquainted with the job, and I want you to let them know that you're the boss, not just their companion.

Andy: Okay, Walt. I don't think I'll have any problems. We've got a bunch of good men working, and they know their job.

Walt: I've heard that before. If you ask me, there is too much goofing off going on. These guys get on the clock and then sit around til a job gets called in. I want them busy whenever possible.

Andy: What do you suggest I have them do, Walt?

Walt: Hell, Andy, they could be sweeping the garages, cleaning out the hopper room, I don't know.... There's a lot that can be done. Those trucks sure need cleaning. Sam says he can't fix anything when the parts are full of cement dust. Tell those guys to get the acid out and clean the back of them. I don't know how long it's been since I saw the name *Falls Church Concrete* on the drums of those trucks.

Andy: We're out of acid, Walt.

Walt: Well, get Nick to order some more. I can't have five guys sitting around at ten dollars an hour each, waiting for a barrel of acid.

Andy: Okay, Walt. It should only take a couple of days. We will have 'em clean as new in a week or so.

Walt: That's what I like to hear! Oh, don't forget about those other things either, Andy. There's a lot to be done.

Andy: I'll get right on it, Walt. No problem.

At this point, Andy got up to leave. Just as he opened the office door, Walt started again.

Walt: One more thing, Andy. These guys are complaining about not getting called in on the light days, but when heavy days come up and we need them, they don't show up on time. We give each guy a day's notice. I want them to know that they are not indispensible. If they don't show up on time, we'll find somebody who will. I'm counting on you, Andy. Don't let me down.

Andy assured Walt that everything would be taken care of. Upon closing the door, however, he breathed a sigh of relief. Andy never thought the job was as difficult as Walt made it seem. He hoped that any responsibilities he might take would not hurt his relationship with the guys. Moreover, he wanted to impress upon Walt and Nick Verenis that he could handle any responsibilities.

It was Thursday, and Falls Church had gotten a sudden surge of work orders. Jack Porter was on vacation, so the remaining five drivers were called in to work. Some of the younger drivers had not worked for several days, so they were all on time, eager to earn a day's wage.

The morning hours were quite busy. A substantial number of loads were already delivered, but it had started to rain. With the rain came order cancellations, and soon work was at a minimum. Andy knew that this provided the drivers with an opportunity to slack off. He, too, was a bit tired from the fast-paced morning, yet he couldn't forget his conversation with Walt. Determined to fulfill his responsibilities, Andy went out to the garage. There he found two drivers, Mike Meade and his cousin Bob Meade, playing cards at the workbench. Andy abruptly suggested that they find something constructive to do.

Mike: Oh, come on, Andy. We work our tails off all morning and we can't even sit down for ten minutes?

Andy: You guys know what my job is. I don't want any trouble from Walt so I've got to keep you working while you're on the clock.

Bob: Since when is it different, Andy? Just two weeks ago you were sitting right here with us.

Mike: I don't know, Andy. Just because you get a promotion doesn't mean you should forget about your friends.

Bob: That's right. Your job is to represent us, anyway. Jack always did. He never gave us much hassle, and they didn't bother him about it.

Andy: You know I don't like to get on your backs. And I'd just as soon tell Walt to go to hell, but he's the one paying me. Now, I promised him that the trucks would be clean by tomorrow, so you guys have got to help me keep that promise.

With that, Mitch Freeman drove his truck into the garage. Getting out, he lit a cigarette and sat down on the bumper.

Mitch had generally kept his truck clean, so Andy didn't intend to say anything to him. Besides, he and Mitch were fairly close, and by now Andy felt he needed a friend.

Bob: What about Mitch, Andy? Don't tell me his truck is clean enough for you?

Mitch: What about me? You guys shouldn't be giving Andy a hard time. You know that's part of his job; and part of yours is to keep your trucks clean.

Andy: We just got a new barrel of acid yesterday. A half hour is all it will take.

Bob: Tell you what. You get us more hours and we'll keep the trucks spotless for you. Mitch doesn't mind doing it because he works every day.

Mitch: That's got nothing to do with it.

Andy: Bob, you know I can't do anything about the hours. Steve's dad, Nick is the one who suggests the number of drivers each day.

Mike: That may be why Steve works pretty often, even when we don't need him.

Bob: Gee, Andy, Steve's truck is the worst of the fleet, and I don't see you or Nick ever getting on his back about cleaning it.

With that, Nick called the garage on the intercom. A contractor wanted to do a floor indoors, and Andy was to load his truck.

Andy: (upon leaving) I expect that, by the end of the day, you two guys will have done what I asked.

All the way to the construction site, Andy reviewed the conversation he had just had. How could he get those guys to cooperate when he had been the same way two weeks earlier? He didn't want to lose their friendship, but he felt he had to prove to Walt that he could handle his new role.

Even if he could convince some of the younger drivers to clean their trucks, how would he approach a guy like Mitch? Sooner or later he would have to ask Mitch to clean the hopper room, shovel stones, or something. Either way, Mitch would resent it. Moreover, what could he do with Steve? Everyone knew that Nick was overprotective of his son.

Andy wasn't quite sure how to handle these problems, and he dreaded driving back to the plant.

**FALLS CHURCH CONCRETE COMPANY
PARTIAL ORGANIZATION CHART**

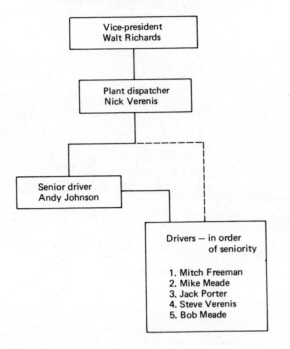

Case Question

1. Does the fact that Andy was so recently a member of the drivers' group make it impossible for him to be effective as their supervisor?
2. What is the "character" of the drivers' group? What factors are shaping their attitudes toward their work?
3. Consider Andy's statement beginning with "You know I don't like to get on your backs." Was this a useful statement for him to make? Why or why not?
4. Imagine you are in Andy's position. Develop a strategy for communicating with the drivers and with your superiors. Given your strategy, what should you say and do right away?

Part IV

Communication in the Total Organization

Chapter 10

Communicating within Organization Structures

Organization Design Issues that Affect Communication
    Division of Labor
    Unity of Command
    Span of Control
    Line-Staff Relationships
    Centralization versus Decentralization
Communication Within Basic Organization Designs
    Forms of Specialization
    Matrix Designs
Organization, Environment, and Communication
Communication and the Informal Organization
    Advantages and Disadvantages of Informal Organization
    The Grapevine

After studying this chapter, the reader should be able to

Define and use the following terms and concepts

Organization structure
Division of labor
Unity of command
Span of control
Line-staff relationships
Centralization
Decentralization
Specialization by function
Specialization by process
Specialization by product

Specialization by customer
Specialization by geography
Matrix design
Two-boss manager
Structure-environment fit
Coordinating roles
Informal organization
The grapevine
Grapevine cluster pattern

Understand

Five fundamental organization design issues
Effects various bases of specialization have on communication

Examples of matrix structures and their effects
How the degree of organization-environment fit can affect communication
Advantages and disadvantages of informal organization
At least three characteristics of grapevines

10

The word *structure* is usually used to refer to the way in which something is built—that is, what parts comprise it and how they fit together. Thus, an organization, such as the crew of a small naval ship, can be said to have a structure that includes a weapons department, operations department, engineering department, and supply department, each lead by a department head, with all department heads reporting to the executive officer. Furthermore, it is useful to include within the concept of structure certain operating mechanisms, such as the rules, decision processes, control procedures, information systems, and reward and appraisal systems that most managements use to reinforce the basic structure.[1]

Every organization, in addition to its basic structure and operating mechanisms, also has an informal structure. The informal structure is the pattern of relationships between individuals and groups that, as Keith Davis puts it, "develops spontaneously as people associate with each other."[2] A look at the informal structure of the small naval vessel, for example, might reveal the engineering officer to be a very influential advisor to the operations officer because of his prior experience as an operations officer himself. All three of these aspects—the basic structure, operating mechanisms, and the informal structure—are important parts of the overall concept of organization structure.

The topics of organization structure and communication are virtually inseparable. It is impossible to talk about one without the other. Chester Barnard, who became a highly respected management scholar after many years of experience as a senior executive, put it this way: "In an exhaustive theory of organization, communication would occupy a central place, because the structure, extensiveness, and scope of the organization are almost entirely determined by communication techniques."[3]

The relationship between organization structure and communication is one of mutual interdependence. Each has important effects on the other.

While these effects are sometimes not recognized too clearly—even by organization members themselves—there are cases where they become public knowledge. The White House provides frequent examples, since political observers keep close watch to see what people and, thus, what information is reaching the president. Under Lyndon Johnson, for example, so much power was vested in the president's appointments secretary, Marvin Watson, that he was said to exercise total control over who saw Johnson. One observer concluded, "It is undeniable that Watson has exercised virtually unlimited authority over many outstanding people."[4] In particular, Johnson cut himself off more and more during his presidency from people who disagreed with his Vietnam policy. As staff members with divergent views saw their access and credibility diminishing, they ultimately resigned, thus reinforcing the limited access structure and the informal norm of "no disagreement" with the president.[5]

The Johnson White House was experiencing a fundamental problem. It had an organization structure that was not adapted to providing the information flows that were needed for the complex task at hand. This example shows that the structure of an organization is not just a chart written on paper but is made up of the actions of people. Patterns of group and individual behavior determine an organization's design as much or more than decisions made by broads of directors and chief executives.

This chapter examines the basic components of the design problem that is faced by all organizations. Major emphasis will be on the choices that organizations and their members have in this area and on some of the specific steps that can be taken to improve structure, communication, and effectiveness.

ORGANIZATION DESIGN ISSUES THAT AFFECT COMMUNICATION

If you were presiding over the setting up of a new organization, you would have to answer certain questions. Who will do what? How will performance be controlled? How many supervisors should there be? How will people and activities be grouped? How will decisions be made? As time passed, you would discover that these matters kept reemerging; they had not been decided once and for all. Their persistence stems from the fact that they reflect the very nature of organizations themselves and the ways that organizations can differ from one another. The sections that follow give attention to these fundamental issues—namely, division of labor, unity of command, span of control, line-staff relationships, and centralization versus decentralization.

Division of Labor

The division of labor issue has to do with the extent to which jobs are specialized. One of the main advantages of having organizations is that they allow job specialization. Instead of having a cook in a hospital also performing duties as a nurse in an intensive care unit, the cook specializes in cooking while the nurse concentrates on caring for patients. Adam Smith gave the classic description of the results of division of labor. In one small pin factory he found that output had been increased from 200 to 48,000 pins per day with no change in the number of workers employed. This increase was achieved by breaking the task into ten subtasks, such as cutting the wire, straightening the wire, making the heads, and putting on the heads.[6]

The advantages of division of labor usually cited are that the worker becomes more proficient in a narrower job, and that simplified jobs can be performed by workers with less skill and training. With such compelling economic advantages, one might well ask, "Why not break pinmaking down into twenty subtasks instead of only ten?"

Adam Smith's answer was that division of labor is limited only by the extent of the market. From a communication standpoint, however, it became obvious that there are additional limiting factors. Highly specialized jobs have to be defined precisely and understood very clearly by the worker—something that cannot always be fully achieved. In addition, specialization requires coordination. Some communication mechanism has to be provided so that the pin head maker will know what size heads are needed and will make necessary adjustments if the heads do not fit the pins properly.

Historically, the most frequent response of organizations to the need for coordination has been to develop managerial roles to handle it. Thus, a new division of labor, a vertical division, comes about, where work is divided between those who physically do the work and those who coordinate the various interdependent, specialized activities. This vertical division of labor in turn brings in new problems. One is the question of how to keep workers motivated if decisions about their activities are being made by others. Another problem is how to divide up managerial work in an organization that is large enough to have many managers. Since division of labor evokes issues of how managerial work should be organized and conducted, four of the most venerable of these issues will be discussed in the sections that follow.[7]

Unity of Command

One of the oldest principles of organization states that each member should be accountable to one and only one superior. In exhibit 10-1, which shows several of the positions in a small manufacturing company, the machining department head clearly reports to the vice-president of manufacturing. The usual rationale behind this principle is that discipline, order, and stability would be threatened without unity of command. It follows from the unity of command principle that there is an unbroken chain of command running to the president from every member of the organization, even the newest drill press operator.

EXHIBIT 10-1
PARTIAL ORGANIZATION CHART OF A SMALL
MANUFACTURING COMPANY

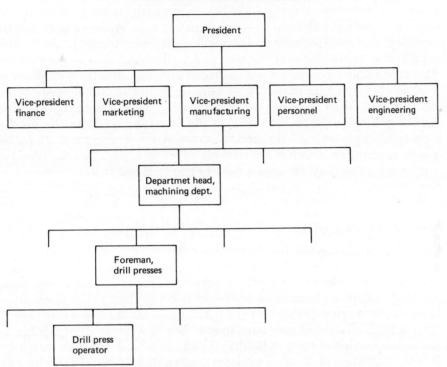

In most organizations, members are well advised to give some attention to the chain of command. The machining department head would likely be offended if the drill press foreman went directly to the vice-president of manufacturing with a problem or grievance. Direct contact between boss and subordinate is clearly important in organizations. Study after study has shown that superiors spend about fifty percent of their time with their subordinates.[8]

Nevertheless, the unity of command rule is widely violated. It would not be uncommon in a small company like the one diagramed in exhibit 10-1 to see the marketing vice-president talking with the drill press foreman about how to speed up work on an order for an important customer who has just called in to complain about late delivery. This might put the foreman in a difficult and awkward situation, depending on how both people handled the conversation, but it might also serve an essential purpose, especially if the company does not have a better way of making minute by minute adjustments in schedules.

In the best of organizations, a manufacturing supervisor would be guided by the personnel department's decisions as to hiring and performance appraisal procedures, the engineering department's product designs, and so forth. It has even proved effective in certain cases to have workers report simultaneously to two supervisors. James Abegglen reports on the use of this double supervisor structure in certain Japanese mines, located in mountain villages, which had been in operation with a locally recruited work force since the seventeenth century. Each supervisory post was held by both a young engineer who knew modern mining methods, and an experienced supervisor with several years in the locality who was sensitive to local customs and traditions.[9] Another instance of dual command occurs in project management. The structural engineer on a bridge construction project, for example, would simultaneously report both to the project manager, who is overall head of the bridge-building effort, and to his permanent boss in the construction firm, the head of structural engineering. The success of command arrangements, whether single or multiple, depends not on their adherence to an abstract principle but on whether they are appropriate to the task and culture and on how they are handled by the participants.

Span of Control

Span of control refers to the number of subordinates who report directly to a given superior. A small span of control would seem to make for more thorough communication between supervisors and subordinates. Small spans of control are expensive, however, because the smaller the spans of control, the more supervisors the organization must have on its payroll. Larger spans of control may save money but may make it impossible for managers to control their subordinates effectively. It has been suggested that the president of the United States is often unaware of what is happening on his own immediate staff because this span of control is too great.[10] Massachusetts recently reorganized its state government after public attention became focused on the fact that over 300 heads of state agencies supposedly reported directly to the governor.

Certain management experts argued for many years that the appropriate span of control was approximately 7, claiming that this number allowed managers to maintain close enough contact with their subordinates and, at the same time, kept the organization's supervisory costs within reason.[11] It is not hard to see that some spans of control are too large and others too small, but 7 is not necessarily the ideal. In a design engineering firm working on sophisticated products, a small span of control can allow a manager time for lengthy discussions of technical problems. Engineering managers generally can handle 5 to 10 subordinates, while supervisors in mass production plants can successfully manage 40 to 50.[12] One retail chain headquarters gave its regional vice-presidents a span of control of 100 because they needed to communicate only with those store managers who were having difficulty. Such problems could be spotted easily by the monthly sales figures, and the other store managers were simply left alone.[13]

Thus, a given span of control can only be said to be too high or too low in reference to the factors that are important in a specific situation. These factors would include the following:[14]

1. Similarity of functions supervised.
2. Geographic closeness of subordinates.
3. Complexity of functions supervised.
4. Direction and control required by subordinates.
5. Coordination required.
6. Planning importance, complexity, and time required.
7. Organizational assistance received by supervisor.

This list shows the central importance of communication to the span of control issue. In a given situation, the span of control can be viewed as both a cause and a result of the amount and quality of communication that exist.

Line-Staff Relationships

Matters relating to the chain of command are important, but they do not address an equally important area—relations between line and staff personnel. Line personnel are usually defined as those who are directly responsible for planning and executing a dominant activity. In the small manufacturing firm in exhibit 10-1, manufacturing would clearly be a line function, while finance, personnel, and engineering contain staff experts whose presence enables the organization to handle more information and make more complicated decisions. In general, line managers are those who make decisions and exercise authority on the basis of information, analyses, and advice provided by staff experts.

In theory, the line and staff functions complement each other perfectly, since the line personnel are the practical realists while the staff members provide specialized inputs. Things do not always go so smoothly, however. As Melville Dalton puts it, "Intermeshing staff and line is the impossible problem of wedding change and habit."[15]

If staff-line debates were strictly matters of professional disagreement, all would be well, but often the relationship takes on a more bitterly competitive nature, where each is trying to look better than the other in order to win rewards from higher management. In such cases, energy goes into maintaining or resolving the conflict instead of into decision making and task performance. Staff members, such as internal auditors and industrial engineers, are often seen as spies by line personnel, sometimes with good reason, and it is not unheard of for the line to sabotage a staff project in order to cast the staff into a bad light.

Uncalled for accommodations are sometimes made by one side to obtain the other's support in an inherently competitive setting. Dalton cites one example of staff units that literally bought tolerance and cooperation from certain line departments by transferring staff research funds to line accounts. In another case, a staff specialist delayed a project for three months as a concession to a line manager.[16]

Ideally, organizations need to work toward the elimination of these nonprofessional kinds of conflict and accommodation so that legitimate task-relevant disagreements can emerge and be dealt with.[17] Realistically, however, most people discover that this ideal has not been fully realized and that part of their interpersonal skill consists in recognizing and coping with the political realities that are contained in the line-staff relationships in most organizations. Again, as with the two issues discussed earlier, it can be seen that communication and organization design are interdependent. Line-staff relationships both affect and are affected by communication quality.

Centralization versus Decentralization

The chart shown in exhibit 10-1 is not the only possible line-staff structure. Another is given in exhibit 10-2, which shows an organization with separate divisions for each of two products, each division having its own line and staff structure. If there are major differences between product A and product B, the decentralized structure provides each with its own set of managers and specialists, allowing decisions to be made at lower levels.

The extent of decentralization can be depicted only in part by an

EXHIBIT 10-2
DECENTRALIZED LINE-STAFF STRUCTURE

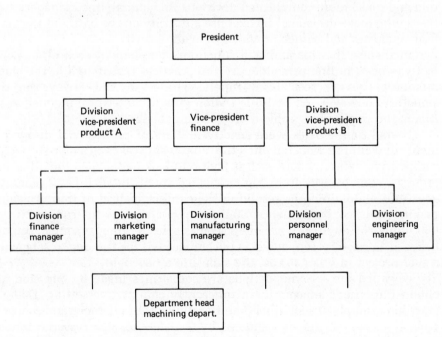

organization chart. A university class, for example, would appear on paper to be a highly centralized organization, since each student reports directly to the professor. But some professors allow the students to decide what their term projects will be, while others specify the project, and still others reach the decision with each student on a joint basis. Decentralization is a matter of degree; it is not absolutely present or absent, and it gets manifested in action, not on the chart.

Several arguments can be made in favor of decentralization. As an organization becomes more complex, it relieves top management of an overload of information and decision making. Decentralization puts decision making in the hands of the managers who are most knowledgeable about their products, customers, and other issues. It creates organizational units small enough for people to identify with fully, and it provides more people with the opportunity to participate in decision making. A more centralized structure, however, puts staff people together in larger groupings, allowing their professional competencies to be developed in greater depth; puts decision making in the hands of people who see the organization's overall needs; and avoids certain dual reporting relationships, such as that of the division finance manager in exhibit 10-2.

Though all of these arguments are persuasive, no one of them is always true or false. Centralization and decentralization can be both sources of communication problems and solutions to communication problems, depending on the circumstances, the nature of the task, and the people involved.[18]

COMMUNICATION WITHIN BASIC ORGANIZATION DESIGNS

All of the issues discussed in the preceding sections come to bear in an organization's decision as to what its basic structure will be—that is, how the organization will be divided into specialized subunits. Every organization makes this choice. If it is a specialty clothing store, should the departments be shoes, dresses, and outerwear, or should all items for a given age group be grouped together: pre-teens, teens, young adults? If it is a professional school in a university, will separate faculties be established for the graduate and undergraduate programs? The basic form of specialization that an organization chooses has a major impact on its climate and character.

Forms of Specialization

The kinds of specialization most often used are specialization by *function, process, product, customer,* and *geography.* An example of specialization by function was provided by the small manufacturing company depicted in exhibit 10-1. This company is said to be organized by function because it has a subunit for each of the major areas of knowledge needed in the business: finance, marketing, manufacturing, personnel, and engineering.

Most university faculties have a functional structure, with each department containing professors in a single field, such as chemistry, philosophy, or French. With such groupings of specialists, the organization can develop depth of competence in the subfields of each functional area but may find coordination between functions hard to achieve.

Specialization by process exists when each of several departments performs one phase of the production or service provided by the organization. An example would be a printing plant where the composing room sets the type, whereupon the plate-making department produces press plates, the pressroom prints the job, the bindery binds it, and the shipping department sends it to the customer. This facilitates coordination between one step and the next but may not encourage adequate special attention to individual products.

Specialization by product refers to the type of organization shown in exhibit 10-2, where major subunits are established for each type of product, these subunits containing the specialized functions and processes needed to design, produce, and market that product. The price often paid for this organization design choice is that professional competencies tend to be spread thin. Engineers, for example, may be occupied with all phases of engineering for the product, making it difficult for them to become experts in a specialized engineering subfield.

For some organizations the primary strategic problem may be marketing to different types of customers or clients. Specialization by customer is a way of addressing the special needs of customers, such as institutions, wholesalers, consumers, and governments, by organizing a department to serve each grouping. Similarly, to serve customers scattered over a wide area best, specialization by geography may be used. Thus, a health clinic may divide into small branch offices located throughout a metropolitan area if making an office more accessible to patients is deemed more important than providing a large number of specialists at a central facility.

As indicated, all forms of specialization have advantages and disadvantages. Customer specialization eases communication between people who are doing work for the same customer but may make it harder for two market researchers who are in different subunits to pool their professional knowledge. Political and social realities often make it hard for people to cross departmental boundaries, even when they have good reasons for doing so. Therefore, many organizations have tried to find ways of retaining the advantages of more than just one form of specialization. One approach that is being used by more and more organizations is an organization design form known as the matrix.

Matrix Designs

As organizations cope with increasingly complex environments, more of them are choosing to respond to two or more environmental sectors si-

EXHIBIT 10-3
MATRIX STRUCTURE

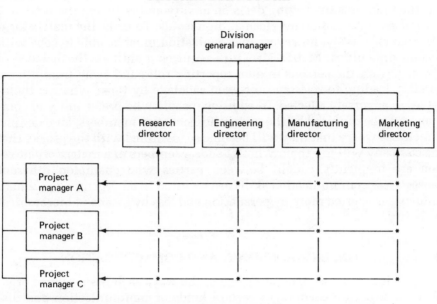

* Project team members having dual reporting relationships

multaneously—to organize by function *and* by project, by service *and* by geographic area at the same time. An example of a matrix design is indicated in exhibit 10-3, which shows a function-project combination.

As exhibit 10-3 shows, the key to matrix structure is that certain individuals have two bosses. For example, such a person in an aerospace firm could be the designer responsible for the engine of a new aircraft the company is developing. This designer might report both to the engineering director and to the project manager in charge of the overall development and production of the aircraft. In this case, the designer would be one member of a team of several functional specialists formed to coordinate the work on the engine done by diverse groups in the company, such as electrical, mechanical, and structural engineers, production planners, and cost accountants, to mention a few.

Two-boss roles are emerging in many fields. In multi-unit retailing the manager of a branch store may report to superiors in both the merchandising and operations areas. In a public accounting firm, the head of the team doing an audit of the Cleveland division of a large New York-based firm might report both to the director of audit teams in the Cleveland office of the accounting firm and to the account director in the New York office. Nursing supervisors in hospitals work for both a head nurse and a chief of service.[19]

The matrix structure can be a way of increasing the ability of an organization to process information. It provides a way of bringing specialists from many subunits to bear on a task, thus facilitating coordination, and permits many decisions to be made by people who have their "hands on" the task, thus improving decision quality and reducing the tendency toward communication overload at high levels. To make the matrix form function effectively, however, an organization must be able to cope with certain difficulties. Matrix structure requires a shift in the balance of power toward the persons in dual reporting roles and away from others, possibly leading to resistance or even sabotage by those who see themselves as adversely affected. In addition, people who prefer unity of command may be confused by the matrix. Project team members, for example, sometimes worry that they will become so identified with the project that the company will fire them when it ends. Members of a matrix organization are frequently caught between parties who champion different causes. New communication skills are required in an organization where influence is exerted more by persuasion and less by means of hierarchical authority.[20]

ORGANIZATION, ENVIRONMENT, AND COMMUNICATION

The previous discussion shows some of the ways each basic type of organization structure encourages certain kinds of communication and discourages others. As noted, for example, functional structure tends to facilitate contact between specialists who are in the same area but to limit interdepartmental contacts. The product structure tends to bring different specialists, say accountants and engineers, into more frequent, spontaneous contact with each other but limits the extent to which an accountant can work exclusively with other accountants.[21] From the standpoint of communication, productivity, and member satisfaction, either form may or may not be satisfactory. Recent research has shown that the difference lies in whether the structure is one that fits the demands of the organization's environment. Joan Woodward's studies in Great Britain revealed that manufacturing firms engaged in different kinds of technologies tend to have different structures. Mass production firms, for example, tend to have more centralized decision making—typefied by more hierarchial levels and wider spans of control—than custom and small batch manufacturers. Interestingly, the more successful firms Woodward studied tended to fit this more centralized pattern much more closely than the less successful.[22]

Other studies have shown the importance of a good fit between the organization's structure and more pervasive aspects of its environment, such as the diversity, rate of change, and degree of environmental predictability with which the organization must cope. In one study by Tom Burns and George Stalker, an organization in a stable environment was found to have a functional structure, precise role definitions, centralized hierarchical control, and a tendency for personal contacts to be mainly between superiors and subordinates. Another organization, this one in a rapidly changing environment, had a more fluid structure, frequent redefinition of roles, wider distribution of authority and control, and a lateral rather than vertical direction of communication.[23] Another study, by Paul Lawrence and Jay Lorsch, supported and added to Burns and Stalkers findings. The extent of departmental specialization and the amount and quality of coordinating effort were found to relate differently to organizational effectiveness depending on the nature of the environment.[24] In this study Lawrence and Lorsch found that success in a dynamic, uncertain environment was associated with having highly specialized departments that were very different from each other and, necessarily, a large amount of effort and many structural devices devoted to achieving coordination between them. Among other things, Lawrence and Lorsch found that in these organizations the people in coordinating roles needed to be skillful in speaking the language of all the various specialized experts, and that they had to exert influence based on technical competence rather than the authority of their position. In a more stable, certain environment, the successful organization was one where departmental differences were not so great, and less integrative effort was required. Here, the top manager was the one who had the information necessary to make the key decisions and so did most of the coordinating.

These studies show that the nature of communication in an organization is related to the extent to which the organization's structure is appropriate to the demands of its environment. If you are working in an organization having a design that fits well with its environment, you will experience very different patterns of communication than if you are in one that does not. An example of the good fit condition is provided by Woodward's description of four engineering firms whose business involved doing a unique job in response to each order from a customer. Appropriately, the firms were organized on a product basis. Because of the need to communicate unique product needs, the sales personnel in these firms were associated very closely with people in other functions. In addition, research and development people spent far more of their time in the production workshops than did their counterparts in other kinds of firms. Development engineers were quick to become involved whenever production engineers ran into difficulties. Coordination between functions depended almost entirely on direct personal contacts, and interdepartmental relations were good.[25] In a different type of industrial environment described by Lawrence and Lorsch—one requiring continuous production of an unchanging product—people were involved with one another in a very different way. Here, communication was not a matter of functional managers mutually influencing and helping each other. Instead, each one gave information to the chief executive so he could make the decisions. The functional managers' morale was as good as it was in Woodward's engineering firms, however, because they saw the structure and communication pattern was appropriate to the task and realized the top manager was competent in decision making.[26]

The low-performing firm in Lawrence and Lorsch's stable environment had a different, less centralized structure. In this single-product organization, production scheduling decisions had been delegated to the manager of each local plant and the regional sales mamager in that area. In addition, a coordinating unit, reporting to the chief executive, had the assigned duty of integrating sales requirements with production at each of the organization's several plants. As might be expected, this structure led to a good deal of confusion about how conflicts were to be resolved. Managers in the plants complained that the sales office had too much influence on production schedules.[27] As one of them put it, "There are thousands of guys involved in the scheduling process around here. It just doesn't work with so many cooks in the stew."[28] By the same token, a salesman expressed dismay that his boss, the regional sales manager, had been "turned into a production scheduler" and did not seem to be able to make decisions that would really stick. He would make them, but disputes with production would cause them to be referred up the line to top management, where they were often reversed.[29]

In a more diverse, unstable environment, an example of poor fit provided by Lawrence and Lorsch is that of a consumer food products firm that was organized on a more centralized basis than was appropriate. The many products and the several kinds of research, marketing, and production expertise involved in each of them made it impossible for top management to know enough to make the many detailed decisions. Researchers and managers at lower levels experienced a high degree of frustration because projects were being taken out of their hands before they were able to complete them. They felt excluded from communication. As a result, the performance of the organization in its industry was poor.[30]

These studies show that the extent to which an organization's structure fits its environment affects the content and quality of communication that its members directly experience. Communication is not automatically good or poor in one or another type of organization, whether it is a highly formal bureaucracy or a more decentralized matrix type. Instead, the question is whether the organization's form fits its environment, allowing its members to communicate in ways that provide them the satisfaction of task accomplishment.[31]

COMMUNICATION AND THE INFORMAL ORGANIZATION

Since the landmark research studies by Fritz Roethlisberger and others in the 1930s at Western Electric Company, it has been widely recognized that networks of informal relationships exist in organizations beyond what is prescribed by the formal structure. At Western Electric workers influenced one another to restrict output, thus hoping to avoid a toughening of production standards by management. Production was thus being controlled through spontaneous contact between workers outside the formal supervisory structure. The researchers also observed that workers' morale could be strongly affected depending upon whether they were being supported or rejected by their informal group.[32] When two accountants regularly join two members of the market research department for lunch, they are contributing to the informal organization. When one office borrows a box of mimeograph paper from another office rather than going through the company's official (but slower) supply system, the informal structure is operating.

Advantages and Disadvantages of Informal Organization

The informal organization can provide communication links that reinforce and add to those charted by the formal structure. On the other hand, informal networks can compete with or even replace the formal design. The informal organization can work against changes desired by management. Charles Savage described a classic example of such resistance in a factory located in a Colombian mountain village where modern methods, introduced by young, recently educated industrial engineers from the city, were resisted by workers who were accustomed to a traditional management style and social organization. Workers respected older members and looked to them for leadership, but the engineers brought in new working arrangements where the older workers no longer had formal leadership positions. The engineers did not recognize the existing social system, nor did they personally interact with the workers in the way of the owner and former manager, a respected resident of the village who knew all the residents and began every conversation by asking the employee about his family. The engineers' failure to adapt to the informal structure resulted in communication breakdown. The engineers could not get valid information from the factory floor because the workers did not trust them, and the owner could not because his informants, the older workers, were no longer in central roles in the formal structure.[33]

On the other hand, the informal structure can reinforce and add to the communication links provided by the formal structure in ways that contribute to the attainment of organizational goals. Research has shown that managers derive needed information from a huge variety of personal contacts far beyond the limits of their formally charted relationships.[34] A very explicit example is the two-door policy used by President John F. Kennedy. Kennedy had an "informal" entrance to his office that was presided over by his warm, understanding personal secretary, Evelyn Lincoln, and a "formal" one guarded by his hard-minded appointments secretary, Kenneth O'Donnell, whose major effort was to protect the president's time and energy. When Kennedy left Mrs. Lincoln's door ajar, it served as a signal to the staff members that they could try coming directly in to see him. This way, key advisors could reach the president without having to schedule an appointment.[35] Even in Russia, where all activities have the outside reputation of being formal, logical, and planned, the informal organization plays a major role. A factory's suppliers, for example, are not always able to deliver the planned raw materials, necessitating the use of informal negotiating channels to obtain the materials from an unofficial source. The well-known production quotas that Soviet managers must attain on pain of severe reprimand or punishment are often not so hard to attain if the manager and his superiors are members of the same mutually supportive informal network and have set the quotas by mutual agreement, as is often the case.[36]

When the formal design of an organization does not fit its environment well, the informal organization may be able to make up the difference. Conversely, an otherwise good organization-environment fit can be negated by an informal structure that acts to reduce task effectiveness. Overall, it is clear that organizational events cannot be understood or managed well if the informal structure is not taken into account.

The Grapevine

Communication in the informal organization is often referred to as the grapevine. This term is said to have arisen during the Civil War to describe the telephone lines the military forces used, which were strung loosely from tree to tree. Since messages using this primitive technology were often incomplete or distorted, it came to be said that any rumor was from the grapevine.[37] Today, many people in organizations still associate the grapevine with unfounded rumor, but wise organization members know differently. They have discovered, and research has proved, that the grapevine is usually a fast, penetrating, accurate communication system.

The speed of the grapevine is shown by an example Keith Davis gives. The wife of a plant supervisor had a baby at 11 P.M., and a plant survey taken the next day at 2 P.M. showed that forty-six percent of the management personnel had heard of it.[38] Since the grapevine comes into action spontaneously out of people's natural desire to communicate, it tends to be most active in transmitting information that is news and high in interest value, such as personnel promotions and transfers, layoffs, or policy changes. In one study of Canadian government engineers who had been transferred, one-third reported that they had first heard about their transfer through the grapevine.[39] The grapevine can often penetrate tight security screens because of its potential for directly involving the people who know the information. Barriers of confidentiality are often lowered in the safety of one-to-one and small group settings, and it is in just these settings that over seventy percent of all grapevine communication occurs.[40]

Research has shown that grapevine information is more than three-fourths accurate.[41] Some organization members do not trust such information, feeling that it has been passed from person to person so many times before it reaches them that it must have become distorted. Anyone who has ever played the parlor game of "rumor" knows how many additions, omissions, and changes can happen to a message as it is passed by word of mouth from one person to another in a chainlike sequence. A simple chain model is not a completely accurate representation of the organizational grapevine, however. Instead, grapevine messages tend to travel in a "cluster" pattern, typefied by the diagram in exhibit 10-4. The diagram indicates the usual pattern of grapevine information flow revealed in research by Davis, who found that most people tell grapevine information to a cluster of other people, not all of whom pass it on.[42] In exhibit 10-4, the longest chain is the one involving four steps to reach person H, while six others were reached in fewer steps. Since information is not as likely to be passed on when it gets old, the chains tend not to be very long. The actual paths followed by the information are influenced by such structural realities as physical locations of people, the flow of work, friendships, and other social and psychological factors. In most organizations there is some degree of predictability as to how information will spread, who usually spreads it, and who always seems to "know what's going on."[43]

EXHIBIT 10-4
THE GRAPEVINE CLUSTER PATTERN

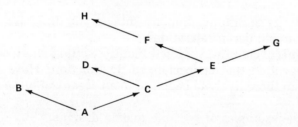

Although one might expect that grapevine rumors would be dangerously inaccurate sources of information, most rumors that have been studied in organizations have proved to be fairly accurate.[44] However, it is true that rumors are sometimes inaccurate, and that they can be destructive. Organization members need to know something of the nature of grapevines in general and the particular forms they take in their own organization. This awareness can enable them to both guard against the dangers of the grapevine and use its positive potential as a fast, accurate, widespread information network.

Summary

This chapter has shown that organization structure and communication are closely intertwined. Each of the classical issues of organization design has communication overtones, as shown in the discussions of division of labor, unity of command, span of control, line-staff relationships, and centralization versus decentralization. Various basic structural types were examined. The functional, process, product, customer, geographic, and matrix forms each were shown to solve certain communication problems but to provoke others. A partial resolution to this dilemma was provided in the discussion of organization and environment. Research and examples reviewed indicated that communication quality and an organization's effectiveness both tend to be higher when the structure of the organization fits its environment. Finally, the topics of informal organization and the grapevine were addressed and seen to be factors that can increase organizational effectiveness or reduce it, in some cases by reinforcing the formal structure and in others by providing a supplement to it.

Questions for Review

1. Why is it impossible to discuss organization structure without discussing communication?
2. How are communication and division of labor related to each other?
3. Why do line-staff relationships often involve communication difficulties?
4. What are the communication advantages and disadvantages of centralization and decentralization?
5. What kinds of communication difficulty would you expect to find in an organization that is specialized by function? How would they differ from those likely to be found in an organization specialized by product?
6. Give three examples of possible matrix designs.
7. What specific communication skills should a successful two-boss manager possess?
8. How does communication within a successful organization in a dynamic, uncertain environment, differ from communication in a successful organization in a stable, certain environment?
9. Why is communication quality likely to be impaired in an organization that does not have a structure that fits its environment? Give an example.
10. What sort of informal action could an individual take to improve the fit between his or her organization and its environment?
11. Can grapevine communication be managed?

References and Notes

1. Jay W. Lorsch, "Introduction to the Structural Design of Organizations," in Gene W. Dalton, Paul R. Lawrence, and Jay W. Lorsch, *Organizational Structure and Design* (Homewood, Ill.: Irwin-Dorsey, 1970), p. 1.

2. Keith Davis, *Human Relations at Work* (New York: McGraw-Hill, 1962), p. 236.

3. Chester I. Barnard, *The Functions of the Executive* (Cambridge, Mass.: Harvard University Press, 1938), p. 91.

4. Patrick Anderson, *The President's Men* (Garden City, N.J.: Doubleday, 1968), p. 387.

5. Richard Tanner Johnson, *Managing the White House* (New York: Harper & Row, 1974), pp. 190–95.

6. Adam Smith, *An Inquiry into the Nature and Causes of the Wealth of Nations* (London: Alex Murray & Company, 1974), pp. 4–5.

7. The discussion of division of labor draws on Jay R. Galbraith, *Organization Design* (Reading, Mass.: Addison-Wesley, 1977), pp. 13–14.

8. Henry Mintzberg, *The Nature of Managerial Work* (New York: Harper and Row, 1973), pp. 44–45.

9. James G. Abegglen, *The Japanese Factory* (Glencoe, Ill.: The Free Press, 1958), pp. 82–83.

10. Arthur M. Schlesinger, Jr., *The Imperial Presidency* (Boston, Houghton Mifflin, Co. 1973), p. 221.

11. See, for example, Lyndall F. Urwick, "The Manager's Span of Control," *Harvard Business Review,* May-June 1956, pp. 39–47; G. A. Miller, "The Magical Number Seven, Plus or Minus Two: Some Limits on our Capacity for Processing Information," *Psychological Review* 63 (March 1956):39–47.

12. Joan Woodward, *Industrial Organization: Theory and Practice* (Oxford: Oxford University Press, 1965), chap. 4.

13. Ross A. Webber, *Management* (Homewood, Ill.: Richard D. Irwin, 1975), p. 391.

14. Harold Stieglitz, "Optimizing Span of Control," *Management Record,* September 1962, pp. 25–29.

15. Melville Dalton, *Men who Manage* (New York: John Wiley & Sons, 1959), p. 107.

16. Ibid., pp. 90–91, 104–6.

17. The discussion of span of control is adapted from K. Tim Hostiuck, *Contemporary Organizations: An Introductory Appraoch* (Morristown, N.J.: General Learning Press, 1974), pp. 191–200.

18. For a discussion of the concept of "goodness of fit" between organizations, tasks, and people, see John J. Morse and Jay W. Lorsch, "Beyond Theory Y," *Harvard Business Review,* May-June 1970, pp. 61–68.

19. The terminology and concept of the "two-boss manager" are developed in Stanley M. Davis and Paul R. Lawrence, *Matrix* (Reading, Mass.: Addison-Wesley, 1977), pp. 21–23, and 50–52. The examples are ones suggested in chap. 7.

20. For data relating to differences in the distribution of influence between two matrix organizations (in the food and plastics industries) and a traditional hierarchical structure (in the container industry), see Paul R. Lawrence and Jay W. Lorsch, *Organization and Environment* (Boston: Division of Research, Harvard Business School, 1967), pp. 141–46.

21. Arthur H. Walker and Jay W. Lorsch, "Organizational Choice: Product versus Function," *Harvard Business Review,* November-December 1968, pp. 129–39.

22. Joan Woodward, *Industrial Organization: Theory and Practice,* pp. 52, 69.

23. Tom Burns and G. M. Stalker, *The Management of Innovation* (London: Tavistock Publications, 1961).

24. Paul R. Lawrence and Jay W. Lorsch, *Organization and Environment* (Boston: Division of Research, Harvard Business School, 1967); idem, "Differentiation and Integration in Complex Organizations," *Administrative Science Quarterly* 12, no. 1 (1967):1–47.

25. Woodward, *Industrial Organization*, pp. 131, 134–35.

26. Lawrence and Lorsch, *Organization and Environment*, pp. 110–20.

27. Ibid.

28. Ibid., p. 116.

29. Ibid.

30. Ibid., pp. 128–29.

31. For a summary of research studies showing the effects of various aspects of organization structures and their appropriateness on communication, see Lyman W. Porter and Karlene H. Roberts, "Communication in Organization," in *Handbook of Industrial and Organizational Psychology*, ed. Marvin D. Dunnette (Chicago: Rand McNally, 1976), pp. 1553–89.

32. Fritz J. Roethlisberger and William J. Dickson, *Management and the Worker* (Cambridge, Mass.: Harvard University Press, 1943), pp. 373–84, 525–48.

33. Charles H. Savage, Jr., *Social Reorganization in a Factory in the Andes* (Ithaca, N.Y.: The Society for Applied Anthropology, 1964), pp. 1–7.

34. Mintzberg, *Nature of Managerial Work*, pp. 44–45.

35. Arthur M. Schlesinger, Jr., *A Thousand Days* (Boston: Houghton Mifflin, 1965), p. 687.

36. Jerome S. Berliner, *Factory and Manager in the U.S.S.R.* (Cambridge, Mass.: Harvard University Press, 1957), pp. 182–230.

37. Keith Davis, *Human Behavior at Work* (New York: McGraw-Hill, 1977), p. 278.

38. Idem, "Management Communication and the Grapevine," *Harvard Business Review*, September-October 1953, p. 44.

39. Ronald J. Burke, "Quality of Organizational Life: The Effects of Personnel Job Transfers," in *Proceedings of the Academy of Management*, ed. Vance F. Mitchell et. al. (Vancouver, B.C.: University of British Columbia, 1973), p. 242.

40. Jay T. Knippen, "Grapevine Communication," *Journal of Business Research*, January 1974, pp. 47–58.

41. In a study by Davis, the grapevine was found to be eighty to ninety-nine percent accurate for noncontroversial company information. Eighty-two percent accuracy was indicated in a study by Walton. See Davis, *Human Behavior at Work*, p. 290, n. 9; Eugene Walton, "How Efficient is the Grapevine?" *Personnel*, March-April 1961, pp. 45–49.

42. Davis, *Human Behavior at Work*, p. 280.

43. Harold Sutton and Lyman W. Porter, "A Study of the Grapevine in a Governmental Organization," *Personnel Psychology* 21 (1968):223–30.

44. Ithiel de Sola Pool, "Communication Systems," in *Handbook of Communication*, ed. Ithiel De Sola Pool and Wilbur Schramm (Chicago: Rand McNally, 1973).

Chapter 11

Managing Conflict in Organizations

Milo Chemical
Guardian Printing
Sources and Effects of Conflict-Laden Communication
  Sources of conflict
    Win-lose and game situations
    Differing subunit goals and perceptions
    Concerns about status and authority
  Effects of conflict
  Effects within groups
  Effects between groups
  Effects of winning or losing a conflict
  Communicating constructively and destructively in conflict situations
Approaches to Managing Conflict Communication
  A cyclical model of the conflict process
  Reactions to intergroup conflict
    Avoiding
    Smoothing
    Forcing
    Compromising
    Collaborating
  Operational steps to managing conflict communication
    Increasing intergroup contacts
    Developing a superordinate goal
    Restructuring the organization
Organization Design and Conflict Management
  Differentiation and integration
Communication and Role Conflict

After studying this chapter, the reader should be able to

Define and use the following terms and concepts

Competition
Conflict
Win-lose situations
Differing submit goals and
  perceptions
Concerns about status and
  authority
Constructive conflict
Destructive conflict
Cyclical model of conflict

Avoiding
Smoothing
Forcing
Compromising
Collaborating
Superordinate goal
Differentiation
Integration
Integrator
Role conflict

Understand

Sources of organizational conflict
Effects of conflict within groups and between groups
Advantages and disadvantages of various reactions to conflict
Specific methods for managing conflict
How differentiation and integration relate to conflict management
Alternative ways of handling role conflict
Characteristics of effective integrators

11

Many battles are fought in organizations. The most persistent of these struggles are the ones that have their roots in the structure of the organization itself. Strong emotions and much energy can be invested in conflicts between design engineers and production engineers in a factory, merchandising managers and the credit office in a department store, and the emergency room staff and the purchasing department in a hospital. These battles may be destructive or constructive; they may weaken or strengthen the organization and the participating parties. The two cases that follow provide examples of each of these two kinds of conflict.

Milo Chemical*

In the Milo Chemical processing plant, top management was very concerned about the need to reduce operating costs. Middle and lower managers learned that their career futures depended on an excellent cost record. One key to controlling the departments' costs was equipment maintenance, which was performed by a separate department. Some operating department heads became skillful at pressuring and bargaining with the maintenance unit so that their departments' equipment would be repaired faster than that of other departments and at lower cost. This inequity led to the establishment of a formal control system run by an independent department, whereby orders would be processed in an impersonal numerical sequence.

Soon a new problem emerged. The maintenance people, initially freed from direct pressure from the operating managers, took it upon themselves to reward those who had not pressured them previously by charging the cost of some of their work to the other department heads. The newly disadvantaged managers now began to spend even more of their time trying to beg favors from maintenance, since they could no longer apply pressure. During this phase, one operating manager was said to have done so well in these covert negotiations that he was able to buy fancy new storm windows, ten new fans, and a 9,000 square-foot paint job he really didn't need. Gradually, as tensions worsened, operating departments began to set up their own internal maintenance units in order to be independent of the intrigues involved in dealing with central maintenance. This not only represented duplication of effort, but it brought conflict *into* the operating departments. The new internal maintenance foremen, responsible to the department head, felt responsible for seeing that all equipment was in top shape, while the operating foremen were angered by such interference. Here, as before, more energy was devoted to the conflict than to solving the problem.

Guardian Printing*

Guardian Printing was a large printer of publications ranging from magazines and catalogs to school textbooks. The business was a competitive one, leading to a continuing conflict between the salesmen and the plant. Salesmen, to attract new customers and hold onto existing ones, argued

---

*Adapted from Melville Dalton, *Men Who Manage,* pp. 31–42. Copyright © 1959 by John Wiley & Sons. Reprinted by permission of John Wiley & Sons, Inc.
*Case drawn from author's personal experience.

strongly and repeatedly for lower-than-normal prices and faster-than-normal schedules on virtually every job they tried to sell. The plant's managers who were evaluated on the basis of profit, not volume, always responded vigorously that prices should be high and that schedules should depend on the existing workload, not the customer's convenience.

Several mechanisms existed for dealing with these conflicts. A separate estimating department, independent of both sales and the plant, set prices initially on the basis of rational standards and then helped mediate the heated discussions of possible price cuts. To control schedule commitments, a sales scheduling unit had to issue a written schedule to the salesman before he was allowed to quote the job to the prospective customer. This small unit was located in sales but run by a former pressman, whose expertise and fairness were widely respected throughout both the plant and the sales force. He typically worked out a difficult schedule directly with plant managers and the salesman before approving it for release to the prospective customer.

Once a job had been sold, a "job manager" was assigned to serve as liaison between the plant and the customer. When unforseen events threatened to throw a job off schedule or decrease its cost, the matter was handled by the job manager as mediator between the plant departments, the salesman, and the customer. Problems tended to be solved on their merits, with the job manager working to obtain a solution to which all parties could agree.

The Milo and Guardian cases show that organizational conflict can have various forms and origins. At Milo it took the form of managers' efforts to outdo one another in the eyes of their superiors. This stemmed partly from the way in which pressure was being applied by the top management and from loose controls that allowed the maintenance department to play favorites. At Guardian the conflict was an on-going debate about goals between sales and the plant, brought about by the difference in goals between these two units, one charged with sales volume and the other with internal efficiency.

The examples also show that conflict can be handled in different ways. This is what makes organizational conflict so much more intriguing than simple "competition" (e.g., a football game or submitting sealed bids for a government contract). In competition the parties play by rules agreed to in advance. In organizational conflict the rules are not so clear, and choices have to be made as to how conflict will be managed.[1] Milo, for a while, allowed the parties to work it out in diverse informal ways. Then the company tried changes in the formal structure. At Guardian, the major burden of conflict resolution was placed on persons who filled several kinds of liaison roles.

Obviously, these different conflict management modes had different results in the two organizations. The sales-plant conflict at Guardian was constructive because energies were channeled into sound problem-solving efforts. Paperwork systems (the estimates and schedules), liaison roles (estimators, sales scheduler, job manager), and the tradition of problem solving by procedures that were widely accepted as fair were all factors that enabled Guardian to avoid the destructive outcomes and reprisals experienced at Milo. The Guardian case shows that conflict is not something to be avoided or minimized but rather to be made more productive.

In accordance with these themes, this chapter gives attention to the forms of conflict that arise in organizations, their origins, and their effects. Conflict management techniques and devices are also addressed. Attention is given to a special manifestation of conflict called role conflict and alternatives available to people who face it.

SOURCES AND EFFECTS OF CONFLICT-LADEN COMMUNICATION

Conflict can be defined as the interaction between two or more parties in an effort to gain advantage over each other where each party sees their goal as incompatable with the other's.[2] The parties may be individuals or groups. Organizations, because they bring together diverse people and groups, provide fertile breeding ground for conflicts of many kinds.

Sources of Conflict

Every conflict that arises has its own special character. A conflict cannot be separated from the individuals, the particular organization, and the unique circumstances in which the problem occurs. There are, however, certain general characteristics of organizations that tend to produce conflicts. Knowing these can sharpen our ability to identify conflict and spot situations that have high potential for conflict. These typical sources of conflict are: (1) win-lose and game situations, (2) differing subunit goals and perceptions, and (3) concerns about status and authority.[3]

Win-lose and Game Situations. Sometimes two people or groups have goals that cannot be attained simultaneously. It is surprising how often organizations set up such circumstances. A frequent example is the situation where one group is charged with inspecting the work of another. It is not unusual for the inspectors to believe sincerely that the manufacturing people are trying to slip bad parts through while they in turn are sure that the inspectors are rejecting even good parts in order to prove they are on the job. Sometimes there is truth to this. An inspector in a manufacturing plant was once asked what would happen if he went a week without rejecting any parts. He replied, "Oh, I couldn't do that. My boss would think I wasn't doing my job."[4]

Another way in which reward systems can bring about a win-lose situation sometimes occurs in decentralized organizational units, such as product divisions, branch plants, or neighborhood branches of community health clinics. Where such units are evaluated and rewarded on the basis of their individual performance, one unit is likely to resist another's requests for loans of supplies or personnel even when such moves would increase the effectiveness of the total organization.

Win-lose conflicts are frequent when resources are limited. For example, many universities currently have a policy of not increasing either the overall size of the faculty or the proportion of tenured professors. Thus, if the engineering department wishes to add a program in environmental engineering but can do this only by hiring two new senior professors, other departments will likely resist.

Conflict is often more subtle and involved than simply "going all out" to beat one's opponent. The best strategy for one party may depend on knowing what the other party will do, and this may be far from certain. The study of such situations is known as *game theory*.[5]

A classic "game" situation is the well-known Prisoner's Dilemma, which involves the following circumstances. Two persons suspected of a crime have been captured by the police. They are being questioned in separate rooms. Each is told either to confess or remain silent. If only one confesses, he or she will be released and given a reward while the other will get a stiff sentence. If both confess, they will both be jailed with light sentences. If both remain silent, the police will have no case and both will be released. If these outcomes, or "payoffs," were expressed in numerical form, they might appear as follows:

$$2 = \text{being released and getting a reward}$$
$$1 = \text{being released}$$
$$-1 = \text{light sentence}$$
$$-2 = \text{stiff sentence}$$

Exhibit 11–1 shows the situation confronting the prisoners.

EXHIBIT 11-1
PRISONER'S DILEMMA PAYOFF MATRIX

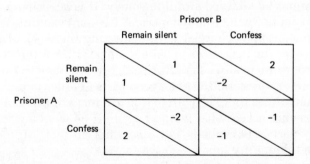

An organizational parallel to the Prisoner's Dilemma could occur when a department manager feels she can get a large increase in her department's budget if she and just a few other departments request increases, but might be seen as greedy if she is the only one to request an increase. Such situations put individuals and organizational units in a quandry because of conflicting motives. Moves have to be made without full awareness of the viewpoints of competing parties, and the payoffs available in future moves, not just the immediate one, have to be considered.

Differing Subunit Goals and Perceptions. The members of an organization are usually in agreement about the organization's general purpose: "We are here to provide good government for this city" or "We are in business to satisfy our customers and make a fair profit." They tend to disagree about more specific goals, however. Production managers, for example, will likely argue for larger inventories, since this would give them more time to adapt to changes in sales requirements, while finance managers will argue that less money should be tied up in inventory. In a teaching hospital, some staff members will argue that increased emphasis should be given to the training of interns and residents, while others will argue that such an emphasis would reduce the quality of patient care.

The presence of specialist groups contributes to this type of conflict. As one respected management writer, James D. Thompson, has put it, "the potential for conflict . . . increases with the variety of professions incorporated."[6] Research directors and sales managers are not likely to see things the same way, nor are professors and university administrators. This is partly because of their differing responsibilities but also stems from the effects of group interaction on perception. Most people tend toward the views of those with whom they are linked. Professors tend to spend their time with other professors and administrators with administrators.[7] In government, this can be observed when the president appoints a cabinet officer. Appointees who were originally loyal to the president can "get captured," sometimes within just a few days, by the permanent staff of their own agency. A former aid to Presidents Kennedy and Johnson has been quoted as saying, "Even the great Cabinet members like McNamara and Freeman were terrible in evading their share of many of our efforts."[8]

Concerns About Status and Authority. Issues of status and authority take several forms, some of the more common being empire building, individuals' desires for autonomy, and inconsistency between authority and prestige differences.

Empire building refers to efforts by a group to increase promotion opportunities for its members by increasing the size of the unit, an effort that other units are not likely to endorse. Empire building can be attempted by any unit within an organization but appears to be more prevalent among the newer staff specialities.[9]

Personal desires for autonomy lead to conflict in various ways. Anxieties about pay raises and promotions can make communication guarded or even overtly hostile between subordinates and their bosses, and between peers who may be competing with each other for advancement or perceive themselves to be. Conflict can also come up around peoples' desire to have increased control over their work and a share in decision making. The importance of this desire is validated by the success of recent programs, such as job enrichment and autonomous work groups. If frustrated, the desire for autonomy can lead to worker alienation, which might be termed a passive form of conflict, or to more active resistance.[10]

Status and authority differences do not automatically produce conflict. Other things being equal, lower-status groups are likely not to resist demands made on them by groups whom they see as having rightfully higher status. In most organizations a request from the president's office gets a rapid conscientious response. Conflict is much more likely when demands are made on a group by another party whose status is seen as inferior. In one reported case, a production unit resisted the directives it received from the company's production engineering unit, a group whose abilities it saw as being no higher than its own. Production personnel spent unreasonable amounts of time searching for errors in the drawings received from production engineering and cheered loudly when one was found. Face-to-face contact between the two departments was almost nil, with communication consisting of memos carried by messengers. Obviously, this was a destructive conflict, since it drained off energies that could have been used by the two groups to arrive more quickly at technically desirable designs.[11]

Effects of Conflict

Conflict can have positive effects, negative effects, or both. For some people conflict motivates and arouses enthusiasm, but for others it constitutes a major threat. In one study, several groups of executives were asked to think about the effects of recent conflicts in their companies. Both positive and negative outcomes were mentioned.[12]

The positive outcomes were: (1) creative thinking was stimulated; (2) new approaches were tried; (3) long-standing problems were addressed and dealt with; (4) people's viewpoints were clarified; (5) interest was heightened; and (6) people were afforded a test of their abilities.

The negative effects of conflict, as seen by the executives, were the following: (1) certain people felt defeated and embarrassed; (2) contact between people was reduced; (3) distrust and suspicion increased; (4) parties that needed to cooperate pursued their own self-interests instead; and (5) some people left as a result of the turmoil.

Researchers have made systematic observations of groups engaged in conflict, the most famous being Sherif's study of 12-year-old boys at a summer camp.[13] Sherif divided the boys into two groups, the Bull Dogs and the Red Devils, housed them in different areas of the camp, and arranged all their activities so that they would be opposed to each other. As conflict between the groups persisted and increased, the researchers noted changes in the boys' behavior toward members of their own group and toward members of the other group. These changes, classified as effects within group and effects between groups, have been replicated in later research, including studies of managers in organization training programs.[14]

Effects Within Groups. The effects that occur within groups as a result of intergroup conflict include the following:

1. *Cohesiveness increases.* Faced with a common enemy, group members tend to become more tightly knit. Internal disputes between members are forgotten and members' loyalty to the group grows.
2. *Members become more task-oriented.* The group "buckles down" to the job of meeting the challenge posed by the other group. Casualness and playfulness decrease. Members become less concerned with individual satisfaction and more concerned with getting work done.
3. *Leadership becomes more autocratic.* Since the group is felt to be in danger, members tolerate or even demand more controlling, less democratic leadership. Leaders tend not to encourage group decision making. Instead, they make unilateral decisions and issue orders to the group.
4. *Group structure becomes more formal.* Members' duties and responsibilities become more clearly defined. Activities are increasingly governed by rules and procedures.
5. *Group norms become stronger.* Conformity is stressed. Members are expected to demonstrate clearly their loyalty to the group and its values. There is little tolerance of members who do not help present a unified stand against the opposing group.

While these may appear to be the kinds of behavior one would expect within a group engaged in real warfare, these patterns do occur in less violent situations as well. Proposal-writing teams are a good example. Formed for the purpose of writing a description of work they hope to perform for some outside customer, proposal teams typically have members from a variety of specialities and are in competition with other similar groups for the award of the work. Dedication to the task usually becomes intense on these teams. Members readily agree to overtime and weekend work is order to meet deadlines and improve choices of winning the award. Team members from different specialties who are normally at odds with one another find themselves cooperating smoothly. Strong leadership evokes dutiful responses, and those who do not contribute what is expected of them are viewed with contempt by others in the group.

Effects Between Groups. When groups are in conflict, relationships between them also tend to change along the following lines:

1. *Each group's perception of the other becomes negative.* The groups no longer see each other as neutral objects but rather as enemies. Derogatory labels are applied to the rival group and its members. In the boys'

camp study, members of one group called the others "pigs" and "bums."

2. *Perceptual distortions occur.* Members see their own group as being right and the opposing group as being wrong. Selective perception develops. Negative facts about one's own group are discounted; positive aspects of the opponent are ignored. When the members listen to confrontations between representatives of the two groups, they tend to hear only part of what is said, listening intently to their own representative but remembering little that is said by the other group's representative.

3. *Hostility increases and communication decreases.* These factors contribute to the negative stereotypes each group has of the other. A decrease in interaction between the two groups reduces the opportunity for perceptual distortions to be corrected.

The earlier example of conflict between production managers and production engineers shows most of these factors. As noted, the two groups kept their distance from each other by communicating through messengers. Interaction was thus held to a minimum, except for hostile contact production initiated whenever they found an engineering error. Production was especially angered when they received engineering change orders from the engineers. In fact, the most common form of conversation among the production managers was to curse the engineers because of their change orders. It is clear that perceptual distortion was occurring, however, since the production managers themselves initiated as many change orders as the engineers did.[15]

Effects of Winning or Losing a Conflict. As discussed earlier, many organizational conflicts arise out of win-lose situations. Therefore, it is useful to continue examining the results of group conflict research to see what happens in winning and losing groups.

In winning groups, cohesiveness tends to remain high. In fact, winning groups sometimes become even more cohesive since their victory gives members another reason to be attracted to the group. Winning groups tend to relax. Tension is released. Members become complacent, feeling their victory confirms their positive stereotype of themselves as well as their negative stereotype of the other group and leaves no reason to reexamine their perceptions. In a winning group, task orientation decreases. Concern for members' needs increases, while concern for task performance declines.

In losing groups there is a strong tendency for members to distort or deny the reality of losing. Excuses are offered, such as "we didn't understand the rules of the games" or "luck was against us." Losing groups tend to splinter. Old internal conflicts reappear as members look for someone to blame for defeat. Members of the losing groups feel the need to work harder, to discover what the group did correctly and incorrectly and what their opponents real strengths and weaknesses are. Because they realize their earlier stereotypes were invalid, the losers are likely to reorganize and become more effective. Since the losers are stronger and unwilling to accept defeat, it is not unusual for intergroup tensions to become even higher and for the conflict to be renewed.

Communicating Constructively and Destructively in Conflict Situations.
    It should be clear from the effects listed above that conflicts can have negative results, but that its outcomes can also be positive. Conflict is constructive to the extent that problems are being brought to light and clarified, creativity is encouraged, and needed information is being sought out and viewed realistically. When conflict has the effects of increasing individual effort and enhancing cooperation, it is clearly acting as a constructive process. However, when the negative outcomes prevail, conflict is destructive. Destructive conflict exists when individuals experience more stress than they can tolerate, cooperation breaks down, perceptions are distorted, patterns of behavior and thought become rigid, and task motivation declines. Ethel Glenn and Elliott Pood have used the term *unregulated confrontation* to refer to this type of conflict.[16] It is characterized by a win-lose, no-holds-barred attitude in which the parties try in overt or subtle ways to injure each other. The goal becomes "eliminate your opponent" rather than "solve the problem." In the remaining sections of this chapter, attention is given to ways that organizational conflict can be managed with the aim of reducing the likelihood of destructive conflict and increasing the likelihood of constructive conflict.

APPROACHES TO MANAGING CONFLICT COMMUNICATION

It is impossible to imagine an organization in which no conflict ever occurs. Differences between peoples' personalities, their job specialties, their group affiliations, and their ideas are sure to produce conflict. Since the nature of organizations makes conflict a certainty, it is important for organization members to understand how conflict processes work. A basic model of the conflict process, as seen in exhibit 11–2, begins to suggest that there are ways conflict can be managed to make it more constructive.

A Cyclical Model of the Conflict Process

When conflict occurs, it tends to take a cyclical form (see exhibit 11–2). Opposed parties are only perodically engaged in manifest conflict. The problems and issues between them may be ongoing, but at a given point in time the conflict may be lying dormant. Then something happens to trigger the conflict and bring it out into the open. The consequences of the conflict may be favorable or unfavorable, but in either case the conflict usually becomes dormant again, to be reawakened by a later triggering event.[17]

EXHIBIT 11-2
A CYCLICAL MODEL OF CONFLICT

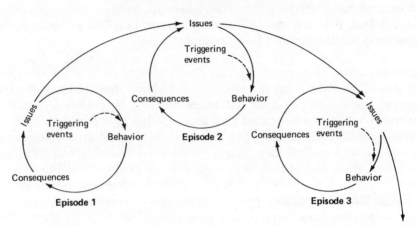

Richard E. Walton, *Interpersonal Peacemaking,* © 1969, Addison-Wesley, Reading, Massachusetts. Fig. 5.1. Reprinted with permission.

The cyclical model indicates that conflicts tend to perpetuate. The results of conflict typically produce more conflict. Thus, the model shows the consequences of conflict behavior acting upon the source problems and issues in ways that make them the sources of a new conflict episode.[18] Further, the model suggests that conflict is a dynamic process. The issues or form of the conflict typically undergo change from episode to episode. The Milo Chemical plant described at the start of this chapter provides a good example. Disputes dividing the line managers and maintenance managers were persistent and ongoing, but the manifest nature of the conflict kept changing as the results of one phase produced a different kind of succeeding phase. This suggests that if the issues producing conflict can be changed it may be possible to change a destructive conflict to a constructive one.

Exhibit 11–2 indicates another important aspect of conflict—namely, that conflict does not always become manifest. If no triggering events occur, the conflict process cannot move forward. This suggests that people wishing to avoid open conflict may be able to do so if they can understand and get control of the triggering factors. The production managers and production engineers mentioned earlier seem to have done this to a degree by breaking off face-to-face contact with each other. On the other hand, latent conflicts that do not get openly expressed sometimes lie beneath the surface, building up pressure until an explosion occurs. The avoidance of triggering events might be useful to provide a cooling-off period. It might be even better, however, for opposing groups to use triggering events to bring disputes up at times when they can deal with them rather than be consumed by them. The various meetings involving pricing and scheduling at Guardian Printing are an example of effective use of triggering events.[19]

Reactions to Intergroup Conflict

The Milo and Guardian cases show that organizations can react to intergroup conflict in different ways. In Milo alone several approaches were used. The operating managers used threats to obtain maintenance services and thereby gain the advantage over each other. Later, others used a technique of forming friendly alliances. Still later, the contending departments simply withdrew from each other by setting up their own maintenance crews. At Guardian Printing, with the aid of past precedent and effective work by liaison personnel, disputes tended to be decided on the basis of the facts of the particular case. Sources of conflict and actual disputes were present in both organizations, but they were reacted to in different ways. The possible reactions to conflict can be divided into five major categories: avoiding, smoothing, forcing, compromising, and collaborating.[20]

Avoiding. One way of dealing with conflict is simply to withdraw from it. The parties may avoid contact with each other altogether or, if meetings are inevitable, engage in pleasantries or evasions in order to avoid confronting the problem. Some groups have an incentive for avoiding disagreements. A university department may feel it can do well on its own, building up a commendable record of research and teaching in its own discipline. Its members may see opportunities for curriculum improvements involving joint programs with other departments but be reluctant to push them for fear of becoming involved in power struggles.

Avoidance can be a useful technique for cooling off the parties or preventing disputes about unimportant matters. Clearly, though, it is not a valid method for achieving long-run solutions to serious, basic issues that divide the contending parties.

Smoothing. Another method often used when the parties have a strong aversion to open conflict is smoothing. Here, discussion is limited to only those matters upon which the parties can agree. All conversation is about positive things; nothing negative is said. In effect, the parties ignore the conflict by sweeping it under the rug. In the short run, such mutual appreciation meetings may be uplifting for all concerned, but, like first aid, they leave the underlying problems unsolved.

Smoothing is sometimes employed in conflicts between superiors and subordinates. The boss may agree to meet with subordinates to discuss their grievances but spend the whole meeting telling them what a great job he thinks they're doing, thus defusing their hostility. In this mode, smoothing overlaps with the forcing process.

Forcing. Forcing occurs (1) when one antagonist wins over another by virtue of having more power in the organization, (2) when the dispute is referred to a shared superior for a decision, or (3) when some other neutral umpire or arbitrator decides the matter. To have someone who can make it stick say, "OK, here's the decision and that's it" is certainly an expedient way of stopping a conflict. Forcing is necessary in emergencies, at times when unpopular courses of action need to be implemented, and when the parties are in an adversary relationship to each other—so totally opposed that no other approach is possible. One drawback might be that the person who is most powerful is not always the most competent to make the decision. Another problem with forcing is that it can evoke bitterness in the losing party. In addition, forcing can condition the parties to become dependent on power to resolve disagreements.

Compromising. Compromise is a process of give-and-take. Each side moves from its original position to one that is somewhere in between. An example of compromise is the bargaining that occurs in labor-management contract negotiations. Another is the trading that takes place in a political setting. As a legislative committee prepares to bring a bill to the floor of the House, one group of members may vote for a provision with which they disagree in order to get others to vote for one they favor.

Like smoothing and forcing, compromising is sometimes the best possible response to conflict, depending on the particular circumstances. It has similar weaknesses, however. The compromise process, once initiated, precludes the search for better alternative solutions to the problem. The outcome is often less than appealing to both sides, and the original issues have not been dealt with according to their merits.

Collaborating. In collaboration, the parties in conflict work to reach a solution that fully satisfies the concerns of each. They first share all relevant facts and feelings, allowing differences to become clarified and admitted. Two kinds of behavior are the keys to collaboration, expressing one's own position as clearly as possible *and* listening fully to the other side's point of view. The full range of possible alternatives is considered in the search for a mutually beneficial outcome.

Collaboration is effective when the conflict stems from semantic misunderstandings, when the insights of diverse people can lead to a better decision, and when the parties are interdependent, open-minded, and desirous of solving the problem, not just exercising power or saving face. The collaboration process usually produces strong commitment to the solution, since the parties have become so highly involved in developing it.

While collaborating has great potential, it is the most difficult process to use. For many people it requires changes in behavior against which they have strong resistance. Some fear that in exploring the conflict situation someone may be hurt (including themselves). Others feel that collaboration is too soft; that one's strength as an individual can only be maintained through a forcing approach. Collaboration also requires a larger amount of time than the other methods. Thus, although it is in many ways the best method, there are situations in which the other means are more practical. Therefore, it is well for managers and other organization members to be aware of avoiding, smoothing, forcing, compromising, and collaborating, and to be able to use them as required.

Operational Steps to Managing Conflict Communication

In some organizations steps are taken to manage conflict more effectively when it becomes destructive. Because of the complexity of conflict and the many varieties of conflict, no single technique can be prescribed that will fit all circumstances. There are, however, three basic kinds of action to consider. One, two, or all three of them might prove to be promising areas for management action in a given conflict situation. The three are increasing intergroup contacts, determining a superordinate goal, and restructuring the organization.

Increasing Intergroup Contacts. One way of changing stereotypes and increasing communication is to bring the conflicting parties into more frequent contact. There is a danger in doing this, however. Sometimes when members of such groups are brought together they devote their time to propaganda, arguing the rightness of their own views and the wrongness of the other side, thus reinforcing the stereotypes.[21] This is especially likely to happen when the parties have made up their minds in advance about all the matters in contention and when the intergroup contact is between representatives who are committed to upholding their own group's position.[22] On the other hand, if such meetings are widely perceived as being for the purpose of developing joint solutions and are seen as rewarding because they generate shared data for problem solving, the outcomes can prove to be highly constructive. This has been proved experimentally as well as in actual practice. In one reported field study in a manufacturing plant, the formation of an intergroup task force not only reduced destructive conflict but also resulted in a sixty percent increase in product quality.[23]

A structured approach called the organizational confrontation meeting has been developed for bringing contending groups together, usually with the aid of consultants.[24] The groups first agree to work on improving their relationships, then each writes down its perceptions of both itself and the other group, and the two groups meet to present these to each other. The groups then separate to analyze and explain the differences in perceptions. Each group attempts to see how its own actions have contributed to the other group's misperceptions. In further joint meetings, the two groups share their analyses and begin to establish mutual goals. The method has been used successfully even in hard-line disagreements, such as those involving union and management.

Developing a Superordinate Goal. In the boys' camp experiments, the most successful tactic used to resolve conflict was developing a superordinate goal.[25] After producing two hostile groups, the researchers tried a number of methods to reduce the destructive effects of conflict—name-calling, aggression, refusal to cooperate—that had resulted. Contacts between groups and between their leaders, jointly attending movies, and other distractions had little effect. Then a series of superordinate goals was devised—ones thought to be important to both groups and which required their cooperation. Included were such projects as finding and fixing a break in the camp water supply, choosing and renting a movie, rescuing a stalled truck carrying camp food, and cooperating to prepare a meal. Tension and hostility were reduced, barriers between the groups began to fall, competition lessened, and friendships began to form across group lines. Three things that these goals had in common were:

1. Both groups desired them.
2. They required cooperation between the two groups.
3. They were successfully accomplished.

One way for antagonists to share a goal is to locate a common enemy. In one revealing example, a management consultant was attending a meeting in which two managers, each heading opposing groups, were in heated debate. A third manager came in and interrupted them, whereupon the two immediately closed ranks against him. After the "intruder" had left, the two resumed attacking one another. The consultant pointed out to them that only minutes before they had worked together to ward off the intruder. Their ensuing discussion of why and how this had happened proved to be a turning point for both managers. Cooperation between them and their groups improved greatly in the weeks that followed.[26] This example is significant because it shows that when the parties in conflict understood what was happening and saw that new behavior was possible, the relationship improved, even though the third manager had since departed. Since superordinate goals and common enemies are not always easy to find, it is encouraging to see such clear evidence that more constructive behavior can be produced *when the parties see a real potential for it.*

Restructuring the Organization. When the source of the conflict is structural, as is often the case, a structural remedy can be effective. Conflicting groups can be separated from each other organizationally, task responsibilities can be redefined, and hierarchies can be decentralized. Sometimes destructive conflict can be eliminated by combining two units that share the same function but have been separated by the design of the organization. These and other structural approaches to the management of conflict can be viewed in clearer perspective when they are considered in the light of the research findings discussed in the next section.

ORGANIZATION DESIGN AND CONFLICT MANAGEMENT

A number of basic organization designs were described in chapter 10. Whatever their differences, all of these designs have two things in common. Each includes a way of dividing an organization into specialized subunits and a way of providing for coordination between them. The geographically specialized organization has territorially defined units coordinated by a common superior. The matrix form provides specialized subunits of more than one kind and puts coordinating responsibility in the hands of two-boss managers as well as hierarchical superiors. Thus, the concepts of specialization and coordination are fundamental dimensions of organization design that cut across all the specific forms.

Two researchers, Paul Lawrence and Jay Lorsch, have used the concepts of differentiation (specialization) and integration (coordination) to describe and measure structural features in ways that highlights important aspects of conflict management.[27]

Differentiation and Integration

Lawrence and Lorsch define differentiation as the degree to which subunits within an organization differ in their formality of structure and in the goals, time orientations, and interpersonal orientations of their members. By formality of structure they mean the number of hierarchical levels and the pervasiveness of rules and formal controls in the subunit. Goals refer to the things the subunit's members see as most important, for example, cost control, technological problems, and market impacts. Time orientation indicates whether members are working on short-range, intermediate, or long-range matters, while interpersonal orientation is an indication of whether the members' approach to people is social and permissive or task-focused and directive. It is easy to see that communication would be very different in a highly formalized subunit where members' orientations center on cost control, immediate results, and the supervision of people—say a manufacturing unit—as compared with a basic research laboratory, where few rules and regulations exist, attention is focused on long-term contributions to knowledge, and relationships are collegial rather than directive. Not only is communication different *in* these two units, but, if they need to work together, destructive conflict *between* them would be likely. Their members think differently and, in a very real sense, talk two different languages.

One of the key findings of the Lawrence and Lorsch studies is that for many organizations, a high degree of differentiation is an important ingredient in the organization's success. This is especially true for organizations in uncertain, rapidly changing environments. These organizations, typified by firms in the plastics and consumer foods industries in the Lawrence and Lorsch researches, had to achieve high degrees of specialization in order to cope with the complexity of their technical and market environments. In these firms the members of the research subunit had to think and communicate like researchers, and the manufacturing personnel had to behave like manufacturers. Too much smoothing of differences across departmental lines could reduce organizational effectiveness. In other words, on-going conflict was necessary in order to keep important specialized points of view from being diluted.

Lawrence and Lorsch defined integration as "the quality of the state of collaboration that exists among departments that are required to achieve unity of effort by the demands of the environment."[28] Obviously, when the environment requires coordination between highly diverse subunits, like the research and manufacturing groups mentioned above, integration can be difficult to attain. In circumstances like this, Lawrence and Lorsch found that it was more likely to be achieved when a number of integrating devices were employed and when behavior patterns leading to effective conflict management were present.

Integrating devices include the managerial hierarchy, information and control systems, direct managerial contact across departmental boundaries, the use of individual integrator roles, temporary or permanent cross-departmental teams, and integrative departments. Where needed coordination is being attained between highly diverse subunits, it is likely that many, if not all, of these devices will be found.

Conflict management behavior involves several factors. The research results showed, for example, that integration tended to be more effective when people in integrator roles (e.g., project team members, product managers, liaison personnel) had goals, time, and interpersonal orientations that were midway between those of the specialists with whom they were working. In addition, integration was aided when power and influence were located at the places in the organization where information needed for problem solving was present, and when integrators derived their influence from technical competence rather than from their position or their control over scarce resources. Finally, integration was best attained when collaboration was the dominant type of response to conflict.

In presenting their findings, Lawrence and Lorsch showed what their results meant in terms of face-to-face communication between people in two highly effective organizations, a plastics firm operating in a complex and dynamic environment, and a container manufacturing firm, which was in a simpler, more stable environment.

> In the plastics organization we might find a sales manager discussing a potential new product with a fundamental research scientist and an integrator. In this discussion the sales manager is concerned with the needs of the customer. What performance characteristics must a new product have to perform in the customer's machinery? How much can the customer afford to pay? How long can the material be stored without deteriorating? Further, our sales manager, while talking about these matters, may be thinking about more pressing current problems. Should he lower the price on an existing

product? Did the material shipped to another customer meet his specifications? Is he going to meet this quarter's sales targets?

In contrast, our fundamental scientist is concerned about a different order of problems. Will this new project provide a scientific challenge? To get the desired result, could he change the molecular structure of a known material without affecting its stability? What difficulties will he encounter in solving these problems? Will this be a more interesting project to work on than another he heard about last week? Will he receive some professional recognition if he is successful in solving the problem. . . .

But these are not the only ways in which those two specialists are different. The sales manager may be outgoing and concerned with maintaining a warm, friendly relationship with the scientist. He may be put off because the scientist seems withdrawn and disinclined to talk about anything other than the problem in which he is interested. He may also be annoyed that the scientist seems to have such freedom in choosing what he will work on. Furthermore, the scientist is probably often late for appointments, which from the salesman's point of view, is no way to run a business. Our scientist, for his part, may feel uncomfortable because the salesman seems to be pressing for immediate answers to technical questions that will take a long time to investigate. All these discomforts are concrete manifestations of the relatively wide differences between these two men in respect to their working and thinking styles and the departmental structures to which each is accustomed.

Between these two points of view stands our integrator. If he is effective, he will understand and to some extent share the viewpoints of both specialists and will be working to help them communicate with each other. . . .

In the high-performing container organization we might find a research scientist meeting with a plant manager to determine how to solve a quality problem. The plant manager talks about getting the problem solved as quickly as possible, in order to reduce the spoilage rate, . . . to meet the current production schedule and to operate within cost constraints. The researcher is also seeking an immediate answer to the problem. He is concerned not with its theoretical niceties, but with how he can find an immediate applied solution. . . . In fact, these specialists may share a concern with finding the most feasible solution. They also operate in a similar, short-term time dimension. The differences in their interpersonal style are also not too large. Both are primarily concerned with getting the job done, and neither finds the other's style of behavior strange. They are also accustomed to quite similar organizational practices. Both see that they are rewarded for quite specific short-run accomplishments, and both might be feeling similar pressures from their superiors to get the job done. . . . Thus they would need no integrator.[29]

These examples are helpful in showing that there is not one universal formula for conflict management. In an organization having a high degree of differentiation, coordination is aided by having integrators present. This allows the specialists to avoid having too much direct contact with each other—contact that might result either in destructive conflict or in compromising necessary differences between the specialists' orientations.

In this organization, the design provides an integrator who confronts each specialist while the specialists tend to avoid one another. In an organization where differentiation is not so great, the design of the organization allows direct collaboration among the specialists and is appropriate. In this setting, an integrator might turn out to be superfluous. Overall, the Lawrence and Lorsch studies show clearly that organization design has an important bearing on conflict management, and that effective conflict management occurs in different ways depending on the particular organizational circumstances.

COMMUNICATION AND ROLE CONFLICT

One of the most intense ways that individuals experience organizational conflict is in the condition social scientists call role conflict. Role conflict exists when a person is expected to behave in incompatibly different ways by two or more important other people. The incompatible demands may come from a manager's own superior and subordinates when, for example, the superior expects reduced costs while subordinates want their budgets increased (exhibit 11-3). Conflicting demands may also come from others on the individual's own level, as when a person's job requires contact with two or more departments in a highly differentiated organization. As organizations become more complex and rapidly changing, role conflict is becoming an increasingly common experience for organization members. It not only occurs frequently but in a wide variety of occupational settings including unskilled workers, educational administrators, school teachers, salesmen, scientists, chaplains, and industrial managers.[30]

It is clear that being in a role-conflict situation puts the individual

EXHIBIT 11-3

A MANAGER IN A CONDITION OF ROLE CONFLICT

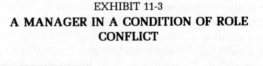

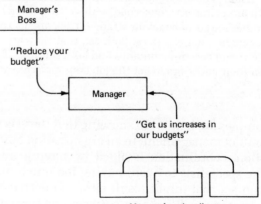

under stress, often resulting in tension and reduced productivity and job satisfaction.[31] It is equally clear, however, that role conflict is an inevitable fact of organizational life. The importance to many organizations of such managerial roles as integrator, liaison person, product manager, and project manager has already been pointed out in this chapter and chapter 10. These positions tend to bring the incumbent into contact with work associates whose viewpoints differ widely, but it is for this reason that these jobs are so important for facilitating flows of information and managing conflict in the organization.[32] The important question, therefore, is not how to make role conflict disappear but how to cope with it effectively.

One can easily begin to see that there are many ways to cope with role conflict. Imagine that your parents want you to come home for the weekend, but your roommate had just managed to get two tickets to a crucial basketball game Saturday night and wants you to go to the game. You have several alternatives. You can simply do what your parents want and ignore your roommate, or vice versa. You can perhaps exert influence on one or the other to try to get them to change their preferences (obviously the parents in this case). Or, you might try to satisfy them both by going home Saturday evening after the game. You might even try to achieve a redefinition of the whole situation by inviting your parents to visit the campus for the weekend and go to the game themselves.

When a member of an organization experiences role conflict, an even larger number of alternatives may be available, and the choice of an approach may be far more difficult to make. Suppose a project manager has been told by the company controller that no more budget revision will be allowed, whereupon the engineering director comes to him and says additional funds will be needed in order to meet schedule. It is likely that the parties to this dispute will be much less ready to change their preferences or accept a redefinition of the situation than the parties in the basketball game example. Department goals and professional judgments are at stake.

Despite the difficulties, it appears that some people are more successful than others in managing role conflict and also less weakened by it. Both conclusions seem well supported by the results of research on the differences between more and less effective managers in integrator roles. Although there is a high degree of role conflict in these jobs, they tend to be handled well by people who have certain characteristics.[33] Intermediate orientations toward time, goals, and personal relationship style were mentioned earlier, as was the importance of exerting influence on the basis of expertise and knowledge. Other characteristics include the following:

1. A preference for taking the initiative.
2. Confidence and persuasiveness.
3. Social poise, spontaneity, talkativeness. A preference for flexible ways of acting.

4. A strong desire to affiliate with people. Moderate but not extreme desires for achievement and power.
5. An ability to reach one's own conclusions despite coercive pressure from others.
6. A view that rewards come from the success of the task or project, not just from personal accomplishment.
7. A tendency to attach high priority to planning and goal-setting activities.
8. Lack of excessive feelings of pressure.
9. General agreement with the policies of the organization.

Personal skills are important, but it is also clear that the organizational surroundings need to be conducive if role conflict is to be managed successfully. In one study in which integrators were found to be performing effectively in a government research laboratory, the organization was designed in a flexible, nonbureaucratic way. Furthermore, top management as well as lower management had agreed to try the integrator concept. Had these circumstances been different, the integrators might not have been able to perform so well.[34]

In short, studies of the integrator role have shown that successful communication is possible even by people who are subjected to role conflict. This success depends, however, on specific kinds of behavior by the individual and on organizational surroundings that reinforce the individual's efforts.

Summary

The major aim of this chapter has been twofold. First, some of the forces in organizations that produce conflict-laden communication were described. Second, it was shown that the communication involved in organizational conflict can be constructive rather than destructive.

Organizational sources of conflict were examined, including win-lose situations, differing subunit goals, and perceptions and concerns about status and authority. The effects of conflict within and between competing groups were reviewed, as were the effects of winning and losing. These effects were found to include both positive and negative factors. Approaches to managing conflict were then discussed, including the general alternatives of avoiding, smoothing, forcing, compromising, and collaborating. Attention was also given to three possible operational steps toward conflict management—the increasing of intergroup contacts, developing a superordinate goal, and restructuring the organization. Factors involved in effective conflict management were then discussed from two standpoints, overall organization design and the individual organization member. From the organization design standpoint, the research studies on differentiation and integration showed that organizations need productive conflict and that certain structural features can help encourage and manage it. From the perspective of the individual, role conflict was discussed along with the factors that enable people experiencing role conflict to cope with it successfully.

Questions for Review

1. Why is it true that the most persistent conflicts are those that have their roots in the structure of the organization itself? Give an example.
2. Give examples from your own experience of instances where conflict was (a) helpful and (b) harmful. What accounts for the difference?
3. At the end of a sports event, what kinds of communication are likely among members of (a) the winning team and (b) the losing team?
4. Are there instances where collaboration is not the best response to conflict? Discuss.
5. How do the concepts discussed in this chapter help explain why conflict is likely to lead to more conflict? Explain.
6. Think of an organization you know about that is highly differentiated. How does this organization manage conflict? How could its conflict management be improved?
7. Why is role conflict likely to act as a barrier to communication?
8. Think of two experiences you have had in a role conflict situation, one that you handled well and one you handled less skillfully. What made the difference?

References and Notes

1. The distinction between competition and conflict has been made by several authors. See Raymond W. Mack and Richard C. Snyder, "The Analysis of Social Conflict," *Journal of Conflict Resolution* 1 (1957); 212–48, especially p. 217.
2. The definition draws upon Kenneth E. Boulding, *Conflict and Defense* (New York: Harper & Brothers, 1962), p. 5; Alan C. Filley, *Interpersonal Conflict Resolution* (Glenview, Ill.: Scott, Foresman, 1975), p. 4.
3. The threefold classification of types of conflict is adapted from Joseph A. Litterer, "Conflict in Organization: A Re-Examination," *Academy of Management Journal* 9, no. 3 (September 1966): 178–86; Victor A. Thompson, *Modern Organization* (New York; Alfred A. Knopf, 1961), pp. 99–108; Richard E. Walton and John M. Dutton, "The Management of Interdepartmental Conflict: A Model and Review," *Administrative Science Quarterly* 14, no. 1 (1969); 73–84; H. Randolph Bobbitt, Jr. et. al., *Organizational Behavior* (Englewood Cliffs, N.J.: Prentice-Hall, 1974), pp. 137–44.
4. Edgar F. Huse and James L. Bowditch, *Behavior in Organizations* (Reading, Mass.: Addison-Wesley, 1977), p. 203.
5. Among many sources for a more complete discussion of game theory in

interpersonal communication are Joyce Hocker Frost and William W. Wilmot, *Interpersonal Conflict* (Dubuque, Ia.: Wm. C. Brown, 1978), pp. 65–77; Kenneth J. Gergen, *The Psychology of Behavior Exchange* (Reading, Mass.: Addison-Wesley, 1969), pp. 51–70; Anatol Rappaport, "Conflict Resolution in the Light of Game Theory and Beyond," in *The Structure of Conflict*, ed. Paul Swingle (New York: Academic Press, 1970), pp. 1–43; Thomas C. Schelling, *The Strategy of Conflict* (Cambridge, Mass.: Harvard University Press, 1960).

6. James D. Thompson, *Organizations in Action* (New York: McGraw-Hill, 1967), p. 139.

7. Huse and Bowditch, *Behavior in Organizations,* p. 206; Thompson, *Modern Organization,* pp. 105–8.

8. Richard Tanner Johnson, *Managing the White House* (New York: Harper and Row, 1974), p. xix.

9. Thompson, *Modern Organization,* pp. 101–3.

10. See, for example, Irving Bluestone, "Worker Participation in Decision Making," in Edgar F. Huse, James L. Bowditch, and Dalmar Fisher, *Readings on Behavior in Organizations* (Reading, Mass.: Addison-Wesley, 1975), pp. 9–24.

11. The discussion of status and authority inconsistency, including the example, draws upon John A. Seiler, "Diagnosing Interdepartmental Conflict," *Harvard Business Review,* September–October 1963, pp. 121–32.

12. Warren H. Schmidt, "Conflict: A Powerful Force for (Good or Bad) Change," *Management Review,* December 1974, pp. 5–10.

13. Muzafer Sherif and Carolyn W. Sherif, *Groups in Harmony and Tension* (New York: Harper and Row, 1953).

14. Robert R. Blake and Jane S. Mouton, "Reactions to Intergroup Competition under Win-Lose Conditions," *Management Science* 4, no. 4 (1961); 420–35; Huse and Bowditch, *Behavior in Organizations,* pp. 208–10; Edgar H. Schein, *Organizational Psychology* (Englewood Cliffs, N.J.: Prentice-Hall, 1965), pp. 96–97.

15. Seiler, "Diagnosing Interdepartmental Conflict," pp. 121–32.

16. Ethel C. Glenn and Elliott Pood, "Groups Can Make The Best Decisions If You Lead The Way," *Supervisory Management* 23 (December 1978); 2–6.

17. The discussion of the cyclical model of the conflict process is based on Richard E. Walton, *Interpersonal Peacemaking: Confrontations and Third Party Consultation* (Reading, Mass.: Addison-Wesley, 1969), pp. 71–73; Louis R. Pondy, "Organizational Conflict: Concepts and Models," *Administrative Science Quarterly* 12, no. 2 (1977); 296–320.

18. Morton Deutsch, *The Resolution of Conflict* (New Haven, Conn.: Yale University Press, 1973), p. 365. Duetsch asserts that the conflict process fits his "crude law of social relations," which is that "processes and effects elicited by a given type of social relationship . . . tend also to elicit that type of social relationships."

19. The discussion of triggering events is based on Edgar F. Huse, *Organization Development and Change* (St. Paul, Minn.: West Publishing Company, 1975), p. 229.

20. Robert R. Blake and Jane S. Mouton, *The Managerial Grid* (Houston: Gulf Publishing Company, 1964); Kenneth Thomas, "Conflict and Conflict Management," in Marvin D. Dunnette, *Handbook of Industrial and Organizational Psychology* (Chicago: Rand McNally, 1976), pp. 889–935; Stephen P. Robbins,

" 'Conflict Management' and 'Conflict Resolution' Are Not Synonymous Terms," *California Management Review* 21 (Winter 1978); 67–75; Eleanor Phillips and Ric Cheston, "Conflict Resolution: What Works?" *California Management Review* 21 (Summer 1979); 76–83.

21. H. Joseph Reitz, *Behavior in Organizations* (Homewood, Ill.: Richard D. Irwin, 1977), p. 454.

22. Deutsch, *Resolution of Conflict,* p. 378; Harold J. Leavitt, *Managerial Psychology* (Chicago: University of Chicago Press, 1964), pp. 284–93.

23. Edgar F. Huse, "The Behavioral Scientist in the Shop," *Personnel* 42, no. 3 (May–June 1965); 50–57. For an experimental study, see Thomas M. Steinfalt, David R. Seibold, and Terry K. Frye, "Communication in Game Simulated Conflicts: Two Experiments," *Speech Monographs* 41 (1974); 24–35.

24. Richard Beckhard, *Organizational Development: Strategies and Models* (Reading, Mass.: Addison-Wesley, 1969). See also Robert R. Blake, Herbert A. Shephard, and Jane S. Mouton, *Managing Intergroup Conflict in Industry* (Houston: Gulf Publishing Company, 1964).

25. Sherif and Sherif, *Groups in Harmony and Tension,* pp. 159–96.

26. Huse and Bowditch, *Behavior in Organizations,* pp. 211–12.

27. Paul R. Lawrence and Jay W. Lorsch, "Organizing for Product Innovation," *Harvard Business Review*, January–February 1965, pp. 109–20; idem, "Differentiation and Integration in Complex Organizations," *Administrative Science Quarterly* 12, no. 1 (1967); 1–47; idem, *Organization and Environment* (Boston: Division of Research, Harvard Business School, 1967).

28. Lawrence and Lorsch, *Organization and Environment,* p. 11.

29. Used by permission of Harvard University Press from *Organization and Environment* by Paul R. Lawrence and Jay W. Lorsch, Boston: Division of Research, Graduate School of Business Administration, Harvard University; Copyright © 1967 by the President and Fellows of Harvard College.

30. J. Ben-David, "The Professional Role of the Physician in Bureaucratized Medicine," *Human Relations* 11, no. 3 (1958); 255–57; Norman Kaplan, "The Role of the Research Administrator," *Administrative Science Quarterly* 4, no. 1 (June 1959); 20–41; Amitai Etzioni, "Authority Structure and Organizational Effectiveness," *Administrative Science Quarterly* 4, no. 1 (June 1959); 43–67; Ronald G. Corwin, "The Professional Employee: A Study of Conflict in Nursing Roles," *American Journal of Sociology* 66, no. 6 (1961); 604–15; J. Paschal Twyman and Bruce J. Biddle, "Role Conflict of Public School Teachers," *Journal of Psychology* 55, no. 1 (1963); 183–98; Robert L. Kahn et. al., *Organizational Stress: Studies in Role Conflict and Ambiguity* (New York: John Wiley & Sons, 1964).

31. See, for example, John T. Gullahorn, "Measuring Role Conflict," *American Journal of Sociology* 61, no. 4 (1956); 299–303; Neil Gross et. al., *Explorations in Role Analysis* (New York: John Wiley & Sons, 1966), pp. 212–21; Kahn et. al., *Organizational Stress.*

32. For a study of role conflict in the integrator role, see Dalmar Fisher, "Entrepreneurship and Moderation: The Role of the Integrator," in *Studies in Organization Design,* ed. Jay W. Lorsch and Paul R. Lawrence (Homewood, Ill.: Irwin-Dorsey, 1970), pp. 153–67. The importance of liaison roles is shown, for example, in Thomas J. Allen, "Communications in the Research and Development Laboratory," in Bernard L. Hinton and H. Joseph Reitz, *Groups and*

Organizations (Belmont, Calif.: Wadsworth Publishing Company, 1971), pp. 108–14; Donald F. Schwartz and Eugene Jacobson, "Organizational Communication Network Analysis: The Liaison Communication Role," *Organizational Behavior and Human Performance* 18, no. 1 (1977); 158–74.

33. Jay W. Lorsch and Paul R. Lawrence, "New Management Job: The Integrator," *Harvard Business Review,* November–December 1967, pp. 142–51; Fisher, "Entrepreneurship and Moderation," pp. 153–67.

34. Stephen A. Stumpf, "Using Integrators to Manage Conflict in a Research Organization," *Journal of Applied Behavioral Science* 13, no. 4 (1977); 507–17.

Cases

for Part Four

The Case of the Missing Time*

At approximately 7:30 A.M. on Tuesday, June 23, 1959, Chet Craig, manager of the Norris Company's Central Plant, swung his car out of the driveway of his suburban home and headed toward the plant located some six miles away just inside the Midvale city limits.[1] It was a beautiful day. The sun was shining brightly and a cool, fresh breeze was blowing. The trip to the plant took about 20 minutes and sometimes gave Chet an opportunity to think about plant problems without interruption.

The Norris Company owned and operated three quality printing plants. Norris enjoyed a nation-wide commercial business, specializing in quality color work. It was a closely held company with some 350 employees, nearly half of whom were employed at the Central Plant, the largest of the three Norris production operations. The company's main offices were also located in the Central Plant building.

Chet had started with the Norris Company as an expediter in its Eastern Plant in 1948 just after he graduated from Ohio State. After three years Chet was promoted to production supervisor and two years later was made assistant to the manager of the Eastern Plant. Early in 1957 he was transferred to the Central Plant as assistant to the plant manager and one month later was promoted to plant manager, when the former manager retired.

Chet was in fine spirits as he relaxed behind the wheel. As his car picked up speed, the hum of the tires on the newly paved highway faded into the background. Various thoughts occurred to him and he said to himself, "This is going to be the day to really get things done."

He began to run through the day's work, first one project, then another, trying to establish priorities. After a few minutes he decided that the open-end unit scheduling was probably the most important; certainly the most urgent. He frowned for a moment as he recalled that on Friday and vice president and general manager had casually asked him if he had given the project any further thought. Chet realized that he had not been giving it much thought lately. He had been meaning to get to work on this idea for over three months, but something else always seemed to crop up. "I haven't had much time to sit down and really work it out," he said to himself. "I'd better get going and hit this one today for sure." With that he began to break down the objectives, procedures, and installation steps

---

*Copyright © 1960, Northwestern University. Reproduced by permission.
[1]All names and organizational designations have been disguised.

301

of the project. He grinned as he reviewed the principles involved and calculated roughly the anticipated savings. "It's about time," he told himself. "This idea should have been followed up long ago." Chet remembered that he had first conceived of the open-end unit scheduling idea nearly a year and a half ago just prior to his leaving Norris's Eastern Plant. He had spoken to his boss, Jim Quince, manager of the Eastern Plant, about it then and both agreed that it was worth looking into. The idea was temporarily shelved when he was transferred to the Central Plant a month later.

A blast from a passing horn startled him but his thoughts quickly returned to other plant projects he was determined to get under way. He started to think through a procedure for simpler transport of dies to and from the Eastern Plant. Visualizing the notes on his desk he thought about the inventory analysis he needed to identify and eliminate some of the slow-moving stock items; the packing controls which needed revision; and the need to design a new special-order form. He also decided that this was the day to settle on a job printer to do the simple outside printing of office forms. There were a few other projects he couldn't recall offhand but he could tend to them after lunch if not before. "Yes sir," he said to himself, "this is the day to really get rolling."

Chet's thoughts were interrupted as he pulled into the company parking lot. When he entered the plant Chet knew something was wrong as he met Al Noren, the stockroom foreman, who appeared troubled. "A great morning, Al," Chet greeted him cheerfully.

"Not so good, Chet; my new man isn't in this morning," Noren growled.

"Have you heard from him?" asked Chet.

"No, I haven't," replied Al.

Chet frowned as he commented, "These stock handlers assume you take it for granted that if they're not here, they're not here, and they don't have to call in and verify it. Better ask Personnel to call him."

Al hesitated for a moment before replying. "Okay, Chet, but can you find me a man? I have two cars to unload today."

As Chet turned to leave he said, "I'll call you in half an hour, Al, and let you know."

Making a mental note of the situation Chet headed for his office. He greeted the group of workers huddled around Marilyn, the office manager, who was discussing the day's work schedule with them. As the meeting broke up Marilyn picked up a few samples from the clasper, showed them to Chet, and asked if they should be shipped that way or if it would be necessary to inspect them. Before he could answer, Marilyn went on to ask if he could suggest another clerical operator for the sealing machine to replace the regular operator who was home ill. She also told him that Gene, the industrial engineer, had called and was waiting to hear from Chet.

After telling Marilyn to go ahead and ship the samples, he made a note of the need for a sealer operator for the office and then called Gene.

He agreed to stop by Gene's office before lunch and started on his routine morning tour of the plant. He asked each foreman the types and volumes of orders they were running, the number of people present, how the schedules were coming along, and the orders to be run next; helped the folding-room foreman find temporary storage space for consolidating a carload shipment; discussed quality control with a pressman who had been running poor work; arranged to transfer four people temporarily to different departments, including two for Al in the stockroom, talked to the shipping foreman about pickups and special orders to be delivered that day. As he continued through the plant, he saw to it that reserve stock was moved out of the forward stock area; talked to another pressman about his requested change of vacation schedule; and a "heart-to-heart" talk with a press helper who seemed to need frequent reassurance; approved two type and one color order okays for different pressmen.

Returning to his office, Chet reviewed the production reports on the larger orders against his initial productions and found that the plant was running behind schedule. He called in the folding-room foreman and together they went over the line-up of machines and made several necessary changes.

During this discussion, the composing-room foreman stopped in to cover several type changes and the routing foreman telephoned for approval of a revised printing schedule. The stockroom foreman called twice, first to inform him that two standard, fast-moving stock items were dangerously low; later to advise him that the paper stock for the urgent Dillion job had finally arrived. Chet made the necessary subsequent calls to inform those concerned.

He then began to put delivery dates on important and difficult inquiries received from customers and salesmen. (The routine inquiries were handled by Marilyn.) While he was doing this he was interrupted twice, once by a sales correspondent calling from the West Coast to ask for a better delivery date than originally scheduled; once by the personnel vice president asking him to set a time when he could hold an initial training and induction interview with a new employee.

After dating the customer and salesmen inquiries, Chet headed for his morning conference in the Executive Offices. At this meeting he answered the sales vice president's questions in connection with "hot" orders, complaints, the status of large-volume orders and potential new orders. He then met with the general manager to discuss a few ticklish policy matters and to answer "the old man's" questions on several specific production and personnel problems. Before leaving the Executive Offices, he stopped at the office of the secretary-treasurer to inquire about delivery of cartons, paper, and boxes, and to place a new order for paper.

On the way back to his own office, Chet conferred with Gene about two current engineering projects concerning which he had called earlier. When he reached his desk, he lit a cigarette, and looked at his watch. It was 10 minutes before lunch, just time enough to make a few notes of the details he needed to check in order to answer knotty questions raised by the sales manager that morning.

After lunch Chet started again. He began by checking the previous day's production reports; did some rescheduling to get out urgent orders; placed appropriate delivery dates on new orders and inquiries received that morning; consulted with a foreman on a personal problem. He spent some 20 minutes at the TWX[2] going over mutual problems with the Eastern Plant.

By midafternoon Chet had made another tour of the plant after which he met with the personnel director to review with him a touchy personal problem raised by one of the clerical employees; the vacation schedules submitted by his foremen; and the pending job evaluation program. Following this conference, Chet hurried back to his office to complete the special statistical report for Universal Waxing Corporation, one of Norris' best customers. As he finished the report he discovered that it was ten minutes after six and he was the only one left in the office. Chet was tired. He put on his coat and headed through the plant toward the parking lot; on the way he was stopped by both the night supervisor and night layout foreman for approval of type and layout changes.

With both eyes on the traffic, Chet reviewed the day he had just completed. "Busy?" he asked himself. "Too much so—but did I accomplish anything?" His mind raced over day's activities. "Yes and no" seemed to be the answer. "There was the usual routine, the same as any other day. The plant kept going and I think it must have been a good production day. Any creative or special project-work done?" Chet grimaced as he reluctantly answered, "No."

With a feeling of guilt, he probed further. "Am I an executive? I'm paid like one, respected like one, and have a responsible assignment with the necessary authority to carry it out. Yet one of the greatest values a company derives from an executive is his creative thinking and accomplishments. What have I done about it? An executive needs some time for thinking. Today was a typical day, just like most other days, and I did little, if any, creative work. The projects that I so enthusiastically planned to work on this morning are exactly as they were yesterday. What's more, I have no guarantee that tomorrow night or the next night will bring me any closer to their completion. This is a real problem and there must be an answer."

Chet continued, "Night work? Yes, occasionally. This is understood. But I've been doing too much of this lately. I owe my wife and family some of my time. When you come down to it, they are the people for whom I'm really working. If I am forced to spend much more time away from them, I'm not meeting my own personal objectives. What about church work? Should I eliminate that? I spend a lot of time on this, but I feel I owe God some time too. Besides, I believe I'm making a worthwhile

---

[2]Leased private telegram communication system using teletypewriter.

contribution in this work. Perhaps I can squeeze a little time from my fraternal activities. But where does recreation fit in?"

Chet groped for the solution. "Maybe I'm just rationalizing because I schedule my own work poorly. But I don't think so. I've studied my work habits carefully and I think I plan intelligently and delegate authority. Do I need an assistant? Possibly, but that's a long-time project and I don't believe I could justify the additional overhead expenditure. Anyway, I doubt whether it would solve the problem."

By this time Chet had turned off the highway onto the side street leading to his home—the problem still uppermost in his mind. "I guess I really don't know the answer," he told himself as he pulled into his driveway. "This morning everything seemed so simple but now...." His thoughts were interrupted as he saw his son running toward the car calling out, "Mommy, Daddy's home."

NORRIS COMPANY

Organization Chart

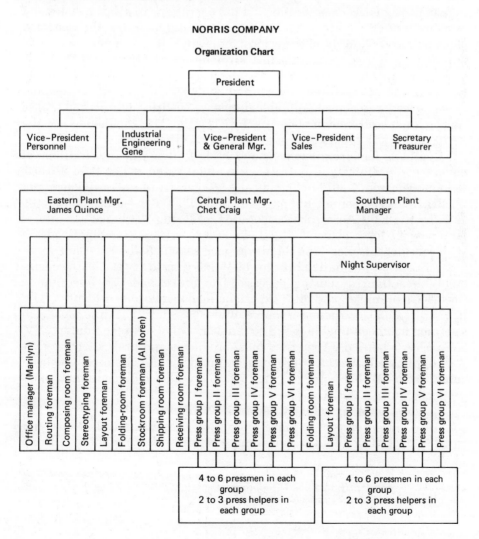

Case Questions

1. How did the things Chet Craig planned to do on the day described in the case differ from the things he actually did do?
2. What is it about Chet's style of communicating with people that leaves him short of time?
3. Consider the organization chart. Does organization design have a bearing on Chet's problem?
4. What changes in communication style, organization design, or both, would you recommend to Chet Craig?

The Aircraft Brake Scandal: A Cautionary Tale in Which The Moral Is Unpleasant*

The B. F. Goodrich Company is what business magazines like to refer to as "a major American corporation." It has operations in a dozen states and as many foreign countries: and of these far-flung facilities, the Goodrich plant at Troy, Ohio, is not the most imposing. It is a small, one-story building, once used to manufacture airplanes. Set in the grassy flatlands of west-central Ohio, it employs only about six hundred people. Nevertheless, it is one of the three largest manufacturers of aircraft wheels and brakes, a leader in a most profitable industry. Goodrich wheels and brakes support such well-known planes as the F111, the C5A, the Boeing 727, the XB70, and many others.

Contracts for aircraft wheels and brakes often run into millions of dollars, and ordinarily a contract with a total value of less than $70,000, though welcome, would not create any special stir of joy in the hearts of Goodrich sales personnel. But purchase order P-237138—issued on June 18, 1967, by the LTV Aerospace Corporation, ordering 202 brake assemblies for a new air force plane at a total of $69,417—was received by Goodrich with considerable glee. And there was good reason. Some ten years previously, Goodrich had built a brke for LTV that was, to say the least, considerably less than a rousing success. The brake had not lived up to Goodrich's promises, and after experiencing considerable difficulty, LTV had written off Goodrich as a source of brakes. Since that time, Goodrich salesmen had been unable to sell so much as a shot of brake fluid to LTV. So in 1967, when LTV requested bids on wheels and brakes for the new A7D light attack aircraft it proposed to build for the air force, Goodrich submitted a bid that was absurdly low, so low that LTV could not, in all prudence, turn it down.

Goodrich had, in industry parlance, "bought into the business." The company did not expect to make a profit on the initial deal; it was prepared, if necessary, to lose money. But aircraft brakes are not something

---

*"The Aircraft Brake Scandal" by Kermit Vandivier from *In The Name of Profit: Profiles in Corporate Irresponsibility* by Robert Heilbroner. Copyright © 1972 by Doubleday & Company, Inc. Reprinted by permission of the publisher.

that can be ordered off the shelf. They are designed for a particular aircraft, and once an aircraft manufacturer buys a brke, he is forced to purchase all replacement parts from the brake manufacturer. The $70,000 that Goodrich would get for making the brake would be a drop in the bucket when compared with the cost of the linings and other parts the air force would have to buy from Goodrich during the lifetime of the aircraft.

There was another factor, besides the low bid, that had undoubtedly influenced LTV. All aircraft brakes made today are of the disk type, and the bid submitted by Goodrich called for a relatively small brake, one containing four disks and weighing only 106 pounds. The weight of any aircraft part is extremely important: The lighter a part is, the heavier the plane's payload can be.

The brake was designed by one of Goodrich's most capable engineers, John Warren. A tall, lanky, blond graduate of Purdue, Warren had come from the Chrysler Corporation seven years before and had become adept at aircraft brake design. The happy-go-lucky manner he usually maintained belied a temper that exploded whenever anyone ventured to offer criticism of his work, no matter how small. On these occasions, Warren would turn red in the face, often throwing or slamming something and then stalking from the scene. As his co-workers learned the consequences of criticizing him, they did so less and less readily, and when he submitted his preliminary design for the A7D brake, it was accepted without question.

Warren was named project engineer for the A7D, and he, in turn, assigned the task of producing the final production design to a newcomer to the Goodrich engineering stable, Searle Lawson. Just turned twenty-six, Lawson had been out of the Northrop Institute of Technology only one year when he came to Goodrich in January 1967. He had been assigned to various "paper projects" to break him in, and after several months spent reviewing statistics and old brake designs, he was beginning to fret at the lack of challenge. When told he was being assigned to his first "real" project, he was elated and immediately plunged into his work.

The major portion of the design had already been completed by Warren, and major subassemblies for the brake had already been ordered from Goodrich suppliers. Naturally, however, before Goodrich could start making the brakes on a production basis, much testing would have to be done. Lawson would have to determine the best materials to use for the linings and discover what minor adjustments in the design would have to be made.

Then, after the preliminary testing and after the brake was judged ready for production, one whole brake assembly would undergo a series of grueling, simulated braking stops and other severe trials called qualification tests. These tests are required by the military, which gives very detailed specifications on how they are to be conducted, the criteria for failure, and so on. They are performed in the Goodrich plant's test laboratory, where huge machines called dynamometers can simulate the weight and speed of almost any aircraft.

A DISMAL BEGINNING

Searle Lawson was well aware that much work had to be done before the A7D brake could go into production, and he knew that LTV had set the last two weeks in June 1968 as the starting dates for flight tests. So he decided to begin testing immediately. Goodrich's suppliers had not yet delivered the brake housing and other parts, but the brake disks had arrived, and using the housing from a brake similar in size and weight to the A7D brake, Lawson built a prototype. The prototype was installed in a test wheel and placed on one of the big dynamometers in the plant's test laboratory. Lawson began a series of tests, "landing" the wheel and brake at the A7D's landing speed and braking it to a stop. The main purpose of these preliminary tests was to learn what tempratures would develop within the brake during the simulated stops and to evaluate lining materials tentatively selected for use.

During a normal aircraft landing, the temperatures inside the brake may reach 1,000 degrees, and occasionally a bit higher. During Lawson's first simulated landings, the temperature of his prototype brake reached 1,500 degrees. The brake glowed a bright cherry-red and threw off incandescent particles of metal and lining material as the temperature reached its peak. After a few such stops, the brake was dismantled and the linings were found to be almost completely disintegrated. Lawson chalked this first failure up to chance and, ordering new lining materials, tried again.

The second attempt was a repeat of the first. The brake became extremely hot, causing the lining materials to crumble into dust.

After the third such failure, Lawson, inexperienced though he was, knew that the fault lay not in defective parts or unsuitable lining material but in the basic design of the brake itself. Ignoring Warren's original computations, Lawson made his own, and it didn't take him long to discover whre the trouble lay—the brake was too small. There simply was not enough surface area on the disks to stop the aircraft without generating the excessive heat that caused the linings to fail.

The answer to the problem was obvious, but far from simple—the four-disk brake would have to be scrapped, and a new design using five disks, would have to be developed. The implications were not lost on Lawson. Such a step would require junking the four-disk brake subassemblies, many of which had now begun to arrive from the various suppliers. It would also mean several weeks of preliminary design and testing and many more weeks of waiting while the suppliers made and delivered the new subassemblies.

Yet, several weeks had already gone by since LTV's order had arrived, and the date for delivery of the first production brakes for flight testing was only a few months away.

Although John Warren had more or less turned the A7D over to Lawson, he knew of the difficulties Lawson had been experiencing. He had assured the young engineer that the problem revolved around getting the right kind of lining material. Once that was found, he said, the difficulties would end.

Despite the evidence of the abortive tests and Lawson's careful computations, Warren rejected the suggestion that the four-disk brake was too light for the job. He knew that his superior had already told LTV, in rather glowing terms, that the preliminary tests on the A7D brake were very successful. Indeed, Warren's superiors weren't aware at this time of the trouble on the brake. It would have been difficult for Warren to admit not only that he had made a serious error in his calculations and original design but that his mistakes had been caught by a green kid, barely out of college.

Warren's reaction to a five-disk brake was not unexpected by Lawson, and, seeing that the four-disk brake was not to be abandoned so easily, he took his calculations and dismal test results one step up the corporate ladder.

At Goodrich, the man who supervises the engineers working on projects slated for production is called, predictably, the projects manager. The job was held by a short, chubby, bald man named Robert Sink. Some fifteen years before, Sink had begun working at Goodrich as a lowly draftsman. Slowly, he worked his way up. Despite his geniality, Sink was neither respected nor liked by the majority of the engineers, and his appointment as their supervisor did not improve their feelings toward him. He possessed only a high school diploma, and it quite naturally rankled those who had gone through years of college to be commanded by a man whom they considered their intellectual inferior. But, though Sink had no college training, he had something even more useful: a fine working knowledge of company politics.

Puffing on a meerschaum pipe, Sink listend gravely as young Lawson confided his fears about the four-disk brake. Then he examined Lawson's calculations and the results of the abortive tests. Despite the fact that he was not a qualified engineer in the strictest sense of the word, it must certainly have been obvious to Sink that Lawson's calculations were correct and that a four-disk brake would never work on the A7D.

But other things of equal importance were also obvious. First, to concede that Lawson's calculations were correct would also mean conceding that Warren's calculations were incorrect. As projects manager, not only was he responsible for Warren's activities, but, in admitting that Warren had erred, he would have to admit that he had erred in trusting Warren's judgment. It also meant that, as projects manager, it would be he who would have to explain the whole messy situation to the Goodrich hierarchy, not only at Troy but possibly on the corporate level at Goodrich's Akron offices. And having taken Warren's judgment of the four-disk brake at face value, he had assured LTV, not once but several times, that about all there was left to do on the brake was pack it in a crate and ship it out the door.

There's really no problem at all, he told Lawson. After all, Warren was an experienced engineer, and if he said the brake would work, it would work. Just keep on testing and probably maybe even on the very next try, it'll work out just fine.

Lawson was far from convinced, but without the support of his superiors there was little he could do except keep on testing. By now, housings for the four-disk brake had begun to arrive at the plant, and Lawson was able to build a production model of the brake and begin the formal qualification test demanded by the military.

The first qualification attempts went exactly as the tests on the prototype had. Terrific heat developed within the brakes, and after a few short simulated stops, the linings crumbled. A new type of lining material was ordered and once again an attempt to qualify the brake was made. Again, failure.

Experts were called in from lining manufacturers, and new lining "mixes" were tried, always with the same result. Failure.

It was now the last week in March 1968, and flight tests were scheduled to begin in seventy days. Twelve separate attempts had been made to qualify the brake, and all had failed. It was no longer possible for anyone to ignore the glaring truth that the brake was a dismal failure and that nothing short of a major design change could ever make it work.

On April 4, the thirteenth attempt at qualification was begun. This time no attempt was made to conduct the tests by the methods and techniques spelled out in the military specifications. Regardless of how it had to be done, the brake was to be "nursed" through the required fifty simulated stops.

Fans were set up to provide special cooling. Instead of maintaining pressure on the brake until the test wheel had come to a complete stop, the pressure was reduced when the wheel had decelerated to around 15 mph, allowing it to "coast" to a stop. After each stop, the brake was disassembled and carefully cleaned, and after some of the stops, internal brake parts were machined in order to remove warp and other disfigurations caused by the high heat.

By these and other methods, all clearly contrary to the techniques established by the military specifications, the brake was coaxed through the fifty stops. But even using these methods, the brake could not meet all the requirements. On one stop the wheel rolled for a distance of 16,000 feet, or over three miles, before the brake could bring it to a stop. The normal distance for such a stop was around 3,500 feet.

NURSING IT THROUGH

On April 11, the day the thirteenth test was completed, I became personally involved in the A7D situation.

I had worked in the Goodrich test laboratory for five years, starting first as an instrumentation engineer, then later becoming a data analyst and technical writer. As part of my duties, I analyzed the reams and reams of instrumentation data that came from the many testing machines in the lab, then transcribed all of it to a more usable form for the engineering department. When a new-type brake had successfully completed the required qualification tests, I would issue a formal qualification report.

Qualification reports are an accumulation of all the data and test logs compiled during the qualification tests and are documentary proof that a brake has met all the requirements established by the military specifications and is therefore presumed safe for flight testing. Before actual flight tests are conducted on a brake, qualification reports have to be delivered to the customer and to various government officials.

On April 11, I was looking over the data from the latest A7D test, and I noticed that many irregularities in testing methods had been noted on the test logs.

Technically, of course, there was nothing wrong with conducting tests in any manner desired, so long as the test was for research purposes only. But qualification test methods are clearly delineated by the military, and I knew that this test had been a formal qualification attempt. One particular notation on the test logs caught my eye. For some of the stops, the instrument that recorded the brake pressure had been deliberately miscalibrated so that, while the brake pressure used during the stops was recorded as 1,000 psi (pounds per square inch)—the maximum pressure that would be available on the A7D aircraft—the pressure had actually been 1,100 psi.

I showed the test logs to the test lab supervisor, Ralph Gretzinger, who said he had learned from the technician who had miscalibrated the instrument that he had been asked to do so by Lawson. Lawson, said Gretzinger, readily admitted asking for the miscalibration, saying he had been told to do so by Sink.

I asked Gretzinger why anyone would want to miscalibrate th data-recording instruments

"Why? I'll tell you why," he snorted. "That brake is a failure. It's way too small for the job, and they're not ever going to get it to work. They're getting desperate, and instead of scrapping the damned thing and starting over, they figure they can horse around down here in the lab and qualify it that way."

An expert engineer, Gretzinger had been responsible for several innovations in brake design. It was he who had invented the unique brake system used on the famous XB70. "If you want to find out what's going on," said Gretzinger, "ask Lawson; he'll tell you."

Curious, I did ask Lawson the next time he came into the lab. He seemed eager to discuss the A7D and gave me the history of his months of frustrating efforts to get Warren and Sink to change the brake design. "I just can't believe this is really happening," said Lawson, shaking his head slowly. "This isn't engineering, at least now what I thought it would be. Back in school, I thought that when you were an engineer, you tried to do your best, no matter what it cost. But this is something else."

He sat across the desk from me, his chin propped in his hand. "Just wait," he warned. "You'll get a chance to see what I'm talking about. You're going to get in the act too, because I've already had the word that we're going to make one more attempt to qualify the brake, and that's it. Win or lose, we're going to issue a qualification report!"

I reminded him that a qualification report could be issued only after a brake had successfully met all military requirements, and therefore, unless the next qualification attempt was a success, no report would be issued.

"You'll find out," retorted Lawson. "I was already told that regardless of what the brake does on test, it's going to be qualified." He said he had been told in those exact words at a conference with Sink and Russell Van Horn.

This was the first indication that Sink had brought his boss, Van Horn, into the mess. Although Van Horn, as manager of the design engineering section, was responsible for the entire department, he was not necessarily familiar with all phases of every project, and it was not uncommon for those under him to exercise the what-he-doesn't-know-won't-hurt-him philosophy. If he was aware of the full extent of the A7D situation, it meant that Sink had decided not only to call for help but to look toward that moment when blame must be borne and, if possible, shared.

Also, if Van Horn had said, "Regardless of what the brake does on test, it's going to be qualified," then it could only mean that, if necessary, a false qualification report would be issued. I discussed this possibility with Gretzinger, and he assured me that under no circumstances would such a report ever be issued.

"If they want a qualification report, we'll write them one, but we'll tell it just like it is." he declared emphatically. "No false data or false reports are going to come out of this lab."

On May 2, 1968, the fourteenth and final attempt to qualify the brake was begun. Although the same improper methods used to nurse the brake through the previous tests were employed, it soon became obvious that this too would end in failure.

When the tests were about half completed, Lawson asked if I would start preparing the various engineering curves and graphic displays that were normally incorporated in a qualification report. I flatly refused to have anything to do with the matter and immediately told Gretzinger what I had been asked to do. He was furious and repeated his previous declaration that under no circumstances would any false data or other matter be issued from the lab.

"I'm going to get this settled right now, once and for all," he declared. "I'm going to see Line [Russell Line, manager of the Goodrich Technical Services Section, of which the test lab was a part] and find out just how far this thing is going to go!" He stormed out of the room.

In about an hour, he returned and called me to his desk. He sat silently for a few moments, then muttered half to himself, "I wonder what the hell they'd do if I just quit?" I didn't answer and I didn't ask what he meant. I knew. He had been beaten down. He had reached the point when the decision had to be made. Defy them now while there was still time —or knuckle under, sell out.

"You know," he went on uncertainly, looking down at his desk, "I've been an engineer for a long time, and I've always believed that ethics and integrity were every bit as important as theorems and formulas, and never once has anything happened to changed my beliefs. Now this. . . . Hell, I've got two sons I've got to put through school and I just . . ." His voice trailed off.

He sat for a few more minutes, then, looking over the top of his glasses, said hoarsely, "Well, it looks like we're licked. The way it stands now, we're to go ahead and prepare the data and other things for the graphic presentation in the report, and when we're finished, someone upstairs will actually write the report.

"After all," he continued, "we're just drawing some curves, and what happens to them after they leave here—well, we're not responsible for that."

I wasn't at all satisfied with the situation and decided that I too would discuss the matter with Russell Line, the senior executive in our section.

Tall, powerfully built, his teeth flashing white, his face tanned to a coffee-brown by a daily stint with a sunlamp, Line looked and acted every inch the executive. He had been transferred from the Akron offices some two years previously, and he commanded great respect and had come to be well liked by those of us who worked under him.

He listened sympathetically while I explained how I felt about the A7D situation, and when I had finished, he asked me what I wanted him to do about it. I said that as employees of the Goodrich Company we had a responsibility to protect the company and its reputation if at all possible. I said I was certain that officers on the corporate level would never knowingly allow such tactics as had been employed on the A7D.

"I agree with you," he remarked, "but I still want to know what you want me to do about it."

I suggested that in all probability the chief engineer at the Troy plant, H. C. "Bud" Sunderman, was unaware of the A7D problem and that he, Line, could tell him what was going on.

Line laughed, good-humoredly, "Sure, I could, but I'm not going to. Bud probably already knows about this thing anyway and if he doesn't, I'm sure not going to be the one to tell him."

"But why?"

"Because it's none of my business, and it's none of yours. I learned a long time ago not to worry about things over which I had no control. I have no control over this."

I wasn't satisfied with this answer, and I asked him if his conscience wouldn't bother him if, say, during flight tests on the brake, something should happen resulting in death or injury to the test pilot.

"Look," he said, becoming somewhat exasperated, "I just told you I have no control over this. Why should my conscience bother me?"

His voice took on a quiet, soothing tone as he continued. "You're just getting all upset over this thing for nothing. I just do as I'm told, and I'd advise you to do the same."

I made no attempt to rationalize what I had been asked to do. It made no difference who would falsify which part of the report or whether the actual falsification would be by misleading numbers or misleading words. Whether by acts of commission or omission, all of us who contributed to the fraud would be guilty. The only question left for me to decide was whether or not I would become a party to the fraud.

Before coming to Goodrich in 1963, I had held a variety of jobs, each a little more pleasant, a little more rewarding than the last. At forty-two, with seven children, I had decided that the Goodrich Company would probably by my "home" for the rest of my working life. The job paid well, it was pleasant and challenging, and the future looked reasonably bright. My wife and I had bought a home and we were ready to settle down into a comfortable middle-aged, middle-class rut. If I refused to take part in the A7D fraud, I would have either to resign or be fired. The report would be written by someone anyway, but I would have the satisfaction of knowing I had had no part in the matter. But bills aren't paid with personal satisfaction, nor house payments with ethical principles. I made my decision. The next morning, I telephoned Lawson and told him I was ready to begin on the qualification report.

I had written dozens of qualification reports, and I knew what a "good" one looked like. Resorting to the actual test data only on occasion, Lawson and I proceeded to prepare page after page of elaborate, detailed engineering curves, charts, and test logs, which purported to show what had happened during the formal qualification tests. Where temperatures were too high, we deliberately chopped them down a few hundred degrees, and where they were too low, we raised them to a value that would appear reasonable to the LTV and military engineers. Brake pressure, torque values, distances, times—everything of consequence was tailored to fit.

Occasionally, we would find that some test either hadn't been performed at all or had been conducted improperly. On those occasions, we "conducted" the test—successfully, of course—on paper.

For nearly a month we worked on the graphic presentation that would be a part of the report. Meanwhile, the final qualification attempt had been completed, and the brake, not unexpectedly, had failed again.

We finished our work on the graphic portion of the report around the first of June. Altogether, we had prepared nearly two hundred pages of data, containing dozens of deliberate falsifications and misrepresentations. I delivered the data to Gretzinger, who said he had been instructed to deliver it personally to the chief engineer, Bud Sunderman, who in turn would assign someone in the engineering department to complete the written portion of the report. He gathered the bundle of data and left the office. Within minutes, he was back with the data, his face white with anger.

"That damned Sink's beat me to it," he said furiously. "He's already talked to Bud about this, and now Sunderman says no one in the engineering department has time to write the report. He wants us to do it, and I told him we couldn't."

The words had barely left his mouth when Russell Line burst in the door. "What the hell's all the fuss about this damned report?" he demanded.

Patiently, Gretzinger explained. "There's no fuss, Sunderman just told me that we'd have to write the report down here, and I said we couldn't." "Russ," he went on, "I've told you before that we weren't going to write the report. I made my position clear on that a long time ago."

Line shut him up with a wave of his hand and, turning to me, bellowed, "I'm getting sick and tired of hearing about this damned report. Now, write the goddamn thing and shut up about it!" He slammed out of the office.

Gretzinger and I just sat for a few seconds looking at each other. Then he spoke.

"Well, I guess he's made it pretty clear, hasn't he? We can either write the thing or quit. You know, what we should have done was quit a long time ago. Now, it's too late."

Somehow, I wasn't at all surprised at this turn of events, and it didn't really make that much difference. As far as I was concerned, we were all up to our necks in the thing anyway, and writing the narrative portion of the report couldn't make me more guilty than I already felt myself to be.

Within two days, I had completed the narrative, or written portion, of the report. As a final sop to my own self-repect, in the conclusion of the report I wrote, "The B. F. Goodrich P/N 2-1162-3 brake assembly does not meet the intent or the requirements of the applicable specification documents and therefore is not qualified."

This was a meaningless gesture, since I knew that this would certainly be changed when the report went through the final typing process. Sure enough, when the report was published, the negative conclusion had been made positive.

One final and significant incident occurred just before publication.

Qualification reports always bear the signature of the person who has prepared them. I refused to sign the report, as did Lawson. Warren was later asked to sign the report. He replied that he would "when I receive a signed statement from Bob Sink ordering me to sign it."

The engineering secretary who was delegated the responsibility of "dogging" the report through publication told me later that after I, Lawson, and Warren had all refused to sign the report, she had asked Sink if he would sign. He replied, "On something of this nature, I don't think a signature is really needed."

NEAR CRASHES

On June 5, 1968, the report was officially published and copies were delivered by hand to the air force and LTV. Within a week, flight tests were begun at Edwards Air Force Base in California. Searle Lawson was sent to California as Goodrich's representative. Within approximately two weeks, he returned because some rather unusual incidents during the tests had caused them to be canceled.

His face was grim as he related stories of several near crashes during landings—caused by brake troubles. He told me about one incident in which, upon landing, one brake was literally welded together by the intense heat developed during the test stop. The wheel locked, and the plane skidded for nearly 1,500 feet before coming to a halt. The plane was jacked up and the wheel removed. The fused parts within the brake had to be pried apart.

That evening I left work early and went to see my attorney. After I told him the story, he advised that, while I was probably not actually guilty of fraud, I was certainly part of a conspiracy to defraud. He advised me to go to the Federal Bureau of Investigation and offered to arrange an appointment. The following week he took me to the Dayton office of the FBI, and after I had been warned that I would not be immune from prosecution, I disclosed the A7D matter to one of the agents. The agent told me to say nothing about the episode to anyone and to report any further incidents to him. He said he would forward the story to his superiors in Washington.

A few days later, Lawson returned from a conference with LTV in Dallas and said that the air force, which had previously approved the qualification report, had suddenly rescinded that approval and was demanding to see some of the raw test data. I gathered that the FBI had passed the word.

Omitting any reference to the FBI, I told Lawson I had been to an attorney and that we were probably guilty of conspiracy.

"Can you get me an appointment with your attorney?" he asked. Within a week, he had been to the FBI and told them of his part in the mess. He too was advised to say nothing but to keep on the job, reporting any new development.

Naturally, with the rescinding of air force approval and the demand to see raw test data, Goodrich officials were in a panic. A conference was called for July 27, a Saturday morning affair at which Lawson, Sink, Warren, and I were present. We met in a tiny conference room in the deserted engineering department. Lawson and I, by now openly hostile to Warren and Sink, ranged ourselves on one side of the conference table while Warren sat on the other side. Sink, chairing the meeting, paced slowly in front of a blackboard, puffing furiously on a pipe.

The meeting was called, Sink began, "to see where we stand on the A7D." What we were going to do, he said, was to "level" with LTV and tell them the "whole truth" about the A7D. "After all," he said, "they're in this thing with us, and they have the right to know how matters stand."

"In other words," I asked, "we're going to tell them the truth?"

"That's right," he replied. "We're going to level with them and let them handle the ball from there."

"There's one thing I don't quite understand," I interjected. "Isn't it going to be pretty hard for us to admit to them that we've lied?"

"Now, wait a minute," he said angrily. "Let's don't go off half-cocked on this thing. It's not a matter of lying. We've just interpreted the information the way we felt it should be."

"I don't know what you call it," I replied, "but to me it's lying, and it's going to be damned hard to confess to them that we've been lying all along."

He became very agitated at this and repeated, "We're not lying," adding, "I don't like this sort of talk."

I dropped the matter at this point, and he began discussing the various discrepancies in the report.

We broke for lunch, and afterward, I came back to the plant to find Sink sitting alone at his desk, waiting to resume the meeting. He called me over and said he wanted to apologize for his outburst that morning. "This thing has kind of gotten me down," he confessed, "and I think you've got the wrong picture. I don't think you really understand everything about this."

Perhaps so, I conceded, but it seemed to me that if we had already told LTV one thing and then had to tell them another, changing our story completely, we would have to admit we were lying.

"No," he explained patiently, "we're not really lying. All we were doing was interpreting the figures the way we knew they should be. We were just exercising engineering license."

During the afternoon session, we marked some forty-three discrepant points in the report; forty-three points that LTV would surely spot as occasions where we had exercised "engineering license."

After Sink listed those points on the blackboard, we discussed each one individually. As each point came up, Sink would explain that it was probably "too minor to bother about," or that perhaps it "wouldn't be wise to open that can of worms," or that maybe this was a point that "LTV just wouldn't understand." When the meeting was over, it had been decided that only three points were "worth mentioning."

Similar conferences were held during August and September, and the summer was punctuated with frequent treks between Dallas and Troy and demands by the Air Force to see the raw test data. Tempers were short, and matters seemed to grow worse.

Finally, early in October 1968, Lawson submitted his resignation, to take effect on October 25. On October 18, I submitted my own resignation, to take effect on November 1. In my resignation addressed to Russell Line, I cited the A7D report and stated, "As you are aware this report contained numerous deliberate and willful misrepresentations which, according to legal counsel, constitute fraud and expose both myself and others to criminal charges of conspiracy to defraud ... The events of the past seven months have created an atmosphere of deceit and distrust in which it is impossible to work ... "

On October 25, I received a sharp summons to the office of Bud Sunderman. Tall and graying, impeccably dressed at all times, he was capable of producing a dazzling smile or a hearty chuckle or immobilizing his face into marble hardness, as the occasion required.

I faced the marble hardness when I reached his office. He motioned me to a chair. "I have your resignation here," he snapped, "and I must say you have made some rather shocking, I might even say irresponsbile charges. This is very serious."

Before I could reply, he was demanding an explanation. "I want to know exactly what the fraud is in connection with the A7D and how you can dare accuse this company of such a thing!"

I started to tell some of the things that had happened during the testing, but he shut me off saying. "There's nothing wrong with anything we've done here. You aren't aware of all the things that have been going on behind the scenes. If you had known the true situation, you would never have made these charges." He said that in view of my apparent "disloyalty" he had decided to accept my resignation "right now," and said it would be better for all concerned if I left the plant immediately. As I got up to leave he asked me if I intended to "carry this thing further."

I answered simply, "Yes," to which he replied, "Suit yourself." Within twenty minutes, I had cleaned out my desk and left. Forty-eight hours later, the B.F. Goodrich Company recalled the qualification report and the four-disk brake, announcing that it would replace the brake with a new improved, five-disk brake at no cost to LTV.

Ten months later, on August 13, 1969, I was the chief goverment witness at a hearing conducted before Senator William Proxmire's Economy in Government Subcommittee. I related the A7D story to the committee, and my testimony was supported by Searle Lawson, who followed me to the witness stand. Air force officers also testified, as well as a four-man team from the General Accounting Office, which had conducted an investigation of the A7D brake at the request of Senator Proxmire. Both Air

Force and GAO investigators declared that the brake was dangerous and had not been tested properly.

Testifying for Goodrich was R. G. Jeter, vice-president and general counsel of the company, from the Akron headquarters. Representing the Troy plant was Robert Sink. These two denied any wrongdoing on the part of the Goodrich Company, despite expert testimony to the contrary by Air Force and GAO officials. Sink was quick to deny any connection with the writing of the report or directing of any falsifications, claiming to have been on the West Coast at the time. John Warren was the man who had supervised its writing, said Sink.

As for me, I was dismissed as a highschool graduate with no technical training, while Sink testified that Lawson was a young, inexperienced engineer. "We tried to give him guidance," Sink testified, "but he preferred to have his own convictions."

About changing the data and figures in the report, Sink said, "When you take data from several different sources, you have to rationalize among those data what is the true story. This is part of your engineering know-how." He admitted that changes had been made in the data, "but only to make them more consistent with the overall picture of the data that is available."

Jeter pooh-poohed the suggestion that anything improper occurred, saying, "We have thirty-odd engineers at this plant . . . and I say to you that it is incredible that these men would stand idly by and see reports changed or falsified. . . . I mean you just do not have to do that working for anybody. . . . Just nobody does that."

The four-hour hearing adjourned with no real conclusion reached by the subcommittee. But the following day, the Department of Defense made sweeping changes in its inspection, testing, and reporting procedures. A spokesman said the changes were a result of the Goodrich episode.

The A7D is now in service, sporting a Goodrich-made five-disk brake, a brake that works very well, I'm told. Business at the Goodrich plant is good. Lawson is now an engineer for LTV and has been assigned to the A7D project, possibly explaining why the A7D's new brakes work so well. And I am now a newspaper reporter.

At this writing, those remaining at Goodrich—including Warren— are still secure in the same positions, all except Russell Line and Robert Sink. Line has been rewarded with a promotion to production superintendent, a large step upward on the corporate ladder. As for Sink, he moved up into Line's old job.

Case Questions

1. What would you have done if you had been in the position of Lawson, Vandiver, or Gretzinger?
2. What does this case have to do with organizational communication? What

communication patterns and characteristics contributed to this situation? What changes in the communication characteristics of this organization would reduce the likelihood that such events could recur?

3. Do you think incidents of this sort are frequent in organizations? Why, or why not?

4. Can people keep their ethics and values and still be successful in an organization?

Don't Ask Dumb Questions*

Paul was very angry when he came stomping into the plant manager's office. "Greg," he said, "you told me that I wouldn't have to fill out this report ever again. You know how much I hate it. The report is senseless. Nothing is gained by it and we should have thrown it away years ago." The conversation then went as follows:

"Paul, you're getting worked up over nothing. Now Andy is sick today and that report has to be filled out within twenty-four hours of the time we receive it. We got it in this morning, and it has to go out before we close today. Look Andy is sick very seldom, and you're the only guy around who knows how to fill it out. Be a pal and do it, will you?"

"Greg, you're missing the point. Why should we fill it out at all? You know as well as I do that there is no good reason why we should send this kind of information to the home office. I'll bet you no one there reads it. We could forget about it and no one would know the difference. In addition, I could get something really important done today."

"If it's going to make you feel better, Paul, I'll admit it's a dumb report. However, there is probably some little man sitting in the home office doing nothing but counting how many of those reports come in from the branch plants, and the minute he spots us not sending one in he'll get on the line and call."

"Then let's call them first and tell them we don't see any logic in filling it out. It's going to take me five hours to get the necessary figures and work out everything they want. Can't we get this straightened out once and for all?"

"Paul, there's nothing to straighten out. The report has to be filled out and that's that."

"You mean we're going to spend company time filling out a useless report so some idiot in the home office will come up with a correct count when he adds up the number of in-coming reports and tallies them with the number he's supposed to have."

"Something like that."

"And you don't question it?"

*From *Cases and Study Guide to Accompany Luthans Organizational Behavior* by Fred Luthans and Richard M. Hodgetts. Copyright © 1973 McGraw-Hill, Inc. Used with permission of McGraw-Hill Book Company.

"Look, Paul, I've been here twenty years. When you have as many years on the job as I do, you don't ask dumb questions, you just do as you're told. I'm not paid to ask questions; I'm paid to respond to the needs of the company. If they say they need to have this report filled out, I get it filled out. They're paying for it; I do it. Why make such a big thing out of a little report?"

"I just think we could increase efficiency around here if we would cut out some of the red tape."

"We're not paid to cut red tape; we're paid to live with it. Now when we get into top management, we can throw out this report. But for now, it has to be filled out. Look, this is a big company. It has a lot of rules and regulations. A lot of dos and don'ts. However, they are there for a reason. If you just try to live with them, it's a lot better than trying to fight the system."

Case Questions

1. What effects did Paul and Greg's organizational surroundings have in bringing about their disagreement?
2. How did Paul and Greg each see the organization and their role in it? Whose view was more accurate?
3. What was accomplished in this conversation in terms of (a) making perceptions more valid, (b) satisfying Paul and Greg's needs, and (c) strengthening the organization and fulfilling its goals?
4. How would you have handled your end of the conversation if you had been in (a) Paul's position, or (b) Greg's position?
5. What is organizational "red tape"? Are there communication processes that can effectively cope with it?

Part V

Improving Organizational Communication

Chapter 12

Counseling and Helping

Counseling in Organizational Life
Listening With Uncerstanding
    Listening orientation
    Reflection: The technique of client-centered listening
        Some dangers to avoid
Counseling in The Broader Perspective of Helping
    The task
    Factors in the individuals
    Nature and stage of the relationship
    Organizational and social surroundings
A Mode of Directive Helping: Confrontation
The Appraisal Interview: A Counseling/Helping Application
    Typical problems in appraisal counseling
    Toward Improved appraisal interviews

After studying this chapter, the reader should be able to

Define and use the following terms and concepts

Listening orientation
Empathy
Acceptance
Congruence
Contreteness
Reflection
Selective choices in reflective
  listening
A general model of a
  helping relationship

Simple assistance
Developmental help
Need for power
Need for affiliation
Stages in a helping relationship
Confrontation
"You-messages"
"I-messages"
Appraisal interviews

Understand

The kinds of situations that provide opportunities for counseling
Four components of listening orientation and their effects
The choices made by the reflective listener
Five dangers to be avoided in reflective listening
How to decide when reflective listening is and is not appropriate
The major factors in the helping process
Characteristics of effective confrontation
How to conduct effective performance appraisal interviews

12

The ability to counsel another person is one of the most valuable skills a member of an organization can possess. By whatever name the process may be called—counseling, helping, coaching, advising, training, or problem solving—opportunities arise often. Consider the following examples:

> A maintenance department manager becomes concerned about one of his best repair crew leaders whose performance has been slipping. The crew leader takes longer to complete jobs than he used to, seems less resourceful, and has often been late to work in recent weeks.

*   *   *   *

> A young accountant is working with a systems analyst from an outside firm that is installing new computer equipment and software in the accountant's company. The accountant and others have been turned off by the systems analyst's cold, factual, logical way of treating people in the company. During a coffee break, the systems analyst asks the accountant, "Why am I treated so defensively in your department? As soon as I walk in here, everyone clams up."

*   *   *   *

> An industrial sales representative observes that her manager is making a number of "human errors" in the way he is relating to his subordinates.

She has discussed this with her peers on the sales force, all of whom seem reluctant to confront the manager with the problem.

*　　*　　*　　*

The executives of a small manufacturing company notice that one of their number, the manufacturing director, is showing signs of "managerial obsolescence." They know the manufacturing director has no intention of stepping aside, but his operating results have been declining and there have been numerous complaints that he is getting too old to understand young employees.

COUNSELING IN ORGANIZATIONAL LIFE

It is clear that someone skilled at counseling another person could perform a critically important function in each of the examples just cited. This is not just a matter of "being good to people." In each case there is an opportunity for someone to help a *person,* but it is also clear that there are economic advantages to be gained. In organizations, the economic and technical realities are interwoven with the human realities. The "coldly factual" systems analyst is experiencing personal discomfort, and, at the same time, the success of the new computer installation may be in jeopardy. Likewise, the case of the apparently obsolete executive is clearly an individual human problem that has a direct bearing on an organization's effectiveness.

While some situations where counseling is needed are largely work-related and some are mainly personal, most have aspects of both. For example, suppose the director of market research for a major consumer products firm is approached by one of her most promising young leaders, who says he has a problem. He has applied and been admitted to a good M.B.A. program and is now trying to decide whether to go to school or stay with the company. The manager would like to keep him, having made tentative plans to promote him to head up a new section in a pending reorganization of the department. She is sure he can move up in the company without having an M.B.A. On the other hand, she does not want to persuade him to pass up an educational opportunity if it is what he really wants. The difficulty is that he himself is ambivalent; he doesn't know what he wants to do. The manager would need to approach this helping situation with caution and sensitivity. She cannot simply give advice. In a sense, the manager faces a tougher job than a professional career counselor would, since she must attend not only to the person but also to the company and her role in it. But *because* of her role as manager, she is the person who is in the best position to give help. This is why it is so important that organization members develop counseling skills. The effective organization member, whether in a line or a staff job at a high or a low level, is a person who is able to be helpful in such situations. Even though professional counseling may be available within the organization or outside, it is the involved coworker who knows the job and career realities and thus can respond best to "the whole person" who has a problem.[1]

Clearly, there is not an obvious, single, simple solution to problems of these kinds. Counseling opportunities come in many different types and varieties. An approach that might be effective with the maintenance crew leader whose job performance has been slipping might be very different from the kind of help the sales manager would find useful. In fact, no two problems are alike, since they intermingle the features of unique individuals and situations. Furthermore, a single case may have two or more possible solutions whose relative merits cannot be seen clearly at the outset by either the helper or the other person. For example, there may not be an objectively "right" answer to whether or not the young market researcher should go for an M.B.A. The success of the solution will depend largely on his degree of enthusiasm for the course of action he adopts.

Because of these two factors—the uniqueness of people and their problems and the importance of the other person's commitment—there is one skill more than any other that tends to distinguish the effective counselor. That skill is listening. Counseling, and helping in general, involve more than just listening (the total process of helping will be discussed later in this chapter), but listening is the early and crucial skill that most often makes the difference between whether help is given and received or not. This is true because for counseling really to be effective, it must be experienced as such from the receiver's point of view. Listening is so important that it has been called a primary skill in counseling, coaching, managing, and problem solving.[2] Listening is important not only because it enables the helper to understand the other person and the problem, but because it conveys something to the person who is listened to.[3] By listening, the helper is saying, "I am not going to charge in and take over the problem. It is your problem. You need to clarify and express an understanding of it, and I believe you are capable of doing that." Listening also conveys that the helper cares about what the other thinks and feels. When a helper does succeed in communicating these messages through skillful listening, it is not unusual for the receiver to become increasingly expressive and willing to examine him or herself and the problem. Oftentimes the receiver also becomes more open to change.[4]

Despite its importance, listening is a skill that most people in organizations are not very good at. The pressure of one's own duties and responsibilities makes it hard to tune in to someone else's point of view. Most people at work are used to talking and telling, not listening and learning. Listening is contrary to many of our spontaneous reflexes. For example, when someone else has a view that is different from our own, we commonly react by stating our own position more emphatically. Also, when a person comes to us with a problem, a typical reflexlike response is to give assurance immediately that everything will work out alright, or give a quick solution from experience. These responses block communication and inhibit exploration of what the other person is experiencing, yet they are very common responses that are made by all of us in encounters that otherwise might have developed into successful helping relationships. Listening is given special emphasis in this chapter because it is the part of the counseling process that is most contrary to the natural tendencies of most people in organizations.

The kind of listening that tends to be helpful to another person is not a passive sitting back and absorbing; it is an exercise of a specific active skill that has to be learned and practiced a great deal. The next section describes an approach to skillful listening that has proved useful and effective in a wide variety of situations.

LISTENING WITH UNDERSTANDING

The approach to listening described in the sections that follow has its foundation in the fields of counseling and psychotherapy, particularly in Carl Rogers's "client-centered" therapy.[5] This is not to say that people in organizations should become therapists, but rather that this area has important implications that can be translated into practical action in many everyday work situations. The professions of counseling and psychotherapy shed light on how to understand others and help others understand themselves. We have seen that most people need to improve these skills. Rogers's approach is emphasized because it has been found to be most applicable in the kinds of human problems people typically face in organizations as well as in their personal lives. It is an approach that is not limited to professional counseling. The process can take place spontaneously, between nonprofessionals and in many settings. The skills it requires can be acquired without prior specialized psychological training. It is not an effort aimed at reshaping another's personality. Obviously, this would be unethical and dangerous in the hands of a layperson. Instead, it is an approach that leaves the decision of how far to go in the hands of the person being helped. Client-centered listening will be described by first discussing the attitude and orientation of the listener and then some of the important techniques involved.

Listening Orientation

There is a substantial amount of evidence showing that successful helping depends as much on the helper's attitudes and orientation as it does on the techniques used.[6] The psychological climate of the relationship is also crucial. Listening and helping cannot be described simply as methods.

The basic attitude that Rogers finds to be essential he calls "the therapist's hypothesis." This is the helper's belief that the capacity for self-insight, problem solving, and growth resides primarily in the other person.[7] This means that the central questions for the helper are not

"What can I do for this person?" or even "How do I see this person?" but rather "What are this person's own capabilities," and "How does this person see himself or herself?" Rogers and others have made the underlying orientation of the listener-helper more specific by noting that it contains four components: empathy, acceptance, congruence, and concreteness.[8]

Empathy is the helper's desire and effort to understand the other person from his or her own internal frame of reference rather than from some external point of view, such as a theory, a set of standards, or the helper's preferences. The empathic listener tries to get inside the other's thoughts and feelings. Empathy is expressed when the listener communicates verbally and nonverbally such messages as "I follow you," "I'm with you," or "I understand." It is the helper's effort to hear the other person deeply, accurately, and nonjudgmentally. A person who sees that a helper is really trying to understand his or her meanings will trust the helper and be willing to talk more and explore problems and self more deeply. Empathic understanding is not simple to achieve or even to try for. As noted before, our natural tendency is to advise, tell, agree, or disagree from our own point of view. It is well worth the effort to become an empathic listener, however. Check your own experience. When you have had important difficulties, haven't the people you have found most helpful been ones who have offered you empathic understanding? Empathy is so powerful a force that even when it is only partially attained the mere attempt can be enough to open up communication.

Acceptance is closely related to empathy. Acceptance means having a deep concern for the other person's welfare along with a respect for the other's individuality and worth as a person. Rogers has used the terms *prizing, caring,* and *valuing* as synonyms for the first of these two aspects, likening the attitude to that of accepting parents who prize their child as a person regardless of the child's behavior at the moment. The second aspect is that the acceptance is as *unconditional* as the helper can make it. This means the helper does not express agreement or disagreement with what the other person is saying. Neither is acceptance a matter of expressing sympathy or being passively tolerant. Instead, the acceptant helper conveys a deep respect for the other's right to think and feel in his or her own way. This attitude by the helper tends to encourage the other to be less defensive and to be willing to explore aspects of self and situation that would otherwise be kept out of awareness. As the helper accepts the other person, the other person becomes more willing to accept self.

Congruence, the third component of listener-helper orientation, refers to openness, frankness, and genuineness on the part of the helper. The concept of congruence has an internal and an external aspect. Internally, the congruent helper is "in touch with" himself or herself. If angry or irritated, for example, the congruent person admits that fact rather than denying it. The external aspect is that the congruent individual communicates what is present in his or her awareness. This person does not stay behind a mask, pretending to be something or to be experiencing something he or she really is not. Congruence, then, is a condition where experience matches awareness and awareness matches communication. Rogers observes from his experience that congruence, or realness, on the part of the helper tends to evoke realness in the other person. When one person comes out from behind a facade, the other tends to do the same.

In a sense, congruence is inconsistent with empathy and acceptance. Suppose, for instance, the helper is annoyed with the other person at a particular moment. At such times, realistically, empathy and acceptance may need to be suspended while the helper expresses and deals with the annoyance, thus "clearing the air." Thus, in the overall relationship between helper and receiver of help, empathy and acceptance, as well as congruence, can be present.

Concreteness, the fourth component, means focusing on specifics rather than vague generalities. Often, one who is experiencing a painful problem will avoid confronting uncomfortable feelings by being abstract, using such expressions as, "most people . . ." or "they say . . .," using the pronoun "you" in place of "I," and talking about the past and future instead of the present. The helper can encourage the other to be more concrete by making responses that are specific even when the other is vague. Consider the following example, in which help is offered to an advertising agency account executive who is discussing a conflict she is having with one of the agency's art directors:

Executive: You just can't trust those art directors. They have a history of putting the account second and their self-interest first.

Helper A: People just don't seem to care sometimes.

Helper B: It disturbed you when the art director went directly to the vice-president.

Notice that Helper A reinforces the executive's vagueness by focusing on "people" rather than by naming the art director, and also by focusing on a vague "sometimes" rather than on a specific current incident. Helper B is more concrete in these respects and also adds an attempt to focus on the feeling the executive herself had experienced (being "disturbed"). The helper who is oriented toward concreteness tends not to let the other person ramble on and on but intervenes rather often with crisp, focused responses.

It is important to add that the acid test of the components of the listener's orientation is whether the other person *experiences* the listener as empathic, accepting, congruent, and concrete. Therefore, the skillful listener tries hard to understand how the other is experiencing the interaction and to respond genuinely to the other's needs rather than adhering dogmatically to textbook definitions of the process. For example, a helper who rigidly refuses to challenge the other person, give advice, or render a personal opinion will probably not be experienced as empathic or accepting by a person who believes that a concerned listener would do one of these. This caution should be kept in mind with respect to the techniques for reflective listening discussed in the next section. These techniques should be thought of as central tendencies around which the behavior of the skillful listener will vary, depending on the needs of the person being helped and other circumstances.

Reflection: The Technique of Client-centered Listening

The elements of listening orientation just discussed can be put into active practive through a method counselors and therapists call reflection. Reflection is a process in which the listener tries to clarify and reflect back what the other person is saying. Skillfully done, this can have a threefold advantage: (1) it can increase the listener's understanding of the other person; (2) it can help the other clarify his or her thoughts and feelings; and (3) it can encourage the other that someone is willing to attend to his or her point of view and wants to help. Listening orientation and reflection are mutually reinforcing. Empathy, acceptance, congruence, and concreteness contribute to the making of reflective responses. At the same time, reflective responses contribute to the development of these conditions.

Reflective technique can be described by listing some of its specific characteristics. It involves the following:[9]

More listening than talking.

Responding to what is personal rather than to what is impersonal, distant, or abstract.

Restating and clarifying what the other has said, not asking questions or telling what the listener feels, believes, or wants.

Trying to understand the feelings contained in what the other is saying, not just the facts or ideas.

Working to get the best possible sense of the other's frame of reference; avoiding responding from the listener's frame of reference.

Responding with acceptance and empathy, not with aloofness, cold objectivity, or fake overconcern.

This list shows that reflection is a highly selective process; it involves choosing to do and say certain very specific kinds of things and avoiding others. The most important choices made by the reflective listener are shown in exhibit 12–1. The boxes in the exhibit contain the choices that

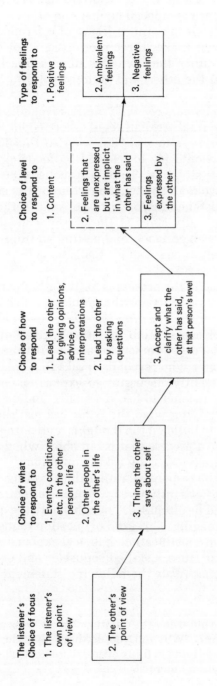

EXHIBIT 12-1

THE CHOICES MADE BY THE REFLECTIVE LISTENER

The listener's Choice of focus

1. The listener's own point of view

2. The other's point of view

Choice of what to respond to

1. Events, conditions, etc. in the other person's life

2. Other people in the other's life

3. Things the other says about self

Choice of how to respond

1. Lead the other by giving opinions, advice, or interpretations

2. Lead the other by asking questions

3. Accept and clarify what the other has said, at that person's level

Choice of level to respond to

1. Content

2. Feelings that are unexpressed but are implicit in what the other has said

3. Feelings expressed by the other

Type of feelings to respond to

1. Positive feelings

2. Ambivalent feelings

3. Negative feelings

Adapted from Anthony G. Athos and John J. Gabarro, *Interpersonal Behavior* (Englewood Cliffs, N.J.: Prentice-Hall, 1978), p. 430; and Arthur N. Turner and George F. F. Lombard, *Interpersonal Behavior and Administration*. Adapted with permission of Macmillan Publishing Co., Inc. Copyright © 1969 by Arthur N. Turner and George F. F. Lombard.

the skillful listener makes. The alternatives that are not enclosed in boxes are behaviors that are avoided. The diagram shows that after the initial decision to listen from the other's frame of reference rather than his or her own, the listener makes three more basic choices: (1) to respond to what is personal rather than what is impersonal, (2) to be responsive rather than to lead the other, and (3) to respond to feelings rather than content.[10]

Responding to what is personal means responding to things the other person says about self rather than about other people, events, or situations. If a work associate were to say, "I'm worried that I'll lose my job," the reflective listener would try to respond by focusing on the worried "I" rather than the job situation. Thus, a response like, "So you are really getting anxious," would be better than, "Maybe the cutbacks won't affect you." When the listener responds to personal rather than impersonal topics, the other usually stays at the personal level, exploring further aspects of his or her experience, and getting an improved understanding of self in the situation and a more realistic, active approach to solving problems.

Because the goal of the process is for the other person, rather than the helper, to take responsibility for the problem, reflective listening means *responding to, rather than leading the other.* Responding means reacting to what the other has said from the other's frame of reference. Leading means directing the other person to talk about things the helper wants explored. The listener who responds speaks in terms of those things the other person is currently discussing or exploring. One way this is often achieved is for the listener to test his or her understanding of the other by restating or clarifying what the latter has just said. This usually encourages the other to build on the thoughts andfeelings just expressed and to explore further—a process that is cut short when the helper leads by giving opinions or advice, or by asking questions.

Questions can be responsive rather than leading, but they very often work to limit the other's initiative by focusing attention on something the listener feels should be discussed. Though small, the question "Why?" can be particularly damaging. This kind of question tends to put the other on the defensive to find a justification or logical explanation that is acceptable to the helper. Edgar Huse, a skilled counselor and organization development consultant, once made the following statement to a class of M.B.A. students:

> I always avoid using the question "Why?" It is a loaded term. It's like a mommy saying, "Why did you do that?" to a kid, and the kid looks up stammering and trying to think of an excuse. Instead, I say, "That's interesting; can you tell me more about it?"

Perhaps most important, the reflective listener tries to *respond to feelings rather than content.* Feelings are the emotional tone expressed, such as anger, disappointment, discouragement, fear, joy, elation, or surprise. Content refers to ideas, reasons, theories, assumptions, descriptions, and so forth. It is often true that when a person is emotionally involved in a problem, the help of another person can be most useful. The listener who responds to feelings communicates a desire to "tune in" to the problem in terms of its emotional relevance to the other, not as an impersonal fact or idea. Carl Rogers notes that a person who is responded to at the emotional level has "the satisfaction of being deeply understood" and can go on to express more feelings and get "directly to the emotional roots" of the problem.[11]

Usually, the listener can be most in touch with the other's frame of reference by responding to feelings that are expressed rather than unexpressed. Since people seldom state their emotions explicitly, this typically means responding to the *emotional tone* expressed implicitly, as in the case of the advertising account executive, where Helper B responded to the "surprise" she had expressed, even though she had not stated it directly.

It is extremely important for the reflective listener to respond to negative and ambivalent feelings because this communicates that the listener accepts the dark, unpleasant sides of the other's experience and is willing to join in exploring them. A major release is provided for a person who has previously felt it necessary to suppress negative feelings. The energy that has been used to keep these feelings in check can now be devoted to exploring the problem.

The basics of reflective listening are summarized in an applied fashion in exhibit 12–2. This short quiz is intended to begin building the reader's skill in applying the concepts just discussed. It is a skill that cannot be learned without practice. Your next step in developing this skill could be to try responding in a reflective way during a portion of a normal social or work-related conversation. You will probably be awkward at first, but the more you practice, the more you may find your comfort increasing. Many who try the technique, even in a small way, report immediate results. Only rarely do most people have the experience of being listened to in this way. As a result, they view even a small exposure to a reflective listener as very satisfying and helpful.

Some Dangers to Avoid.　Although the reflective technique looks good on paper, those who try it out usually find that at the outset it does not come easily. As already noted, most of us have strong tendencies when communicating to give self-centered rather than reflective responses. Some of the more typical and important of these errors are the following:[12]

> *Stereotyped responses*—the constant use of the same repeated phrase, such as "You feel that. . . ." or "You're telling me that. . . ." Parroting back the other's exact words is also to be avoided, as in the use of cliches.

EXHIBIT 12-2
A QUIZ ON REFLECTIVE LISTENING

A computer programmer, Jack Phillips, does work both for you and for another member of your department, Joyce Carlton. One morning you walk up to Jack's desk and he greets you as follows:

Jack: What am I supposed to do about Joyce? She throws more work at me than I can possibly handle. I've told her but she won't listen. I don't want people to think I'm trying to get out of doing my job, but she's really got me totally buried.

Which of the responses listed below that you might make would represent reflective listening, and which would not? (Answers appear at the end of the references and notes for this chapter.)

1. Hang in there; I'm sure it will work out eventually.
2. I will talk with Joyce about it.
3. It sounds like this is really getting you down.
4. You're worried others might think you are looking for a soft deal.
5. Joyce is really unfair, huh?
6. Have you discussed it with your boss?
7. You were discouraged when Joyce seemed so unresponsive.
8. Why have you let things go on like this?
9. So you are fed up with the situation and really want to see something done about it.

Pretended understanding—trying to indicate you understand the other when you really do not. The helper conveys more genuineness and respect to the other by saying, "Sorry, I got distracted and didn't follow you; could you say that again?"

Overreaching—going too far beyond what the other has expressed, such as by giving psychological explanations ("psychologizing") or otherwise stating interpretations that the other experiences as going too far.

Underreaching—repeatedly missing the feelings conveyed by the other or making responses that understate them. An example of the latter would be responding to an intensely anxious person by saying, "You're bothered."

Long-windedness—giving very long or complex responses. These put more emphasis on the helper's massive effort to understand than they do on the other person's point of view. Short, simple responses tend to be much more effective.

Inattention to nonverbal cues—facing or leaning away from the other, not maintaining eye contact, lack of relaxation, presenting a "closed" posture by crossing the arms, and so forth. "Correct" verbal responses are of little use when accompanied by nonverbal signals that contradict them.

Violating the other person's expectations—giving client-centered responses when they are clearly not appropriate to the situation. For example, if the other person asks a direct question and obviously expects an answer, it is best to answer it.

As the last item on this list begins to indicate, the circumstances are not always right for reflective listening. Being skillful at counseling means developing one's ability to sense when the time is right for using a reflective technique. This sense is important to exercise in everyday working encounters, where reflective technique can often be useful even when counseling is not an expressed purpose of the conversation. Furthermore, at times when we are explicitly trying to give help, it is important to be able to choose wisely whether reflective listening or a more directive style of helping is more appropriate. The next section offers some guidelines for making this choice within the framework of a general model of the helping process.

COUNSELING IN THE BROADER PERSPECTIVE OF HELPING

Although reflective listening can be powerful and effective, it is just one of many possible approaches to counseling and, more broadly, to the process of helping. Other forms of help can be wanted, needed, and useful. Sometimes a person is helped by reassurance, criticism, questions, suggestions, or by having another person take over the problem and handle it for them. The type of help that is effective in a particular situation depends on the type of task or problem, on factors within the individuals, on the nature and stage of their relationship, and on the organizational and social surroundings. These factors are diagrammed in exhibit 12–3 and discussed in the following sections.

The Task

The diagram indicates that tasks around which helping occurs can range from simple assistance at one extreme to developmental help at the other. Simple assistance tasks are ones best handled by having the helper direct or do the task for the other; developmental help tasks are those where the goal is to increase the other's own ability to do the task, or ones like it, that come up in the future. An example of simple assistance would be a computer programmer who writes a program to be used by a marketing executive. An example of developmental help would be the programmer's

EXHIBIT 12-3
**A GENERAL MODEL OF A HELPING
RELATIONSHIP**

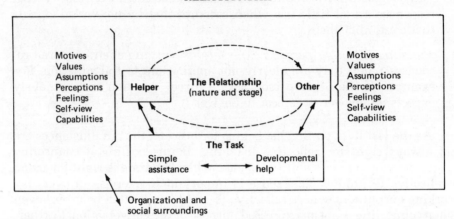

Adapted from Lawrence M. Brammer, *The Helping Relationship,* © 1973, p. 48; and David A. Kolb and Richard E. Boyatzis, "On the Dynamics of the Helping Relationship," in D. Kolb, I. M. Rubin, and J. M. McIntire (Eds.), *Organizational Psychology: A Book of Readings, Second Edition,* © 1974, p. 372. Reprinted by permission of Prentice-Hall, Inc., Englewood Cliffs, New Jersey.

efforts to help the executive to be more able to recognize marketing problems that can be aided by computer applications. Notice from this example that the kind of communication two people need to engage in in order for help to be effective can change due to a change in the task. Note also that effective helping requires that the helper and the other both perceive accurately the nature of the task.

Factors within the Individuals

The personal characteristics of the helper and the other person are important factors influencing the kind of helping relationship that emerges and its degree of success. Consider, for example, two human motives, the need for power and the need for affiliation, which can vary greatly in strength between different people and can also show wide variations within the same person at different times.[13] Need for power refers to the extent to which the person has an urge to influence others' behavior. Need for affiliation is the desire to have friendly, close interpersonal relationships. A person with a very strong need for power would probably have a hard time doing a good job of reflective listening. Similarly, someone with a high need for affiliation might be so anxious to have a friendly social relationship with the other person that the two would not get around to working on the task. Very low levels of these needs can also block the helping process in some instances. For example, a person with a very low affiliation need might not value associating with a helper enough to permit useful communication to take place. In the case of helpers, one study has shown that effective helpers tend to have needs of intermediate strength—neither extremely high nor extremely low.[14] Obviously, the other personal attributes (such as values, assumptions, and perceptions) listed in exhibit 12–3 can also have a major influence.

Nature and Stage of the Relationship

When two people have become solidly entrenched over time in a certain pattern of communication, the range of possible helping approaches may be limited. A manager who has always given rigid orders to a certain subordinate, never asking for suggestions or delegating any authority, would likely have a hard time making an effort at reflective listening seem plausible. The employee would wonder, "What's he up to this time?" and "What does he want me to say?" More directive help might be the only kind this subordinate would believe. A shift to another helping mode could take several tries over a considerable span of time.

Effective helping relationships often take time and involve a development through various phases. Gerard Egan, for example, has proposed the time-phased model of helping shown in exhibit 12–4. According to Egan's model, the helper takes a reflective listening approach in the prehelping

EXHIBIT 12-4
STAGES IN THE DEVELOPMENT OF A HELPING RELATIONSHIP

Stage	Helper's Goal	Other's Goal
Prehelping phase: Attending	Listening attentively to the other	
Stage I: Responding/ self-exploration	Facilitate other's self-exploration	Self-exploration of problems and feelings
Stage II: Integrative understanding/dynamic self-understanding	Teach the other to put pieces of the problem together to see the whole picture	See the need for change; identify resources for change
Stage III: Facilitating action/acting	Work out action programs with the other; offer support	Practice new skills; develop new resources

Adapted from *The Skilled Helper* by G. Egan. Copyright © 1975 by Wadsworth, Inc. Reprinted by permission of the publisher, Brooks/Cole Publishing Company, Monterey, California.

phase and in Stage I, becomes much more directive in Stage II, and then works on a mutual basis with the other person in Stage III. Every successful helping effort does not conform exactly to Egan's stages, but the point that different styles of communication may be needed in different phases of the helping process is an important one to note.

Organizational and Social Surroundings

Surroundings refer to such factors as the degree of comfort and freedom from distraction as well as to the norms and climate surrounding the helping effort. In a highly structured, power-oriented group or organization, for example, a reflective approach to helping may not be credible or possible. Similarly, directive help is hard to give effectively in an atmosphere of collegiality where the people involved are all of equal status (e.g., all are project engineers or department heads).

Obviously, these many variables do not fit together into a neat, simple formula. One of them—say the receiver's need for power—might be the dominant factor in one situation, while a combination of factors might be important in another. But surroundings do help indicate the kinds of questions to ask before deciding on the type of help to offer a particular person in a given set of circumstances.

Two questions can be especially useful ones for a prospective helper to ask.[15] The first is, *Whose point of view do I want to understand?* If the answer is, "I'd like to understand things as the other person sees them," then reflective listening would be appropriate. Learning more about the other might have been the helper's purpose from the outset, or it might emerge as the helper senses that the other seems to be leaving important things unsaid or is so confused or conflicted that help is needed to sort things out. The second question is, *Who owns the decision?* Whose problem is it and who has to make the choice, the helper or the other? If the other person is facing a personal decision that only he or she can make, then reflective listening may well be appropriate. A clear example is the successful young market researcher mentioned earlier who is undecided about leaving the job to work on an M.B.A. degree. The reflective technique may also be useful when the helper and the other share the problem or when the helper owns the decision, but the other will be affected by it. For instance, before making an organizational change, a manager might "sound out" how key subordinates see the situation.

There clearly are circumstances where the reflective mode is not appropriate. An example would be where it is the helper's job to provide certain advice and information, as when a department head asks the personnel director what procedures the organization requires in making performance appraisals of employees. Another example would be when it is the other's legitimate expectation that the helper (who could be a friend, coworker, or superior) will offer advice. The ability to share one's experience and to give direction are things that people value in others and that most organizations reward. Reflective listening also would not fit at times when open debate is the necessary purpose of the exchange (though even here it might play some part in helping clarify what an opponent's point of view is), or when feelings are running so hot that they make listening impossible. In the latter case, an attempt to be reflective would probably be interpreted by the other person as deceitful or phony. To summarize, a useful helping method is one that is appropriate to the person helped, to the helper, and to the situation. The effective helper develops skill in making these three discriminations.

A MODE OF DIRECTIVE HELPING: CONFRONTATION

Reflective listening has been emphasized in this chapter because it is a very useful skill—underdeveloped in most people—and an approach that is often the first step to other forms of helping. We have seen, however, that this nondirective style of helping cannot be used universally. It is therefore appropriate to give attention to help of the more directive type. Some examples would include instructing, coaching, disciplining, praising, and critiquing, where the distinguishing feature is that the helper takes the initiative and expresses his or her own point of view. A key ingredient that often contributes to effectiveness in this kind of helping is a process called confrontation (sometimes also referred to as feedback). This process is described now, with emphasis on how it can be accomplished most effectively.

Confrontation takes place when the helper directs the other person to reflect upon or change some aspects of his or her behavior.[16] This broad definition suggests, rightly so, that there are many degrees and kinds of confrontation, both constructive and destructive. It is important for a helper to know how to use confrontation effectively. Suppose, for example, a supervisor is about to speak to a subordinate about his frequent late arrivals to work. Assuming the supervisor has decided to take ownership of the problem and to confront the subordinate, what approach is likely to be most useful?

Thomas Gordon suggests that a basic difference between less effective and more effective confrontation is whether the person doing the confronting is sending "you-messages" or "I-messages."[17] Very often, ineffective efforts to confront begin with or contain the word *you*. For example:

You were late again today.

You need to start getting here on time.

You are a poor influence on others in the office.

If *you* don't improve, . . .

You don't seem to feel being here on time is important.

These messages stand a good chance of provoking resistance rather than cooperation. The subordinate may feel, for example, that she's been working hard and effectively, but what's the use if the boss only cares about punctuality?

"I-messages" differ in that they simply report how some unacceptable behavior is making the confronter feel.

> *I* have been concerned that others in the office may start coming in late, too.

> *I* get discouraged when I think of all the work we have to do, and then see an empty desk at 9 A.M.

> When there are unexplained absences, *I* just can't concentrate on the other work I need to get done.

> *I'*m afraid the division director will come around and want to know why everyone isn't here.

> When you come in late to work, *I* figure you don't care about your job, and *I* get angry.

"I-messages" are usually more effective than "you-messages" because they are nonjudgmental. They do not accuse the other or put the other into a category that may square with the helper's frame of reference but not be acceptable from the other's point of view. "I-messages" simply report the fact of the effect the other's behavior has had on the helper in a way that is hard to argue with. "I-messages" are also more effective because they put the responsibility for corrective action within the other without demeaning or antagonizing that person. This accurately represents the situation in all instances where corrective action ultimately has to be taken by the other.

The following list itemizes several important characteristics of effective confrontation. The list includes the characteristics of "I-messages" and adds other factors as well. Effective confrontation typically conforms with these rules.[18]

1. *Give immediate feedback.* The best confrontation usually takes place as soon as possible. Delay tends to reduce its effectiveness.
2. *Show concern for helping the other.* The helper's concern for the other makes confrontation more acceptable to the other.
3. *Be descriptive rather than evaluative.* Facts tend to be much more acceptable to the other than do the helper's judgments.
4. *Focus on behavior.* It is better to describe clear, outward actions than to try to attribute inner motives to the other.
5. *Describe the effects.* Useful confrontation states how the other's behavior affects the helper's thoughts and feelings. The "I-messages" listed earlier are good examples.

6. *Be specific rather than general.* Refer to concrete events instead of trying to tell what the other person "is like."

7. *Confront when the other person is ready to accept it.* Try to insure the confrontation is in tune with the situation, the nature of the relationship between the helper and other, and the other's readiness to handle such information at this particular time.

8. *Confront only on matters the other is able to do something about.* There is no point in confronting someone about physical characteristics or personal history.

Confronting takes a certain amount of courage, but it usually turns out to have been worth the risk. There are two major fears that tend to keep helpers from sending confronting messages. The first is the fear that the other person will be offended, leading to some form of retaliation or the end of the relationship. A manager, for example, might be reluctant to confront a suborbinate for fear of losing a good employee. The second fear is not wanting to reveal too much of one's self to another person. Here the question is, "Will the other person still accept and respect me when he knows how I really feel about his behavior?"

Ironically, though, when people do not confront, they often choose the even more risky alternative of sending a "you-message," which puts the blame on the other person and thus likely evokes a defensive stance from them. Furthermore, one's feelings toward another person usually come out one way or another, directly or indirectly, sooner or later. It generally promotes the helping process if the helper gives honest feedback about the other's behavior at the time it occurs.

Probably the strongest argument for the helper to use confronting behavior is that it stimulates the other to do the same thing. The other gets to know what the helper's reactions are, which encourages the other to reveal more. This not only provides more "data" for problem solving but also builds the levels of honesty and openness, making the helping relationship one that is truly *interpersonal* rather than merely a cool, distant exchange of information.[19]

THE APPRAISAL INTERVIEW: A COUNSELING/HELPING APPLICATION

Most organizations require superiors to meet periodically with each of their subordinates to review the latter's job performance. While there are many times, scheduled and spontaneous, when the principles of counseling and helping have application, this appraisal interview is perhaps the most important and difficult.

Appraisal interviews are typically intended to achieve many, if not all, of the following purposes:[20]

To let subordinates know how they are viewed and what the future holds.

To recognize good work subordinates have done.

To identify areas where improvement is needed.

To clarify the job to be done.

To relate subordinates' goals to the organization's goals.

To stimulate subordinates' motivation.

To enhance communication between superior and subordinates.

To foster subordinates' growth and development.

The importance of these goals is self-evident, but the list also highlights the difficulty of appraisal communications. The large number of goals makes the process a complex one. Also, some of the goals are ones that run a high risk of evoking defensiveness on the subordinate's part (e.g., letting subordinates' know how they are viewed and noting where improvement is needed). Because it deals with the assessment of a person's contribution and ability, the appraisal interview is one of the most emotionally charged of all organizational activities and is an activity whose goals, though everyone views them as desirable, often are not fulfilled.

Typical Problems in Appraisal Counseling

Three factors are the most prominent causes of failure in appraisal interviews. These are defensiveness (resulting from criticism and other factors), faulty criteria, and the time factor.

People tend to become defensive when they are criticized. A study conducted within a unit of General Electric Company showed a strong relationship between comments addressing subordinate weaknesses in an appraisal interview and defensive comments made by the subordinates.[21] As the number of critical comments increased, subordinate defensiveness increased. Even more importantly, the researchers found that people who received an above-average number of criticisms typically performed more poorly ten to twelve weeks later than those who received fewer criticisms.

The superior may also have defensive reactions to the appraisal process. Harry Levinson notes that many managers experience appraisal as a hostile act on their own part, producing personal feelings of guilt that make it extremely difficult for them to be constructively critical of subordinates.[22]

Another reason for defensiveness is that salary action is often discussed in the same interview in which the performance review is attempted. In this case, the superior's effort to justify the recommended salary tends to dominate the discussion to such a degree that neither party is in a mood to discuss constructively how performance can be improved.

The criteria used to judge performance are a frequent source of difficulties. For some managers, a subordinate's results are "never good enough." The manager's aim is to apply pressure for improvement, but the subordinate may take this pressure as an admonition never to make any mistakes and decide the best way to avoid errors is to avoid taking any initiative.[23] Managers sometimes judge subordinates on how well they have helped the manager meet his or her own needs. This becomes a problem in cases where the subordinate's job requirements are not a carbon copy of the superior's, as, for example, within organizations designed in the matrix form (see chapter 10). Another problem with performance criteria occurs in organizations where the evaluation system requires a forced ranking of people into categories, such as "best ten percent," "second ten percent," and on down to the "lowest ten percent."[24] Such categorizations are almost sure to produce defensiveness in at least half of the people rated, since most people do not like to think of themselves as "below average." Superiors' thinking is also adversely affected in that the rating method leads them automatically to think of some of their people as being at the "bottom," regardless of how well these people may actually be doing.

Finally, a major problem in appraisal interviews is time. The appraisal and goal-setting relationship is often limited to certain times the organization has officially marked out on the calendar (a one-hour interview every six months, for example). Appraisal then becomes a rule to be complied with (another item of "red tape" to be gotten out of the way) rather than a real part of the management process.[25] Effective appraisal and developmental counseling take time, but many managers feel they cannot and should not devote time to vague goals, like "develop subordinates," that are hard to quantify and do not appear to lead directly to the rewards for which the manager is working.

Toward Improved Appraisal Interviews

Researchers, consultants, and skilled practioners suggest many ways that appraisal interviews can be improved. The recommendations that follow are not all-inclusive and need to be tailored to the particular situation and people involved. However, they do suggest steps that can be taken to avoid the problems discussed earlier.[26]

1. *Prepare for the interview.* First, the purpose of the interview should be determined. Do not try to do everything in one interview (e.g., discuss salary, promotions, performance, and career planning). The general model of a helping relationship presented in exhibit 12-3 suggests that limiting and specifying the task will make the choice of a helping approach clearer. Once the task is established, the superior should prepare by reveiwing documents and records relating to the subordinate's performance. Consultation with others who know the subordinate's work can also be useful. To allow the subordinate to prepare, many organizations in which rating forms are used provide

the subordinate with a blank form to fill out in advance so his or her conclusions can be compared with the superior's as a basis for discussion during the interview.

2. *Establish rapport and obtain the subordinate's involvement.* The subordinate should be put at ease and reminded of the purpose of the interview and the overriding goal of improving his or her success on the job. The subordinate should be an involved participant in the body of the appraisal interview, not a passive listener. Research has shown the importance of the subordinate's participation. Those who participate more tend to see the appraisal process more favorably and tend to perform better subsequent to the interview.[27] Therefore, subordinates should be asked to give their opinions of their strengths and development needs. Some writers advise that the subordinate do fifty percent of the talking. Others say that the superior may talk most of the time when the subordinate is new and still unfamiliar with the job. The discussion earlier in this chapter of factors determining the type of help that is likely to be effective in a particular instance has bearing on this issue. In connection with establishing rapport and involving the subordinate, the two approaches to helping discussed in some detail in this chapter—reflective listening and confrontation—can enhance the effectiveness of an appraisal interview if used when appropriate. Both are techniques that tend to reduce the other person's defensiveness, thus countering one of the most serious problems in the appraisal process.

3. *Focus on analysis and performance development.* A climate of analysis is preferable to a climate of judgment in appraisal interviews. An employee would rather be helped to discover why his or her performance has been below expectation, and, therefore, how it can be improved, than to be labeled as an inferior person. Obstacles to improved performance typically can be identified, including poor service from another department, conflicting orders, lack of authority, and areas in which the employee has not yet developed adequate skill or knowledge. Areas of strong performance, and the contributing factors, should also be identified. Since the superior may not be fully aware of these factors, listening orientation and the reflective technique can be used to help the employee take initiative in the analytic task. A progression through Egan's stages of helping, discussed earlier, often makes an effective session. The appraisal interview procedures outlined by several writers compare rather closely with Egan's phases.[28] After factors affecting performance have been identified, the superior begins to do more of the talking, helping the subordinate to see an overall pattern formed by the separate factors. The superior and subordinate then mutually discuss and agree upon specific goals for the future.

4. *Mutually determine specific future goals.* To make the interview truly developmental, the superior and subordinate should jointly de-

cide on specific steps that should be taken to improve the employee's performance. These steps, of course, should be consistent with the factors affecting performance that have been identified. Performance goals should be agreed to and set in such a way that the subordinate knows what actions will lead to improved performance ratings. It is useful for the superior to recap the interview, summarizing the points both have agreed to as areas for improvement and the methods for achieving that improvement.

5. *Continue coaching on a day-to-day basis.* When a superior and subordinate discuss performance once or twice a year, the process is usually not very effective. Many performance problems are better dealt with when they occur and need not be "saved up" for a formally scheduled interview. Furthermore, studies of the learning process have shown that feedback is more effective when it is received soon after the particular situation.

6. *Include appraisal of the appraiser.* In some organizations, the appraisal program includes periodic appraisals of superiors by their subordinates. This stimulates the superior to put effort into developing subordinates, helps the superior learn how to improve as an appraiser, and makes it more likely that the organization will reward managers partly on the basis of how well they do in this area. Systematic appraisals by subordinates are far preferable to behind-the-back complaints that seldom serve as the basis for corrective action.

Summary

This chapter began with examples showing that there are frequent opportunities for helping in organizations. It should be emphasized that many of these occur spontaneously, not as formally arranged advising or counseling meetings. An increment of help can be given and received during brief minutes, or even seconds, within a conversation devoted primarily to other purposes. Because opportunities for helping arise so frequently and unpredictably, helping in an organization—if it is to be adequate—cannot be practiced only by professional counselors. This is why any person who possesses helping skills is valuable to an organization. The "helper" and "other" referred to in this chapter are not formal job titles but could refer to any two people in an organization who are attempting to give and receive help.

A helping skill given major emphasis in this chapter was that of reflective listening, based primarily on the method of Carl Rogers. Listening *orientation,* including empathy, acceptance, congruence, and concreteness, and the *reflective technique,* based on a selective process whereby the helper makes certain important response choices, were discussed in detail. The reasons for this strong emphasis on reflective listening are its power as a helping method, the fact that most people's listening skills are badly underdeveloped, and that the method does not require specialized training and can be developed through on-the-job practice.

A broader perspective of helping was provided through the general model of a helping relationship (exhibit 12–3). This model indicated that the task, factors within the individuals, the nature and stage of their relationship, and their organizational and social surroundings are important considerations in determining the type of helping approach most likely to be successful. Two questions were seen as particularly important ones for the helper to consider: (1) Whose point of view do I want to understand? and (2) Who owns the decision? The helper's decision to offer more or less directive help hinges on these issues.

The topic of directive helping was addressed, emphasing *confrontation.* A basis approach, the sending of "I-messages," was explained, followed by a more detailed set of rules for effective confrontation. This discussion showed that directive helping does not necessarily have to be demeaning to the person helped and does not require that person to become dependent on the helper. Like active listening, confrontation places the responsibility for corrective action on the person, not the helper. In all cases it is ultimately the client who determines whether or not an attempt at helping has been successful. The chapter concluded with an important application of counseling and helping, the performance appraisal interview.

Questions for Review

1. Why is it important for a member of an organization to possess skill as a helper? Why is listening an important skill for organization members to develop?
2. Why are both listening orientation *and* the reflective technique necessary for the effective practice of reflective listening?
3. Why are responses that accept and clarify ambivalent or negative feelings generally helpful for the other person?
4. Think of a recent instance where you tried to help another person. Use the general model of a helping relationship to explain why your effort was successful, wasn't successful, or was successful only in part.
5. Why are "I-messages" a better method of confrontation than "you-messages?"
6. Describe an incident from your own experience where you could have confronted another person but did not. Why didn't you? What could you have said that likely would have been an effective confrontation?
7. Should all performance appraisal interviews be conducted in the same manner? Consider this question in connection with the general model of a helping relationship (exhibit 12–3).

References and Notes

1. Lawrence M. Brammer, *The Helping Relationship* (Englewood Cliffs, N.J.: Prentice-Hall, 1973), p. 9.
2. See Jerry C. Wofford, Edwin A. Gerloff, and Robert C. Cummins, *Organizational Communication* (New York: McGraw-Hill, 1977), pp. 208–9. Also, Anthony G. Athos and John J. Gabarro, *Interpersonal Behavior* (Englewood Cliffs, N.J.: Prentice-Hall, 1978), p. 402.
3. Arthur W. Combs, Donald L. Avila, and William W. Purkey, *Helping Relationships* (Boston: Allyn and Bacon, 1971), p. 269; Charles M. Rossiter, Jr., "Defining 'Therapeutic Communication,'" *Journal of Communication* 25, no. 3 (1975). 127–30.
4. Carl R. Rogers, *Freedom to Learn* (Columbus, Ohio: Merrill, 1969), pp. 231–37.
5. Carl R. Rogers, *Counseling and Psychotherapy* (Boston: Houghton-Mifflin, 1942); idem, *Client-Centered Therapy* (Boston: Houghton-Mifflin, 1951).
6. Brammer, *The Helping Relationship,* p. 18, Combs, Avila and Purkey, *Helping Relationships,* pp. 3–17; Carl R. Rogers, *On Becoming a Person* (Boston: Houghton-Mifflin, 1961), pp. 39–50.
7. Rogers, *Client-Centered Therapy,* pp. 20–24.
8. The discussion of components of listening orientation draws on ideas contained in Athos and Gabarro *Interpersonal Behavior,* pp. 406–11; Brammer, *The Helping Relationship,* pp. 29–35; Gerard Egan, *The Skilled Helper* (Monterey, Calif.: Brooks/Cole, 1975), pp. 100–106; Kim Giffin and Bobby R. Patton, *Fundamentals of Interpersonal Communication* (New York: Harper and Row, 1971), pp. 213–17; Rogers, *On Becoming A Person,* pp. 338–46; Carl R. Rogers, "Being In Relationship," in Bobby R. Patton and Kim Giffin, *Interpersonal Communication* (New York: Harper and Row, 1974), pp. 466–77; Harold S. Spear, "Notes on Carl Rogers' Concept of Congruence and His General Law of Interpersonal Relationships," in Robert E. Coffey, Anthony G. Althos, and Peter A. Raynolds, *Behavior in Organizations* (Englewood Cliffs, N.J.: Prentice-Hall, 1975), pp. 179–85.
9. Adapted from Athos and Gabarro, *Interpersonal Behavior,* © 1978, p. 417. Reprinted by permission of Prentice-Hall, Inc., Englewood Cliffs, New Jersey.
10. The ideas concerning the basic choices of the client-centered listener are drawn primarily from Athos and Gabarro, *Interpersonal Behavior,* pp. 418–28; Rogers, *Counseling and Psychotherapy,* pp. 131–49.
11. Rogers, *Counseling and Psychotherapy, p. 141.*
12. The list of dangers to avoid in client-centered listening is adapted from Athos and Gabarro, *Interpersonal Behavior,* pp. 434–38, 441–44; Gerard Egan, *You and Me* (Montery, Calif.: Brooks/Cole, 1977), pp. 114–16, 156–62; James B. Stull, "Rewards for Openness," *Journal of Communication* 28, no. 1 (1978); 124–29.
13. For further information relating to need for power and need for affiliation, see *Motives in Fantasy, Action, and Society,* ed. John W. Atkinson (Princeton, N.J.: Van Nostrand, 1958); David C. McClelland, *The Achieving Society* (Princeton, N.J.: Van Nostrand, 1961).
14. David A. Kolb and Richard E. Bayatzis, "On the Dynamics of the Helping Relationship," in *Organizational Psychology,* ed. David A. Kolb, Irwin M.

Rubin, and James M. McIntyre (Englewood Cliffs, N.J.: Prentice-Hall, 1974), pp. 371–87.

15. The ideas that follow concerning when client-centered listening is and is not appropriate come from Athos and Gabarro, *Interpersonal Behavior,* pp. 448–51; Eileen Morley, "Interpersonal Skills and Helping Relationships," in Athos and Gabarro, *Interpersonal Behavior,* pp. 470–80; Thomas Gordon, *P.E.T.: Parent Effectiveness Training* (New York: Wyden, 1970), pp. 63–70; Arthur N. Turner and George F. F. Lombard, *Interpersonal Behavior and Administration* (New York: Free Press, 1969), pp. 430–46.

16. Gerard Egan, *Face to Face* (Monterey, Calif.: Brooks/Cole, 1973), p. 107.

17. Gordon, *P.E.T.,* pp. 115–38. For an experimental study indicating, as Gordon would predict, that "you-messages" evoke more defensiveness than "I-messages," see Rebecca J. Cline and Bonnie McDaniel Johnson, "The Verbal Stare: Focus of Attention in conversation," *Communication Monographs* 43 (1976); 1–10.

18. The "rules" of confrontation are adapted from John Anderson, "Giving and Receiving Feedback," in Paul R. Lawrence, Louis B. Barnes, and Jay W. Lorsch, *Organizational Behavior and Administration* (Homewood, Ill.: Irwin-Dorsey, 1976), pp. 103–11; Joseph A. DeVito, *The Interpersonal Communication Book* (New York: Harper and Row, 1976), pp. 218–20; Egan, *Face to Face,* pp. 133–34; Aubrey C. Sanford, *Human Relations* (Columbus, Ohio: Merrill, 1977), pp. 307–8.

19. The ideas relating to fears about confronting draw upon Gordon, *P.E.T.,* pp. 119–20; Sanford, *Human Relations,* p. 306.

20. Norman R. F. Maier, "Three Types of Appraisal Interviews," *Personnel,* March-April 1968, pp. 27–40; Harry Levinson, "Management by Whose Objectives?" *Harvard Business Review* 48 (1970); 125–34; Paul H. Thompson and Gene W. Dalton, "Performance Appraisal: Managers Beware," *Harvard Business Review* 48 (1970); 149–57.

21. Emmanuel Kay, Herbert H. Meyer, and John R. P. French, "Effects of Threat in a Performance Appraisal Interview," *Journal of Applied Psychology* 50 (1965); 311–17. See also Herbert H. Meyer, Emmanuel Kay, and John R. P. French, "Split Roles in Performance Appraisal," *Harvard Business Review* 43 (1965); 123–29.

22. Levinson, "Management By Whose Objectives?"

23. Harry Levinson, "A Psychologist Looks at Executive Development," *Harvard Business Review* 40 (1962); 69–75.

24. Thompson and Dalton, "Performance Appraisal."

25. Lee H. Hansen, "A Model for Subverting Management by Objectives," in Edgar F. Huse, James L. Bowditch, and Dalmar Fisher, *Readings on Behavior in Organizations,* (Reading, Mass.: Addison-Wesley, 1975), pp. 248–51.

26. Donald P. Crane, *Personnel* (Belmont, Calif.: Wadsworth, 1979), pp. 383–87; Richard C. Huseman, James M. Lahiff, and John C. Hatfield, *Interpersonal Communication in Organizations* (Boston: Holbrook, 1976), pp. 160–63; Levinson, "Management By Whose Objectives?": Robert L. Mathis and John J. Jackson, *Personnel: Contemporary Perspectives and Applications* (St. Paul: West, 1976), pp. 228–30; Norman R. F. Maier, *The Appraisal Interview: Three Basic Approaches* (La Jolla, Calif.: University Associates, 1976); Meyer, Kay, and French, "Split Roles in Performance Appraisal."

27. E. Bruce Kirk, "Appraisee Participation in Performance Interviews," *Personnel Journal* 44 (1965); 24; Ronald J. Burke and Douglas S. Wilcox, "Characteristics of Effective Employee Performance Review and Development Interviews," *Personnel Psychology* 22 (1969); 291–309.
28. See, for example, Edgar F. Huse, "Putting In A Management Development Plan That Works," *California Management Review* 9, (1966); 73–80; Huseman, Lahiff, and Hatfield, *Interpersonal Communication in Organizations,* pp. 160–63; Mathis and Jackson, *Personnel,* pp. 228–30; Crane, *Personnel,* pp. 383–87.

Answers to exhibit 12–2, "A Quiz on Reflective Listening:" responses representing reflective thinking are 3, 4, 7, and 9.

Chapter 13

Influence
through Communication

Influence Success and Failure: Hovey and Beard Company
Reinforcement Theory
    Characteristics of reinforcement
    Schedules of reinforcers
    Inadvertent reinforement
    Punishment
Phases in the Influence Process
    Unfreezing
    Changing
    Refreezing
Some Major Factors Affecting the Influence Process
    Source
    Message
    Receiver
    Group and organizational settings
        Group Factors
        Organizational Factors
Some Specific Persuasive Tactics

After studying this chapter,
the reader should be able to

Define and use the following terms and concepts

Positive reinforcement
Negative reinforcement
Self-reinforcing behavior
Group reinforcement
Reinforcement schedules
Inadvertent reinforcement
Punishment
Unfreezing, changing, refreezing
Identification

Scanning
Factors affecting the influence process
Source credibility
Sleeper effect
Message structure
Message content
Cognitive dissonance
Persuasive tactics

Understand

The characteriestics of effective reinforcers
What makes punishment effective or not effective
Three schedules of reinforcement and their relative merits
The influence process in terms of Lewin's three phases of change
Four major factors affecting the influence process
Several specific persuasive tactics

13

From the point of view of a manager, probably the most important communication that occurs in an organization involves efforts to exert influence. How can I get the work force to increase their effort? Can I convince my superiors to approve bonus payments for my best supervisors? What can we do to get our customers to accept a price increase? What can I say to persuade an exceptional recent graduate to come to work in my department?

Both inside and outside the organizational setting, people make frequent attempts to influence other people, and their batting averages are mixed. Sometimes they succeed, sometimes they don't, and they feel their average should be higher than it is. An example of this mixture of success and failure is shown in the following case. Here, management was trying to influence a group of workers to increase their productivity.

Influence Success and Failure: Hovey and Beard Company*

The Hovey and Beard Company manufactured various kinds of wooden toys. It was in the paint shop that trouble began.

The toys were sent to the paint shop after having been formed, partially assembled, and dipped in shellac in other departments. Most of the toys were two-colored, with each color requiring a separate trip through the paint shop.

---

*Adaptation of "Group Dynamics and Intergroup Relations" by George Strauss and Alex Bavelas (pp. 90–94) from *Money and Motivation* by William F. Whyte. Copyright © 1955 by Harper and Row, Publishers, Inc. Reprinted by permission of the publisher.

For years, the toys had been hand painted, but the company's industrial engineers had recently completed work on a new design for the operation. In the new method, the eight women who did the painting were to sit along a continuously moving chain of hooks. Each woman was enclosed in her own paint booth, designed to stop the excess paint and carry away fumes. In the new procedure, the worker would take a toy from a tray, place it in a fixture inside the booth, spray on the paint according to a pattern, then hang the toy on a passing hook, which would carry it into the drying oven. The hooks moved at a rate, calculated by the engineers, such that a worker when fully trained should be able to put a painted toy on each hook before it passed beyond her reach.

The new system included a group bonus plan. While the operation was new to them, the women were to receive a learning bonus, scheduled to decrease over a six-month period, by which time it was expected they would be able to exceed the established production quota and thereby earn the group bonus on their own.

Soon after the new method was begun, problems arose. Productivity was below expectations, and the workers expressed several complaints: the hooks went by too fast; the room was too hot; the bonus was not being calculated correctly. The team spirit that management had felt would develop as a result of the group bonus system had not materialized. One woman who was regarded by the group as its leader (and by the management as the "ringleader") was especially vocal in her complaints to the supervisor. Clearly management's efforts to influence the workers up to this point had been unsuccessful.

The supervisor brought in a consultant to help. After several conversations with the consultant, the supervisor made a decision to call the workers together to discuss working conditions. A series of meetings were held, resulting in a number of changes, each of them suggested first by the workers and then argued up the line long and vigorously by the supervisor until approval was obtained from the engineers and higher management.

The early meetings served to reduce tension and show the workers that their ideas were being given consideration. The women were especially encouraged when fans were purchased at their suggestion to provide cooling and ventilation. At a subsequent meeting the workers asked for authority to regulate the speed of the line itself. They argued that they could keep up with the hooks for short periods, but didn't want to if it meant they would be expected to do so all day long. After several conferences with the engineers, the supervisor had a control dial mounted in the booth of the group leader. The workers were delighted and spent their lunch hours deciding how the speed of the hooks should be varied hour by hour throughout the day. Production soared to more than thirty percent above the production quota the engineers had originally expected. Management's attempt to exert influence by being responsive to the workers' suggestions had proved highly successful.

A new problem arose, however. The women were now collecting the group incentive bonus as well as the learning bonus. Thus, their pay had risen to a level higher than that of many skilled workers in other parts of the plant, who now began complaining to management about this inequity. Acting on the complaints, the superintendent, without consultation, decided to return the operation to its original status. The learning bonus was removed and the hooks were restored to the speed originally set by the engineers. Production dropped to a low level, and within a month most of the women had quit.

The Hovey and Beard case shows that behavior in organizations can be influenced and changed through communication. This is attested to by the workers' greater work effort and less frequent complaining during the period when they were allowed to participate in decision making. But the case also shows that some people (the superintendent, for example) can be stubbornly resistant to change. After completing this chapter, the reader might try considering the superintendent again. Could anything have been done that might have influenced the superintendent to act differently, and if so, what?

The case also shows that influence includes a process of rewarding. The workers were given something they liked—the chance to affect decisions about their working conditions. In return, they did what was necessary to keep receiving this reward. They made the decisions responsibly, and they worked hard. When management stopped providing the reward, the workers stopped providing their side of the bargain. This notion of influence as a process of rewarding is part of a set of principles called *reinforcement theory.* In the next section reinforcement theory is examined in some detail because of its importance in explaining when and why influence occurs.

REINFORCEMENT THEORY

People tend to repeat behavior that leads to results they like.[1] Reinforcement refers to any stimulus that serves to strengthen a behavioral response. In general, reinforcement may be positive or negative. Positive reinforcement involves providing something desirable to a person for producing a certain kind of behavior. Negative reinforcement involves withdrawing or withholding an undesirable consequence.[2]

An example of positive reinforcement would be a commendation from a supervisor to a worker for a job well done. Negative reinforcement could be typified by the supervisor's visiting the workplace periodically to insure that the worker is on the job. In the latter case the worker, by keeping busy, avoids the unpleasant consequence of being reprimanded for goofing off. Negative reinforcement should not be confused with *punishment* (discussed later). In fact, the two are opposite in their effects. Reinforcement, whether positive or negative, rewards and strengthens behavior, while punishment weakens and decreases behavior.

The conditions under which reinforcement by an influencer produces a change in a target individual are suggested in an extensive body of theory. Some of the most important of these conditions are discussed in the next section.

Characteristics of Reinforcers

To be effective, a reinforcer has to be something the target person wants. Since individuals differ in their motivations, it is important for the influencer to get to know the likes and dislikes of the person or persons who are to be influenced. Persuasion can fail to occur when a reinforcer that is meaningful to the persuader is not seen the same way by the receiver. In one classic case, the productivity of splitters and trimmers in a slate rock processing mill had fallen off after the introduction of methods changes. The changes reduced the skill level of the workers' jobs and broke up their accustomed work groups. Since the workers placed high values on their chance to exercise their skill and on group membership, they responded to the changes by reducing their output. When management tried to stimulate higher output by instituting a wage increase, production did not increase. The wage increase was not what the workers were concerned about and thus did not act as a reinforcer.[3]

Reinforcers need to be seen by the receiver as profitable, not just rewarding. The value of the reinforcer to the receiver must be greater than the cost involved in performing the behavior desired by the persuader.[4] It is a principle of reinforcement theory that the less a person's profit (rewards minus costs) on a particular activity, the more likely it is that the person will shift to some other kind of activity. An example occurred in a certain office of a federal law enforcement agency where agents had widely varying levels of experience and knowledge. When less knowledgeable agents encountered a complicated legal question, they could ask one of the expert agents for help. This sometimes occurred, but close partnerships seldom formed between more and less expert agents because of the admission of incompetence that was implied in going to an expert for help. Instead, regular helping partnerships formed between agents of roughly equal experience levels. Going to an equal for help yielded less valuable information, but it was obtained at a low cost, thus providing a margin of profit.[5]

It is important that reinforcers be selected whose effectiveness does not diminish with repeated use. Reinforcers have to be used over and over again in order to influence behavior. Expressions of liking or encouragement, for example, are reinforcers whose value deteriorates with frequent use. If you want to win someone's esteem by telling him you like his shirt, don't do so twice in the same day. By the same token, a manger who tries to reward a subordinate with an approving comment for every desirable activity, however minor, will soon be seen as patronizing rather than encouraging.

Used more wisely, however, feedback about receiver performance can be one of the most effective reinforcers. The discussion of counseling and performance appraisal in the previous chapter showed that when the process is handled well, people can use information about their behavior as a stimulus to change. In such cases, the receiver learns to use the feedback information to produce behavior that is self-reinforcing as well as satisfactory to the influencer. The internally generated reward of changing performance to one's own satisfaction can often be an even more powerful and long-lived reinforcer than a reward given by the persuader. An example would be a music teacher who has students listen to tapes of their own performances. Another is the approach to selling life insurance in which the sales agent collects comprehensive information from the prospect and has it run through the company's computer. After viewing the resulting printout showing what the family's income would be if he or she were to die, the prospect then makes the choice as to how much insurance is needed.

When the goal is to influence a number of people, an especially useful form of reinforcement is group reinforcement. In group reinforcement, the reinforcing function is spread around the group. Members reinforce each other rather than having all rewards emanate from a single leader. When the reward is something the members value highly and is contingent upon satisfactory performance by the entire group, the group will likely begin to exert social pressure. Uncooperative members who jeopardize the group's success will become targets for disciplinary action by the group instead of requiring external regulation by a formal leader. The Hovey and Beard case is a clear example of a group whose members were more responsive to reinforcement from within the group than to external influence by the engineers and management.

Schedules of Reinforcement

The success of reinforcement varies, depending on the schedule of reinforcement that is used. While many variations are possible, there are three basic schedules for an influencer to choose from: continuous reinforcement, fixed ratio reinforcement, and variable ratio reinforcement.

Continuous reinforcement means that behavior is reinforced every time it occurs. Under this schedule the receiver quickly learns that the desired behavior will produce the reward. A disadvantage of continuous reinforcement, however, is that the receiver may rather quickly become satiated—so fully rewarded that further units of the reward cease to be worth the cost of obtaining them.

Fixed ratio reinforcement is a schedule in which the ratio of reinforced to nonreinforced occurrences is constant—that is, the behavior is rewarded after it occurs a fixed number of times. An example would be paying a salesperson a commission for every third sale. With this schedule it is usually found that just after reinforcement there is a pause before the person being reinforced resumes the activity at the same rate as before. Thus, the salesperson might decide to take a day or two off after receiving each commission payment.

A more intriguing type of schedule is one known as variable ratio reinforcement. Here, the ratio of reinforced to nonreinforced occurrences varies. Sometimes a performance might be rewarded after seven occurrences, sometimes after two. Under this schedule, the receiver doesn't know when reinforcement will occur and thus is more likely to produce the desired behavior at a steadier rate, without pauses. Suppose, for example, a child is given a dime upon completing each of three pages of a reading assignment. Another child is placed on a variable ratio schedule, with an *average* rate of reinforcement of one out of every three times. It is likely that the child who is given dimes on a variable schedule will continue reading longer and read more than the one who is given a dime after reading every page. This would be true even though the total number of dimes given is the same under both schedules.[6] The variable ratio schedule seems to be more effective because the uncertainty about when the reward will be received makes the receiver persist longer. Variable ratio reinforcement is also the most subtle of the various schedules. In some cases, the persuader does not want to be seen as an obvious manipulator. The use of variable ratio reinforcement may help the persuader maintain a lower profile.

An overall program of reinforcement, then, might begin with continuous reinforcement, shift as soon as possible to a variable ratio schedule, and then gradually reduce the ratio of reinforced to nonreinforced behavior. If successful, this would allow the desired behavior to be maintained with a very small amount of reinforcement. Obviously, the success of a particular reinforcement program will depend upon the specific situation in which it is used.

Inadvertent Reinforcement

Often a performance is maintained because it is being reinforced in a subtle fashion, so subtle that the person doing the reinforcing is unaware of what is happening. A mother, for example, may believe she is punishing a child for certain behavior, while the child, wanting the mother's continued attention, may keep producing the behavior. This phenomenon is not limited to parents and children. The boss who warmly greets a certain employee each morning communicates approval to the employee. If the employee is not performing satisfactorily on the job, the boss may be inadvertently reinforcing the poor performance. People frequently persuade others of things even when they do not intend to do so and are unaware of the process. Actually, every time you speak you are attempting to persuade someone at least to listen to you. Thus, all interpersonal behavior contains some aspects of the influence process and can be explained at least in part by the principles of reinforcement theory.

Punishment

Reinforcement theory usually emphasizes the application of reinforcers rather than punishment. The effects of punishment are harder to predict. Research has shown that while punished behavior does tend to decrease in frequency, undesired side effects can develop, such as a tendency to avoid the situation or aggression toward the punishing agent.

When punishment is unavoidable, it is most likely to be a successful reinforcer under these conditions: (1) when the person being punished cannot avoid the situation, (2) when the punishment is begun at a severe level and is maintained at the same level of severity rather than increased or decreased, and (3) when the punishment is administered on a continuous schedule and is given immediately after the unwanted behavior occurs. The most important of these conditions appears to be severity. Moderate punishment does not produce lasting changes, while severe punishment does.[7]

While punishment may sometimes be appropriate, it is still useful to employ positive reinforcers, given so as to reward the specific new behavior that is desired. Used alone, punishment may reduce a certain unwanted behavior, but it does not assure that new behavior will be that which is desired.

The moral and ethical issues involved in reinforcement theory, as well as in the overall topic of influence, should be mentioned at this point. Obviously there is the chance, whether in business, academic life, or professional practice, that someone will make irresponsible use of the principles of persuasion. This does not mean that these principles should not be taught, but rather that they should be used for constructive rather than destructive purposes.

PHASES IN THE INFLUENCE PROCESS

Influence does not happen in one instantaneous flash. The simplistic notion that a new idea or experience will immediately convince people to change their behavior and attitudes just does not square with the facts. Reinforcement theorists recognize this by saying that rewards may initially be given for "good mistakes"—that is, for behavior that is in the *direction* of what is desired.[8] Thus, to train a child who is always sloppy at the dinner table to become neat, one must first begin by giving a reward when the sloppiness is a little less than usual. Thus begun, the process of influence and change may then proceed into further phases.

A useful conception of the change process is the three-phase model advanced by Kurt Lewin and elaborated by Edgar Schein and others.[9] Lewin's phases—*unfreezing, changing,* and *refreezing*—are summarized in exhibit 13–1.

EXHIBIT 13–1
PHASES IN THE INFLUENCE PROCESS

Phase 1. *Unfreezing*: arousing motivation to change
Mechanisms: (a) Lack of confirmation or disconfirmation
(b) Reduction of threat or removal of barriers to change
Phase 2. *Changing*: developing new attitudes and behavior based on new information
Mechanisms: (a) Identification: information from a single source
(b) Scanning: information from multiple sources
Phase 3. *Refreezing*. stabilizing and integrating the changes
Mechanisms: (a) Integrating new responses into personality
(b) Integrating new responses into significant ongoing relationships through reconfirmation

Adapted from Warren G. Bennis, Edgar H. Schein, Fred I. Steele, and David E. Berlew, eds., *Interpersonal Dynamics: Essays and Readings in Human Interaction,* Rev. Ed. (Homewood, Ill.: The Dorsey Press, 1968), p. 339. © 1968 by The Dorsey Press.

Unfreezing

For a change to take place in response to an influence attempt, unlearning has to happen before new learning can occur. This is especially so when the change involves a move away from strongly held beliefs or habits. This sort of change tends to be resisted because it implies an admission of personal inadequacy. Thus, change must begin with upsetting the person's initially stable equilibrium.

Schein suggests two ways in which unfreezing can come about: (a) disconfirmation (or lack of confirmation) of the person's existing attitudes or behavior and (b) reduction of threat. Disconfirmation occurs when the person's attitudes or behavior begin to receive a negative reaction. Lack of confirmation, on the other hand, happens when the person's viewpoints or actions simply find no support. In the Hovey and Beard case, the new production line—with its constant, preset speed—was a disconfirmation of the workers' idea of what their jobs should be like. This was a first step in the influence process, even though it was not in the direction intended by management. The worker's dissatisfaction opened up their willingness to search for new solutions.

Another way that unfreezing can be brought about is by reducing threat or removing barriers to change. The reflective listening technique discussed in chapter 12 is an example. The reflective listener, by concentrating on understanding the other person's point of view, provides a nonthreatening atmosphere in which the other person is encouraged to explore problems more openly and thoroghly than he or she would in the presence of someone viewed as judgmental or challenging.

Changing

After unfreezing has made the individual open to new information, the change process itself involves the actual assimilation of new information and the formation of new ideas and plans of action. According to Schein, information can be acquired by two means; *identification* and *scanning.*

Identification involves getting information from a single source. If the influencer is a person whom the receiver trusts and respects, the change may be dramatic, with the receiver modeling himself or herself after the attitudes and actions of the influencer. By contrast, the receiver may experience an involuntary form of identification with a persuader who is seen as exercising coercive power, forcing the receiver to change. In this case, change may occur, but it is likely to be a more stilted and ritualized copying of the persuader's behavior. Here, the receiver is simply going along with the persuader in order to avoid disconfirmation and likely would not act the same way in the absence of the persuader.

In identification, a strong emotional relationship exists between the influencer and the receiver. Information may, however, be gained from more emotionally neutral sources. This process of scanning involves searching among multiple sources of information rather than focusing on just one. An example would be a group member who receives reactions and information from many members of the group and attempts to integrate all the data obtained. Scanning may be a more difficult process than identification, requiring large amounts of time and effort before reliable, useful information is located. The solution is likely to fit better into the receiver's personality, however, because it has been accepted voluntarily. The term *internalization* has been used to describe information acquired in this way, since the receiver accepts it because of personal preference for the information rather than because of someone else's desires.[10]

Refreezing

If the receiver is to stay influenced, it is necessary that the new behavior fit well with the rest of the receiver's personality. It is also important that it be accepted by those whose opinions are important to the receiver. The influence process often fails at this step. Managerial and supervisory training programs frequently produce changes in behavior that disappear when the trainee returns to the job if coworkers disconfirm the attitudes and behavior learned during training.[11] The paint shop workers in the Hovey and Beard case eventually received a disconfirming response from their organizational surroundings, leading to another unfreezing and change when many of them decided to leave the company.

An influencer who is really concerned about inducing stable change must make adequate provisions for the refreezing of new behavior. In practice, this means that the successful persuader communicates not just with the primary receiver of influence but also with those others whose impact on the receiver is significant.

It should be noted that the means by which the change is introduced can have a bearing on the ease or difficulty of refreezing. Scanning—producing solutions that are self-selected—tends to lead to changes that are well integrated into the person's total personality. Such solutions may be more desirable in cases where the persuader has little control over the reactions of significant others. On the other hand, changes produced by identification remain stable only if the relationship between the receiver and the model remains stable. They also require integration into other parts of the receiver's self and acceptance by people other than the model. The problem for the influencer, then, is to judge whether or not the changes induced will fit the receiver's needs and be reinforced by others.

Obviously, the unfreezing-changing-refreezing model does not provide a sure, simple rule for an influencer to follow. Interpersonal influence is an extremely complex process about which much remains unknown. However, the model does help us to become less naive about the process of influence and to begin to face its complexities head-on. Influence is indeed a complex phenomenon, involving a multitude of factors that go toward determining whether or not unfreezing, changing, and refreezing take place. There are many more such factors than have been discussed thus far, more than can be considered in a single chapter. Research findings relating to some of the most important of these factors are reviewed in the next section.

SOME MAJOR FACTORS AFFECTING THE INFLUENCE PROCESS

A convenient way to organize the key factors relating to influence is to think in terms of *who* says *what* to *whom,* and with what *effect.* The first three italicized terms in this formula may be recognized as the components of the Berlo model presented in chapter 2: source, message, and receiver. According to this formula, the effect—that is, the extent to which influence occurs—depends on these three determinants. Exhibit 13–2 is a diagram of these relationships. The exhibit shows the addition of a fourth determinant, the group and organizational setting, which may be seen as analogous to the channel in Berlo's model.

The factors relating to influence are discussed in the sections following. The chapter will then conclude with a list of strategies and tactics for influence.

EXHIBIT 13–2
FACTORS AFFECTING THE INFLUENCE
PROCESS

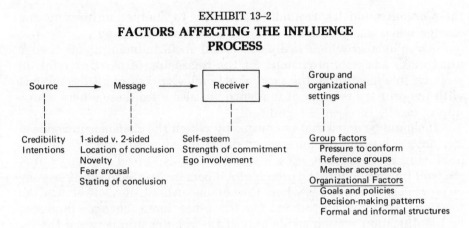

Adapted from Irving L. Janis and Carl I. Hovland, *Personality and Persuasibility* (New Haven: Yale University Press, 1959), p. 4; and Jonathan L. Freedman, J. Merrill Carlsmith and David O. Sears, *Social Psychology* (Englewood Cliffs, N.J.: Prentice-Hall, 1974), p. 266.

Source

One of the most straightforward and reliable findings from research on influence is that the more credible the source, the greater the persuasive effect. Source credibility means the extent to which the influencer is seen by the receiver as being a qualified expert, trustworthy, well intentioned, and dynamic.[12] If someone tells you a certain poem is a good one, you will be much more likely to agree if that someone is T. S. Eliot than if it is the local gas station proprietor. The reverse, of course, would be true concerning carburetor problems.

Regardless of the sender's expertise, it is extremely important that the receiver trust the sender's intentions. People tend to trust others who are similar to themselves and who initially express some views with which they agree. They also tend to trust communicators who are not seen as making an open attempt to exert influence. Studies have shown that when there is a forewarning of an intent to persuade, the listeners will then go through a mental checking off of whether the arguments support or disagree with their own position.[13] Open attempts at influence are not necessarily rejected, however, if other aspects of the transaction are highly favorable. One well-known study, for example, showed that men were persuaded more by a person they liked when they knew the persuader was trying to influence them than when the influence attempt was less obvious.[14] The more open the influence attempt, the more likely the target person will feel, "I'd better go along, or I'll be jeopardizing a good friendship."

Persuasiveness tends to be more effective when a sender argues against his or her own best interest. This was shown in a study revealing that prosecuting attorneys who gave arguments for reducing the power of prosecutors were believed more than those who argued the opposite.

The same study showed that criminals who advocated that prosecutors should have more power were much more effective than prosecutors who argued the same position.[15]

An interesting phenomenon connected with the source variables discussed thus far is the so-called sleeper effect. The source of a communication apparently has its strongest effect immediately after the transmission of the message and is much less important some time later. One experiment exposed audiences of high school students to a speech arguing for lenient treatment of juvenile delinquents.[16] With different audience groups, the speaker was made to appear either competent, fair, and attractive, or uninformed, biased, and unattractive. The students were asked their attitudes on the issue right after the speech and again three weeks later. The immediate effect of the more credible speaker was greater than that of the less credible speaker. After three weeks, however, the effect of the credible speaker had declined, while the effect of the less credible speaker had increased. This is called the sleeper effect because the effect of the less credible communicator is greater than it appears at first. The explanation appears to be that people forget the source of a message sooner than they forget its content. Interestingly, it was found that the effects of source credibility could be reinstated if the subjects were reminded of the source before being asked for their opinion after the three-week period. When this was done, the students who had heard the more credible speaker again showed markedly more agreement with the message than did the others. Source credibility is obviously very important, but it is also clear that persuasive effects can take place even when the source is not seen as highly appealing.

Organization members are often aware they will not be seen as credible by persons they would like to influence (for example, their more experienced seniors or members of a rival department). They conclude, "There's no point in saying anything to them; they'd never pay attention to me." The sleeper effect phenomenon should encourage such members to make the effort to exert influence. Despite their low credibility, persuasion can still take place, particularly if the content of the message has strong enough merit and impact that it can, over time, become dissociated from its source in the receiver's thinking.[17]

Message

Obviously, the message itself has an effect on the extent to which persuasion occurs. Both the form and the content of the message are important.

In terms of form, for example, research has shed some light on the relative merits of one-sided versus two-sided messages and on the sequencing of different parts of a persuasive message. It appears that under most circumstances, greater effect is obtained with a two-sided message —that is, one that mentions arguments both for and against the conclusion being advocated. If you are trying to persuade an employee to accept a change in job assignment, you probably should mention both the advantages and disadvantages of the new assignment, not just the advantages. Most people in organizations today are relatively well educated and well informed and are not likely to be convinced by a simplistic, one-sided argument. An added advantage of two-sided arguments is that they tend to "immunize" the receiver against subsequent counterarguments, since the original persuasive message has taken opposing views into account.[18] A one-sided appeal may be more persuasive, however, if the listener is already favorably disposed toward the message, is unaware of opposing arguments and will not be exposed to them, and has little formal education.[19] It should be noted that research continues on the relative effects of one-sided versus two-sided messages. More remains to be learned, and judgment should be used in applying the suggestions just given and those that follow.

Research results offer some suggestions about other aspects of message structure. Among these are placement of supporting and refuting arguments in a two-sided message, whether to present problems or solutions first, and where to place points of common agreement.[20]

Though research is limited, it can be tentatively concluded that positive arguments should be given first, followed by refutation of opposing arguments. This tends to establish the listener on the side of the persuader first before the counterarguments are discussed.

When the persuasive message proposes a solution to a problem, it has been found more effective to state the problem first, then the solution. This sequence is usually more interesting, and a listener who has first heard the problem described can understand the proposed solution better.

In most cases the persuader agrees with the listener(s) in some respects and disagrees in others. Research indicates that it is best to first discuss the points of common agreement and then move to areas of disagreement. If all goes well, discussing agreed-on points will heighten the listener's evaluation of the persuader, making the listener more receptive to the persuader's claims in the disputed area.

In terms of message content, one factor that almost always helps persuade is novelty of the information presented. An audience is more willing to change when given new facts that presumably they have not considered before. Even if information is not new, it is more persuasive if it can be made to seem new.[21]

In most cases, arousing fear increases the persuasiveness of a message. The ads by the American Cancer Society noting the dangers of smoking are good examples of fear-arousing messages. It is possible that extreme fear can so disrupt the receiver that he or she becomes defensive and denies the validity of the message. Moderate fear appeals may be generally more effective, with the optimum level depending upon the circumstances and message contents. Fear-arousing messages that include specific instructions as to how, when, and where the receiver can act to remove the danger have been shown to be more effective than those that threaten but do not provide a clear remedy.[22]

A final point that should be emphasized concerning message content is that it is almost always useful for the persuader to state the conclusion rather than to just give the facts and leave the conclusion up to the audience. This has been found to be true for all arguments except for those of extreme simplicity.[23]

Receiver

When a message reaches its intended receiver, the problems of persuasion are not yet over. Various characteristics of the receiver are important determinants of his or her reaction to the message. Research has established connections between persuasiveness and the receiver's self-esteem, strength of commitment, and ego involvement.

The general rule relating to self-esteem is that receivers who have lower self-esteem are more easily influenced. This is most likely to be true in cases where self-esteem has been reduced by a specific recent failure and where the persuasive message is a simple one and does not arouse the receiver's fear. Receivers with low self-esteem seem to be relatively unwilling or unable to comprehend messages of these latter kinds.[24]

A crucial factor in being persuaded is the strenth of the receiver's commitment to his or her present position.[25] A person who has just bought a car is more committed to the belief that it is a fine car than if the purchase had not yet been made. A change in the opinion has much broader implications after the purchase than before.

Two factors that work to strengthen commitment are action taken on the basis of the belief and public commitment to the belief. It also appears that the opportunity to choose a position freely, rather than being forced, produces stronger commitment. In one study, subjects were asked to rate the acceptability of a candidate for graduate school. Some of the subjects were told they were free to make up their own minds, while others were made to feel they had little to do with the decision and had been forced to select a certain rating. After making their ratings, each subject was exposed to information that strongly contradicted their initial rating and was given the opportunity to change the rating. Those who had made the first rating with a sense of free choice changed less than those in a low-choice situation.[26]

Commitment is also affected by the extent to which the current attitude is intertwined with other attitudes and behaviors. It is probably relatively easy to change most people's attitudes on the fluoridation of drinking water, for example. People might strongly favor it, but this attitude probably stands by itself to a large extent. If they were to change their attitude from favorable to unfavorable, it would involve few other changes in their cognitive systems. By contrast, consider a dentist who has been telling patients the merits of fluoridation for years, has been coating teeth with fluorides, reading literature supporting fluoridation, and has donated money to fluoridation campaigns. Changing the dentist's opinion would be very difficult since it would require many changes in a tightly interconnected system of many cognitions and behaviors.

A particularly sensitive portion of the cognitive system is a person's self-concept. An influence attempt may fail when an influencer advocates a belief or action that has negative implications for the receiver's self-view. The importance of self-concept is shown vividly in the classic "cognitive dissonance" experiment conducted by Leon Festinger and James Carlsmith.[27]

In this study, subjects performed very boring tasks, such as packing and unpacking boxes of spools. After completing the tasks, the subjects were asked to tell a certain student who was waiting in the hallway that the experiment had been an interesting one. Some subjects were offered twenty dollars to tell the waiting student that the experiment had been interesting, while others were offered one dollar to perform this same task. The researchers predicted that those who had been paid just one dollar would change their attitudes to correspond with their behavior more than would those who were paid twenty dollars.

The researchers based their prediction on the notion that people will tend to form attitudes that are consistent with a favorable view of self. The subjects who argued the boring task was interesting, contrary to their real belief, had to resolve somehow the discrepancy between their lying behavior and their views of themselves as honest people. For those who had been paid twenty dollars, the money apparently provided an adequate justification. For those who lied for the small sum of just one dollar, however, the most comfortable resolution came by convincing themselves that the boring task really was not so boring after all.

Since the smaller reward yielded the greater attitude change, the Festinger and Carlsmith study is used by some commentators as an argument against reinforcement theory. Looked at another way, however, the experiment supports reinforcement theory. The subjects paid one dollar found their new belief that the task had been interesting to be highly reinforcing because it restored their views of themselves as reasonable, valuable people.

For the communicator who is trying to be persuasive, this study shows the need to maintain or increase the receiver's feeling of personal responsibility and voluntary commitment. It also suggests that it might often be useful to follow up a successful persuasive message with additional information to help the receiver resolve discrepancies within the self-concept. The Hovey and Beard case at the beginning of this chapter supports both of these recommendations. The workers' improved performance on the job was obviously reinforced through a sense of personal responsibility deriving from the fact that they themselves had developed the new work methods and they themselves enforced them. The importance of follow-up information is shown by its absence in the Hovey and Beard case. The case gives no indication that the plant superintendent was provided with follow-up information about the newly developed sense of worker responsibility in the paint shop. If this had been done, the superintendent might have felt less threatened by the wage imbalance problem that developed and more willing to give the paint shop workers a voice in solving it.

Group and Organizational Settings

The Hovey and Beard case showed that group and organizational factors can help and hurt a persuasive effort. The worker group, *as* a group, successfully resisted the engineers' initial attempt to get the production line running smoothly. Then the supervisor's effort to change the women's morale and effort received strong support from the group and was dramatically successful. The supervisor did not take adequate account of the total organization, however. Other departments and the superintendent ultimately became forces that worked to reverse the change. Some of the ways in which group and organizational factors can effect the influence process are now addressed.

Group Factors. A persuasive message can gain great strength by having the force of group support behind it. This was shown vividly in a famous experiment on group pressure conducted by Solomon Asch.[28] Asch formed groups consisting of one naive subject and several of his own confederates. The group members were asked to state their individual judgments of three lines displayed on a screen. Specifically, each member in turn was asked to say which of the displayed lines was most similar to a fourth line shown separately. The confederates, all of whom had been primed to give the same incorrect answer, were asked first. In many experiments and many trials the naive subjects conformed with the group about thirty-five percent of the time, even though this meant giving an answer that was at odds with their clear visual perception.

Some studies have indicated that conformity increases with the number of sources of information, up to four sources. This suggests that an influencer should try to get four associates of the receiver to confirm the message. The effect of such social pressure is probably mediated by the receiver's degree of confidence or lack of confidence in his or her own attitude and the extent to which the opinion must be stated in public. A receiver who lacks confidence and is being observed publicly is probably more susceptible to group pressures.[29]

The availability of outside reference groups also affects the degree to which a person will be influenced in a given group situation. A medical doctor is more likely to stick to a professional opinion than to be swayed by a group of nonprofessionals.[30]

A group can exercise greatest control over members who are moderately accepted by the group. Those who feel fully accepted or who feel rejected accept little influence. Individuals who are already accepted tend not to worry about complying in order to gain additional acceptance, and those who are rejected see little chance of gaining the group's favor even if they do accept influence.[31]

Groups can, then, exert a powerful effect on the persuasive process, either in favor of the message or against it. The direction and degree of this effect depends, however, on the specifics of the situation.

Organizational Factors. Organizations, by their nature, put limitations on the extent to which their members can influence each other. Policies, decisions, and actions of people outside the immediate influencer-receiver relationship may strongly affect the success of influence attempts. Among the most important organizational factors bearing on the influence process are the organization's formal and informal structures.[32]

It is generally more difficult to influence an organization member to act counter to the goals, policies, or rules of an organization and easier to encourage behavior that conforms with them. Thus, it behooves the influencer to know what those goals are and to stay within them. Messages cast in terms of an organizational goal are likely to be more persuasive. Thus, if the organization is currently emphasizing cost control, a recommendation for the purchase of new equipment will fare better if it emphasizes its cost-saving advantages rather than its technical sophistication. The successful persuader is likely one who knows what the organization's problems are and is aware that a communication offering a solution to one or more of them is apt to be well received. It usually helps also if the influencer knows something about the way similar organizations operate, particularly successful ones. In proposing new programs, products, or services, for example, the influences can present the experience other organizations have had with similar efforts.

The persuader needs to be aware of the decision pattern in the organization. If it is centralized, the persuader's strategy will need to be geared toward reaching and convincing top management. If it is decentralized, the appropriate target may be a subunit manager or even a key technician at a low organizational level. If many people tend to participate in decisions, the persuader will need to discover who they are and reach as many of them as possible. Political realities obviously need to be considered. If the people who have the most real power in the organization can be won over to a proposal, it is well on its way. In line with the earlier discussion of source credibility, a persuader who has limited credibility alone may become highly successful by convincing one or more persons who do have high credibility within the organization.

The formal and informal structures of the organization include numerous variables that can help or hinder an influence attempt. As discussed in chapter 11, the formal design of an organization typically establishes subunits whose self-interests differ from one another. This suggests that an attempt to influence members of more than one subunit may need to involve making more than one type of appeal and separate contact with people from different units. Subunit differences also account for the fact that most new ideas introduced in an organization generate conflict. The persuader needs to be aware of the likelihood of conflict and ready to work for its resolution in a way that is acceptable to the organization.

A formal structure containing large differences between individuals in terms of status and prestige can be a barrier to the influence process, but in a different way so can a "flatter" structure, where people are considered to be near equals. In the steep hierarchy, persuasive attempts by senior persons, for example, may be resisted by lower-level personnel who fear further domination. In the flat structure, an influencer may seem to be violating the norm of equality and hence be resisted. In such cases, the influencer may increase the likelihood of success by depersonalizing the message and emphasizing the ways in which the proposed change will give power to the receivers rather than amass power to the persuader.

These points relating to formal structure apply equally to informal structure, which has its own factions and norms. The successful influencer does well to know and use the informal organizational grapevine. Special mention should be made of the informal structure's ability to bridge the boundaries between formal subunits. In most organizations, the informal communication network puts certain individuals in contact with members of several groups other than their own. Research has shown these liaison persons to be more influential within organizations than members whose contacts are restricted within a single group.[33] A persuader could be greatly aided by an awareness of who these "opinion leaders" are.

SOME SPECIFIC PERSUASIVE TACTICS

This chapter has focused on the major processes and factors involved in influence. It will now conclude with a brief description of several specific persuasive tactics. The list is not exhaustive, nor are all of the techniques applicable to every situation, but the tactics are ones that have proved effective over the years to many successful influencers.[34]

1. *The Numerous Agreements Technique.* Ask the receiver several questions in a planned series, making sure that each question is one demanding a yes answer. When the habit of saying yes has become established, the likelihood is increased that the receiver will say yes to the persuader's proposition.
2. *Win Friends.* People like to be liked. When it is possible to say something nice about the receiver, do so. Smiling, maintaining eye contact, and calling the receiver by name are also important. Flattery can be overdone, but recognition for accomplishments and plain warmth are appreciated by virtually everyone.
3. *Simulated Indifference.* Persuasive success is often increased if the

persuader does not seem too anxious about the outcome. The reason may be that the receiver is then able to concentrate on his or her own situation and the proposal rather than on the vested interest the persuader has in "making the sale."

4. *Transfer.* Transfer is the effect that the physical surroundings have on the outcome of an influence attempt. Positive transfer occurs when the surroundings help the persuasive effort, and negative transfer happens when the surroundings interfere. Job applicants, for example, tend to be favorably impressed when they are interviewed in an attractive office.

5. *Use Facts.* It is next to impossible to convince someone else of something you yourself do not understand. A persuader who lacks knowledge may well be worried and may unintentionally transmit this worry to the receiver. Thorough knowledge and use of facts help the persuader to meet challenges in a positive frame of mind.

6. *Address the Receiver's Self-interest.* Assume that the question the receiver wants answered most thoroughly is, "What's in it for me?" The successful persuader discovers what the receiver's personal concerns are and tailors the message to that person.

7. *Point to the Bandwagon.* Show the receiver evidence that other people are accepting the idea. As the Asch experiments showed, people are more prone to conform than one might think.

8. *Give the Choice of Either Buying or Buying.* Whenever possible, offer the receiver the choice of *something* and *something else* instead of *something* or *nothing.* When two or more alternatives are suggested as possibilities, the receiver tends to focus on selecting the best one. If just one possibility is recommended, the receiver can think only of accepting or rejecting it. The "which, not if" tactic is well suited to proposals that are complex. A recommendation to build a new building or change a production line can usually be presented in several forms, all of which are acceptable to the persuader.

9. *Welcome Objections.* The receiver who talks and expresses his or her objections is much easier to persuade than the receiver who is silent. Objections show the areas where more persuasive effort is needed. The alert persuader treats objections as requests for further information and as aids in getting to know the receiver's needs and wants.

10. *Horse Trading.* In horse trading, the persuader does something for the receiver, thus establishing an obligation on the part of the latter to do something in return. An example is the sales representative who gives a free sample in exchange for the opportunity to present the full sales pitch. Beginning an influence attempt by sharing valued information with the receiver is another example of horse trading.

11. *Be Something of a Pest.* This tactic can backfire but, when used skillfully, can also be a powerful aid to persuasion. It consists of being

just irritating enough that the receiver will not explode but will do what you want in order to get rid of you. The trick is to avoid being obvious in your attempt to annoy the receiver. Many sales persons and all children are experts in this technique.

The reader can undoubtedly make associates between many of these techniques and the concepts and research findings discussed earlier. "Horse trading" and "being a pest" can be techniques for unfreezing the receiver, for example, while "welcoming objections" provides a way for the persuader to discover the very factors affecting the receiver's point of view. It must be cautioned again, however, that these tactics should be used selectively rather than blindly and must be tailored to the specific circumstances. They can comprise *part* of a successful influence attempt, but they are not the whole story.

Summary

This chapter began by conceiving of the influence process as an exchange between the influencer and the receiver of influence. In this connection, reinforcement theory was introduced as a set of concepts having broad applicability to many aspects of the influence process. The characteristics of reinforcers were discussed, with emphasis on the notion that the receiver must experience the reinforcer as rewarding and profitable if influence is to take place. The effects of various reinforcement schedules were considered, as were the topics of inadvertent reinforcement and punishment. The influence process was then described in terms of Lewin's phases of unfreezing, changing, and refreezing. This discussion indicated the importance of these three phases by showing how influence attempts can result in failure if any one of these phases is not fulfilled. The multidimensional nature of the influence process was then examined, with attention given to the source, the message, the receiver, and the group and organizational settings surrounding the persuasive effort. Research studies were presented supporting several useful principles of persuasion. While these principles were of broad applicability, the persuasion researches taken as a whole showed the complexity of the persuasive process and the need to shape the specifics of an influence attempt to fit the situation in which it is used. With this reservation in mind, the chapter concluded with a list of eleven specific persuasive tactics that have been used with frequent success by skilled practitioners.

Questions for Review

1. Using reinforcement thory, explain the success or failure of an instance where you tried to influence someone. Consider both the char-

acteristics of the reinforcer(s) and the schedule of reinforcement you used.

2. What is meant by a program of reinforcement? Give an example.

3. Explain the concept of inadvertent reinforcement, and give an illustration.

4. What is a "good mistake"? Why is this concept an important one for an influencer to be aware of?

5. Explain how an attitude change that a person arrives at by identification is likely to differ from one achieved through scanning.

6. What are the key elements in the "refreezing" process? How well were they fulfilled in the Hovey and Beard case?

7. State four ways in which a communicator may establish source credibility.

8. Discuss the relative merits of one-sided versus two-sided messages as vehicles for persuasion.

9. Describe the methods and results of the cognitive dissonance experiments performed by Festinger and Carlsmith and the conformity studies conducted by Asch. What implications can be drawn for improving the success of persuasive communications?

10. Give an example of how organizational factors can act as barriers to the influence process and an example of how they can aid it.

11. Think about an unsuccessful persuasive attempt you have been involved in or observed. What specific persuasive tactics could have increased the likelihood that this attempt could have been successful?

References and Notes

1. Edward L. Thorndyke, *Animal Intelligence* (New York: Macmillan, 1911), p. 244.

2. The discussion of reinforcement theory draws primarily upon Erwin P. Bettinghaus, *Persuasive Communication* (New York: Holt, Rinehart and Winston, 1968), pp. 52–66; George C. Homans, *Social Behavior: Its Elementary Forms* (New York: Harcourt, Brace & World, 1961), pp. 17–68; Albert Mehrabian, *Tactics of Social Influence* (Englewood Cliffs, N.J.: Prentice-Hall, 1970); Fred Luthans, *Organizational Behavior* (New York: McGraw-Hill, 1977), pp. 291–302. For a more recent study explaining persuasive communication in terms of reinforcement, see Nathan Maccoby and John W. Farquhar, "Communication for Health: Unselling Heart Disease," *Journal of Communication* 25, no. 3 (1975): 114–26.

3. "Superior Slate Quarry," in Paul R. Lawrence, Louis B. Barnes, and Jay W. Lorsch, *Organizational Behavior and Administration* (Homewood, Ill.: Irwin, 1976), pp. 591–97.

4. See William F. Whyte, "Pigeons, Persons and Piece Rates: Skinnerian Theory in Organizations," *Psychology Today,* April 1972, pp. 67–68, 96–110.

5. The federal law enforcement agency example comes from Peter M. Blau, *The Dynamics of Bureaucracy* (Chicago: University of Chicago Press, 1955), p. 109. The explanation in terms of profitability is given by Homans, *Social Behavior,* p. 365.

6. This example is suggested by Mehrabian, *Tactics of Social Influence,* p. 20, based on animal experiments reported in C. B. Ferster and B. F. Skinner, *Schedules of Reinforcement* (Englewood Cliffs, N.J.: Prentice-Hall, 1957), pp. 391–414.

7. Tbe conclusions about punishment presented in this section are from research summarized in Nathan H. Azrin and W. C. Holtz, "Punishment," in *Operant Behavior: Areas of Research and Application,* ed. Werner K. Honig (New York: Appleton-Century-Crofts, 1966), pp. 380–446.

8. Mehrabian, *Tactics of Social Influence,* pp. 26–28.

9. Edgar H. Schein, "The Mechanisms of Change," in Warren G. Bennis et al., *The Planning of Change* (New York: Holt, Reinhart and Winston, 1969), pp. 357–65. See also Warren G. Bennis et al., *Interpersonal Dynamics* (Homewood, Ill.: Dorsey Press, 1968), pp. 333–68.

10. Herbert C. Kelman, "Compliance, Identification, and Internalization," *Journal of Conflict Resolution,* 2, no. 1 (1958): 51–60 .

11. Edwin A. Fleishman, "Leadership Climate, Human Relations Training and Supervisory Behavior," *Personnel Psychology* 6 (1953): 205–22.

12. Carl I. Hovland, Irving L. Janis, and Harold H. Kelley, *Communication and Persuasion,* (New Haven: Yale University Press, 1953): 19–36; James B. Lemert, "Dimensions of Source Credibility" (Paper presented to the Association for Education in Journalism, August 26, 1963); Lawrence R. Wheeless, "Attitudes and Credibility in the Prediction of Attitude Change: A Regression Approach," *Speech Monographs,* 41 (1974): 277–81; James C. McCroskey and David W. Wright, "A Comparison of the Effects of Punishment-Oriented and Reward-Oriented Messages in Persuasive Communication," *Journal of Communication* 21, no. 1 (1971): 83–93.

13. William J. McGuire and Susan Millman, "Anticipatory Belief Lowering Following Forewarning of a Persuasive Attack," *Journal of Personality and Social Psychology* 2, no. 4 (1965): 471–79; Jonathan L. Freedman and David O. Sears, "Warning, Distraction, and Resistance to Influence," *Journal of Personality and Social Psychology* 1, no. 3 (1965); 262–66.

14. Judson Mills and Elliot Aronson, "Opinion Change as a Function of Communicator's Attractiveness and Desire to Influence," *Journal of Personality and Social Psychology* 1, no. 2 (1965): 173–77

15. Elaine Walster, Elliot Aronson, and Darcy Abrams, "On Increasing The Persuasiveness of a Low Prestige Communicator," *Journal of Experimental Social Psychology* 2 (1966): 325–42.

16. Herbert C. Kelman and Carl I. Hovland, "Reinstatement of the Communicator in Delayed Measurement of Opinion Change," *Journal of Abnormal and Social Psychology,* 48 (1953): 327–35.

17. Charles L. Gruder, "Empirical Tests of the Absolute Sleeper Effect Predicted from the Discounting Cue Hypotheses," *Journal of Personality and Social Psychology* 36 (1978): 1061–74.

18. William J. McGuire, "Inducing Resistance to Persuasion," in *Advances in Experimental Social Psychology,* vol. 1, ed. Leonard Berkowitz (New York:

Academic Press, 1964), pp. 191–229; James C. McCroskey, Thomas J. Young, and Michael D. Scott, "The Effects of Message Sidedness and Evidence on Inoculation Against Counterpersuasion in Small Group Communication," *Speech Monographs* 39 (1972): 205–12.

19. Thomas J. Crawford, "Theories of Attitude Change," in Bernard Seidenberg and Alvin Snadowsky, *Social Psychology* (New York: Free Press, 1976), p. 204.

20. Michael B. Burgoon and Judee K. Burgoon, "Message Strategies and Influence Attempts," in *Communication and Behavior,* ed. Gerhard J. Hanneman and William J. McEwen (Reading, Mass.: Addison-Wesley, 1975), pp. 149–65.

21. David O. Sears and Jonathan L. Freedman, "Effects of Expected Familiarity of Arguments upon Opinion Change and Selective Exposure," *Journal of Personality and Social Psychology* 2, no. 3 (1967): 420–25.

22. Howard Leventhal, "Findings and Theory in the Study of Fear Communications," *Advances in Experimental Social Psychology* 5 (1970): 119–86.

23. William J. McGuire, "Personality and Susceptibility to Social Influence," in *Handbook of Personality Theory and Research,* ed. E. F. Burgather and W. W. Lambert (Chicago: Rand McNally, 1968), pp. 1130–87.

24. Arthur R. Cohen, "Some Implications of Self-Esteem for Social Influence," in *Personality and Persuasibility,* ed. Carl I. Hovland and Irving L. Janis (New Haven: Yale University Press, 1959), pp. 102–20; Miriam Zellner, "Self-Esteem, Reception and Influenceability," *Journal of Personality and Social Psychology* 15, no. 1 (1970): 87–93.

25. The discussion that follows on commitment draws upon Jonathan L. Freedman, J. Merril Carlsmith, and David O. Sears, *Social Psychology* (Englewood Cliffs, N.J.: Prentice-Hall, 1974), pp. 296–97.

26. Jonathan L. Freedman and John D. Steinbruner, "Perceived Choice and Resistence to Persuasion," *Journal of Abnormal and Social Psychology* 68, no. 6 (1964): 678–81.

27. Leon Festinger and James M. Carlsmith, "Cognitive Consequences of Forced Compliance," *Journal of Abnormal and Social Psychology* 58, no. 2 (1959): 203–10.

28. Solomon E. Asch, "Effects of Group Pressure upon the Modification and Distortion of Judgments," in *Groups, Leadership and Men,* ed. Harold Guetzkow (Pittsburgh: Carnegie Press, 1951), pp. 177–90.

29. Stephen W. King, *Communication and Social Influence* (Reading, Mass.: Addison-Wesley, 1975), pp. 43–44.

30. Leon Festinger and John Thibaut, "Interpersonal Communication in Small Groups," *Journal of Abnormal and Social Psychology* 46 (1951): 92–99.

31. James E. Dittes and Harold H. Kelley, "Effects of Different Conditions of Acceptance upon Conformity to Group Norms," *Journal of Abnormal and Social Psychology* 53 (1956): 100–117.

32. The discussion of organizational factors given here is a much abbreviated adaptation of one contained in Bettinghaus, *Persuasive Communication,* pp. 224–54. See also, Jerry C. Wofford, Edwin A. Gerloff, and Robert C. Cummins, *Organizational Communication* (New York: McGraw-Hill, 1977), pp. 216–24.

33. Donald F. Schwartz and Eugene Jacobson, "Organizational Communication Network Analysis: The Liaison Communication Role," *Organizational Behavior and Human Performance* 18, no. 1 (1977): 158–74.

34. The ideas contained in the list of eleven persuasive techniques are drawn from Ernest G. Borman et al., *Interpersonal Communication in the Modern Organization* (Englewood Cliffs, N.J.: Prentice-Hall, 1969), pp. 233–41; Kenneth Brooks Haas and Enos C. Perry, *Sales Horizons* (Englewood Cliffs, N.J.: Prentice-Hall, 1968), pp. 52–80; Rollie Tillman and Charles A. Kirkpatrick, *Promotion: Persuasive Communication in Marketing* (Homewood, Ill.: Irwin, 1968), pp. 148–55.

Chapter 14

Organization Development and Communication

The Process of Organizational Change
Specific Approaches to OD
    Individuals
    Dyads, Small Groups, or Teams
    Intergroup Relations
    The Total Organization
Communication Problems and Strategies in OD
    Causes of Resistance to OD
    Strategies for Decreasing Resistance
Communication Approaches for the OD Practitioner

After studying this chapter, the reader should be able to

Define and use the following terms and concepts

Dalton's subprocesses of
    organizational change
Greiner's six phases of
    organizational change
Change as an on-going
    cyclical process
T-group
Survey feedback
Classroom training and OD
Job enrichment
Counseling
Interpersonal peacemaking

Process consultation
Team building
Intergroup team building
Organization mirror
Confrontation meetings
MBO
Structural approaches
Communication appraisals
Causes of resistance to change
Strategies for decreasing
    resistance
OD practitioner guidelines

Understand

How organization development and communication are related
The four subprocesses of change
Greiner's six phases of successful change
Several specific organization development techniques

14

Organization development (OD) can be defined as a planned, sustained effort, based on behavioral science knowledge, to change the human and social processes of work groups and organizations in the direction of improved problem solving and renewal processes.[1] Here are some examples:

> In 1972, following a year of detailed planning, the city government of Tacoma, Washington began an extensive series of organizational improvement measures aided by two outside consultants. The program included quarterly interview feedback and problem-solving workshops for the city manager and his top staff, "team-building" workshops at the department level, a job attitude survey of city employees used to stimulate discussions between superiors and subordinates, role and goal clarification sessions for the city council, and a number of other activities. As of 1977 the program was still on-going. It had produced a more open, cooperative approach to problem-solving, many examples of improved work group effectiveness, an improved budget process that reduced interdepartmental rivalry, and the solution of many long standing problems.[2]

*   *   *   *

> A manufacturing plant a department assembling hotplates by an assembly line method was experiencing an 8% rate of absenteeism, poor worker morale and a 23% error rate. The supervisor of the line, working with a plant engineer and OD consultants decided to break up the assembly line and have each worker assemble an entire hotplate. It was also decided to post schedules so the workers would know how many of each model were needed for the manufacturing period. By six months later absenteeism had dropped to 1%, the error rate was down from 23% to 1%, and productivity was up by

84%. Later, as quality continued to increase, the full time inspector who had been inspecting hotplates was reassigned to another department, and the operators began doing their own inspection, signing their name to each completed instrument.[3]

* * *

Certain executives in a commercial bank became concerned that the institution's international banking department was not developing future strategies for competing in a rapidly changing worldwide market. The department's procedures and its personnel were attuned to getting daily "production" out but not to digging in depth into complex, long range strategic problems. With a consultant's aid, the department members held special meetings, away from their offices and telephones, in which they learned techniques for solving unstructured problems (multichannel communication, free questioning, reduction of hierarchical control, etc.). Task forces were set up to work in this mode and then present their proposals at three-day off site meetings held periodically. Daily routine work was still handled as before, but the department now began to develop impressive new strategies and programs. The international department has been rated as outstanding by the bank's top management during each of the years since the start of the new approach.[4]

As these examples suggest, OD includes many types of approaches to planned change that can involve people from the highest to the lowest levels in all kinds of organizations. Hospitals, clinics, police departments, metropolitan transit authorities, schools, and universities are just a few of the settings where OD has been applied.[5] OD appears to have grown beyond the stage where it might have been considered a fad to become one of the primary methods for helping organizations adapt to change.

One driving force behind OD is that today's world is changing so rapidly that organizations are hard pressed to keep up. Technological innovations are multiplying at an increasing rate, such basic resources as energy are becoming increasingly expensive, government regulation is becoming more and more pervasive, environmental and consumer interest groups are exerting greater influence, and the drive for social equality continues to grow. A second reason why OD is needed is the pressure for change arising within organizations themselves. Changes in methods, technologies, and managerial policies are frequent as management tries to cope with a changing environment. Growth in the size and diversity of organizations makes coordination and control increasingly difficult. Paradoxically, at the same time management is trying to automate and simplify work, a contrary force is increasing the changing composition of the work force. Younger, higher-educated, more mobile workers bring changes in the values people place on their jobs. As people become more intellectually committed to their work, they require more autonomy but also more involvement and participation. All these forces work to heighten the importance of solving the human and social problems occurring in organizations. Since that is what OD is all about, its use has become more and more widespread during the past two decades.

Not all changes that occur in organizations are the exclusive province of the OD specialist. Such changes as designing and installing a computerized information system, building new facilities, or redesigning existing ones are, of course, the work of systems analysts and architects. However, it has often proved wise in such cases to have an OD practitioner working with the engineers and others to help keep human system realities in mind.

Communication considerations are pervasive in OD.[6] The outcome of a successful OD intervention is basically a change in communication patterns. Typically, the organization has been kept from changing in the past largely by the persistence of old, outmoded communication patterns. OD is undertaken so that the organization can develop more valid and useful communication.

In addition to being central to the *goal* of OD, communication is also paramount in the *process* by which OD is undertaken. We will see, for example, that diagnosis is a critically important ingredient in OD, requiring especially skillful communication. We will also see the importance of feedback communication in order that an on-going test-and-response link can be maintained throughout the change process. As one writer has put it, "Communication *is* the process by which organizations change."[7]

THE PROCESS OF ORGANIZATIONAL CHANGE

Chapter 13 outlined a basic model of the change process. This was Kurt Lewin's concept of the three-phase sequence: unfreezing, changing, and refreezing (exhibit 13-1). This model, which served as a useful starting

EXHIBIT 14-1
SUBPROCESSES OF ORGANIZATIONAL CHANGE

Away from	and	Toward
Generalized goals	———▶	Specific objectives
Former social ties built around previous behavior patterns	———▶	New relationships which support the intended changes in behavior and attitudes
Self-doubt and a lowered sense of self-esteem	———▶	A heightened sense of self-esteem
An external motive for change	———▶	An internalized motive for change

From Gene Dalton, Paul Lawrence, and Larry Greiner, *Organizational Change and Development* (Homewood, Ill.: Richard D. Irwin) p. 233. © 1970 by Richard D. Irwin, Inc.

point for understanding interpersonal influence, can now help us understand organizational change. In order to change, organization members have to become dissatisfied or uninhibited enough to want to change (unfreezing); they need to acquire new attitudes and behavior (changing); and the changes have to be reinforced if regression back to old ways is to be avoided (refreezing). Important as these steps are, the Lewin model leaves out some vital details of how successful change happens in organizations. These include the following:

1. Change happens at several levels simultaneously. There is not just a single change process occurring.
2. There are more than just three steps involved in bringing about a change.
3. Successful organizational change does not end; it is ongoing.

The first of these points, that a change involves many simultaneous changes, was made by Gene Dalton, based on his comparison of several successful change efforts with less successful ones.[8] He concluded that the overall process of change consists of subprocesses occurring on four levels: goals, social, self-esteem, and motivational. In successful change, the organization's goals become less vague and more specific. Prior social ties are modified or ended, and new relationships are formed around changed activities. Self-esteem increases as people see their task accomplishments improving. At the motivational level, people are encouraged to perform in new ways, depending less on direction from powerful bosses or consultants. The four subprocess are shown in exhibit 14-1. Dalton's scheme points out that change is a multidimensional set of processes that cannot be usefully understood in terms of simplistic abstract terms, like "better communication." It is equally clear that communication is central to each of the four subprocesses.

The second point, that effective organizational change involes more than Lewin's three steps, is made by Larry Greiner, who breaks the developmental process down into six phases, illustrated in exhibit 14-2.[9]

Phase 1: Pressure and Arousal. As Lewin suggests, people must be hurting before they begin to desire change. Greiner stresses the importance of top management's commitment to the need for change so that they will provide the resources necessary to keep the change effort going.

Phase 2: Intervention and Reorientation. Intervention refers to the entry of a full-time OD practitioner—frequently, though not always, a consultant from outside who enters at the top of the organization. At this stage it is important that the organization's power structure suspend its habitual ways of defining (perhaps presuming) what the "real" problems are.

EXHIBIT 14-2
DYNAMICS OF SUCCESSFUL ORGANIZATION
CHANGE

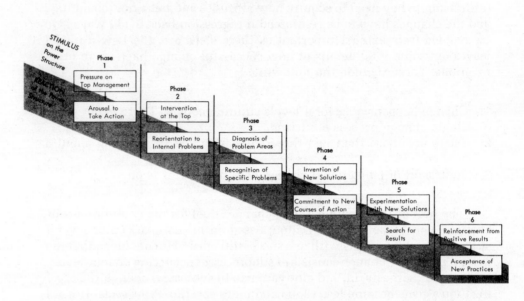

Phase 3: Diagnosis and Recognition. Here, managers and the OD practitioner cooperate on getting information. Open communication between superiors and subordinates is important in this phase so that the information base for recognizing problems is established and so that people at all levels will sense that they are meaningfully included in the change effort.

Phase 4: Invention and Commitment. In successful change efforts, organization members resist the temptation to apply old, outworn solutions to problems. Typically, the OD practitioner assists in a widespread search for creative solutions. Broad participation in this effort by organization members helps develop their support and commitment.

Phase 5: Experimentation and Search. Large-scale changes usually are not implemented quickly and without resistance. Normally, there is an atmosphere of tentativeness for a time as subordinates watch to see if their bosses are really supporting the new methods, and everyone checks closely to determine whether or not the changes are producing tangible results and improvements.

Phase 6: Reinforcement and Acceptance. Improvements and results, of course, tend to have a strong reinforcing effect. The changes themselves are thus reinforced but, in addition, so are the methods used to bring about the change. For example, the use of superior-subordinate collaboration to identify prolems is likely to become an accepted day-to-day mode in the organization rather than something that is done only in times of unusual crisis.

The Greiner model, based (like Dalton's) on a review of a number of well-documented, successful change efforts, is valuable in that it reveals the groundwork and patience that change requires. Organizational change is a multiphased, methodical process. It does not happen in one fell swoop.

The last phase in Greiner's model also helps make the third point—namely, that successful change is ongoing. Organization members' learn to accept not just the change itself but the change process. Such an organization can become what William Torbert calls a "liberating structure," meaning an organization in which collaborative inquiry, problem identification, and experimentation recur on a regular basis.[10] Organization development is not a one-shot event in which *a* change is made to solve *a* problem. The "D" in OD stands for the development of both the ability and the propensity of an organization's members to evaluate results, locate problems, plan and take new action, evaluate results again, and so forth. Exhibit 14-3 represents this cyclical process, including, in the circle, the organization's growing resources for keeping the process going and under control.

SPECIFIC APPROACHES TO OD

OD had its beginnings in the 1940s with the development of two techniques for stimulating change in organizations. One of these was the T-group ("T" for "training"), originated by Kurt Lewin and others at Massachusetts Institute of Technology and carried forward by the National Training Laboratories. A T-group is a small group in which a trainer helps participants improve their interpersonal sensitivity and skill. The second technique, called survey feedback, involves reporting back to organization members data on their attitudes and opinions collected on questionnaires. Survey feedback was also begun by colleagues of Lewin, who founded the Survey Research Center at the University of Michigan, which later became the Institute for Social Research.[11]

Since these beginnings, a large number of diverse techniques have become associated with OD, leading to a certain amount of confusion as to what OD actually is. In a recent article, Sam White and Terrence Mitchell suggest that OD approaches can be classified in terms of who the *target* for change is, what *level* of change is desired, and the *relationships* involved in the change.[12] The target could be individuals, subgroups of people, or the total organization (three possibilities). The level of desired

EXHIBIT 14-3
**THE ONGOING PROCESS OF ORGANIZATION
DEVELOPMENT**

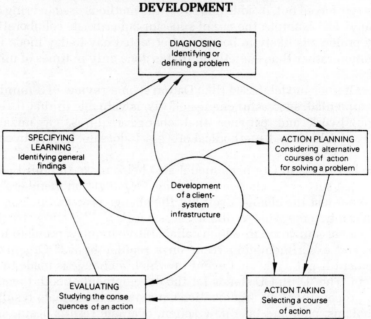

Reprinted from "An Assessment of the Scientific Merits of Action Research" by Gerald I. Susman and Roger D. Evered, published in *Administrative Science Quarterly,* Vol. 23, No. 4, by permission of The Administrative Science Quarterly © 1978 by Cornell University.

change could be a change in people's thinking, in their behavior, in work rules and procedures, or in the organization's structure (four possibilities). The relationships involved might be intrapersonal (one's attitudes and behavior toward one's self), interpersonal, intragroup, intergroup, or organizational (five possibilities). Survey research, for example, might be used as an approach targeted at individuals to let them know people's thinking about the overall organization. Since three times four times five possibilities add up to a total of sixty different approaches, it is not hard to see why OD has been understood differently by different people.

To give a more concrete picture of the kinds of approaches used in OD, several specific techniques are described in the sections that follow. For the sake of simplicity, the techniques are grouped according to whether the target of change is individuals, small groups or teams, intergroup relations, or the total organization. These groupings and the specific techniques to be described are listed in exhibit 14-4.

Individuals

Classroom training is a part of an OD effort based on the reasoning that in a given organizational situation, people need certain concepts, skills,

EXHIBIT 14-4
EXAMPLES OF SOME TECHNIQUES USED IN OD

Target of Change	Technique
Individuals	Classroom training T-groups Job enrichment Counseling
Small Groups or Teams	Interpersonal peacemaking Process consultation Team building
Intergroup Relations	Intergroup team building Organization mirror
The Total Organization	Confrontation meeting MBO Structural approaches Survey feedback Communication appraisals

items of information, and shared terminology to proceed with change competently. Conventional classroom methods, including lecture, case discussion, role playing, and other experience-simulation techniques, can be effective if well presented and if what is learned is what the participants truly need. It is sometimes possible for classroom sessions, after starting with a focus on concepts and prototypical examples, to shift attention to the participants' own organization, so that the beginning of the "real" problem identification process begins to take place right in the classroom. This probably should be done only when there is assurance that the actual problem-solving process will be allowed to continue outside the classroom.

T-groups (often called sensitivity training or laboratory training), as noted earlier, aim at building the interpersonal competence of individuals. They are face-to-face groups of ten to fifteen people who meet together for anywhere from two days to two weeks. With the help of a professional trainer, each participant tries to become more aware of his or her effects on others. No agenda is planned in advance, and an atmosphere of "psychological safety" is created, which helps participants to examine their own and others' attitudes, values, feelings, and behavior in a nondefensive way and to experiment with new behavior. The competence of the trainer is crucial in this process. The effectiveness of T-groups also depends on whether the trainee returns after the T-group to a work environment that supports or rejects the newly learned behavior. Thus, as an OD approach, T-groups are not too likely to be effective when used as the only intervention technique in an organization.[13] Though T-groups are being used less frequently as more alternative OD techniques are being developed, they can be very helpful for individual learning.

Job enrichment. The example of the hotplate department given at the start of this chapter is an example of job enrichment. Job enrichment is an attempt to make jobs more motivating by building into the work more responsibility, decision-making opportunity, worker autonomy, opportunity for achievement and recognition, and feedback about performance. It could be said that job enrichment builds the self-renewing characteristic into the organization at the level of the individual worker's job specifications. "Enriched" jobs give the worker responsibility for deciding on his or her own work methods and for identifying and solving problems. As the hotplate example suggests, job enrichment can produce major increases in worker commitment and productivity. Many successful applications have been made, but results have been unfavorable where unions have resisted the effort, where supervisors and managers have not fully supported the effort, and where the workers themselves have not really wanted greater responsibility.[14]

Counseling. Many organizations provide help for individuals who are experiencing difficulties in handling job-related tensions. Less frequently, counseling is used as a means for developing leadership and managerial competence and, thus, for enhancing the organization's capacity for on-going change. It is a sign of organizational health when managers and others who do want this kind of help are able to find it, either in the person of a specialist, consultant, or trusted colleague. In OD interventions, the OD practitioner can help organization members identify and work on problems that are blocking their participation in the change effort. In this situation, the counselor typically takes an active role in helping the individual discover new solutions and methods for use on the job.[15]

Dyads, Small Groups, or Teams

Interpersonal peacemaking. A consultant may serve as a third party to help change a destructive conflict between two persons. A major problem in such conflicts is what Richard Walton terms "malevolent cycling"—a process wherein the parties keep introducing new issues that keep the conflict rolling on and on (see exhibit 11-1).[16] The consultant tries to interrupt such cycles by such tactics as increasing the weaker party's power by involving more allies, encouraging more openness, delaying confrontation, or helping the parties bargain to resolve their differences. It is important that the consultant be neutral with respect to the conflict and not in a position of power over the principals. The consultant also must have strong professional expertise in the area of social processes.

Process consultation typically involves a consultant working with on-going groups or teams to help them develop skills in diagnosing and solving problems that arise relating to social processes. By reporting to the group observations of their process, the consultant develops the group's skill in identifying communication patterns, roles and functions of group members, decision-making methods being used, group norms, and patterns of authority and leadership. The consultant helps the group to see these hidden issues that have been influencing them, their consequences, and the ways in which they can be changed.[17] Process consultation has been used successfully by groups ranging from a unit manager and his or her subordinates to boards of directors.

Team building. Unlike process consultation, which takes place during a group's normal work meetings, team building involves special meetings by the group to identify group problems and improve the group's effectiveness. Specific approaches vary, but typically, the consultant begins by gathering data through questionnaires, interviews, or process observation. After summarizing and feeding this data back to the group, the consultant helps the group identify problems, set priorities, and decide on specific action steps for improving group performance. A two- or three-day series of meetings with later follow-up meetings to appraise results is a typical pattern. Task-related problems are often given the highest priority. For example, a group being assigned new work responsibilities may undertake team building to decide how to handle them. Even in such cases, a part of the time is used for examining how the group is solving its problems. Thus, the group becomes more skillful at both the task and process levels.[18]

Intergroup Relations

Intergroup team building. Interdependent units in an organization often expend much energy in destructive competition (see chapter 10 on organization structure and chapter 11 on conflict). OD methods provide ways of improving intergroup communication and cooperation. One approach includes the following steps: Each group meets separately to list its attitudes, feelings, and perceptions of the other group and, on a second list, its predictions of how the other group sees them. The groups come together and share their lists. Groups in conflict usually have a number of misperceptions of each other, which the sharing of the lists helps to expose. Next, the groups return to separate meetings to list priority issues that need to be resolved between the two groups. In another combined meeting these two lists are merged into a single prioritized list. Together, the two groups decide on action steps to be taken on each item and who will take them. Later, follow-up meetings help insure that momentum is maintained.[19]

Organization mirror. In this variation on intergroup team building, a given organizational unit—the host group—gets feedback about how it is perceived and regarded from several other groups in the organization, not just one. The host group asks key people from the other groups to a meeting that begins with interview data feedback by the consultant, then moves to an uninterrupted discussion by the visitors of how they see the host group, followed by questions directed to the visitors by the host group. These questions are carefully monitored by the consultant to make sure they are questions of clarification ("You mean you see us as follows: ...?") rather than efforts at rebuttal or self-justification ("Are you aware that our department acts as it does because of ...?") Subgroups composed of host group and visitor group representatives then convene to identify key problems. The total group then receives reports from the subgroups, and action plans are made.[20] Like the intergroup team-building technique, the mirror approach helps clear up intergroup misconceptions, gets problems identified, and starts remedial action within a short period of time.

The Total Organization

The confrontation meeting. As developed by consultant Richard Beckhard, this technique is a one-day meeting of the entire management of the organization.[21] After introductory speeches by the top manager and the consultant, small groups of seven or eight members are formed, each group's membership being drawn from a variety of units and levels of the organization. Bosses and subordinates are not put on the same team. The groups list organizational problems and needed changes, which are subsequently reported back to the total group. A meeting leader then groups the problems into major categories. Next, the participants form into their normal, everyday work teams, each headed by its top manager. These groups decide what action they are prepared to take on the problems related to their area that have been identified and decide what steps they feel top management should take, At the end of the day, top management meets to determine what action it should take, based on what has been learned during the day. All the action plans are communicated to the total group. Four to six weeks later the total group meets again to review the actions and progress that have resulted.

MBO (management by objectives) is a term applied to a wide array of different methods for setting individual and organizational goals, comparing performance against them, and periodically resetting new goals. Approaches vary, but prominent writers in the OD field stress that two features are especially important to include. First, subordinate managers should be allowed to participate in and influence the setting of their own individual performance goals. To encourage this, one method is to have subordinates prepare their list of goals independently before discussing it with their bosses. Training in collaborative decision making may also be included. Second, MBO programs need to be coordinated on an organization-wide basis due to the interdependent nature of managerial jobs. Thus, the program may include such steps as an initial diagnosis of organizational problems, goal setting at the total organization, unit, and team levels prior to starting work on individual goal setting, and extensive discussion of individuals' goals by the work team before considering them final. Since MBO depends so much on collaborative decision-making, preliminary training in the associated skills may be necessary in many organizations.[22]

Structural approaches. As OD has been undertaken by larger and larger units, efforts to modify the structural properties of organizations have become more prominent. This does not always mean making organizations more egalitarian, democratic, and decentralized. It is now well known that the "right" structure for an organization is one that enables it to cope well with its particular environment (see chapters 10 and 11). When an organization is experiencing increasing complexity, uncertainty, and change in its environment, innovative structural forms are often needed. These can include matrix structure, new temporary or permanent task forces, and integrator roles. An intriguing possibility, developed by Dale Zand, is that an organization might develop two "collateral" structures, one for daily routine tasks and another for dealing with unusual problems. An illustration is Zand's example at the beginning of this chapter about the bank that improved its strategic planning ability.

Fritz Steele has analyzed the effects physical surroundings can have in changing organizational behavior. Improved physical settings can help increase individual motivation and morale, support the development of new social systems, and improve problem solving.[23]

Survey feedback involves collecting questionnaire, interview, or observational data within one or more work groups in an organization. The data, after being compiled or summarized, are then reported back and used by those who generated the data as an aid to diagnosing problems and developing action plans for solving them. Questionnaire content can cover people's attitudes toward management, the organization's policies and climate, job satisfaction, and other areas. Well-designed standardized questionnaire instruments have been developed for organizational surveys.[24] A limitation of survey methods is that organization members may view the data as unreal—"just a bunch of numbers." This is overcome if participants use the data as a stimulus to open and honest discussion about real problems, and if the survey operation is followed up by meaningful action planning and later monitoring of results.

Communication appraisals. A number of techniques and instruments have been developed for the analysis of communication behavior in an organization.[25] Practitioners in this area borrow from the accounting profession the concept of an audit—a periodic monitoring to show how well the present communication system, or key parts of it, are helping the organization fulfill its goals, deal with problems, or cope with change. A wide array of tools are available for collecting information at various levels of the communication system: individual/personal level, interpersonal level, network level, or, as is the approach frequently used, several of these levels simultaneously. Examples of a number of these diagnostic tools are listed and briefly described in exhibit 14-5.

EXHIBIT 14-5

SOME DIAGNOSTIC TOOLS FOR COMMUNICATION APPRAISALS

Levels	Diagnostic Tools	Description
For individual/ personal data:	Cognitive Stretch Test	Focuses on problem-solving styles of individual managers
	Kirkpatrick's Supervisory Inventory on Communication	Assesses individual's listening, speaking, and writing skills
	Communication Apprehension Tests	Indicates individual's tendency to avoid communication
	Rokeach's Dogmatism Scale	Measures individual's open- versus closed- mindedness
For interpersonal data:	Disparity Tests	Tests for differences between boss and subordinate perceptions of authority, ability and responsibility
	Accuracy Tests	Measures degree of accuracy of managers' knowledge about information dissemination in the organization
	Falcione's Credibility Test	Examines subordinates' perceptions of their supervisors' credibility

For network data:	Observational Studies	Selected individuals' communication activities are recorded in "diaries" by themselves or by trained observers
	ECCO Analysis	Charts "episodic communication channels in the organization" by tracking a particular set of messages through their travels
	Network Analysis	Computer-generated comparisons of patterns of communication pathways, e.g., actual versus expected, regulative versus innovative
For multilevel data:	The ICA Communication Audit	Uses five instruments: questionnaires, interviews, experience descriptions, diaries, and network analysis. Data are collected, analyzed, and fed back to the organization in a planned way.
	The OCD Audit System	Offers a single questionnaire aimed at locating dissatisfactions and defects related to many aspects of communication in the organization

For further descriptions and sources of these and other instruments, see Richard V. Farace et.al., *Communicating and Organizing* (Reading, Mass.: Addison-Wesley, 1977), pp. 209–225; Gerald Goldhaber et.al., *Information Strategies* (Englewood Cliffs, N.J.: Prentice-Hall, 1979), pp. 222–250, 270–280; and Gerald Goldhaber, *Organizational Communication* (Dubuque, Ia.: Wm. C. Brown, 1979), pp. 338–380.

Communication appraisals have several advantages. They allow problems and dissatisfactions to be expressed that might not come to the surface spontaneously. Current patterns and weaknesses can be identified as an aid to organizational redesign. Measurements can be taken before and after to note the effects if new programs or organizational changes. In general, communication appraisals can provide objective, systematic data so that management does not have to rely on mere impressions about the state of communication in the organization.

Managers and consultants undertaking communication appraisals should exercise caution. Careful planning is necessary to insure the relevance and validity of such studies. Further, the participants are personally sensitive to the data, which must be handled accordingly. Among the more important safeguards are the following:

1. Define clear research goals, keyed to the nature of the particular organization, its strategy, and its problems.
2. Insure that all organization members are informed of the purposes of the appraisal and how their responses will be used.
3. Maintain participants' anonymity where appropriate (e.g., data showing a subordinate's dissatisfaction with a supervisor).
4. Be an objective, impartial diagnostician. Do not become an ally of some faction in the organization (e.g., management, labor, or a certain department).
5. Do not use complex methods requiring large time inputs by participants without a definite commitment to follow up by taking action based on the results of the study.
6. Keep monitoring on a recurring basis. An apparaisal done at one point in time may not reveal important trends.

It should be clear, as mentioned earlier, that the OD approaches described in the preceding sections can lead to profound changes in communication patterns and effectiveness in an organization. But it should also be obvious that no single technique in and of itself constitutes the kind of pervasive change in organizational climate whereby the organization becomes spontaneously self-critical and self-renewing on an ongoing basis. The list simply indicates some of the tools organizations have to choose from to help begin the change process and to sustain and further develop a self-renewing climate once it exists.

The nature of the organization and its circumstances governs what OD approach or integrated cluster of approaches is appropriate. A consultant or a manager who becomes locked into a single technique may find success to be elusive. Many different situations and kinds of problems are to be found within a complex organization, and situations change over time. The example at the beginning of the chapter about the city of Tacoma illustrates how a number of approaches can be used over an extended time period.

There are many more OD techniques than have been described here. The ones above are meant to indicate the range of possibilities and show that organizations do not have to rely solely on conventional management practice to bring about needed changes in communication and performance.

COMMUNICATION PROBLEMS AND STRATEGIES IN OD

Although OD is gaining widening acceptance, it still strikes many managers as wishful thinking. They are aware that change does not come about readily. "People resist change" is the conventional wisdom they are prone to express. The truth of the matter is that while people often do resist change, they do not always do so. If the family has been served hot dogs for supper every evening for a week, they probably will not resist a change; nor are workers likely to resist a substantial pay increase. But changes in complex organizations are usually not this easy, since they involve moving many things that can be tough to move—goals, established social ties, and self-perceptions, for example—as the Dalton model suggested. It is worth examining the major operational problems encountered by OD programs and some strategies for overcoming them. The points are relevant to OD in particular but also have general relevance to all action-oriented managerial communication.[26]

Causes of Resistance to OD

1. Inadequate diagnosis. When change approaches are aimed at work methods or organization structure but ignore human relationships, they are likely to be resisted. The same is true of people-focused approaches, such as T-groups, when they ignore task realities. Organization members are not naive. They rightly resist change proposals that overlook important problems. Change that is undertaken for change's sake, or because management demands "immediate action," cannot be substituted for an approach that includes methodical, thorough diagnosis.

2. Perceived threat or manipulation. When people sense a threat to their status, a realignment of their duties, an interruption of valued interpersonal relationships, or fear that they may not be able to handle new responsibilities, resistance is normal. When people are uncertain about the effects of a change and sense they are being manipulated, the likelihood is high that they will resist.

3. The magnitude of the change. When change is opposed, the amount of opposition tends to be proportional to the size of the change. The greater the change, the more likely it will threaten people's security, status, responsibility, relationships, and so forth.

4. The frame of reference and behavior of the OD practitioner. Some consultants are "self-preoccupied." Perceiving themselves to be experts in a particular area, such as job enrichment or process consultation, they may not realize that their objectivity is limited. When challenged, they vigorously defend their approach, which in turn increases the resistance. The more skillful practitioner sees the challenge as useful data rather than a threat.

Strategies for Decreasing Resistance

1. Thorough diagnosis. Motivation for change can be aroused by providing organization members with objective, current information about how their unit or group is functioning. Information that is desired by the group and is new to them is especially helpful in arousing a desire for change. Adequate information gathering and diagnosis also enables the OD practitioner and other proponents of change to empathize with others involved, including resisters.

2. Appeal of the changes. To the people involved, a change is not threatening if they see it as helpful. Resistance will be less to the extent that the change seems to them to reduce their burdens and to be interesting and in accord with their values.

3. Use existing pressures for change. Where change is favored by informal groups or opinion leaders, or by respected formal leaders, these people can be mobilized as key participants in the change effort. A relatively small change that has this kind of support can be a good way to start a long-term change effort. Credibility and interest are enhanced and resistance reduced by early success experiences. Change should generally be introduced using the minimum amount of external pressure necessary to begin showing results.

4. Participation. Resistance to change is reduced when those who advocate the change and those who are to be changed have a strong sense of belonging to the same group, especially if they see this group as attractive and long-lasting. When these conditions exist, the change process is aided. All participants join in diagnostic efforts, and actions are undertaken on the basis of decisions supported by group consensus.

COMMUNICATION APPROACHES FOR THE OD PRACTITIONER

If there is a single most important factor in overcoming resistance to change and making OD efforts successful, it is the OD practitioner. Practitioners may be external consultants or they may be full-time employees of the organization, though there is evidence that external consultants have certain advantages. External consultants appear to have freer access to top management than do their internal counterparts. They also tend to find it easier to make their role clearly understood to people in the organization. Furthermore, external consultants appear to be less easily drawn into the organization's norms and thus are freer to examine the organization from a broad, overall viewpoint.[27] This is not to say that internal OD consultants are ineffective. Many organizations, including General Electric, Polaroid, Corning Glass, TRW, and General Motors make successful use of internal OD staffs.

Whether external or internal, the OD practitioner needs to be a person who can get outside the frame of reference of the organization.[28] The organization needs someone who can help it begin to look at itself in a new, more objective way. Typically, effective practitioners are a-hierarchial; they can talk openly to all levels, for example serving as a megaphone for reluctant subordinates. They establish unconventional communication channels without necessarily undermining conventional channels. They enable people to hear the views and share the experience of others in the organization with whom they ordinarily do not communicate. This is one of the fundamental ways the practitioner breaks down the organization's tendency to act the same as it has in the past.

Based on the OD literature as well as their experience as consultants, Wendell French and Cecil Bell offer several important guidelines for OD practitioner effectiveness.[29] Among them are the following:

1. *See the organization, not an individual, as the client.* While there is usually a key individual client, it is important that the practitioner not be seen as secretly implementing this person's wishes. Both the practitioner and the key client need to see the system as the real client.
2. *Develop mutual trust.* At the outset, the key client may fear that OD will unleash massive complaints by subordinates, and subordinates may fear manipulation. Trust will not be immediate; the practitioner has to earn it.
3. *Avoid being "the expert."* If the practitioner gives much substantive advice, there will be a strong tendency for an adversary role to develop, where the practitioner must constantly defend his or her recommendations against those who disagree. The practitioner does better to help organization members develop their own solutions to problems. The practitioner needs to be an expert but not act like one.
4. *Intervene at the appropriate depth.* "Deeper" interventions are those where the target of change is the attitudes and feelings of individuals. Less deep interventions aim at such targets as the organization's formal design, goals, and rules. In general, the consultant should not intervene at a level deeper than that required to obtain lasting solutions to the problems at hand and no deeper than the client personnel are able to accept.[30]
5. *Avoid becoming part of the culture.* To remain objective, the practitioner must avoid being caught up in the norms, values, and politics

of the organization. Obviously, the practitioner needs to participate in the culture enough to build rapport and trust, but getting too absorbed can mean a loss of effectiveness.

6. *Practice what you preach.* Inevitably, the practitioner is looked to as a model of the characteristics he or she is trying to build into the organization. The values of objectivity, inquiry, and problem solving need to be practiced by the practitioner/key client team and by the practitioners working as a team to set an example for working groups within the client organization. Furthermore, if the practitioner team does not conduct its own internal communication in a skillful way, their diagnoses and interventions will be adversely affected.

In summary, the OD practitioner must be a master of organizational communication. But while the above skills are especially highly developed in effective OD practitioners, they are ones that usually can be developed by organization members as well. Indeed, when the OD practitioner has succeeded to the fullest degree, these skills will have been built into the fabric of the organization so they can be practiced by its members on an ongoing basis.

Summary

Organization development includes a wide range of approaches that are being applied more and more as the pressure on organizations for change increases. In its fullest sense, OD means building an organization's capability to be self-renewing—that is, not just to find and solve problems once but to continue to do so whenever the need occurs. The Greiner and Dalton models help to clarify that successful change is a recurring multistage process and that it occurs along several dimensions simultaneously.

Specific techniques used in OD include approaches targeted at individuals, at small groups, at intergroup problems, and at the total organization. OD is not really these techniques, although it is often thought of as such. Rather, it involves developing an organization using appropriate combinations of these and other techniques to produce a lasting increase in the system's problem-solving capacity. OD is not an exact science. Furthermore, its practice requires considerable experience and skill. When practitioner knowledge and skill are lacking, the organization is likely to resist the change process. Resistance is less likely, however, when diagnosis is done thoroughly, when the changes are ones that appeal to the organization's members, when existing pressures for change are mobilized, and when participation in the change process is widespread. OD practitioners can enhance their effectiveness to the extent that they maintain their objectivity, develop trust, avoid either threatening people or rendering them dependent, and serve as visable models of skillful problem solving. These communication skills are valid not just for OD practitioners on special occasions but for all organization members on a daily basis.

Questions for Review

1. Explain what is meant by OD as a continuing, cyclical process in an organization.
2. Are OD and OD techniques one in the same? Explain.
3. Discuss ways in which problem diagnosis is important in OD.
4. How can an OD practitioner develop mutual trust with organization members and still keep from "becoming part of the culture?"
5. Might an OD practitioner experience a conflict between his or her desire to diagnose thoroughly versus the principle of intervening at the appropriate depth? Discuss.
6. Think of an organization that you feel is not sufficiently able to adapt to change. What is the evidence of this? What OD approaches might be useful in this organization, and why?
7. Rearrange the thirteen OD techniques listed in exhibit 14-4 in order of depth of intervention, from least deep to deepest.
8. Does OD lead to making organizations more democratic? Less bureaucratic? Decentralized? Discuss.

References and Notes

1. For a review of several of the definitions of OD that have been suggested in the literature, see Wendell L. French, Cecil H. Bell, Jr., and Robert A. Zawacki, *Organization Development: Theory, Practice, and Research* (Dallas: Business Publications, Inc., 1978), pp. 6–7.
2. Cecil H. Bell, Jr., and James Rosenzweig, "Heighlights of an Organization Improvement in a City Government," in French, Bell, and Zawacki, *Organization Development;* pp. 380–92.
3. Edgar F. Huse and Michael Beer, "Eclectic Approach to Organizational Development," *Harvard Business Review,* September-October 1971, pp. 103–12. Additional information about the hotplate department has been provided to the author by personal communication from Professor Huse.
4. Dale E. Zand, "Collateral Organization: A New Change Strategy," *Journal of Applied Behavioral Science* 10 (1974):63–89.
5. Clayton P. Alderfer, "Organization Development," *Annual Review of Psychology* 28 (1977):197–223.
6. John W. Lewis III contributed the ideas contained in this paragraph and the one following.
7. Bonnie McDaniel Johnson, *Communication: The Process of Organizing* (Boston: Allyn and Bacon, 1977), p. 358. Italics added.
8. Gene W. Dalton, "Influence and Organizational Change," in Gene W. Dalton, Paul R. Lawrence, and Larry E. Greiner, *Organizational Change and Development* (Homewood, Ill.: Irwin Dorsey, 1970), pp. 230–58.

9. Larry E. Greiner, "Patterns of Organization Change," *Harvard Business Review,* May-June 1967, pp. 119–30.
10. William R. Torbert, "Educating Toward Shared Purpose, Self-Direction and Quality Work," *Journal of Higher Education* 49, no. 2 (1978):109–35.
11. The origins of OD are discussed more fully in Edgar F. Huse, *Organizational Development and Change* (St. Paul: West, 1975), pp. 24–26; Wendell L. French and Cecil H. Bell, Jr., *Organization Development* (Englewood Cliffs, N.J.: Prentice-Hall, 1978), pp. 20–27.
12. Sam E. White and Terrence R. Mitchell, "Organization Development: A Review of Research Content and Research Design," *Academy of Management Review* 1 (1976):57–73.
13. Michael Beer, "The Technology of Organization Development," in *Handbook of Industrial and Organizational Psychology,* ed. Marvin D. Dunnette (Chicago: Rand McNally, 1976), pp. 937–93.
14. For more on job enrichment, see William J. Paul, Jr., Keith B. Robertson, and Frederick Hertzberg, "Job Enrichment Pays Off," *Harvard Business Review,* March-April 1969, pp. 61–78; J. Richard Hackman and Greg R. Oldham, "Development of the Job Diagnostic Survey," *Journal of Applied Psychology,* 60 (1975):159–70; David Sirota and Alan D. Wolfson, "Job Enrichment: What are the Obstacles?" *Personnel* 49, no. 3 (1972):8–17.
15. Beer, "The Technology of Organization Development," pp. 968–69.
16. See Richard E. Walton, *Interpersonal Peacemaking* (Reading, Mass.: Addison-Wesley, 1969).
17. Edgar H. Schein, *Process Consultation* (Reading, Mass.: Addison-Wesley, 1969).
18. For more detailed information on approaches to team building see Beer, "The Technology of Organization Development," pp. 955–61; French and Bell, *Organization Development,* pp. 117–30; Huse, *Organizational Development and Change,* pp. 230–38.
19. This description is based on Richard Beckhard, *Organization Development: Strategies and Models* (Reading, Mass.: Addison-Wesley, 1969), pp. 34–35. For the original development of the method, see Robert R. Blake, Herbert A. Shepard, and Jane S. Mouton, *Managing Intergroup Conflict in Industry* (Houston: Gulf Publishing Co., 1965).
20. The organization mirror is discussed in detail in Jack K. Fordyce and Raymond Weil, *Managing with People* (Reading, Mass.: Addison-Wesley, 1971), pp. 124–30.
21. Richard Beckhard, "The Confrontation Meeting," *Harvard Business Review,* March-April, 1967, pp. 149–55.
22. For a review of the literature and a detailed description of an organization-wide collaborative MBO program, see Wendell L. French and Robert W. Hollmann, "Management by Objectives: The Team Approach," *California Management Review* 17, no. 3 (1975):13–22.
23. The aspects of structural change mentioned in this section are drawn from Paul R. Lawrence and Jay W. Lorsch, *Organization and Environment* (Boston: Harvard Business School, Division of Research, 1967); Jay R. Galbraith, "Organization Design: An Information Processing View," *Interfaces* 4, no. 3 (1974):28–36; Zand, "Collateral Organization," pp. 63–89; Fred I. Steele, *Physical Settings and Organization Development* (Reading, Mass.: Addison-Wesley, 1973).

24. See French and Bell, *Organization Development,* pp. 152–56; Huse, *Organization Development and Change,* pp. 163–74; Beer, "The Technology of Organization Development," pp. 947–49.

25. For more on communication appraisal methods, see Richard V. Farace, Peter R. Monge, and Hamish M. Russell, *Communicating and Organizing* (Reading, Mass.: Addison-Wesley, 1977), pp. 205–47. Howard H. Greenbaum, "The Audit of Organizational Communication," *Academy of Management Journal* 17 (1974):739–54; Gerald Goldhaber et.al., *Information Strategies* (Englewood Cliffs, N.J.: Prentice-Hall, 1979), pp. 219–69; Gerald Goldhaber, *Organizational Communication* (Dubuque, Ia.: Wm. C. Brown, 1979), pp. 338–80.

26. The points relating to causes of resistance to change and strategies for reducing resistance draw upon Allan R. Cohen et.al., *Effective Behavior in Organizations* (Homewood, Ill.: Irwin, 1976), pp. 248–51; Goldhaber, *Organizational Communication,* 327–28, Huse, *Organizational Development and Change,* pp. 110–15; Paul R. Lawrence, "How to Deal with Resistance to Change," *Harvard Business Review,* January-February 1969, p. 4f; Harold J. Leavitt, "Applied Organizational Change in Industry: Structural, Technical and Human Approaches," in William W. Cooper II et.al., *New Perspectives in Organization Research* (New York: John Wiley & Sons, 1964), pp. 55–71; Max D. Richards and Paul S. Greenlaw, *Management Decision Making* (Homewood, Ill.: Irwin, 1972), pp. 324–27; James A. F. Stoner, *Management* (Englewood Cliffs, N.J.: Prentice-Hall, 1978), pp. 377–79.

27. Carol Weiss Heine, "The Internal Consultant: Issues and Questions," in *Readings on Behavior in Organizations,* ed. Edgar F. Huse, James L. Bowditch, and Dalmar Fisher (Reading, Mass.: Addison-Wesley, 1975), pp. 373–78. See also French and Bell, *Organization Development,* pp. 183–85, 209–10; Huse, *Organizational Development and Change,* pp. 314–16.

28. The ideas in this paragraph were suggested by John W. Lewis III.

29. French and Bell, *Organization Development,* pp. 200–215.

30. Roger Harrison, "Choosing the Depth of Organizational Intervention," *Journal of Applied Behavioral Science* 6 (1970):181–202.

Sea Pines*

In the spring of 1977, the coastal town of Sea Pines, Maine, retained a New York consulting engineer to study the effect of greatly expanding the town's sewage system and discharging the treated waste into the harbor.

At that time, fishermen in the town were experiencing massive lobster kills in the harbor and were concerned that the kills were caused by the effluent from the present Sea Pines sewage treatment plant. They were convinced that any expansion of the plant would further aggravate the problem. The fishermen invited Tom Stone, the engineer, to the monthly meeting of the local fishermen's organization to discuss their concerns. On the night of the meeting, the American Legion Hall was filled with men in blue jeans and work jackets, many of whom were drinking beer. An account of this meeting follows, with Fred Mitchell, a local fisherman, speaking first.

Mitchell: Well, as you all know, Mr. Stone has been kind enough to meet with us tonight to explain his recommendations concerning the town's sewage disposal problem. We're all concerned about the lobster kills, like the one last summer, and I for one don't want to see any more sewage dumped into that harbor.
(Murmurs of assent are heard throughout the hall.)
So, Mr. Stone, we'd like to hear from you on what it is you want to do.

Stone: Thank you. I'm glad to get this opportunity to hear your concerns on the lobster situation. Let me say from the outset that we are still studying the problem closely and expect to make our formal recommendation to the town about a month from now. I am not prepared to discuss specific conclusions of our study, but I am prepared to incorporate any relevant comments into our study. As most of you are probably aware, we are attempting to model mathematically, or simulate, conditions in the harbor to help us predict the effects of sewage effluent in the harbor. We ...

Mitchell: Now wait a minute. I don't know anything about models

---

*This case was written by Terence P. Driscoll.

except the kind I used to make as a kid. (Laughter) I can tell you that we never had lobster kills like we have now until they started dumping that sewage into the harbor a few years back. I don't need any model to tell me that. It seems to me that common sense tells you that if we've got troubles now in the summer with the lobster, that increasing the amount of sewage by ten times the present amount is going to cause ten times the problem.

A Fisherman: Yeah, you don't need to be an engineer to see that.

Stone: While it's true that we're proposing to extend the sewage system in town, and that the resulting sewage flow will be about ten times the present flow, the area of the sewage discharge will be moved to a larger area of the harbor, where it will be diluted with much more sea water than is the present area. In addition, if the harbor is selected for the new discharge, we will design a special diffuser to mix the treated sewage effluent quickly with ocean water. As I indicated, we are attempting to use data on currents and water quality that we collected in the harbor and combine it with some mathematical equations in our computer to help us predict what the quality in the harbor will be.

Mitchell: I don't understand what you need a computer to tell you that for. I've been fishing in this area for over thirty-five years now, and I don't need any computer to tell me that my lobster are going to die if that sewage goes into the harbor.

Stone: Let me say before this goes too far that we're not talking about discharging raw sewage into the harbor. The sewage is treated and disinfected before it is discharged.

Mitchell: Isn't the sewage that's being dumped into the harbor right now being treated and disinfected, Mr. Stone?

Stone: Yes, it is, but . . .

Mitchell: The lobster still die, so it's clear to me that "treated and disinfected" doesn't solve the problem.

Stone: Our model will predict whether the treatment provided will be sufficient to maintain the water quality in the harbor at the state's standard for the harbor.

Mitchell: I don't give a damn about any state standard. I just care about my lobster and how I'm going to put bread on the table for my kids! You engineers from New York can come up here spouting all kinds of things about models, data, standards, and your concern for lobster, but what it really comes down to is that it's just another job. You can pick your fees for your study, go back to your office, and leave us holding the bag.

Stone: Now wait a minute, Mr. Mitchell. My firm is well established in New York, and we didn't get that way by giving our clients the fast shuffle and making a quick exit out of town. We have no intention of leaving you with an unworkable solution to your sewage problems. We also will not solve your sewage problem and leave you with a lobster kill problem. Perhaps I have given you the wrong impression about this modeling. We regard this as one method of analysis that may be helpful in predicting future habor conditions, but not the only method. We have over forty years' experience in these harbor studies, and we fully intend to use this experience, *in addition to* whatever the model tells us, to come up with a reasonable solution.

Mitchell: Well, that's all well and good, but I can tell you, and I think I speak for all the lobstermen here, that if you recommend dumping that sewage into the harbor, we'll fight you all the way down the line! (Shouts of agreement) Why can't you pipe the sewage out to the ocean if you're so concerned about dilution? I'm sure that your model will tell you there's enough dilution out there.

Stone: I agree that the ocean will certainly provide sufficient dilution, but the whole purpose of this study is to see if we can avoid a deep ocean outfall.

Mitchell: Why?

Stone: Because the cost of constructing a deep ocean outfall in this area is very expensive—say about $500 per foot. Now, if the length of the outfall is 6,000 feet, don't you think that it makes good sense to spend a few thousand dollars studying the harbor area if we can save you millions?

Mitchell: All that money that you're going to save the town doesn't do much for the lobstermen who'll be put out of business if that sewage goes into the harbor.

Stone: As I said, we wouldn't recommend that if we thought, based on our modeling and our experence in this area, that the quality of water in the harbor would kill any lobster or any other aquatic life.

Mitchell: Well, I'm telling you again, if you try to put that stuff in our harbor, we'll fight you all the way. I think we've made our position clear on this thing, so if there are no further comments, I vote that we adjourn the meeting. (Seconded)

When the meeting ended, the fishermen filed out, talking heatedly among themselves, leaving Mr. Stone standing on the platform.

Case Questions

1. Why weren't Mitchell and the other lobstermen persuaded by Stone's arguments?
2. Consider Stone's opening speech. How do you suppose the lobstermen heard these remarks?
3. What things could Stone have said or done to achieve more persuasive success?
4. Was a public meeting of this sort a good setting for constructive communication on this matter? Why or why not? What alternative communication arrangements, if any, would you recommend, and why?

Judd Curtis*

In August 1979, senior accounting officer Mark Stewart of Neuschaffer, Inc., a large financial institution, had just completed a performance evaluation of Judd Curtis, a management trainee. Stewart, in his late thirties, had been with Neuschaffer for ten years and had earned his B. S. degree attending school part-time. Curtis, a recent graduate of a local university, had been with the organization for two years.

In the evaluation, Stewart had given Curtis outstanding marks on all aspects of his performance and the highest allowable salary increase. In concluding the interview, Stewart offered to answer any questions Judd might have, and the following conversation took place:

> **Curtis:** Well, Mark, now that I've been here for two years, I'm wondering what sort of future I have here in Corporate Accounting.
>
> **Stewart:** I think with more experience and additional exposure to other jobs within the section you'll be in good shape.
>
> **Curtis:** Well, that's fine, but I've done the income statement consolidation for about a year now, and I think that's enough. I'd like to get into another responsibility.
>
> **Stewart:** I agree, but you know the difficulties of cross training. If I move you around, I've got to change all the players, and some just aren't ready to make a change. A great many of these tasks are done on a quarterly basis, and an individual needs to do these jobs at least three or four times to understand them fully. So, you're talking about a year for each assignment.
>
> **Curtis:** I don't see why I should be penalized because others in the section aren't up to speed. Also, turnover in this section is unbelievable. I'm "senior man!" If people continue to leave or transfer, complete cross training will never be possible.

---

*This case was written by Donald P. Bock.

Stewart:	What is it that you want?
Curtis:	I guess I'm looking for some varied responsibilities within the section. I'm really getting bored. Also, since I'm a management trainee, I should have the opportunity for some supervisory experience.
Stewart:	Well, maybe a bit further down the road ...
Curtis:	A bit further? How long? You just gave me an outstanding performance appraisal! It seems to me that there is no formal training program in here. All you're interested in is getting bodies to meet the deadlines for financial reporting. It seems that you almost welcome the turnover so that you don't have to deal with people like me who are still around after a couple of years. I don't think you know what to do with me.
Stewart:	Judd, as I've mentioned before, if you feel you want out, I'll be happy to write you top-notch recommendations and help you in any way I can. If something comes up within the organization, you know Peters, vice-president of finance, will look in corporate accounting first. We're the "favorite sons" of the division.
Curtis:	(agitated) Don't give me that garbage again. You know all the openings recently were filled by outside people. What's worse is that you don't hear about the ones outside of the immediate area until they're filled. Why don't they have internal job postings like other companies?
Stewart:	Well, there was an immediate need to fill those openings with experienced individuals ...
Curtis:	Well, how the heck will any of us out there get qualified when you don't allow us increased responsibilities? You keep everything of importance close to you, and all we do is push the numbers!
Stewart:	(sharply) Look, if you think you're qualified to be a controller at one of our branches, let me know and I'll speak to Peters and ...
Curtis:	Mark, all I'm saying is that our training should be more formalized, like in the Credit Department. The people in that program know they will become commercial lending officers if they do well. They even know the length of the program. I really think that after X number of years there should be an officer slot available, provided the individual has performed well. I like the work and the challenge here, but I need a carrot held out there for me as an incentive.
Stewart:	We can't make guarantees like that. I want to move up also, but I can't until Willis, my superior, moves up the ladder. Peters is only fifty, so things may be status quo for

a while, but who knows? Things can happen fast at the administrative level.

Curtis: Yeah, and when they do I want to be prepared to move up and be able to fill your shoes if I can. I don't want to see them hire someone from the outside because I'm not adequately prepared! I know the others in the group are watching what happens to me, and if it's not good, you're going to have a morale problem and probably more turnover.

Stewart: If people can't cut it, I'll just hire some people who can, that's all. No one ever said this is an easy area. There is plenty of overtime and pressure. The problem is that you people want everything delivered to you right away; promotions, money, but none of the aggravation that goes with it! Look, I'll talk to Willis when I get a chance about this problem. I'm afraid now I've got to get those figures to Peters. I'm glad we had this talk.

Curtis: (rising to leave) Yeah, I am, too.

Following their meeting, Curtis left with his fellow workers for lunch. At this time, Curtis commented about his "closed door" meeting with Stewart. "Well, I feel a little better now that I spoke up. I won't feel guilty at all now if something better comes along. I've given them their chance to do something for me. Mark got all hyper, like usual. He's going to be burned out by the time he's forty. I'm convinced that if you don't speak up, you'll stay right where you are. We'll see, though, if any action comes out of all this."

Meanwhile, Stewart, at a meeting with Willis, commented, "Judd is really impatient. I have trouble making promises about advancement in the division when the environment is so stagnant. My task is trying to make the jobs interesting enough to maintain everyone's interest without sacrificing the accuracy and timeliness of the reporting. Cross training is great in theory, but the logistics in practice are a headache. It's really tough! Anyway, I don't think Curtis is officer material right now, but how to prove that to him is difficult. He does great work, but he needs more time to develop personally as well as broaden his job skills to see how all the pieces fit together. I just hope he can wait it out. I don't want to lose him, but. . . ."

Case Questions

1. Could Stewart have proved to Curtis that he is not "officer material right now"? If so, how?
2. Appraise Stewart's performance as someone who is being asked for help by another person. Could he have communicated in a more helpful way? If so, where, specifically, during the conversation, and how?

3. Did Curtis help his chances for early promotion by his performance in this conversation?

Alice*

The Organization for Women in Management (OWM) at Hillendale College was organized in 1975 because of growing concern about discrimination against women in the field of management. It is a preprofessional organization designed to enhance the awareness and professionalism of women seeking to launch executive careers. Among other things, OWM invites successful women managers to speak about their careers and sponsors programs on such topics as two-career families and dressing for the job. I have been an officer of OWM since its inception and currently serve as secretary. (Fig. 1 at the end of this case provides background data on the officers of OWM.)

This semester the officers of OWM faced a particularly sensitive problem involving the behavior of another officer. Publicity is essential to our success. Members must be notified of programs and events, and our public image is important to maintain credibility. To the rest of the officers it seemed that Alice, our new publicity director, was intentionally and willfully neglecting her duties.

Officer meetings are held weekly, and during September Alice attended only two. She was the last to arrive and sat at the back of the room near the door. During these meetings Alice would agree to do any task we asked but never followed through on it. She did not participate in the discussions, even to ask questions. Alice missed the next three meetings and made no attempt to find out what she missed or to inform us she could not attend. She offered only feeble excuses for her absence, such as, "I fell asleep" and "I simply forgot." Consequently, the other officers were obliged to do her job—make posters and phone calls, place ads in the college newspaper, and so on—in addition to their own duties. This made the officers resentful. Immediately we begn to wish someone had run against her. Being quite intolerant of people who shirk their responsibilities, I strongly urged that she be replaced.

The president, being more level-headed, felt that she should have a private talk with Alice. This she did and Alice responded positively, saying she had been too busy and would be sure to attend the next meeting. But Alice did not come. I gave this some thought and decided her behavior might be attributable to some source we had not considered. I thought it might help to try to see the situation from Alice's point of view.

I arranged to meet with her under the pretense that we would make posters together, at which time I hoped to talk to her. Needless to say, I was disconcerted when Alice did not meet me, particularly when I had gone through the inconvenience of getting over to the central campus.

---

*This case was written by Debra Pasterczyk.

However, I still wanted the chance to try talking with Alice and so proposed to the group that I go to her apartment. They were at first reluctant to approve my idea. It is not the secretary's job to handle such matters, and, knowing my usually abrasive style, they thought I would end up screaming at her. By this time, I really felt challenged, and I managed to prevail upon the other officers to let me give it another try.

What follows is the conversation I had with Alice in her apartment.

> **Debra:** Hi, Alice, I was in the vicinity so I thought I'd stop in and say hello. Are you busy?
> **Alice:** Uh, no, come on in. (She appeared embarrassed.)

I sat down and asked how her classes were going and about her boyfriend (a mutual aquaintance) in order to put her at ease and relax the atmosphere. After these preliminaries, we continued.

> **Debra:** Alice, you know we missed you at the last meeting. We could have used your ideas on planning the next program. (I was trying to give her a feeling of acceptance, showing her that we respected and needed her opinions.)
> **Alice:** Oh, yeah, I *had* to study.
> **Debra:** It sounds like you have a tough schedule.
> **Alice:** Well, I want to keep my chin up.
> **Debra:** Yeah, I know how you feel. What about your other responsibilities, though? When you took an office, you made a commitment to help out.
> **Alice:** Well, I never held an office before, and no one really helped me.
> **Debra:** You mean you felt unsure about procedures?
> **Alice:** Well, that, and I felt like everyone was against me.
> **Debra:** You felt like an outsider?
> **Alice:** Well, you guys all seemed to know what you were doing, and I was afraid of asking dumb questons.
> **Debra:** You felt intimidated by the other officers?
> **Alice:** Yeah, you know what I mean. You guys always knew what was going on, and you all know each other and no one talked to me. (I realized, unfortunately, that this was true.)
> **Debra:** Is that why you didn't come to the meetings?
> **Alice:** Yeah, I thought it was a waste of time because I never did anything anyway.

At this point, I did not want to press her any further. She was near tears, and I felt that I now knew why she had not been participating. It was an unfortunate reason, and I felt personally responsible for not having helped her and for having been insensitive to someone's need for inclusion and affection. The discussion ended with Alice telling me that she no longer wanted the office because she felt that the situation was hopeless.

I reported our conversation to the officers. They also felt shaken that we had unintentionally intimidated Alice.

I called her the next day and asked if she would meet me for lunch in the Commons. She came, which showed a marked increase in trust between us. We talked about all sorts of things—parties, the local restaurants, and "back home."
Enthusiastically, I told her about our upcoming OWM program.

Debra: Alice, we need you on publicity. Why not come to the meeting tonight? Sharon and Jean said they would still like you to organize the publicity.

Alice: Really? They said that?

Debra: Sure. How about if I stop by and we'll go down together?

Alice: That would be great.

We went to the meeting together, and at first she was hesitatnt to talk. This was about a month ago. After a few more meetings, she is now a full-fledged, participating officer.

BACKGROUND DATA ON OWM OFFICERS

Name	Office	Years as member	Previously an officer	Age	Year	Major	Home
Sharon	President	2	X	21	Senior	Accounting	New Jersey
Jean	Vice-president	2	X	21	Senior	Economics	New York
Debra	Secretary	2	X	20	Sophomore	Marketing	New Jersey
Phyllis	Treasurer	1	X	19	Sophomore	Accounting	New York
Alice	Publicity director			19	Sophomore	Undecided	Connecticut
Dawn	Faculty relations	2	X	20	Junior	Accounting	Tennesee

Case Questions

1. What approach did Debra use in her effort to solve the problem and to be helpful to Alice?
2. What attitudes and assumptions (explicit or implicit) did Debra and the other officers hold that enabled problem solving and helping to take place?
3. What attitudes, assumptions, and actions by Alice made it possible for her to be helped?

Subject Index

Abstracting, 101–103
Acceptance, 330
Action language, 120
Adapting, 85–87
Adult ego state, 149–150
Affection needs, 146–147
Allness, 107
Appraisal interviews, 343–347
  improvement of, 345–347
Authoritarian style of leadership, 229–230
Authority, 281–282
Avoidance, 83–84
Avoiding as reaction to conflict, 287

Barriers, communication, 8–9, 53–55
Blindering, 108
Body language, 122–27
Body motion, 120
Body types, 122
Brainstorming, 226
Bypassing, 107

Centralized line-staff structure, 260–261
Changing phase of change process, 361–362
Channel redundancy, 27
Child ego state, 151
Classroom training, 386–387
Client-centered therapy, 329
Closure, 76
Coalition formation, 203–204
Cognitive dissonance, 368
Collaborating, 288
Collateral structures, 391
Compromising, 288
Communication appraisals, 391–395
Communication barriers, 8–9
Communication load, 51–53
Communication networks, 200–202
Communication overload, 52–53
Communication underload, 53
Competition anxiety, 46
Complementary transactions, 151–152
Conceptual system, 82–87
Concreteness, 331
Confirmation, partial, 285
Conflict, constructive, 285
  cyclical model of, 285–287
  definition of, 279
  destructive, 285
  effects of, 282–285
  effects of winning or losing, 284–285
  intergroup, 287–289
  management of, 289–290
  organizational, 13
  role, 294–296
  sources of, 279–282
Conformity, 369
Confrontation, 341–343
Confrontation meetings, 390
Congruence, 330–331
Connotative function, 97–98
Consensus decision-making, 225
Constructive conflict, 285
Context, 77, 104–105
Contingency theory of leadership, 230–232
Continuous reinforcement, 358
Control needs, 146–147
Counseling, 13–14, 327–329, 388
Crossed transactions, 152
Cyclical model of conflict, 285–287

Decentralized line-staff structure, 260–261
Decision-making, consensus, 225
  individual, 224
  group mechanisms for, 224–226
  majority, 225
  minority, 224–225
Decoding, 27–28
Defense mechanisms, 83–85
Defensive climates, 85–87
Delphi technique, 226–227
Democratic style of leadership, 229–230
Denial, 83–84
Denotative function, 97–98
Destructive conflict, 285
Detection, 75
Differentiation, 291–294
Directive function, 99
Disconfirmation, 155–156
Downward communication, 44–46
  barriers to, 44–46
Dress, 123

Ectomorph, 122
Ego states, 149–151
  adult, 149–150
  child, 151
  parent, 149–150
Elementalism, 100–101
Empathy, 330
Encoding, 27–28
Endomorph, 122
Environment, 127–132
  and organizational structure, 264–266
Etc., 109–110
Exposure, 158
Expressive function, 98
Extensional meaning, 103
Eye contact, 125–126
Eye gaze, 125–126

Facial expression, 125
Fayol's bridge, 49
Fear arousing message, 366–367
Feedback, 28–29, 41, 158
Fixed ratio reinforcement, 358–359
Force field analysis, 54–55
Forcing, 288
Formal groups, 194–195
Formal structure of an organization, 370–371
Forming, 198
Frozen evaluations, 107–108
Function, 34

Game situations, 279–280
Games, 153–154
Game theory, 280–281
Gaze, 125–126
General semantics, 95–97
Gestures, 123–124
Grapevine, 268–169
  definition of, 193
Group building and maintenance roles, 205
Group cohesiveness, 206–207
Group controls, 33
Group decision quality, 220–228
Group decision-making mechanisms, 224–226
Group development, phases of, 197–199, 223
Group factors in influence, 369–370
Group member compatibility, 222
Group member heterogeneity, 222

Group norms, 207–209
Group pressure, 369–370
Group risk taking, 227–228
Group structures, 33, 199–206
Groups, 12–13
 and influence process, 369–370
 composition of, 222
 criteria for effectiveness in, 233–234
 decision-making mechanisms for, 224–226
 formal, 194–195
 informal, 194–195
 leadership in, 228–233
 losing, 285
 primary, 193–194
 reference, 194, 369–370
 risk taking in, 227–228
 secondary, 193–194
 size of, 221–222
 winning, 284

Halo effect, 78
Helping, 13–14
Helping relationships, 337–343
Horse trading, 372

Identification, 362
I-messages, 341–343
Implicit assumptions, 41–44
Inadvertent reinforcement, 359
Inclusion needs, 146–147
Index of influence, 202
Indexing, 110
Indiscrimination, 107–108
Individual decision-making, 224
Individual roles, 205
Inferences, 103–104
Influence, 14–15, 202–203, 354–356
 group factors in, 369–370
 index of, 202
 and groups, 369–370
 and organizational factors, 370–371
 and organizational settings, 370–371
 and self-concept, 368–369
 message factors in, 365–367
 phases in, 360–363
 receiver factors in, 366–369
 source factors in, 364–365
Informal groups, 194–195
Informal organization, 266–269
Informal space, 129
Informal structure of an organization, 370–371
Integration, 291–294
Intensional meaning, 103
Intensional orientation, 123
Interaction model, 26–29
Interaction Process Analysis, 222–224
Intergroup conflict, 287–289
Intergroup relations, 389–390
Intergroup team building, 387
Interpersonal dynamics, 11–12, 141–164
Interpersonal need compatibility concept,
 146–147
Interpersonal needs, 146–147
Interpersonal peacemaking, 388
Interpersonal reflex, 148–149
Internalization, 362
Interpretation, 75–76
Interviews, appraisal, 343–347

Jargon, 96
Johari Window, 158–159
Job enrichment, 388
Judgments, 103–104

Kinesic behavior, 120
Kinesic slips, 124

Language, 10–11
 action, 120
 and thought, 105–106
 body, 122–127

functions of, 97–100
improvements in, 109–111
misuses of, 106–109
object, 120
sign, 120
Lateral communication, 44
 barriers to, 49–51
Leadership, 45–46, 228–233
 authoritarian, 229–230
 contingency theory of, 230–232
 democratic, 229–230
 as functions, 232–233
 in groups, 228–233
 path-goal theory of, 231–232
 trait theory of, 228–230
Line-staff relationships, 259–260
Line-staff structure, centralized, 260–261
 decentralized, 260–261
Linear models, 24–29
Load, communication, 51–53
Lockstep reciprocal, 157
Losing groups, 285
Listening, 328–337
Listening orientation, 329–332

Macrobarriers, 41–42
Maintenance roles, 205
Majority decision making, 225
Maladaptive relationships, 155–158
Management by objectives (MBO), 390–391
Managing conflict, 289–290
Matrix structure, 262–264
Mesomorph, 122
Message, 25–26
 content of, 366–367
 factors in influence, 365–367
 fear arousing, 366–367
 I-message, 341–343
 one-sided, 365–366
 structure of, 366
 two-sided, 365–366
 you-message, 341–343
Metacommunication, 159–160
Microbarriers, 41
Minority decision making, 224–225
Models, 22–23
 interaction, 26–29
 linear, 24–29
 one-way, 25–26
 organic, 30–35
 reflective thinking, 218–220
 two person communication, 7–8
 system, 32–35
 two person relationship, 30–32
MUM effect, 48

Need, affection, 146–147
 control, 146–147
 inclusion, 146–147
 interpersonal, 146–147
 compatibility, 146–147
Negative reinforcement, 356
NGT technique, 226–227
Noise, 28
Nominal group technique (NGT), 226–227
Nonverbal communication, 11, 117–139
 implications for managers, 134–135
 and verbal messages, 121
 functions of, 120–121
Norming, 198
Norms, group, 207–209

Object language, 120
One-sided message, 365–366
One-way communication, 44–45
One-way model, 25–26
Operational attitude, 110–111
Organic models, 30–35
Organization mirror, 389–390
Organizational change, 382–385

Organizational conflict, 12, 275–328
Organization design, 13, 253–266
  specialization forms in, 261–262
  matrix structure, 262–264
  division of labor, 255–256
  span of control, 258–259
  unity of command, 256–258
Organization development, 15–16, 380–382
  definition of, 380
  decreasing resistance to, 395–396
  specific approaches to, 385–395
Organization development practitioners, 397–398
  guidelines for, 397–398
Organizational settings, influence and, 370–371
Organizational structure, environment and,
  264–266
Overload, communication, 52–53
Overreaching, 336

Paralanguage, 120, 126–127
Parent ego state, 149–150
Partial confirmation, 156–157
Path-goal theory of leadership, 231–232
Perception, 9–10, 60–90
  consistency tendency and, 78–79
  and organizational subunits, 281
  stability tendency and, 79–80
  defense and, 73
  selectivity of, 74–77
Perceptual defense, 73
Perceptual selectivity, 41, 74–77
Perceptual set, 71–74
Performing, 198
Person-mindedness, 109
Persuasive tactics, 371–373
Polarization, 107–108
Positive reinforcement, 356
Posture, 123
Power patterns, 202–203
Primary groups, 193–194
Prisoner's dilemma, 280–281
Process consultation, 389
Projection, 83–84
Proxemics, 120, 127–132
Punishment, 360

Rationalization, 83–85
Receiver, 367–369
Receiver factors in influence, 366–369
Reference group, 193, 369–370
Reflective thinking model, 218–220
Reflection, 332–337
Reforming, 199
Refreezing 361–363
Reinforcement, 356–360
  continuous, 358
  fixed ratio, 358–359
  inadvertent, 359
  negative, 356
  positive, 356
  schedules of, 358–359
  variable ratio, 359
Reinforcers, 357–358
  feedback and, 358
Relationships, helping, 337–343
  line-staff, 259–260
  maladaptive, 155–158
  two-person, 145–155
Reports, 103–104
Repression, 83–94
Responses, stereotyped, 335
Risk taking in groups, 227–228
Risky shift, 227–228
Role conflict, 294–296
Role taking patterns, 205–206
Roles, 205–206
  group building, 205
  individual, 205

maintenance, 205
self-oriented, 205
task, 205

Scanning, 362
Scripts, 154–155
Secondary groups, 193–194
Self-concept, 80–82
  transactional model of, 81
  and influence, 368–369
Self-esteem, 80
Self-oriented roles, 205
Semantic differential, 97–98
Semantics, general, 95–97
Serial communication, 41
Sign language, 120
Sleeper effect, 365
Smoothing, 287
Social structuring function, 98–99
Source credibility, 365
Source factors in influence, 364–365
Status, 281–282
Status anxiety, 46
Status incongruence, 202
Status patterns, 202–203
Stereotyped responses, 335
Storming, 198
Structural approach to organizational
  development, 391
Subgrouping, 203–205
Subsystem, 34
Supportive climates, 85–87
Survey feedback, 391
Symbolic process, 100–105
Symbols, 96
System, 34
  conceptual, 82–87
System model, 32–35

Task characteristics, 33
Task roles, 205
Team buiding, 15–16, 389
Territoriality, 128–129
T-groups, 385, 387–388
Therapy, client-centered, 329
Time, 132–133
Time-binding, 95–96
Time structuring, 133–154
Total organization, 13
Touching, 124
Trait theory of leadership, 228–230
Transactional analysis, 149–155
Transactions, 151–153
  complimentary, 151–152
  crossed, 152
  ulteri or, 152–153
Triggering events, 285–287
Two-person communication model, 7–8
Two-person relationship, 145–155
Two-person relationship model, 30–32
Two-sided message, 365–366

Ulterior transactions, 152–153
Uncalculated risk, 107
Unstated contracts, 157
Undelayed reaction, 108
Underload, communication, 53
Underreaching, 336
Unfreezing, 361–362
Unregulated confrontation, 285
Upward communication, 44
  barriers to, 46–49

Variable ratio reinforcement, 359
Voice, 126–127

Winning groups, 284
Win-lose situations, 279–280

You-messages, 341–343

Name Index

Abegglen, James, 258
Abrams, Darcy, 365
Agarwala-Rogers, Rekha, 51
Aiken, Michael, 50
Albaum, Gerald, 50
Alderfer, Clayton P., 381
Alexander, Elmore R., III, 46, 49
Allen, Richard K., 44, 49, 51
Allen, Thomas, 119, 295
Alloway, Thomas, 126
Allport, Gordon W., 81
American Cancer Society, 366
Anderson, John, 342–343
Anderson, Patrick, 255
Ardrey, Robert, 128
Argyle, Michael, 124, 125
Argyris, Chris, 55, 161
Aristotle, 25
Aronson, Elliot, 122, 232, 364, 365
Asch, Solomon, 78, 369
Athanassiades, John C., 46
Athos, Anthony G., 80, 123, 131, 157, 328, 329–337, 340–341
Atkinson, John W., 338
Avila, Donald L., 328
Azrin, Nathan H., 360

Bach, George R., 160
Back, Kurt W., 203, 206
Baird, John E., Jr., 46, 49
Bales, Robert F., 148, 198, 222–224, 232
Ballachey, Edgerton L., 106
Barnard, Chester I., 254
Barnes, Louis B., 342, 357
Barnlund, Dean C., 30, 83, 121
Bass, Bernard M., 224–225
Bavelas, Alex, 179, 200–201, 354–356
Bayless, Ovid L., 220
Beavin, Helmock, 145, 156, 159
Becker, Selwin W., 131
Beckhard, Richard, 15, 16, 289, 389, 390
Beer, Michael, 381, 388, 389, 391
Beier, Ernest G., 121
Bell, Cecil H., 380, 385, 389, 391, 397
Bem, Daryl J., 80, 227
Ben-David, J., 294
Benne, Kenneth D., 205
Bennis, Warren, 46, 198, 360
Berkowitz, Leonard, 122, 366
Berkowitz, Norman H., 46
Berleson, Bernard, 73, 74
Berlew, David E., 361
Berliner, Jerome S., 268
Berlo, David, 26
Berne, Eric, 149
Berry, Paul C., 226
Berscheid, Ellen, 122
Bettinghaus, Erwin P., 356
B. F. Goodrich Company, 306–319
Biddle, Bruce J., 294
Bion, W. R., 198
Birdwhistel, Ray L., 118, 124
Blake, Robert R., 80, 283, 287, 289, 389
Blanchard, Kenneth H., 123
Blau, Peter M., 357
Block, Clifford H., 226
Bluestone, Irving, 282
Bobbitt, H. Randolph, Jr., 279
Bock, Donald P., 405
Borgatta, Edgar F., 223, 224, 232
Bois, J. Samuel, 95

Borgatta, Edgar F., 148
Borman, Ernest G., 371
Borman, Walter C., 79
Boulding, Kenneth E., 279
Bowditch, James L., 6, 12, 72, 240, 279, 281, 282, 290, 345, 397
Bowers Richard J., 228
Boyatzis, Richard E., 338, 339
Boyd, John A., 27
Brammer, Lawrence M., 328, 330–332, 338
Brooks, William D., 81, 98, 106, 118, 126
Brown, Bruce L., 127
Brown, David S., 41
Brown, Roger, 73, 105–106, 148
Bruce, David, 104
Bruner, Jerome S., 80
Budd, Richard W., 49, 109
Bundy, McGeorge, 40
Bunker, Douglas R., 233
Burgather, E. F., 367
Burgoon, Michael, 233, 366
Burgoon, Judee K., 366
Burke, Ronald J., 268, 346
Burns, Tom, 264–265
Burnstein, Eugene, 228

Cameron, Juan, 48
Campbell, Jim, 119
Caplow, Theodore H., 203–204
Carlsmith, J. Merrill, 78, 364, 367, 368
Carroll, Archie B., 46
Carson, Robert C., 148, 156
Cartright, John A., 207
Cartwright, Dorwin, 200, 206, 207
Cathcart, Robert S., 72
Cecil, Earl A., 228
Chase, Stuart, 109
Chertkoff, Jerome M., 228
Cheston, Ric, 287
Chomsky, Noam, 106
Christensen, C. Roland, 202
Chrysler Corporation, 307
Churchill, Winston, 94
Clement, Donald A., 30
Cline, Rebecca, 341
Coffey, Robert E., 330–332
Cohen, Allan R., 157, 395
Cohen, Arthur R., 367
Cole, James K., 125
Collins, Barry E., 216
Combs, Arthur W., 80, 82, 83, 328
Condon, John C., 95, 96, 100, 102–103, 109
Cooley, Charles H., 193
Coon, Arthur M., 226
Cooper, Joel, 119
Cooper, Lane, 25
Cooper, William W., II, 395
Corning Glass Company, 397
Corwin, Ronald G., 294
Costanzo, Philip R., 80
Costello, Timothy W., 77
Crutchfield, Richard S., 106
Cottrell, Leonard S., 148
Crane, Donald P., 345
Cummings, Robert C., 26, 83, 328, 370

Dalton, Gene W., 233, 254, 343–344, 382–383, 385
Dalton, Melville, 259–260, 277
Dance, Frank E. X., 83
D'Angelo, Gary, 120, 143
Darnell, Donald K., 30, 98

Davis, Keith, 254, 268–269
Davis, Sheldon, 13
Davis, Stanley M., 263
Dean, Janet, 125
Dearborn, DeWitt C., 9
Delbecq, Andre L., 226
Deep, Samuel, 44
Delia, Jesse, 78
DePaulo, Bella N., 11, 119
De Sola Pool, Ithiel, 269
Dessler, 229
Deutsch, Morton, 286, 289
DeVito, Joseph A., 154, 342–343
Devoe, Shannon, 127
Dewey, John, 218–220
Dickson, William J., 207–208, 266–267
Dittes, James E., 370
Donaghy, William C., 109
Donnelly, James H., Jr., 229
Downey, H. Kirk, 231
Downs, Anthony, 52
Driscoll, Terence P., 402
Duncan, Starkey, 120
Dunnette, Marvin D., 79, 160, 266, 287, 388
Dutton, John M., 279

Ebbesen, Ebbe B., 228
Edwards Air Force Base, 316
Egan, Gerard, 330–332, 335–337, 339–340, 341,
   342–343, 346
Ehrlichman, John, 123, 127
Eisenberg, Abne M., 128
Eisenhower, Dwight D., 126
Ekman, Paul, 11, 119, 120, 125, 134
Eliot, T. S., 364
Ellyson, Steve L., 126
Ellsworth, Phoebe C., 125
Emmert, Philip, 81, 98, 106, 118, 126
Etzioni, Amatei, 221, 294
Evans, Gareth, 165
Evered, Roger D., 386
Exline, Ralph V., 126

Farace, Richard V., 51, 52, 201, 391, 393
Farquhar, John W., 356
Fayol, Henri, 49
Federal Bureau of Investigation, 316
Feldman, S. D., 122
Ferris, Susan, 11
Ferster, C. B., 359
Festinger, Leon, 368, 369
Fiedler, Fred E., 229–230
Filley, Alan C., 279
Fink, C. F., 221
Fink, Stephen L., 157
Fisher, B. Aubrey, 233
Fisher, Dalmar, 6, 81, 161, 217–218, 282, 295, 345,
   397
Fleenor, C. Patrick, 177
Fleishman, Edwin A., 362
Fordyce, Jack K., 390
Frandsen, Kenneth D., 30
Freedman, Jonathan L., 78, 364, 366, 367
French, John R. P., 206, 344, 345
French, Wendell L., 380, 385, 389, 391, 397
Freshley, Dwight L., 127, 227
Friesen, Wallace W., 125, 134
Frost, Joyce Hocker, 280
Frye, Terry K., 289

Gabarro, John J., 80, 123, 131, 157, 328, 329–337,
   340–341
Gadon, Herman, 157
Galbraith, Jay R., 50, 256, 391
Gardella, Mary Louise, 4
General Accounting Office, 318
General Electric Company, 344, 397
General Motors Corporation, 397
Gergen, Kenneth J., 280
Gerloff, Edwin A., 26, 83, 328, 370

Gershenfeld, Matti K., 198, 233
Ghisell, Edwin E., 228
Gibb, Cecil A., 232
Gibb, Jack R., 86–87
Gibson, James L., 229
Giffin, Kim, 157, 330–332
Gilchrist, J. C., 52
Glenn, Ethel, 285
Glidewell, John C., 148
Goffman, Erving, 78, 122, 123
Golden, Burton, 122
Goldhaber, Gerald M., 16, 44, 120, 125, 128–129,
   130, 216, 391, 393, 395
Gordon, Thomas, 340–342, 343
Greenbaum, Howard H., 391
Greene, Charles N., 231
Greenlaw, Paul S., 395
Greiner, Larry E., 382–385
Gross, Neil, 295
Gruder, Charles L., 365
Grunes, Willa F., 73
Guest, Robert, 123
Guetzkow, Harold, 216, 369
Gullahorn, John T., 295
Gunther, John, 122
Gustafson, David H., 226

Haas, Kenneth Brooks, 371
Habbe, S., 44
Hackman, J. Richard, 388
Hage, Jerald, 50
Haiman, Franklin, 122
Haire, Mason, 73
Halberstam, David, 40
Haldeman, H. R., 127
Hall, Edward T., 11, 128, 129, 132
Hall, Jay, 158–159, 216–217
Haney, William V., 72, 73, 77, 106–109
Hanneman, Gerhard J., 366
Hansen, Lee H., 345
Harburg, Ernest, 79
Hare, Paul A., 221, 223, 224, 232
Harris, Thomas A., 149, 154
Harrison, Randall, 119, 132
Harrison, Roger, 82, 85, 397
Hart, Roland J., 127
Hartley, Eugene L., 232
Hastorf, Albert H., 79
Hatfield, John C., 345, 346
Hayakawa, S. I., 7, 72, 80, 98, 101, 109
Hayes, Merwin A., 127
Hearn, Gordon, 131
Heider, Fritz, 79
Helper, Hal, 119
Heine, Carol Weiss, 397
Henley, Nancy M., 123, 124, 127
Heraclitus, 100
Hersey, Paul, 123
Hertzberg, Frederick, 388
Heston, Judee K., 233
Hinton, Bernard L., 295
Hodgetts, Richard M., 320, 321
Hodgson, Richard C., 232
Hoffman, L. Richard, 97, 222
Hollman, T. D., 79
Hollmann, Robert W., 391
Holtz, W. C., 360
Homans, George C., 12, 14, 34, 155, 207, 356, 357
Honig, Werner K., 360
Hook, L. Herman, 131
Hooven, J. G., 97
Hostiuck, K. Tim, 260
House, Robert J., 231
Hovland, Carl I., 364, 365, 367
Howells, Lloyd T., 131
Hoxie, Gordon, 40
Huse, Edgar F., 6, 12, 72, 240, 279, 281, 282, 287,
   289, 290, 345, 346, 381, 385, 389, 395, 397
Huseman, Richard C., 46, 49, 127, 227, 345, 346

Ingham, Harry, 158
Insel, Paul M., 129
Institute for Social Research, 385
Ivancevich, John M., 229
Izard, Carroll E., 121

Jackson, Don D., 145, 156, 159
Jackson, John J., 345, 346
Jacobson, Eugene, 295, 371
Jacobson, Lenore, 80
James, Muriel, 149–155
Janis, Irving L., 12, 364, 367
Johnson, Bonnie McDaniel, 341, 382
Johnson, David W., 119
Johnson, Lyndon B., 40, 124, 255
Johnson, Richard Tanner, 40, 126, 255, 281
Johnson, Robert B., 46
Johnson, Thomas W., 231
Johnson, Wendell, 96, 100
Jones, Stephen C.,
Jongeward, Dorothy, 149–155

Kahn, Robert L., 294
Kamiya, Joe, 224
Kaplan, Norman, 294
Kay, Emmanuel, 344, 345
Kees, Weldon, 120
Kelley, Harold H., 203, 364, 370
Kelly, George A., 30
Kelman, Herbert C., 362, 365
Kennedy, John F., 267
Kim, John Y., 29
King, Stephen W., 369
Kirk, E. Bruce, 346
Kirkpatrick, Charles A., 371
Kitch, John W., 81
Kleinhaus, Bruce, 193
Klemmer, E. T., 4
Knapp, Mark L., 120, 121, 127
Knippen, Jay T., 268
Knott, Peter L., 245
Knudson, Harry R., 177
Kogan, Nathan, 227
Kolb, David A., 338, 339
Koontz, Harold, 95
Korzybski, Alfred, 95–96, 101, 109
Kotter, John P., 10
Krames, Lester, 126
Kretch, David, 106
Kreisberg, M., 216

LaFrance, Marianne, 123, 127
Lahiff, James M., 345, 346
Lambert, W. W., 367
Lamm, Helmut, 226
Lanzetta, John T., 52
Larson, Carl E., 83, 220
Laudon, Kenneth, 221
Lawrence, Paul R., 10, 33, 50, 82, 233, 254, 261,
    263, 264, 265–266, 291–294, 295, 342, 357,
    382–383, 391, 395
Leary, Timothy, 148–149, 155
Leathers, Dale G., 216
Leavitt, Harold J., 200–201, 289, 395
Lecky, Prescott, 82
Lemert, James B., 364
Lenneberg, Eric, 105–106
Lerner, Alan Jay, 118–119
Leth, Pamely C., 30
Leventhal, Howard, 367
Levinson, Daniel J., 232
Levinson, Harry, 343–344, 345
Lewin, Kurt, 54, 360–363, 382, 385
Lewis, John W., III, 233, 238, 382, 397
Lewis, Phillip V., 41, 74
Likert, Rensis, 10, 44, 47, 233
Lindgren, Henry Clay, 129
Lindzey, Gardner, 232
Lincoln, Evelyn, 267
Lipson, Susan, 221

Litterer, Joseph A., 279
Logue, Cal M., 127, 227
Lombard, George F. F., 8, 31, 333, 340–341
Long, Barbara, 126
Lorr, Maurice, 148
Lorsch, Jay W., 33, 50, 233, 254, 261, 264, 265–266,
    291–294, 295, 342, 357, 391
Lott, A. J., 206
Lowe, Frederick, 118–119
LTV Aerospace Corporation, 306
Ludwig, Linda M., 125
Luft, Joseph, 158–159
Luthans, Fred, 320–321, 356

Maher, Brendan, 30
McCarty, Kenneth, 119
McCaskey, Michael B., 131
McClelland, David C., 338
Maccoby, Eleanor E., 232
Maccoby, Nathan, 356
McCroskey, James C., 79, 233, 364, 366
McEwen, William J., 366
McGuire, William J., 364, 366, 367
Machaver, William, 46
McIntyre, James M., 338, 339
Mack, Raymond W., 278
McKersie, John B., 14
McLuhan, Marshall, 27
McNair, Douglas M., 148
McNamara, Robert, 40
Maier, Norman R. F., 97, 220–221, 222, 343–344,
    345
Mann, Floyd, 9–10
Mann, John M., 148
March, James G., 72
Marett, Cora Bagley, 50
Marquis, Donald G., 227
Maslow, Abraham H., 130
Massachusetts, Commonwealth of, 258
Massachusetts Institute of Technology, 385
Mathis, Robert L., 345, 346
Mathies, Leslie H., 10
Mayo, Clara, 123, 127
Meadow, A., 226
Meers, Peter, 210
Megginson, Leon C., 63
Mehrabian, Albert, 11, 119, 122, 123, 126, 130,
    356, 359, 360
Mellinger, Glen, 45
Meyer, Herbert H., 344
Michigan, University of, 385
Milgram, STanley, 209
Millar, Dan P., 94
Millar, Frank E., 94
Miller, G. A., 258
Millman, Susan, 364
Mills, Judson, 364
Mintz, N. L., 130
Mintzberg, Henry, 256, 267
Mitchell, Terence R., 225, 385
Mitchell, Vance F., 268
Molloy, John T., 131
Moment, David, 12, 81, 142–144, 148–149, 161, 202,
    205, 206, 217–218, 225
Monge, Peter R., 51, 52, 201, 391
Morley, Eileen, 340–341
Mortensen, C. David, 30
Moss, Sylvia, 123, 124
Mouton, Jane S., 283, 287, 289, 389

Napier, Rodney, 233
Nichols, Ralph G., 44, 45
Napier, Rodney W., 198
National Training Laboratories, 385
Nebergall, Roger E., 74
Neely, Cathie A., 220
Newcomb, Theodore M., 79, 232
Newman, Pamela Jane, 109
Nilson, Thomas R., 41–44, 159
Nixon, Richard M., 48, 123, 127

Odiorne, George, 44
O'Donnell, Kenneth, 267
Ofner, J. Allen, 216
Ogden, C. K., 98
Oldham, Greg R., 388
Olshan, Karen, 79
Opinion Research Corporation, 44
O'Reilly, Charles A., III, 46
Osborn, Alexander F., 226
Osgood, Charles E., 97
Oster, Harriet, 11, 119
Owen, James L., 155

Page, Paul A., 155
Parnes, S. J., 226
Pasterczyk, Debra, 408
Patton, Bobby R., 157, 330–332
Paul, William J., Jr., 388
Pearce, W. Barrett, 158
Perry, Enos C., 371
Pfungst, O., 118
Phillips, Eleanor, 287
Planty, Earl, 46
Pliner, Patricia, 126
Polaroid Corporation, 397
Polefka, Judith, 79
Ponder, O., 49
Pondy, Louis R., 285–286
Pood, Elliott, 285
Porter, Lyman W., 266, 269
Powers, William G., 75, 81
Price, Kendall O., 79
Proxmire, William, 318
Purkey, William W., 328
Pyke, Sandra W., 220

Rappaport, Anatol, 280
Raynolds, Peter A., 330–332
Read, William H., 46, 97
Reese, H., 226
Reitz, H. Joseph, 289, 295
Rheaume, Robert D., 171
Richards, I. A., 98
Richards, Max D., 395
Richetto, Gary M.,
Rintye, Edward D., 72
Robbins, Owen, 127
Roberts, Donald, 26
Roberts, Karlene H., 46, 266
Robertson, Keith B., 388
Roby, Thornton B., 52
Roethlisberger, Fritz J., 7, 100, 202, 207–208,
    266–267
Rogers, Carl R., 328, 329–335, 347
Rogers, Everett M., 51
Roosevelt, Franklin D., 122
Rosen, Sidney, 46, 48
Rosenberg, Seymour, 79
Rosenthal, Fred, 99
Rosenthal, Robert, 80
Rosenzweig, James, 380
Rossiter, Charles M., Jr., 328
Roy, Donald, 12
Ruben, Brent C., 29, 49, 109
Rubin, Irwin M., 338, 339
Ruesch, Jurgen, 120
Russell, Hamish M., 51, 52, 201, 391

Samovar, Larry A., 72
Sanford, Aubrey C., 342–343
Sapir, Edward, 105
Savage, Charles H., Jr., 267
Schachter, Stanley, 207, 208–209
Schaefer, Earl S., 148
Scheflen, Albert E., 123, 124
Scheflen, Alice, 124
Schein, Edgar H., 193, 233, 360–363, 389
Schelling, Thomas C., 280
Schiffenbauer, Allen, 84
Schiffman, H. R., 97

Schlesinger, Arthur M., Jr., 258, 267
Schmidt, Warren H., 229, 282
Schneider, Anne M., 59
Schneider, Arnold E., 109
Schneider, David J., 79
Schram, Wilbur, 26, 269
Schutz, William C., 146–147, 148, 155, 198, 222
Schwartz, Donald F., 295, 371
Schwartz, Milton, 97
Schwitter, Joseph P., 50
Scott, Michael D., 75, 79, 81, 366
Sears, David O., 78, 364, 366, 367
Seashore, Stanley E., 207
Seibold, David R., 289
Seidenberg, Bernard, 193, 366
Seiler, John A., 34, 82, 282, 284
Senger, John, 77
Sereno, Kenneth, 30
Shannon, Claude F., 26
Sharp, Stewart M., 158
Shaver, Kelly G., 75, 78
Shaw, Marvin, 131, 193, 199, 201, 222, 226
Sheats, Paul, 205
Sheehan, Michael E., 79
Sheldon, Alan, 33
Sheldon, William H., 122
Shelley, M. W., 52
Shepard, Herbert A., 198, 289, 389
Shepherd, Clovis R., 233
Sheridan, John E., 231
Sherif, Carolyn, 74, 282, 290
Sherif, Muzafer, 74, 208, 282, 290
Shuter, Robert, 129
Sieberg, Evelyn, 155
Siegel, Bertram, 122
Simon, Herbert A., 9, 72
Sirota, David, 388
Skinner, B. F., 359
Slater, Phillip E., 148, 221, 232
Slobin, Dan I., 106
Slocum, John W., 231
Smith, Adam, 256
Smith, Ralph R., Jr., 128
Smith, Ronald L., 49
Snadowsky, Alvin M., 193, 201, 366
Snyder, F. W., 4
Snyder, Richard C., 278
Snygg, Donald, 80, 82, 83
Sommer, Robert, 128, 131
Spear, Harold S., 330–332
Stalker, G. M., 264–265
Stark, Harry F., 97
Steele, Fred I., 119, 130, 361, 391
Steiglitz, Harold, 259
Steinberg, Alfred, 124
Steinbruner, John D., 367
Steiner, Gary A., 73, 74
Steinfalt, Thomas M., 289
Stewart, John, 30, 120, 134
Stinson, John E., 231
Stone, Phil, 224
Stoner, James A. F., 395
Strauss, George, 15, 354–356
Strodtbeck, Fred L., 131, 198, 224
Stull, James B., 335–337
Stumpf, John, 121
Stumpf, Stephen A., 296
Succi, George J., 97
Survey Research Center, 385
Susman, Gerald I., 386
Sutton, Harold, 269
Swanberg, Charles, 242
Swingle, Paul, 280

Tacoma, City of, 380
Tagiuri, Renato, 80
Tannenbaum, Percy H., 97
Tannenbaum, Robert, 229
Taylor, Dalmas A., 193

Taylor, Donald W., 226
Terkel, Studs, 53
Tesser, Abraham, 46, 48
Thelen, Herbert A., 198
Thibaut, John W., 203, 369
Thomas, E. J., 221
Thomas, Kenneth, 160, 287
Thompson, James D., 281
Thompson, Paul H., 343–344, 345
Thompson, Victor A., 279
Thorndike, Robert L., 225
Thorndyke, Edward L., 356
Tillman, Rollie, Jr., 221, 371
Tomkins, Silvan S., 121, 125
Torbert, William R., 385
Trager, George L., 126
Trausch, Susan, 131–132
Triandis, Harry C., 75
Trommsdorf, Gisela, 226
TRW, Inc., 397
Tubbs, Stewart L., 123, 124, 148
Tuckman, Bruce W., 198
Turner, Arthur N., 8, 31, 333, 340–341
Twyman, J. Paschal, 294

Urwick, Lyndall F., 258

Vandemark, JoAnne F., 30
Van de Ven, Andrew H., 226
Vandivier, Kermit, 306–319
Verba, Sidney, 207
Vinokur, Amiram, 228
von der Gabelentz, G., 98

Walker, Arthur H., 264
Wall, Victor P., 27
Wallach, Michael A., 227
Walster, Elaine, 122, 365
Walton, Eugene, 50, 268
Walton, Richard E., 10, 14, 54, 279, 285–286, 388
Ward, Charles D., 122

Watson, Marvin, 255
Watson, O. Michael, 129
Watzlawick, Paul, 145, 156, 159
Weaver, Warren, 26
Webber, Ross A., 228, 258
Weil, Raymond, 390
Wells, William D., 122
Western Electric Company, 207
Wheeless, Lawrence R., 364
White, Lee C., 40
White, Robert W., 81
White, Sam E., 385
Whitehead, Alfred North, 34
Whorf, Benjamin Lee, 105
Whyte, William F., 354, 357
Wiener, Morton, 119, 127
Wilcox, Douglas S., 346
Willits, Robin D., 157
Wilmot, William, 145, 156, 280
Wilson, Paul R., 122
Wofford, Jerry C., 26, 83, 328, 370
Wolfson, Alan D., 388
Wood, Julia T., 232
Woodward, Joan, 258, 264, 265
Word, Carl O., 119
Wright, David W., 364
Wyden, Peter, 160

Young, Thomas J., 366

Zaleznik, Abraham, 12, 44, 45, 46, 49, 142–144, 148–149, 202, 205, 225, 232
Zalkind, Sheldon, 77
Zana, Mark P., 119
Zand, Dale E., 226, 381, 391
Zander, Alvin, 200, 206, 207
Zawacki, Robert A., 380
Zellner, Miriam, 367
Zima, Joseph P., 49
Zimmerman, Gordon I., 155

†